DATE DUE

NOV 2 3 2015	

Before They Could Vote

Wisconsin Studies in Autobiography

William L. Andrews
General Editor

Before They Could Vote

American Women's Autobiographical Writing, 1819–1919

Edited by

SIDONIE SMITH

And

JULIA WATSON

THE UNIVERSITY OF WISCONSIN PRESS

This book was published with the support of
the Anonymous Fund for the Humanities of the
University of Wisconsin–Madison.

The University of Wisconsin Press
1930 Monroe Street
Madison, Wisconsin 53711

www.wisc.edu/wisconsinpress/

3 Henrietta Street
London WC2E 8LU, England

5   4   3   2   1

Printed in the United States of America

Library of Congress Cataloging-in-Publication Data
   Before they could vote: American women's autobiographical
writing, 1819–1919 / edited by Sidonie Smith and Julia Watson.
      p.   cm.—(Wisconsin studies in autobiography)
      Includes bibliographical references.
ISBN 0-299-22050-8 (cloth: alk. paper)
ISBN 0-299-22054-0 (pbk.: alk. paper)
   1. Women—United States—Biography.   2. Women—United
States—History—19th century—Sources.   3. Women—United
States—History—20th century—Sources.   4. Women's studies—
United States—Biographical methods.   5. Autobiography—Women
authors.   I. Smith, Sidonie.   II. Watson, Julia, 1945-   III. Series.
   HQ1412.B44   2006
   305.4092'273—dc22   2006006984

To our grandmothers,

ARLENE KINSEL PAULEN
MARY EVE HOMMAN SMITH
JULIA MINEHAN WATSON
MARY BRIDGET MONAHAN RYAN

Contents

Acknowledgments

As we conceptualized, proposed, and prepared this anthology, we benefited from the generosity and expertise of numerous scholars, editors, and students. We thank our reviewers, especially Anne E. Goldman, for helpful suggestions that expanded our thinking about the heterogeneity of narratives from the period. For his unstinting encouragement, erudition, and advice, we are especially grateful to William L. Andrews, editor of the University of Wisconsin Press series in autobiography. At the University of Wisconsin Press we had the unqualified enthusiasm and support of former and current editors Mary Elizabeth Braun, Raphael Kadushin, and Sheila Moermond.

We are deeply indebted to historian Ann Fabian, who led an inspiring seminar on "Biography, Autobiography, and Personal Narrative" at the American Antiquarian Society in the summer of 1999. This seminar, supported by the superb staff of the AAS, particularly John B. Hench and Joanne D. Chaison, helped us to better understand the material culture of the book in the nineteenth century. We thank historians Omar Valerio-Jimenez and Catherine Komisaruk for suggestions about indigenous women writers in Spanish California, offered to Julia during the 2001 University of California Humanities Research Institute seminar on "Confession and Conquest: Autobiography in the Americas." We are also grateful to Paul Baepler for his knowledgeable suggestions about women's captivity narratives and hoaxes of the Barbary and other coasts, and to Carroll Smith-Rosenberg and Mary Kelley for their groundbreaking work on women's social lives in the nineteenth century. Sidonie thanks the College of Literature, Science and the Arts of the University of Michigan for research support; and the staff at the William L. Clements Library for help in locating original manuscripts. Finally, we could not have produced this anthology without the help of University of Michigan doctoral students Emma Crandell, Emily Lutenski, John Cords, Tamara Bhalla, Lauren Lafauci, and Elspeth Healey. Their diligence, doggedness, and dedication to research made this volume a reality.

We thank the Bancroft Library at the University of California, Berkeley, for permission to reprint the Eulalia Pérez dictation, in translation by Vivian Fisher, as published by the Friends of the Bancroft Library, 1988. We thank Penguin Group (USA) Inc. for permission to quote from the footnotes from *Women's Indian Captivity Narratives,* edited by Kathryn Zabelle Derounian-Stodola, copyright © 1998 by Kathryn Zabelle Derounian-Stodola. We thank Oxford University Press for permission to excerpt from pages 85 to 89 of the *Oxford Companion to Women's Writing in the United States,* edited by Cathy N. Davidson and Linda Wagner-Martin, 1995. We thank the William L. Clements Library, University of Michigan, for permission to reprint the 1824 version of the captivity narrative of Mary Jemison. Marjorie Housepian Dobkin's *The Making of a Feminist: Early Journals and Letters of M. Carey Thomas* (1979) provided the text for Thomas's early journals.

Before They Could Vote

Introduction

Living in Public

SIDONIE SMITH and JULIA WATSON

American women's autobiographical writing of the nineteenth and early twentieth centuries, other than slave narratives, suffragist tracts, and Civil War diaries, has received relatively little attention from literary critics and cultural historians. For literary and cultural critics, autobiographical writing has often been seen as a poor relation to the novel and to poetry, the genres in which American women writers created substantial bodies of work and about which significant bodies of scholarship have emerged. For their part, scholars of American women's history have read the autobiographical writings of nineteenth-century women primarily as documentary texts upon which to build careful descriptions of the nature of women's everyday lives and the gendered discourses through which everyday life was organized. In the first case, scholars approach women's autobiographical writing of the century as trivial or marginal to other literary forms. In the second case, scholars read women's autobiographical texts as primarily evidentiary. Neither approach to this rich and diverse field of cultural production does justice to the energy of specific women's texts and the complexity of diverse and changing practices of autobiographical writing in the nineteenth century. Assigning women's autobiographical writing to the zone of merely personal writing or reading it solely for its informational value skews our understanding of how widely women both wrote and read and how many imagined themselves as active agents within the context of public life.

Even the field of autobiography studies has been inattentive to much of American women's life writing.[1] *Before They Could Vote: American Women's Autobiographical Writing, 1819–1919* attempts to redress this inattention by presenting a collection of twenty-four personal narratives written or told by American women, some complete and some excerpted from longer works.[2] These women narrate lives of action, passion, and changing social relations throughout what we are calling the "forgotten" century in the United States, the decades between the early Federalist republic and the post–World War I inception of universal suffrage. We have selected writers from a broad range of regions, ages, ethnic backgrounds, and social and work locations in order to challenge outmoded notions about women's personal writing in the nineteenth century: that there was a pervasive bifurcation of private and public spheres, a gendered world in which women were assigned to the home and imagined themselves through the affective prism of sentimentality and domestic femininity; and that women who went public with their personal stories were primarily white, middle-class women from the Northeast writing within and about their domestic domains.

This introduction discusses several concepts and themes that inform our selections and the ways they might be read: approaches to reading autobiographical discourses, autobiographical genres in this period, public life and the woman writer, shifts in critical approaches to women's writing, and classroom uses and research prospects for this collection.

Reading the Autobiographical

Let us begin with a few theoretical remarks about autobiographical acts before turning to a consideration of women's participation in American autobiographical discourses.

Assuming her experiential history as a reference base and point of departure, an autobiographer represents her life story in order to share it with others. Her "experience" and the "memory" through which it is routed are already interpreted phenomena and thus at least once removed from any pure facticity. After all, autobiographers sometimes take liberty with that most elementary fact, the date of birth, choosing for themselves a more propitious moment or purposefully confusing the date. And memory is selective and untrustworthy. What truth we come to know in reading autobiography derives not from the *facts* of a life truly remembered, though they may be of interest if we can find them, but from the *meanings* the autobiographer assigns to and extracts from the representation of her life. She reads meaningful reality into her life and we read her reading. Because of the interpretive nature of any autobiographical act, then, the distinction between autobiographical narrative and fiction remains elusive. Autobiography is always a story in time interweaving historical fact and fiction.

The meanings the autobiographer reads into her life are historically and culturally contingent. Telling her story, she negotiates—sometimes with little, sometimes with discerning self-consciousness—the cultures of subjectivity available to her, the discourses of identity circulating around her, and the narrative frames commonly used to tell stories. These identities and frames establish what goes into the text, as part of an intelligible and official story, and what remains outside, as unintelligible and unofficial excess—a kind of noise troubling conventional meanings. In effect, then, she reads her life through her readings of other life stories.

But discourses within the dominant culture are multiple, their calls to normative subjectivity often contradictory, their effects on a specific autobiographical subject unpredictable. And each specific autobiographical subject speaks not from a single location within the community but simultaneously, from multiple locations determined by gender, race, class, nationality, ethnicity, religion, and sexuality among other markers of identity. Moreover nondominant communities conserve their own alternative discourses of identity and modes of storytelling. They too circulate heterogeneous calls to subjectivity. Given this multiplicity of the "real," the autobiographical subject does not necessarily imitate prevailing cultural scripts in passive conformity. (And in fact, an imitation by a marginalized subject creates its own kind of noise in the system.) From her specific location within a complex experiential history she may quietly contest, critically adjust, or actively resist normative autobiographical meanings. The impact of her autobiographical mediation depends on the narrative adjustments she makes as she pursues her narrative act, her audience, the models available to her, and her social context and historical circumstances. Autobiographical practice, then, is neither static nor uniform.

Autobiographical Genres in the "Forgotten" Century and the History of American Autobiography

Our choice of time frame, 1819 to 1919, might seem unusual, bridging as it does two centuries. We have skewed this framing of the century in order to de-emphasize the centrality of the Civil War and to focus instead on multiple shifts in what constitutes the territories and boundaries of the nation and thus the changing status of American Indians, African Americans, immigrants, and disenfranchised women as workers and writers. Ranging from the end of the early republic to the passage of the twentieth amendment to the Constitution in 1919 enfranchising women, these narratives link a range of autobiographical genres to broad social transformations, geopolitical, economic, technological, social, and cultural. They offer opportunities to consider the forming, deforming, and reforming of identities in the dynamic context of American myths of identity and belonging. And they focus on what might be called the "forgotten" century for American women's life writing, a time whose myriad and diverse autobiographical forms have as yet not been carefully studied or organized as a canon.

As we have argued elsewhere, the autobiographical is not a single genre but a conceptual umbrella incorporating different forms that serve diverse audiences, purposes, and narrative strategies.[3] Personal narratives are not merely transparent "accounts" of some past experience, or exact records of historical events in people's lives or the life of the nation. Rather, they are performances of self-narrating through which the meanings of the past are produced for the occasions and social identities of the present and the future. Therefore, we cannot assume an unproblematic relationship between autobiographical remembering and the events of the past. Nor can we regard life narratives as merely private acts or acts marginal to literary and cultural production. These modes provide a forum for interrogating issues in gendered experience that change throughout the century: literacy and education; coming-of-age and the life cycle; the nature of work, marriage, and family; mobility and adventure; sexuality and experimentation with identity; and shifting notions of personal and collective identity.[4]

In sum, autobiographical modes are not static. Rather, they are changing, improvisatory, in motion, hybrid modes always in dialogue with the specificities of personal remembering and the cultural expectations generated by the contours of a life story. Autobiographical narratives are always compelled to satisfy certain cultural conventions, the forms, patterns, and rhetorical styles of stories tellable and intelligible at a particular historical moment. They are motivated by particular audiences, contexts of publication, consumption, and desires. They are mediated by publication practices and venues, as well as editorial intermediaries and policies.[5] Yet, however constrained, the modes of the autobiographical continue to be fluid and improvised, and thus malleable to the individual teller's understanding of her past and negotiation of her identity in the present.

Before commenting on autobiographical practices during this "forgotten" century, we want to comment briefly on the relationship of gendered autobiographical discourses and "America." The history of "America" and the history of autobiographical practices are intimately connected. Autobiographical writing emerges as a compelling cultural activity in the West at approximately the same historical moment that European colonists and enslaved Africans began settling into the space described as "the New World," a world well known to its indigenous inhabitants. This New World, laid out in all its abundance before the colonists, invited ever-new opportunities for recreating self and community. America called for autobiographical subjects. Of course the earliest first-person written narratives were accounts of travel and travail through which male Europeans mapped their encounters with and projections of new geographies, peoples, experiences, and identities.

In the Puritan colonies, self scrutiny saturated the environment as what Daniel B. Shea calls "the ur-narrative of God's saving activity in time," a salvation history at once personal and communal that justified and sustained the beleaguered community (1991). In these close communities, soul searching and community building coincided. Individual lives affirmed and secured communal norms; those norms organized the spiritual lives of individuals, including the lives of women, for whom marriage was an economic necessity and public anonymity the mark of God-given femininity.

Despite the dutiful femininity expected of them in this Old World of gender relations, women left accounts of their lives. Autobiographical forms—the poetry of Anne Bradstreet (1612–1672), the captivity narrative of Mary Rowlandson (1682), the diaries of Sarah Kemble Knight (1704–1705) and Elizabeth House Trist (1783–1784), the journal of Esther Edwards Burr (1754–1757), the spiritual testimonies of Quakers Jane Hoskens (1771) and Elizabeth Ashbridge (1774)—provided ready and intimate vehicles through which colonial women simultaneously heeded the cultural call to feminize subjectivity and negotiated their personal and often eccentric responses to unsettling experiences. These are the autobiographical inscriptions of women undomesticated, if only temporarily, by captivity, by travel, or by ministry. Traversing new, often hostile, assuredly fluid environments, these undomesticated subjects end up disrupting communal constructions of femininity. Disputatious women, they adventure through a frontier of their own, reinventing femininity.

By the late eighteenth century heterogeneous autobiographical forms circulated through the vast space of what was becoming a new republic. These included conversion narratives, spiritual journals, adventure narratives, travel diaries, captivity narratives, sea adventures, gallows narratives (or criminal confessions), and slave narratives—all of which contributed powerful cultural myths and communal models of identity to a colony becoming a nation with its own incipient identity. The most influential of these personal narratives was *The Autobiography of Benjamin Franklin,* begun in 1771 but not published as a complete work until 1868. Through his adroit manipulation of the rhetoric of self-fashioning, Franklin creates an exemplary type of American subject: the national, communally-located self-made man, bourgeois, optimistic, flagrantly individualistic, and decidedly masculine. The legacy of his model American continued throughout the nineteenth century. But another autobiographical mode emerged, influenced by Romanticism and Transcendentalism, that celebrates an intensified, sometimes secularized, antinomianism in which the autobiographical *I* as creator of the world defies all provided frames and selves. In either mode the autobiographical subject assumes its participation in the making of an American history.

Not everyone in the nineteenth century, however, had equal access to the official status of the new republican subject or assumed equal access to the making of autobiography and, with autobiography, the making of history. The republican subject remained normatively white, male, and bourgeois, even in its rebellions. Its exclusions were manifold and manifest: bourgeois white women, Native Americans, slaves, exslaves, Mexican Americans, recent immigrants, and members of the working class. When such marginalized subjects turned to autobiographical writing, then, they brought to the official stories unofficial and eccentric histories.

Throughout the one hundred years from 1819 to 1919, women adopted and adapted a range of autobiographical forms to bring personal stories into print and public circulation. Certainly they turned to diaries, journals, and letters as convenient modes of self-inscription, as documented by a number of scholars (see Bloom, Bunkers, Buss, Culley, Gwin, Huff, Schlissel, Temple, Wink). Such genres were understood as properly feminine forms of the autobiographical for literate women during the nineteenth century. These sheltered scribblings were intimate, personal, and colloquial. They focused on the quotidian and were circulated within a vibrant private circuit of exchange among sisters and friends, rather than the marketplace, as chronicled in Carroll Smith-Rosenberg's groundbreaking study *Disorderly Conduct: Visions of Gender in Victorian America.* There were, however, many more modes of the autobiographical to which they turned as they registered their forays into public worlds, and these additional forms were of interest to the expanding outlets for publication. These additional autobiographical genres included confession, captivity narrative, slave narrative, spiritual autobiography, travel narrative, coming-of-age story, collective autobiography, personal essay, ethnographic history, manifesto, immigrant narrative, as-told-to narrative, testimony, and oral witness.

Some of the narratives included here, such as Mary Jemison's captivity narrative, are among the most important genres of life writing in the nineteenth century. Some unfold through plots common to their era. Mary Antin's narrative of immigrant assimilation to an idealized America tells a different story than does Zitkala-Ša's "Sketches," but immigration narratives inevitably identify tensions between American and ethnic discourses, as Betty Bergland notes (144). Most of the narratives included here are less well known or less commonly thought of as autobiographical, such as Fannie Barrier Williams's "The Club Movement Among Colored Women in America." All of the included narratives complicate the assumption that women's writing was confined to particular genres of the "personal." The spiritual autobiography of Jarena Lee, for instance, not only documents an African American woman's public mission but also attests that the slave narrative was not the only genre of life writing taken up by African American women in the first half of the nineteenth century. Thus, the narratives included here turn the focus of women's writing from domesticity and the home to aspects of public life—work, travel, social movements, and political struggles.

The juxtaposition of these twenty-four narratives in their hybrid and diverse modes of subjectivity reveals how much women writers experiment with the cultural forms permeating private and public worlds. That is, they perform subjectivity in ways that undermine any simplistic binary opposition of public and private. As can be seen here, women's practices of autobiographical writing were multifaceted and wildly divergent. At different moments and in various regions, the audiences addressed and the modes used differed, depending upon the politics of publication, the desire of the public for narratives, and the social and cultural pressures for certain kinds of stories. Perhaps this very mobility and malleability of life writing accounts for why autobiographical practice flourished as an enabling means to articulate and reform subjectivity for many diversely located women. Life writing was restricted neither to middle-class women, nor to women of the northeast, nor to white women. Nor was it restricted to a dialogue sustained only between African American and white women. Life writing flourished during this century-long period as an enabling means of articulating and re-forming subjectivity, re-authoring a previously written self, or reflecting on the writer's professional roles for many kinds of women who were otherwise differently advantaged and situated (see Boardman, Lee, Ling, Namias).

Women's Life Writing and Print Culture

Over this century, women took up autobiographical genres for the multiple possibilities of subjectivity these forms made available. They used the existing media available through small and large publishers and in newspapers and magazines for the dissemination of their life stories to an American reading public. And it was not just the literati and the reasonably well-off and educated people of the northeastern states who participated in these thriving publication and circulation ventures. The poor, the vagrant, the criminal, the mobile, and women, too, became not only consumers of other people's writing but also tellers or producers of print culture in very public ways. In his exploration of the history of the book in nineteenth-century America, David D. Hall suggests that "several factors coalesced to bring about this transformation: new printing and paper making technologies that reduced the price of books, improvements in how books were marketed, a rapid increase in the rate of literacy, and a general speeding up of communication. With abundance came the introduction of new literary genres" (37). People began to recognize that writing one's story was not only an "American" thing to do; it brought social status, public recognition, and economic gain as well.

Autobiographical genres of self-narration multiplied. "A market economy, evangelical religion, and romanticism all encouraged people to think of themselves as free agents, characters in the making (and on the make) on the stage of their own devising," suggests Scott Casper (14). Personal stories could circulate far beyond the local community, materializing elsewhere as a commodity of self-locating. With the expansion of print culture, "a pamphlet," writes Ann Fabian, "created 'a memorial' more permanent than either the gossip of the street or the coverage of the press" (55). Autobiographical writing thus became a strategy for making one's way in the world, making the world attentive to one's passions, commitments, and goals, and making oneself as a world.

Casper points out that, for some people, life stories were the only capital readily available to them, a kind of personal property that could be turned into some modicum of profit for immediate return from audiences and readers. Those who were non-literate could dictate their stories to an intermediary or a publisher. The literate could write down their stories and either self-publish them or find a willing printer. Editors could publish the confessions of the non-literate, the renegade, the downtrodden, and the condemned. Travelers could produce chapbooks that focused on true-life adventures. Publishers increasingly directed their attention to "marginal figures who otherwise would not have survived in print: Indian captives, victims of shipwreck, eccentrics" (Casper 156). Accounts of criminal acts, a popular form of storytelling in America since the late seventeenth century (Fabian 52), became profitable publishing ventures for "printers, confessors, and some literate convicts" (51), and were peddled to an increasing working-class readership.[6] Exploring the kinds of narratives told by the poor, Fabian notes the importance of confessions of sinners and criminals, such as the narrative of the condemned Rose Butler that profited her editor rather than her, while still incorporating her narrative of her brief life.

Writing and publication histories are revealing for what they suggest about the political contexts and the emergent venues of life writing, as well as public responses to particular kinds of stories. What began as a rather brief narrative, such as Mary Jemison's "as-told-to" captivity narrative first published by James Seaver in 1824, was repeatedly reprinted and expanded with supporting materials to become a substantial book later in the century, including such materials as photographs, letters, and testimonials. What was written at one historical moment might be published at a much later moment. Frances Anne (Fanny) Kemble's *Journal of a Residence on a Georgia Plantation*, written in 1838 and 1839, did not appear in published form until 1863 when Kemble decided to

go public with her reflections on the degraded life of the slave plantation to counter English support for the Confederacy during the Civil
War. At the turn of the twentieth century, many of the narratives we include here appeared originally in national magazines or newspapers,
among them *The Independent, The Atlantic Monthly,* and the *Boston Globe,*
and in local newspapers such as the *Butte Evening News.*

By the 1850s an increasing number of women began to make their
living as writers—journalists, novelists, magazine writers (see Bauer
and Gould, Kelley). Publishers recognized the money to be made by
directing attention to the consumer public, especially middle-class
women. With the market for print material expanded, middle-class
white women could establish and sustain themselves as professional
writers, along the lines that George Sand so profitably did in France
and George Eliot in England. Margaret Fuller, Lydia Sigourney, Sarah
Orne Jewett, Lucy Larcom, Elizabeth Phelps, and Rebecca Harding
Davis are among the nineteenth-century women who made their living
as writers, something unheard of for women writers before Margaret
Fuller.[7] Not restricted to domestic life, these women were publicly
active and vocal. Their narratives, however, testify to the cultural pressures of official bourgeois femininity. In each narrative the autobiographical subject has to constitute femininity as well as national subjectivity and construct it in such a fashion as to legitimate her claim to
narrative authority. By the early twentieth century, however, the aspiring professional writer, such as Mary Antin or Mary Hunter Austin,
could assert her life story as simultaneously the making of the writer.

Writers sought to publish autobiographical narratives for a variety
of purposes. The possibility of earning money from publishing one's
life story, as noted above, could be very important, as it was for Adele
Jewel, who helped support her family through reprintings of her brief
life story of growing up as a deaf woman. In the case of Mary MacLane,
the publication of her 1902 life narrative led to national celebrity and
public hunger for more of her spicy stories of life as a single woman.
Important too was the possibility of modeling a transformed life. Jarena
Lee was motivated to write her life story as a way of calling others to
God's purpose and validating her own "call." Sometimes the purpose
was at once individual and collective. The ante-bellum speeches of abolitionist activists Sojourner Truth and Harriet Tubman referenced their
own experience as representative of that of enslaved African women.
The post-bellum narratives of Elizabeth Keckley, *Behind the Scenes; or,
Thirty Years a Slave, and Four Years in the White House* (1868), and Anna

Julia Cooper, *A Voice from the South* (1892), shift the emphasis away from
the horrors of slavery and the moral dilemma of the African American
woman's sexual concubinage, to the representation of the African American
woman as the independent self-supporting member of an emerging
black bourgeoisie desirous of participating in the Franklinian myth (see
Santamarina). Autobiographical narrative becomes a means to affirm
the subject's identification with the mainstream values of American life,
and to affirm it on behalf of the collectivity. This was the case at the
dawn of the twentieth century when Booker T. Washington gathered
essays and polemical writings in *A New Negro for a New Century,* including Fannie Barrier Williams's essay on the club movement entitled "The
Colored Woman and Her Part in Race Regeneration" (1900).

For other writers the motivation for collecting life stories was linked
to gathering the alternative histories of disappearing cultures in the
United States. Although there were indigenous forms of oral and picto-
graphic personal narratives in Native American cultures (Hertha Wong
1992), only after contact with white Americans did written autobiography by Native American women emerge as a bicultural product,
whether written alone or in collaboration with a white amanuensis/ed-
itor.[8] This communal identification is signaled in the titles of such narratives as Catherine Brown's *Memoirs of Catherine Brown, a Christian Indian of the Cherokee Nation* (1824) and Sarah Winnemucca's *Life Among
the Piutes: Their Wrongs and Claims* (1883). Yet the narrator weaves this
alternative notion of communal subjectivity through narrative patterns
influenced by the individualistic ethos of the dominant culture. Brown
is influenced by Christian conversion narratives; Winnemucca may
have been influenced as much by protest narratives as by traditional
coup tales that establish communal stature (David Brumble, *American
Indian Autobiography,* 1988). In these cultural contexts the ideologies of
gender they engaged differentiate the narrative spheres of men and
women.

The personal testimonies of nineteenth-century Mexican American
women have only recently been recovered from various archives, primarily the archive of Western historian Hubert H. Bancroft, who collected over one hundred personal narratives (most in oral history form)
of native Californians in the 1870s. In the late nineteenth century Bancroft hired assistants to collect oral histories of California pioneers and
indigenes for his history of California, published from 1884 to 1890.
One of the women Thomas Savage interviewed was Eulalia Pérez,
whose testimony here marks a past that was being appropriated and

suppressed by the national narrative of the new state of California. Pérez's life narration provides a lively testimony countering the official history of an emergent nation. These women's personal narratives, according to Genaro M. Padilla, reveal common preoccupations: the affirmation of a distinct cultural heritage and a way of life forever changed by the Anglicization of California, the recording of the personal experiences of cultural disruption, and the braiding of domestic and social histories. But Padilla also notes that these women variously reflect upon and critique the gender arrangements deployed in the community and affirm their ability to find forms of empowerment in public life within the constraints of a patriarchal, racist society (*My History* 111).

Many autobiographical narratives of culturally eccentric subjects emerged through collaborative ventures. Often the narratives had to be authenticated by white patrons/editors who testified to their veracity and thereby legitimated the "life." In other cases the autobiographical occasion became entirely collaborative. White editors, whether amateur political activists or (later) professional anthropologists, collected the narrative, framed it, organized it, and in the process conformed both narrative mode and autobiographical subject to their ideological agenda. Nonetheless, autobiographical acts, even if collaborative, also became a medium of cultural critique and resistance. Women like Harriet Jacobs implicitly challenged the exclusionary bases upon which cultural notions of white feminine identity rested, bases implicating racial, ethnic, and class identifications. In the process these subjects reproduced different forms of femininity. They thereby undermined the assumed naturalness of sexual and racial differences, simultaneously affirming and troubling the meaning of American lives by turning their own specific lens upon the process of forced Americanization.

By the early decades of the twentieth century, great masses swelled the populations of urban centers, including large numbers of immigrants who established ethnic communities in America's cities. Like African Americans, Native Americans, and Mexican Americans, these immigrants and their children struggled with hyphenated identities and the different histories determinative of those identities. Thus each group of immigrants and each generation of ethnic Americans confronted the dynamic tension between assimilation to a normative American identity that devalued cultural difference and the immigrant's allegiance to the culture of origin and its indigenous traditions, which continued over generations, as Sau-ling Cynthia Wong's critique makes clear. Autobiographies of immigrant and ethnic women reveal how these tensions are exacerbated by multiple gender histories. Gender arrangements line up differently in different cultural contexts, their effects on women influenced by generational position, class status, ethnic group, and racial identification. Autobiographers negotiate competing histories of normative femininity and, in those negotiations, make gender adjustments. The destabilizing possibilities of adjustments to and in a new land, to and in a multicultural identity, are evident in the succession of names Mary Antin adopts in her autobiography, *The Promised Land* (1912), as well as in the undoing and reinvention of identity in Lillian Wald's *The House on Henry Street* (1915) and Anzia Yezierska's *Children of Loneliness* (1923).

Women's Life Narratives in the Reconfiguration of American Studies

The selection of autobiographical works by women in this collection is intended to contribute to ongoing debates in American studies about its changing canon and praxis. The reconfigured concept of the nineteenth-century United States as a nation with imperialist ambitions articulated by Amy Kaplan, Donald Pease, John Carlos Rowe, Robyn Wiegman, and others finds support in several of these narratives, which attest to internal colonization (Fanny Kemble, Zitkala-Ša) and inequitable access for working class and non-white people (Lucy Larcom, Fanny Barrier Williams, "Madeleine"). Several of these narratives also suggest how seemingly disenfranchised women, such as Sarah Winnemucca and Eulalia Pérez, negotiated the boundary of the American nation transnationally. Notions of the dominance of the Eastern states—New England, mid-Atlantic, the South—are also challenged by the work of women writers publishing not just in private, daily forms but publicly throughout many regions of the nation: for instance, Mary Hunter Austin in California and the Southwest or Mary MacLane in the northern Rockies.

Compelling support for reconfiguring American studies as a site of comparative ethnic studies is also offered in the focus on ethnicity and class position in writers as diverse as African American preacher Jarena Lee and Russian Jewish immigrant Mary Antin, both of whom figure "Americanness" across multiple axes of identification. We have only to turn to Sui Sin Far's brief autobiographical essays to note how inadequate any single characterization of her ethnicity would be, or how her texts intervene in simplistic notions of ethnic identity formation by critiquing stereotypes of the Chinese in North America. Each of these reconfigurations of literary and cultural activity in the period between 1819 and 1919 redefines the nation as transnationally situated, as a site of the colonization of some and the enfranchisement of others.

American literary culture becomes a marketplace of heterogeneous forms of writing and testimony through which seemingly marginal subjects exert their claims to a subjective agency not necessarily grounded in being of European descent, male, prosperous, or Christian. Most strikingly, perhaps, as texts ranging from Rose Butler's public confession in 1819 to Harriet Quimby's narrative of flight in 1912 suggest, this collection contests an early dictum about gendered difference: that women's worlds in the nineteenth and early twentieth centuries constituted a separate sphere. Because this notion has been so pervasive in American literary studies and is implicitly challenged by the narratives in this collection, it requires further discussion.

"Separate Spheres" arguments, an orthodoxy of 1970s and 1980s theorizing of women's history in the United States, asserted a binary opposition between public and private spheres, with women situated in an increasingly privatized zone of domestic femininity and men active within the public zone organized according to masculine values, behaviors, attitudes, and practices.[9] As the essays in *No More Separate Spheres!* make clear, the separate spheres model was productive in the early stages of feminist theorizing of the historically specific construction of gender and gendered roles in nineteenth-century America.[10] It provided, as Linda Kerber notes, a "device" through which women's historians could explore the lives of nineteenth-century women and the social organization of gendered bodies, practices, and discourses (37). Although enabling as a framework for constructing the gendered differences of and in women's lives and cultural production, that model has become increasingly problematic for understanding the intersection of gender with other vectors of identity, including race, ethnicity, class, sexuality, and regional location. Separate spheres arguments universalize "woman," equate public powerlessness with the privatized virtues of pliant femininity, attach sentimentality to women and the feminine, depoliticize the home and family, and reproduce a rigid binary of private and public. In so doing, this bifurcated model belies the diversity and complexity of gendered lives.

For one thing the private sphere invoked through this schema tended to be a particular private sphere, one characterizing only particular households—the bourgeois households of the expanding white middle and upper classes. For millions of immigrants and for slaves—captive, escaped, and eventually "freed" by the Emancipation Proclamation—the household remained a space of labor commanded through slavery, indenture, and economic exigency. Then too, on the ever-moving western "frontier," the amorphous spheres of people's lives were constantly reconfigured and renegotiated through the demands of life on the prairies, in the mountains, and along the coasts. Finally, the intersection of gender with race, ethnicity, and sexuality suggests that feminized spaces could be spaces inhabited by men alone, and that within women's relationships the organization of gendered difference maps unequally across cultural locations. Indeed, as Amy Kaplan argues, in the age of Manifest Destiny, the 1830s through the 1850s, when U.S. boundaries were in continuing fluctuation, domesticity relied on and reproduced the contradictory logic of nationalist expansion. Far from being a "separate sphere," the domestic served as "an ambiguous third realm between the national and the foreign," and even women's texts dedicated to household management—such as those of Catherine Beecher and Sara Josepha Hale—inscribe the "racial underpinnings" shared by domestic and imperialist discourses (584).

A focus on autobiographical narratives written and/or published between 1819 and 1919 exposes the limitations of early feminist mappings of women's separate spheres. The women whose narratives are included here come from regions as far-flung as New England and Mexican California, the Rocky Mountain west and the tenement streets of New York, the Georgia plantation and the Mojave desert. They are not constrained in spaces understood problematically as "domestic." Certainly there are spaces of constraint exposed in these narratives, but they are diverse spaces of negotiation, both public and private. The brothel in Butte, Montana, for instance, is at once a place of labor, domesticity, and public entertainment. And the separate spheres that Zitkala-Ša negotiates are not those of feminized consumption and masculine labor but of the Lakota reservation and the Carlisle Indian School, with their differing political practices, ideas of education, and spiritual belief systems. Moreover these women are moving, adventurous, and questing intellectually, spiritually, physically, and geographically. They emerge from a range of domestic spheres, though not idealized ones, to become agents in their worlds, making, mapping, negotiating, and sometimes changing those worlds.

Collectively these twenty-four narratives challenge easy assumptions about what women were doing, during the century that led up to women's suffrage, that took them outside the home, and outside the imminent foreclosure of sentimental fiction's plots of marriage, childbirth, and/or death. Collectively they challenge our assumptions about what characterized their pursuit of action and agency in public worlds, the worlds of labor (physical and intellectual) and professional work, the world of communities, and the worlds beyond the borders of the expanding nation. Even when these women reflect on domestic life in the home, they do so as accomplished writers, not simply recalling an early life but telling stories about coming of age as a process of encountering and negotiating constraints of gendered, sexual, and ethnic difference. These narratives foreground the continually fluid, and at times migratory, social locations occupied by American women during the nineteenth and early twentieth centuries. They also expose the variety and the vagaries of becoming American and the gendered and racialized identities subsumed in the national narrative.

Classroom and Research Uses of This Collection

The autobiographical texts chosen here suggest a larger story, beginning with the 1819 as-told-to confession of the nineteen-year-old Rose Butler, sentenced to death for alleged arson in a poor rooming house; to the transgressive narratives of women as disparate as the prostitute "Madeleine," the aviator Harriet Quimby, the accomplished writer Sui Sin Far (Edith Maude Eaton), and the American Indian activist author and opera composer Zitkala-Ša in the early twentieth century. While this is no simple story of triumphant emergence onto a public stage, these women all intervened in the social, racial, and religious constraints that aimed to keep them fixed in domestic life, without, in most cases, renouncing the communities that sustained them and their activist commitments to important issues of their times. From Jarena Lee refusing to suppress her preaching in the African Methodist Episcopal Church, to Fanny Kemble protesting the wrongs of slavery on Butler Island, Georgia, to Sarah Winnemucca asserting the rights of the Paiute nation through her narrative of broken promises, to Eulalia Pérez telling a complex story of empowerment and compliance at the California mission, to the Massachusetts mill worker Lucy Larcom chronicling her humble beginnings and rise to literary eminence, to Fannie Barrier Williams's prominence in the African American middle-class in Chicago, these writers all tell stories of making their way in the multiple, changing public worlds of American life.

Yet few of these women became as famous in their own time as did writers Margaret Fuller, Sarah Orne Jewett, Mary Hunter Austin, Mary Antin, and Bryn Mawr College president M. Carey Thomas or activists Sojourner Truth and Harriet Tubman. Many of the autobiographical narratives included here have remained little known. The three brief testimonies published in *The Independent* describe the tensions of daily life between African American and white women in the aftermath of the Civil War and their changing sense of American public life. And a few "forgotten" writers such as Mary MacLane are included both for their piquant sense of the costs and pleasures of autobiographical writing and to introduce them to a wider public. Taken together, all these women, through their life narratives, produce a complex portrait of the challenges and costs of aspiring to self-affirming lives.

By collecting these narratives as *Before They Could Vote*, we argue against the tendency to overinvest in the sentimental modes of cultural production in the nineteenth century, and call for a more nuanced understanding of the affective dimensions of writing in the myriad modes of the everyday. We dispute a reading of the "forgotten" century as predominantly a period of suffragist reform negotiated in domestic spheres prior to the Nineteenth Amendment and call for approaching this time as one generating heterogeneous narratives of activism and adventuring. We counter the tendency to approach this hundred-year span methodologically through the lens of a black-and-white binary of slavery versus freedom and to see its multicultural and transnational complexity. We assert that assimilation to an "American" identity was invariably complicated by the ambivalent relationship of women at multiple sites of immigration to the prospect of American citizenship. Finally, we hope that users of this collection will take as much pleasure as we did in encountering some previously unknown autobiographical writers and texts.

Before They Could Vote is designed to stand as the sole primary resource or to supplement a more extensive reading list in courses in nineteenth- and early-twentieth-century American women's history or in American women's autobiographical literature and culture. While we could not encompass the wealth of women's autobiographical writing produced during this time, we made our selections so as to include: (1) a range of women writers throughout a hundred-year span, diverse in regional location and ethnic background, who became publicly visible as writers or activists in their communities; (2) a wide scope of autobiographical genres including such forms as confession, as-told-to

testimony, coming-of-age narrative, manifesto, captivity narrative, jus-
tificatory essay, and narrative of place; and (3) a diverse group of narra-
tions by women of varying degrees of literacy and education and with
a range of social affiliations who nonetheless craved lives beyond the
confines of domesticity and attempted to become active agents in public life. Of course we could not include all the writers and texts we
learned about in researching this project, but we hope this selection will
encourage others to make their own lists and continue the work of re-
trieving and engaging a "forgotten" century.

As a supplementary text, this collection will complement readily
available, affordable book-length narratives in print by well-known
American women writing in the century spanning from 1819 to 1919.
These include the autobiographical narratives of Harriet Jacobs, Mary
Prince, Louisa Picquet, Elizabeth Cady Stanton, Jane Addams, Helen
Keller, Loreta Janeta Velazquez, Elizabeth Keckley, Catharine Maria
Sedgwick, and others. For instance, it can enliven and complicate a
course focused on the narratives of reformers who employ personal
narrative and personal essay as a call to action on such urgent social
questions as women's suffrage (Elizabeth Cady Stanton and Susan B.
Anthony), the household (Catherine Beecher), and social welfare (Jane
Addams). *Before They Could Vote,* by providing a fascinating "pre-
history," can also complement reading lists that explore the "golden
age" of Modernist women's narratives postdating this period, with narratives by such writers as Emma Goldman, Charlotte Perkins Gilman,
Edith Wharton, Isadora Duncan, H.D., Ida B. Wells, Anzia Yezierska,
Gertrude Stein, Zora Neale Hurston, and the later work of Mary Hunter
Austin.

We hope this collection prompts students and scholars to engage in
their own explorations of, research on, and new thinking about
women's life narratives at the intersection of American studies, women's
studies, literary studies, and cultural studies.[11] Perhaps they will be encouraged to seek out other obscure, less easily available narratives, such
as Mormon women's life stories of "faithful transgressions" against the
doctrinally sanctioned practice of polygamy; women's travel narratives, such as Susan Shelby Magoffin's narrative of her travels in Mexico; and the diaries and journals of such self-conscious writers as Alice
James and Louisa May Alcott.[12]

This collection also suggests prospects for future research. New explorations of women's autobiographical cultures, contexts, genres, and
rhetorical strategies might address prevailing understandings of the

"canon" of nineteenth-century autobiographical writing—through which individuals, communities, and the nation negotiated national belonging and the organization of everyday life. After reading these narratives, how might we read more canonical American autobiographical texts such as those by Walt Whitman, Ralph Waldo Emerson, Henry David Thoreau, Frederick Douglass, Booker T. Washington, and Henry Adams differently? How might we understand the organization of gendered social systems and the socially constituted boundary between the zone of domesticity and the zone of public activity in the nineteenth century without recourse to a "separate spheres" model? How might attending to works by lesser known writers and the little-known works of well-known writers, such as Sarah Orne Jewett and Margaret Fuller, offer a more nuanced picture of the cultural meanings and uses of writing lives in the decades prior to suffrage? If the "self-made man" is a trope that informs many male autobiographical narratives of the time, from Frederick Douglass's to Edward Bok's, what complex terms and contingencies might inform the pressures on and impulses to self-making among "undomesticated" women? We leave it to readers to explore possible responses to these questions and to generate many others.

Notes

We thank Oxford University Press for giving us permission to excerpt sections of Sidonie's essay on "Autobiography" from *The Oxford Companion to Women's Writing in the United States.*

1. In a 1991 essay on "Nineteenth-Century Autobiographies of Affiliation: The Case of Catharine Sedgwick and Lucy Larcom" in the influential collection *American Autobiography: Retrospect and Prospect,* Carol Holly acknowledged that her reading of these neglected texts was only a step toward the "comprehensive contextual study of nineteenth-century autobiography by literary women, indeed by all nineteenth-century American women" (227).

2. Fewer than half (ten) of the women included here are subjects of entries in the encyclopedic *Oxford Companion to Women's Writing in the United States,* published in 1995 (edited by Cathy N. Davidson and Linda Wagner-Martin), suggesting that autobiographical narratives still may be seen as "sub-literary."

3. For an expanded discussion of the types and terms of autobiographical writing, including fifty-three genres of self-narrating, see our *Reading Autobiography.* See also the *Encyclopedia of Life Writing* edited by Margaretta Jolly.

4. As many of these women attest, becoming literate was critical to identity formation (Zagarri on literacy, 33, note 7). Acquisition of literacy was a major achievement for Zitkala-Ša, Sarah Winnemucca, and Sui Sin Far, among others.

5. All punctuation, spelling, italics, capitalization, etc. in the selected excerpts have been retained from the original texts. Where words are indecipherable in the originals we have inserted ellipsis points inside brackets. Information that appeared in the original front matter of each excerpt has been included if available.

6. Such personal stories were seen to give "authentic voice" to those confessing and, as Fabian points out, to persuade readers to accept their truth as authoritative, despite the fact that they were often lurid and sensationalized narratives, designed to capture their audiences through titillation and revelation. Sometimes the authenticity was fictional, but powerful and compelling nonetheless, as in the case of certain Barbary Coast narratives written as women's adventures of being captured by pirates but written by men (see Baepler, cited in Fabian 52).

7. Lawrence Buell points out that Sigourney's *Letters of Life* (1866) was "the first full-dress autobiography written by an American author of either sex whose primary vocation was creative writing" (60).

8. The narrator constitutes herself as an autobiographical subject through what Arnold Krupat calls a synecdochic sense of self "where narration of personal history is more nearly marked by the individual's sense of himself [*sic*] in relation to collective social units or groupings" (xx).

9. See Linda Kerber's essay on feminist scholarship of the nineteenth century, especially the work of Barbara Welter in *The Cult of True Womanhood* and Aileen Kraditor on the notion of the cult of domesticity. See also Frances Cogan's alternative of Real Womanhood. These critiques help us see how the notion of women's constitutive domesticity was "a normative ideal [*for white women*] rather than a description of reality" (Zagarri 33, our interpellation).

10. For critiques of the separate spheres argument, see Dana Nelson and Cathy N. Davidson and Jessamyn Hatcher.

11. For an exploration of twenty years of critical work on women's autobiographical practice and an extensive introduction on the modes of theorizing women's life writing, see our *Women, Autobiography, Theory: A Reader*.

12. See Laura L. Bush, *Faithful Transgressions in the American West: Six Twentieth-Century American Mormon Women's Autobiographical Acts*.

1

An Authentic Statement of the Case and Conduct of Rose Butler, who was tried, convicted, and executed for the crime of arson (1819)

R O S E   B U T L E R

R O S E   B U T L E R (1799–1819) remains a mystery except for the details we learn from the pamphlet that calls itself the "authentic account of the case and conduct of Rose Butler." She was born in November 1799 in Mount Pleasant, New York. Until her imprisonment for arson in 1818, she lived in various households in Mount Pleasant and New York City. She was executed in July 1819. Benjamin G. Jansen submitted this "authentic account" of the non-literate woman's story to the Court of the Southern District of New York where it was "reviewed and approved" by the Rev. John Stanford, chaplain to the prisons. The "case and conduct" seems to have been written and published in order to decry the criminal act of arson (as a violation of the people's "right of habitation" and their "entitle[ment] to hold property") and warn potential arsonists of the fate that awaits them: "Let every intentional incendiary take timely warning, lest they also fall into the same condemnation."

Historian Ann Fabian suggests that gallows confession narratives proved a popular form of life writing in the early nineteenth century because they were instructive and moralistic but also titillating. Prisoners recognized the economic potential of their stories; publishers capitalized on the desire of a broader public to witness vicariously the fate of the condemned (56–59).

Reviewed and Approved by the Rev. John Stanford, M.A.
Chaplain to the Public Institutions.
New-York:
Printed and Sold by Broderick and Ritter,
No. 20 James-Street,
1819.

An Authentic Statement of the Case and Conduct of Rose Butler, who was tried, convicted, and executed for the crime of arson

Southern District of New-York, ss.

Be it remembered, that on the sixteenth day of July, on the forty-fourth year of the Independence of the United States of America, *Benjamin G. Jansen*, of the said district, hath deposited in this office the title of a book, the right whereof he claims as proprietor, in the words following, to wit:

"An Authentic Account of the Case and Conduct of Rose Butler, who was Tried, Convicted, and Executed for the crime of Arson. Reviewed and approved by the Rev. John Stanford, M.A. Chaplain to the Public Institutions."

In conformity to the act of the Congress of the United States, entitled "An Act for the encouragement of Learning, by securing the copies of Maps, Charts, and Books to the authors and proprietors of such copies during the time therein mentioned." And also to an Act, entitled "An

Act, supplementary to an Act entitled an Act for the encouragement of Learning, by securing the copies of Maps, Charts, and Books to the authors and proprietors of such copies, during the times therein mentioned, and extending the benefits thereof to the arts of designing, engraving, and etching historical and other prints."

Gilbert Livingston Thompson,
Clerk of the Southern District of New-York.
By William Ironside, Ass't. Clerk

Rose Butler was born in the month of November, in the year 1799, at Mount Pleasant, West-Chester County, State of New-York; consequently, at the time of her execution, she was aged nineteen years and eight months. She first resided in the family of Col. Straing, at Mount Pleasant—afterwards, when about the age of ten years she came to reside with Mr. Abraham Child of this city, where she continued till the age of sixteen, when lastly, she went to reside in the family of William L. Morris, Esq. where she continued till the 5th day of March, 1818, when she was committed to prison for the crime of which she was afterwards convicted at a court of Oyer and Terminer held in the city of New-York in November last, before the Hon. Smith Thompson, His Honour C. D. Colden, and one of the aldermen.

A question of law, however, was reserved by this court, for the decision of the Supreme Court—viz. "Whether the turning in this case was sufficient, within the meaning of the statute, to constitute it a capital offence, and punishable with death; or, "whether it was only an offence at common law, and punishable with imprisonment?"

At the last May term of the Supreme Court held in the city of New-York, Rose Butler was brought before the court, and after a very eloquent and able argument, by David Graham, Esq. counsel for the prisoner, and Pierre C. Van Wyck, Esq. district attorney—Chief Justice Spencer delivered the unanimous opinion of the court—"That the burning in this case was sufficient to bring it within the meaning of the statute, which constituted it a capital offence, and punishable with death."

After which, the prisoner was arraigned according to law by the Clerk, and asked if she had any thing to say why the Court should not then pass sentence upon her agreeable to law. To which she answered—She had nothing to say—Judge Woodworth then pronounced the awful sentence of death upon her in the following eloquent and impressive words:

"*Rose Butler:* The crime for which you are to suffer is justly considered among the most atrocious of human offences. In all civilized countries its punishment has been marked with severity. No prudence or human foresight can protect as against the midnight incendiary—We can resist the highwayman, and sometimes defeat the attack of the hired assassin; but in the hour of repose, when nature has sunk to rest, what guard can shield us against the wicked purposes of those in whom we are obliged to place confidence?

"Formerly, the crime of arson was punishable with death; but when our criminal law became the subject of review, the Legislature tender of human life, and anxious to promote the reformation of the criminal by every mean consistent with the safety of society, substituted imprisonment instead of the sanguinary code which then prevailed.

"This system with all its imperfections, has on the whole, been consoling to the friends of humanity.—From its adoption until about the year 1813, arson was punished by imprisonment in the state prison. At this time the Legislature distinguished the case of *burning an inhabited dwelling house,* by declaring that every person convicted of this offence should suffer death for the same.

"Under this law you have been tried and convicted. You had the benefit of counsel to advise with you, and assist you on the trial. The evidence of your guilt was clear and satisfactory—your case has been submitted to this court, and ingeniously argued. After the most mature deliberation, we are of opinion that it falls within the statute under which you have been convicted.

"Your crime originated in a wicked and depraved heart—you was a servant in the family—confidence was placed in you: you owed fidelity and obedience—their lives and property were in some measure placed within your power—you selected a time best calculated to effect your purpose: in the hour of imaginary security set fire to this dwelling-house. The fire took effect—two or three of the kitchen stairs were consumed; a number of persons were asleep at the time in the upper part of the house; being alarmed by the noise of fire they awoke and extinguished it. You was offended with one of them for having reprimanded you, and for this cause determined on revenge. The remainder of the family had never injured you or given you the least provocation, and yet you intended to involve all in one common destruction.—They retired to rest without suspicion; and had it not been for that mysterious Providence which governs and controls the occurrences of time, and so often brings to naught the counsels of the wicked, they had been consumed. If you are not completely hardened in guilt, you cannot look back and reflect on your conduct without horror.

"You appear to be young. I understand you are quite *intelligent,* and have had the benefit of *instruction,* yet it is necessary that you be cut off from society by an ignominious death. You are now to be sentenced by a human tribunal; but you must shortly appear in the presence of your Creator, who possesses infinite purity and boundless perfection; who will by no means clear the guilty. Death is but the commencement of being—a state of happiness or misery awaits you beyond the grave. You have but a short time to live—*improve that space to prepare to die.* I know not whether you have been religiously instructed, but I know that you live in a country where the Christian religion is acknowledged and revered—send for the ministers of this religion; they will not deny you the benefit of their counsel, instruction and prayers.—The Gospel of Christ contains the plan of salvation—one of its divine features is, that it is adapted to the meanest capacity. The great essentials of the word of life are plain and obvious—read and meditate on its truths; repent truly of your sins; pray for the illumination of the Holy Spirit: look for the blood of Christ as alone sufficient to purify you—as the fountain that is opened for sinners. To do this I recommend you as the only foundation of hope. Although your sins are great, you need not despair if you cast yourself on the merits of the Saviour with confiding hope and humble trust—'If we confess and forsake our sins, God is faithful and just to forgive us our sins, and to cleanse us from all iniquity.'

"It now remains that I discharge the painful duty of the Court in pronouncing the sentence of the law. You are to be taken to the place from whence you came, and from thence, on the 11th of June next, to the place of execution, and between the hours of one and three o'clock in the afternoon, be hanged by the neck until you are dead—and may God have mercy on your soul."

After Rose Butler had received sentence of death, she was remanded to Bridewell, and placed in the condemned room at which time she behaved with extreme impropriety. Shortly after this, the high sheriff, as is usual, gave the ministerial charge of her to the Rev. John Stanford, Chaplain to the Public Institutions. In addition to this, she received frequent visits from other clergy of different religious denominations, for the purpose of affording her instruction suited to her wretched situation. All these humane efforts were without apparent effect; and to some of the ministers, and others, she behaved in a very insulting

manner. The humane visits of the Rev. Mr. Strong, she received with cor-
diality; and we wish we could say with benefit to her miserable soul;
but, her perverseness was in the extreme. During her confinement, she
had females to attend her, and from Mr. Sickels and his family she received those nourishments and that attention which her wretched condition required. As it became the province of the chaplain to make necessary enquiries of the criminal, not only concerning the state of her soul
in the sight of her God, but of those circumstances which related to her
public offence, he committed to writing the communications he received; so much of which as is proper to be made public, we have permission to insert in this paper.

Communication of Rose Butler.

I lived with Mrs. Morris about three years. With Mrs. Morris I had
frequent disputes, and was determined to be revenged on her. On Monday, the 4th of March, a year ago, she came down in the kitchen, and
we had some high words together. She then asked me why I did not
clean up the kitchen and the wooden things? I told her it was impossible to do so and get dinner in time. But all these I cleared up against
night. I went to bed about half past ten. There was not any fire in the
kitchen, it had all went out. Mr. Morris was the last person that was up
in the house. About 1 o'clock in the morning he went down into the
kitchen, and every thing was right—he went up stairs again, and did
not go to bed till 2 o'clock. Shortly after this the alarm of fire was made
in the house. They went down and found the stair-case on fire; and two
pails, a washing machine, and the broom, all on fire, placed on the third
step from the kitchen floor. A person in the back house, with Mr. Morris, broke open the front door, as they could not go down into the
kitchen any other way. A great many persons came in, and among the
others, the two men who had set the place on fire. They asked Mr. Morris if he knew the girl that lived with him? He said yes; she had lived
with me a great while. They then turned about and went off. Next day
morning I was accused of having set fire to the house; to which I said I
had not; but I did not say who did it, or who did not do it. Mrs. Morris
sent over the way to Mrs. Cashier, to enquire after a fortune teller, and
although it was a dreadful stormy afternoon, she went to Division-
street to see her; and she told Mrs. Morris that it was I that did it, and
none but me. Mrs. Morris gave her money before she told her. Mrs.
Morris told me I must go to my aunt's and stay there, for she would

not have me in the house. I did so, and she sent a watchman for me who took me to the watch-house. I was examined in the Police-office and committed to Bridewell.

About three weeks before the fire, two white men followed me to the pump, it was very dark; they asked me many questions about Mrs. Morris, but I did not choose to answer them. They then asked my name, and I said, It is Jane. I asked their names, and they said A—— B—— and B—— C——, and wished me not to tell Mrs. Morris; but I did tell her. They were in snuff coloured clothes, and wore large brimmed hats. Two weeks after, on Monday, I met these two men as I was going to market; they asked me if I was married? and I told them yes; and they wanted me too meet them in the evening, but I would not. Tuesday week after, while I was sweeping the walk, they were coming past, and asked me to let them light a segar, and they went into the kitchen and did so. They had eight or nine keys on a string. They advised me to burn the house, and I refused. The shortest of the men said he "would burn her out;" and further said, If I told of their conversation they would take away my life. The day before the fire they passed the window several times, but did not speak to me.

Ques. Can you give me any further account about those two men?

Ans. They told me that they were constables in a compting office, or store, near the batters. They were about the age and size of —— ——, the turnkey, thick and short; but one was a little taller than the other. One was of a dark complexion, with black hair, the other had sandy hair.

Ques. Did you put the pails and other things on the stairs when they set them on fire?

Ans. I did not; the men did it. [This she afterwards contradicted.]

Ques. How did they get in?

Ans. By a false key.

Ques. How did you know that the house was burnt the last time, while you were in Bridewell?

Ans. I heard the bells ring, and I supposed so. But a letter was sent to me in a loaf of bread, which told me that they had done it; and as the writing was bad, I got Mrs. Scott to read it, and I then burnt it.

Ques. Who was Mrs. Scott?

Ans. A short fat white woman that afterwards went to the Penitentiary.

Ques. Can you recollect what was in the letter?

Ans. It was something like this:—

"Jane,—We are going away, and we shall come back again. You are in no danger—you will be cleared. We have consumed the house pretty near down. Do not tell what we have said to you."

This is as much as I remember

Ques. What name was to the letter?

Ans. It was so queer and bad we could not make it out; but it must have come from one of the men.

Ques. Did your young master, Mr. William L. Morris, always behave with perfect propriety towards you?

Ans. He always did.

Ques. Have you ever had any children?

Ans. No, I never had, and my mother knows I never had one

————

The following Communication was made by Rose Butler to Eliza Duell, a white woman, who was placed in the apartment to take care of her:—

Whilst I lived with Mr. Childs, I was in the constant practice of stealing, and giving articles to a colored woman in the neighborhood, who sold them for me. Thread and silk, I pilfered from the store in considerable quantities. I carried her a dozen pounds at one time, for which she gave me $1, saying that she could get no more for it! One day Mr. C. hung his waistcoat on the back of a chair, and went out of the room—I seized the opportunity and took $15 out the pocket. I was not discovered—this emboldened me, and when I went to live with Mrs. Morris, I continued pilfering whatever I could lay my hands on. I at one time stole $10 from her: at another time I stole $300, in silver, ten of which I gave to a man in Division-street, who kept a Grocery store, for changing part of it into notes. I left most of the money with him, and, a short time before I was committed to prison, he gave me a due bill for $50 which he owed me. The due bill I gave to my aunt Sally who lives with Mr. C——— in Williams-street. My aunt did not know that I had robbed my mistress until sometime towards after. I purchased a silk dress with part of the money, and made a present of it to my aunt, with which she was very much pleased. I went a carriage riding with her and several others, and paid all the expenses. On the 4th of July I went with some girls on board the steam-boat on a party of pleasure and paid the charges; and $15 of it I spent at Mrs. Bundys, at Corlaer's Hook, on a frolic! It was in this manner I squandered away the money I had stolen—in frolicking and rioting in the dance-houses and other places at the Hook.

On the 2d of June, 1819, after she had made a confession to the Rev. Mr. Stanford, in which she stated that the house was in the first instance set on fire by two men, being reminded of some circumstances connected with it, and solicited to tell the truth, and nothing else, she replied that she would, and then preceded as follows:—

"The statement I made in the Police-office was true—I DID set the house on fire MYSELF, but I was advised to do it by two men whose names were A—— B—— and B—— C—— with whom I became acquainted while in company with —— ——: they gave me the matches, and advised me when and how to set the house on fire. The evening previous to the fire, I affixed a string on the outside of the front kitchen door, to prevent the family escaping the flames in that way, and also cut the door a little, with an old knife, that the family might think some person had broken in, and not suspect any one in the house. Two or three days after I had been committed to prison (Sunday), Mrs. Scott was also committed, and was bailed out on the Tuesday following; on that day, before Mrs. S. went out of prison, I received a loaf of bread, in the centre of which I found a note from the men whom I before mentioned, stating that they had succeeded in burning the house of Mrs. Morris. Not being able to read writing, I requested Mrs. S. to read it for me—she did."

Ques. Are you certain it was not more than a week from the time you was committed till the time of receiving the note?
Ans. I cannot be mistaken as to time—I am sure it was not a week.

[The fire alluded to in the note that she says she received, did not take place until twenty days after her commitment—the story, therefore, as to that part is at least improbable.]

Rose being earnestly solicited to tell the reason why she entertained such malignity and revenge towards her mistress, she replied, "My mistress was always finding fault with my work, and scolding me. I never did like her."

On being informed that there was no hope for her now—that her days were very short; and being entreated to think of her sins—her awful death, and to look for mercy from God alone, she coolly and deliberately answered "They are not so sure of hanging me yet, there are more ways of getting out of the world than one." Being reminded that she never showed such a hardened and wicked disposition while she lived in Mrs. Morris' family, and being asked why she had become so altered? she answered, "I have been kept in prison so long that it hath hardened me—I shall never be otherwise!"

The following is another Communication which she also made to the same woman.

On the day preceding the fire, whilst Mrs. M. was scolding me for not hurrying with my work, A—— B——, alias R—— L, came in the kitchen and heard her; he said to me "The d——d old bitch why don't you burn her out?" to which I replied, "I don't care how quick it is done." He then said it should be done that night. He made me promise to come down and open the door after the family were asleep. Mr. Morris went to bed about 2 o'clock, and when I supposed him to have been asleep, I went down, and found the man cutting the door, which I opened and let him in. He took from his pocket some newspapers and matches, and put them in the pail, together with my wet frock; they were set on fire by a rush-light which he brought in with him. He then advised me to go to bed, saying that the fire would not burn much before day-light. He then went away. I bolted the door, and fastened it with string, to prevent the family making their escape. I frequently met this man at the Hook, and on the night of the fire he promised me $25, and told me at the time we were setting fire that he had not got it. This man used frequently to come and enquire for ashes: and at one time I gave him $19 part of the $300 which I stole from my mistress.

Some few days after, in speaking of the man, she called him by a different name; being told of it, she said laughing, "I thought you would have forgotten that."

The Governor, from humane intentions, having respited her for five weeks longer, gave her a desirable period to indulge reflections on her miserable state, and look to the Saviour of mercy to prepare her for the solemn scene, and for an eternal world. Although no signs of contrition appeared in her, the nearer she approached her end, she became less turbulent. On the morning of her execution, at half past 10 o'clock, the Chaplain, in presence of Mr. Strong, in the most solemn manner addressed her on the subjects he had received from her in relation to her offence; and with apparent seriousness she asserted them to be true.

A little before 1 o'clock, she was brought down to the yard, when the chaplain made an address to the assembled officers of justice, and many other spectators, and afterwards offered a solemn prayer to God, for the soul of the criminal, when the procession moved.

Early in the morning of the day of execution, a large concourse of people assembled in the Park in front of the Bridewell. Such was the novelty (the execution of a woman) that thousands of people from the neighbouring towns and villages flocked into the city to witness the last struggles of an expiring mortal. Oft no occasion, for a number of years, has there been such a general excitement apparent in the minds of all classes, of our citizens. It was not until near 1 o'clock, p.m. that every thing could be got in readiness for the procession to move. After clearing a passage in front of the yard on Broadway, they formed, and proceeded in the following order to the place of execution:—

A troop of horse, which had been ordered on duty for that day, formed an oblong square, open in the rear, into which the High Sheriff entered, accompanied by his deputies; next the carriage containing the prisoner (owing to her weak state, and the humanity of the Sheriff she was permitted to ride in one), accompanied by a Deputy Sheriff, the visiting Physician, a Minister of the Gospel, and a pious Quaker lady; next one of the Deputy Keepers of the Prison, followed by a platoon of civil officers, and then a carriage filled with ministers and pious persons followed in the rear; the whole surrounded by marshals and constables with their staff's of office. When the last of the officers entered, the troops closed the square. The concourse of spectators in the street was so great that it was with the utmost difficulty the procession could proceed. The windows and doors of the houses were filled with men, women and children, to witness a fellow being conducted by the ministers of the law to expiate her offences against the community by suffering an ignomious death. How awful—how solemn was that scene! Thousands were urging themselves forward, each one striving to be first at the place of execution—a death-like silence seemed to pervade the whole assembly—nought to be heard but the shuffling of their feet upon the pavement. Every eye was bent upon the prisoner. She appeared perfectly collected and reconciled to her fate. During the procession the physician asked her how she felt? she replied, "My head feels wild" She was then asked if she would have some water? She said "No: I do not feel thirsty;" but some water being procured, she was requested to drink, and did; and also ate part of an orange. Several questions were then asked her by the Reverend Gentleman who accompanied her, among which were the following:

Ques. Is there nothing, Rose, that lays heavy upon your mind that you would wish to disclose previous to your being launched into eternity?
Ans. No, Sir.
Ques. Would you not wish that your accomplices should suffer a punishment in proportion to their crime?
Ans. Yes, Sir.
Ques. Have you nothing to disclose—no particular word to send to any of your near friends?
Ans. No, Sir;—I am willing to be hanged.

After some conversation respecting her situation, she remarked, "What a dusty road they have taken—it fills my clothes full of dirt. What a great number of people are going to see one person. I was once going myself to see a person hanged, it was through persuasion; I went about twenty yards, and would go no further. I returned." When a short distance from the place of execution she was asked by the same gentleman, "Would you wish that I should say any thing particular for you at the place of execution?" She replied, "No sir; nothing in particular." He then said, "Would you not wish that I should offer up a prayer to the Throne of Grace for the benefit of your dying soul?" To which she answered, "If you think proper, Sir."

On arriving at the place of execution, the procession halted, and after a few moments were past in arrangements of a trifling nature, she was assisted by two of the Deputy Sheriffs in ascending the scaffold. On the platform she displayed a firmness unparalleled—not the least concern or dread of her awful situation was visible in her countenance. She was seated on a stool provided for her, and supported on it by the lady who accompanied her from the prison. A fervent prayer was offered up to the Throne of Grace, in her behalf, by those who accompanied her on the scaffold, during which she appeared to be somewhat attentive. A hymn was then sung; after which, taking a final farewell of her surrounding friends, she was launched into eternity—not a murmur or a sigh escaped her—she died almost without a struggle. After hanging about thirty minutes, her body was taken down and interred in Pottersfield, a few yards from the place of execution. The conduct of those who witnessed this awful scene was truly becoming, and comported with the solemnity of the occasion.

The Crime of Arson.—Arson, from *ardere*, to burn, is the malicious, willful burning the house or out-house, the property of another person; and which is felony by the statute. The atrocity and frequency of the commission of this crime, to the injury of individuals, and the annoyance of the public, have induced the Legislature of this state, in their session of 1818 to revise and amend the law in this case provided; and of which the following is a copy:

"*Be it enacted by the People of the State of New-York, Represented in Senate and Assembly,* That every person who shall hereafter be duly convicted or attainted of any manner of treason against the People of this State; or any kind of murder, or of aiding or abetting or procuring any kind of murder to be committed; or of willfully harming any inhabited dwelling house, shall suffer death for the same, and be hanged by the neck until such person be dead." Cap. 29, §1.

The malignity of the crime of Arson above all others must be at once obvious, and needs only to be contemplated to fill the breast with horror! It is a violation of the right of habitations acquired by the law of nature, as well as by the laws of society. Particularly so in America, where every class and colour of citizens are entitled to hold property with each other, guaranteed by the laws of the country. If to behold a dwelling on fire by accident creates sympathy, confusion and horror: how highly criminal must be the act of an incendiary, maliciously and deliberately by fire to endanger the existence of a whole neighbourhood? Admitting that this be done from a principle of private revenge against the owner or occupant of the dwelling for a real or supposed offence: is it not in contempt of the laws of his country which stand ready to redress his grievance? This diabolical act is worse than theft; because the thing stolen only changes its owner, and remains in substance for the benefit of others; whereas by burning, the very substance is either partially or wholly destroyed. In the eye of the law, as well as to common sense, this malicious burning is worse than murder; which, atrocious and horrible as it is, seldom extends beyond the person or persons first intended: whereas fire frequently involves in the common calamity, persons unknown to the incendiary.

Let us view the fatal consequences of this criminal act of burning. Husband and wife, parents and children, the aged, the sick, and the infirm, retire to their beds, for nature's repose—when lo! in the dark shades of night the wretch advances with his infernal match, and envelopes the whole in flames! In a moral point of view, may we not ask, were all of such family prepared to meet their God and Judge? Perhaps not. In what other aspect then can we behold the incendiary, than the infernal messenger of satan to call such unprepared persons to his dread abode before their time? The effects of burning on the interest of the public and the beauty of a city must not be forgotten. The conflagration in Mott-street will not soon be effaced from our memory. The awfulness of the scene, the destruction of property, the ruin of the industrious labourer and mechanic, together with the total demolition of a noble edifice erected for public worship—these constitute a calamity long to be deplored! But, was this dreadful disaster produced by the immediate hand of the Almighty, who has the vivid lightning at his command? No. It was the act of vile incendiaries. Was it for revenge against an individual from whom they had received an injury? It was for the most wicked purpose of collecting plunder from the affrighted, suffering inhabitants; and thereby to aggravate the criminality of their depredations on the public.

From this statement of the nature and consequences of the horrid crime of arson, combined with the ignominious death of Frazer, the perpetual confinement of Vanderpool, together with the more recent death of this ill-fated woman, let every intentional incendiary take timely warning, lest they also fall into the same condemnation.

THE END.

2

A Narrative of the Life of Mrs. Mary Jemison (as told to James E. Seaver) (1824)

MARY JEMISON

MARY JEMISON (1743–1833) was born of Scotch-Irish immigrant parents aboard a ship during a voyage to the "New World" in 1743. She grew up in a Marsh Creek settlement near what is now Gettysburg, Pennsylvania. In the spring of 1758, during the French and Indian Wars, she and her family (with the exception of two brothers) were taken captive by a faction of French soldiers and Shawnee warriors. Although her family and the rest of the captives were killed, Mary and a young neighbor boy were separated for sale. At Fort Duquesne Mary was sold to a group of Seneca Indians who adopted her and named her Dehgewanus ("Two Falling Voices"). She assimilated to the Seneca lifestyle, married a Delaware Indian named Sheninjee, and bore two children of whom one, Thomas, survived. The family set out for Sheninjee's homeland along the Genesee River in New York, but Sheninjee died during the journey. Welcomed by the Seneca people, however, Jemison soon remarried a man named Hiokatoo, with whom she had six children.

During the Revolutionary War an army of 5,000 soldiers dispatched by George Washington attacked the Seneca nation, which supported the British. The assault devastated their settlements and separated Jemison's family. Eventually reunited, the family reorganized in a deserted town, Gadaho, where they lived for nearly sixty years. After Seneca lands were expropriated and divided into twelve reservations, Dehgewanus secured some land for her family. In the continuing tension between natives and settlers in the early decades of the nineteenth century, three of her sons were murdered. Some settlers in the valley, however, welcomed her, referring to her as "the White Woman of the Genesee."

In late 1823 James Everett Seaver, a doctor and writer, interviewed the eighty-old Jemison for three days in a cabin near her home. He compiled her story and published it the following year with J. D. Bemis and Co. of Canandaigua, New York. That is the version included here. An immediate bestseller, the narrative went through numerous reprintings and increasingly expanded editions, at least nineteen by 1918. Various editors added sections on such topics as the Seneca language and Letchworth Park. In the 1990s scholar June Namias published the currently definitive edition of Jemison's captivity narrative. In the latter half of the nineteenth century, Jemison's story fueled the growth of romantic myths about America's indigenous peoples, myths that obscured the real conditions of native life—expropriation of native lands, forced acculturation of native peoples, and deprivation of treaty rights.

In *Women's Indian Captivity Narratives*, Kathryn Zabelle Derounian-Stodola notes that, although her interlocutor (Seaver) used a lengthy preface and introduction to confer credibility on the narrative, Jemison makes interpolations throughout that rely on oral Seneca traditions of self-narrating (120). As she suggests, Jemison was a "transculturated captive" and "so thoroughly a Seneca woman that she learned to manipulate and maneuver white cultural practices in order to privilege herself and her adopted culture" (121). In this way, a "captive" subverted the narrative expectations of the dominant culture.

A narrative of the life of Mrs. Mary Jemison, who was taken by the Indians, in the year 1755, when only about twelve years of age, and has continued to reside amongst them to the present time.

Containing an Account of the Murder of her Father and his Family; her sufferings; her marriage to two Indians; her troubles with her Children; barbarities of the Indians in the French and Revolutionary Wars; the life of her last Husband, &c.; and many Historical Facts never before published.

Carefully taken from her own words, Nov. 29th, 1823.

Canandaigua [N.Y.]:

Printed by J.D. Bemis and co. 1824.

James Everett Seaver took this down.

A Narrative of the Life of Mrs. Mary Jemison

Preface.

That to biographical writings we are indebted for the greatest and best field in which to study mankind, or human nature, is a fact duly appreciated by a well-informed community. In them we can trace the effects of mental operations to their proper sources; and by comparing our own composition with that of those who have excelled in virtue, or with that of those who have been sunk in the lowest depths of folly and vice, we are enabled to select a plan of life that will at least afford self-satisfaction, and guide us through the world in paths of morality.

Without a knowledge of the lives of the vile and abandoned, we should be wholly incompetent to set an appropriate value upon the charms, the excellence and the worth of those principles which have produced the finest traits in the character of the most virtuous.

Biography is a telescope of life, through which we can see the extremes and excesses of the varied properties of the human heart. Wisdom and folly, refinement and vulgarity, love and hatred, tenderness and cruelty, happiness and misery, piety and infidelity, commingled with every other cardinal virtue or vice, are to be seen on the variegated pages of the history of human events, and are eminently deserving the attention of those who would learn to walk in the "paths of peace."

The brazen statue and the sculptured marble, can commemorate the greatness of heroes, statesmen, philosophers, and blood-stained conquerors, who have risen to the zenith of human glory and popularity, under the influence of the mild sun of prosperity: but it is the faithful page of biography that transmits to future generations the poverty, pain, wrong, hunger, wretchedness and torment, and every nameless misery that has been endured by those who have lived in obscurity, and groped their lonely way through a long series of unpropitious events, with but little help besides the light of nature. While the gilded monument displays in brightest colors the vanity of pomp, and the emptiness of nominal greatness, the biographical page, that lives in every line, is giving lessons of fortitude in time of danger, patience in suffering, hope in distress, invention in necessity, and resignation to unavoidable evils. Here also may be learned, pity for the bereaved, benevolence for the destitute, and compassion for the helpless; and at the same time all the sympathies of the soul will be naturally excited to sigh at the unfavorable result, or to smile at the fortunate relief.

In the great inexplicable chain which forms the circle of human events, each individual link is placed on a level with the others, and performs an equal task; but, as the world is partial, it is the situation that attracts the attention of mankind, and excites the unfortunate vociferous eclat of elevation, that raises the pampered parasite to such an immense height in the scale of personal vanity, as, generally, to deprive him of respect, before he can return to a state of equilibrium with his fellows, or to the place whence he started.

Few great men have passed from the stage of action, who have not left in the history of their lives indelible marks of ambition or folly, which produced insurmountable reverses, and rendered the whole a mere caricature, that can be examined only with disgust and regret. Such pictures, however, are profitable, for "by others' faults wise men correct their own."

The following is a piece of biography, that shows what changes may be effected in the animal and mental constitution of man; what trials may be surmounted; what cruelties perpetrated, and what pain endured, when stern necessity holds the reins, and drives the car of fate.

As books of this kind are sought and read with avidity, especially by children, and are well calculated to excite their attention, inform their understanding, and improve them in the art of reading, the greatest care has been observed to render the style easy, the language comprehensive, and the description natural. Prolixity has been studiously avoided. The line of distinction between virtue and vice has been rendered distinctly visible; and chastity of expression and sentiment have received due attention. Strict fidelity has been observed in the composition: consequently, no circumstance has been intentionally exaggerated by the paintings of fancy, nor by fine flashes of rhetoric: neither has the picture been rendered more dull than the original. Without the aid of fiction, what was received as matter of fact, only has been recorded.

It will be observed that the subject of this narrative has arrived at least to the advanced age of eighty years; that she is destitute of education; and that her journey of life, throughout its texture, has been interwoven with troubles, which ordinarily are calculated to impair the faculties of the mind; and it will be remembered, that there are but few old people who can recollect with precision the circumstances of their lives (particularly those circumstances which transpired after middle age.) If, therefore, any error shall be discovered in the narration in respect to time, it will be overlooked by the kind reader, or charitably placed to the narrator's account, and not imputed to neglect, or to the want of attention in the compiler.

The appendix is principally taken from the words of Mrs. Jemison's statements. Those parts which were not derived from her, are deserving equal credit, having been obtained from authentic sources.

For the accommodation of the reader, the work has been divided into chapters, and a copious table of contents affixed. The introduction will facilitate the understanding of what follows; and as it contains matter that could not be inserted with propriety in any other place, will be read with interest and satisfaction.

Having finished my undertaking, the subsequent pages are cheerfully submitted to the perusal and approbation or animadversion of a candid, generous and indulgent public. At the same time it is fondly hoped that the lessons of distress that are portrayed, may have a direct tendency to increase our love of liberty; to enlarge our views of the blessings that are derived from our liberal institutions; and to excite in our breasts sentiments of devotion and gratitude to the great Author and finisher of our happiness.

THE AUTHOR.
Pembroke, March 1, 1824.

Introduction.

The Peace of 1783, and the consequent cessation of Indian hostilities and barbarities, returned to their friends those prisoners, who had escaped the tomahawk, the gauntlet, and the savage fire, after their having spent many years in captivity, and restored harmony to society.

The stories of Indian cruelties which were common in the new settlements, and were calamitous realities previous to that propitious event; slumbered in the minds that had been constantly agitated by them, and were only roused occasionally, to become the fearful topic of the fireside.

It is presumed that at this time there are but few native Americans
that have arrived to middle age, who cannot distinctly recollect of
sitting in the chimney corner when children, all contracted with fear,
and there listening to their parents or visitors, while they related stories
of Indian conquests, and murders, that would make their flaxen hair
nearly stand erect, and almost destroy the power of motion.

At the close of the Revolutionary war all that part of the State of
New-York that lies west of Utica was uninhabited by white people, and
few indeed had ever passed beyond Fort Stanwix, except when engaged in war against the Indians, who were numerous, and occupied a
number of large towns between the Mohawk river and lake Erie. Sometime elapsed after this event, before the country about the lakes and on
the Genesee river was visited, save by an occasional land speculator, or
by defaulters who wished by retreating to what in those days was
deemed almost the end of the earth, to escape the force of civil law.

At length, the richness and fertility of the soil excited emigration, and
here and there a family settled down and commenced improvements in
the country which had recently been the property of the aborigines.
Those who settled near the Genesee river, soon became acquainted with
"The White Woman," as Mrs. Jemison is called, whose history they anxiously sought, both as a matter of interest and curiosity. Frankness characterized her conduct, and without reserve she would readily gratify
them by relating some of the most important periods of her life.

Although her bosom companion was an ancient Indian warrior, and
notwithstanding her children and associates were all Indians, yet it was
found that she possessed an uncommon share of hospitality, and that
her friendship was well worth courting and preserving. Her house was
the stranger's home; from her table the hungry were refreshed;—she
made the naked as comfortable as her means would admit of; and in all
her actions, discovered so much natural goodness of heart, that her
admirers increased in proportion to the extension of her acquaintance,
and she became celebrated as the friend of the distressed. She was the
protectress of the homeless fugitive, and made welcome the weary
wanderer. Many still live to commemorate her benevolence towards
them, when prisoners during the war, and to ascribe their deliverance
to the mediation of "The White Woman."

The settlements increased, and the whole country around her was
inhabited by a rich and respectable people, principally from New-
England, as much distinguished for their spirit of inquisitiveness as for
their habits of industry and honesty, who had all heard from one source

and another a part of her life in detached pieces, and had obtained an idea that the whole taken in connection would afford instruction and amusement.

Many gentlemen of respectability, felt anxious that her narrative might be laid before the public, with a view not only to perpetuate the remembrance of the atrocities of the savages in former times, but to preserve some historical facts which they supposed to be intimately connected with her life, and which otherwise must be lost.

Forty years had passed since the close of the Revolutionary war, and almost seventy years had seen Mrs. Jemison with the Indians, when Daniel W. Banister, Esq. at the instance of several gentlemen, and prompted by his own ambition to add something to the accumulating fund of useful knowledge, resolved, in the autumn of 1823, to embrace that time, while she was capable of recollecting and reciting the scenes through which she had passed, to collect from herself, and to publish to the world, an accurate account of her life.

I was employed to collect the materials, and prepare the work for the press; and accordingly went to the house of Mrs. Jennet Whaley in the town of Castile, Genesee Co. N. Y. in company with the publisher, who procured the interesting subject of the following narrative, to come to that place (a distance of four miles) and there repeat the story of her eventful life. She came on foot in company with Mr. Thomas Clute, whom she considers her protector, and tarried almost three days, which time was busily occupied in taking a sketch of her narrative as she recited it.

Her appearance was well calculated to excite a great degree of sympathy in a stranger, who had been partially informed of her origin, when comparing her present situation with what it probably would have been, had she been permitted to have remained with her friends, and to have enjoyed the blessings of civilization.

In stature she is very short, and considerably under the middle size, and stands tolerably erect, with her head bent forward, apparently from her having for a long time been accustomed to carrying heavy burdens in a strap placed across her forehead. Her complexion is very white for a woman of her age, and although the wrinkles of fourscore years are deeply indented in her cheeks, yet the crimson of youth is distinctly visible. Her eyes are light blue, a little faded by age, and naturally brilliant and sparkling. Her sight is quite dim, though she is able to perform her necessary labor without the assistance of glasses. Her cheek bones are high, and rather prominent, and her front teeth, in the lower jaw, are sound and good. When she looks up and is engaged in conversation her countenance is very expressive; but from her long residence with the Indians, she has acquired the habit of peeping from under eye-brows as they do with the head inclined downwards. Formerly her hair was of a light chestnut brown—it is now quite grey, a little curled, of middling length and tied in a bunch behind. She informed me that she had never worn a cap nor a comb.

She speaks English plainly and distinctly, with a little of the Irish emphasis, and has the use of words so well as to render herself intelligible on any subject with which she is acquainted. Her recollection and memory exceeded my expectation. It cannot be reasonably supposed, that a person of her age has kept the events of seventy years in so complete a chain as to be able to assign to each its proper time and place; she, however, made her recital with as few obvious mistakes as might be found in that of a person of fifty.

She walks with a quick step without a staff, and I was informed by Mr. Clute, that she could yet cross a stream on a log or pole as steadily as any other person.

Her passions are easily excited. At a number of periods in her narration, tears trickled down her grief worn cheek, and at the same time a rising sigh would stop her utterance.

Industry is a virtue which she has uniformly practised from the day of her adoption to the present. She pounds her samp, cooks for herself, gathers and chops wood, feeds her cattle and poultry, and performs other laborious services. Last season she planted, tended and gathered corn—in short, she is always busy.

Her dress at the time I saw her, was made and worn after the Indian fashion, and consisted of a shirt, short gown, petticoat, stockings, moccasins, a blanket and a bonnet. The shirt was of cotton and made at the top, as I was informed, like a man's without collar or sleeves—was open before and extended down about midway of the hips.—The petticoat was a piece of broadcloth with the list at the top and bottom and the ends sewed together. This was tied on by a string that was passed over it and around the waist, in such a manner as to let the bottom of the petticoat down half way between the knee and ankle and leave one-fourth of a yard at the top to be turned down over the string—the bottom of the shirt coming a little below, and on the outside of the top of the fold so as to leave the list and two or three inches of the cloth uncovered. The stockings, were of blue broadcloth, tied, or pinned on, which reached from the knees, into the mouth of the moccasins.—Around her toes only she had some rags, and over these her buckskin moccasins. Her gown was of undressed flannel, colored brown. It was made in old yankee style, with long sleeves, covered the top of the hips, and was tied before in two places with strings of deer skin. Over all this, she wore an Indian blanket. On her head she wore a piece of old brown woollen cloth made somewhat like a sun bonnet.

Such was the dress that this woman was contented to wear, and habit had rendered it convenient and comfortable. She wore it not as a matter of necessity, but from choice, for it will be seen in the sequel, that her property is sufficient to enable her to dress in the best fashion, and to allow her every comfort of life.

Her house, in which she lives, is 20 by 28 feet; built of square timber, with a shingled roof, and a framed stoop. In the centre of the house is a chimney of stones and sticks, in which there are two fire places. She has a good framed barn, 26 by 36, well filled, and owns a fine stock of cattle and horses. Besides the buildings above mentioned, she owns a number of houses that are occupied by tenants, who work her flats upon shares.

Her dwelling, is about one hundred rods north of the Great Slide, a curiosity that will be described in its proper place, on the west side of the Genesee river.

Mrs. Jemison, appeared sensible of her ignorance of the manners of the white people, and for that reason, was not familiar, except with those with whom she was intimately acquainted. In fact she was (to appearance) so jealous of her rights, or that she should say something that would be injurious to herself or family, that if Mr. Clute had not been present, we should have been unable to have obtained her history. She, however, soon became free and unembarrassed in her conversation, and spoke with a degree of mildness, candor and simplicity, that is calculated to remove all doubts as to the veracity of the speaker. The vices of the Indians, she appeared disposed not to aggravate, and seemed to take pride in extoling their virtues. A kind of family pride inclined her to withhold whatever would blot the character of her descendants, and perhaps induced her to keep back many things that would have been interesting.

For the life of her last husband, we are indebted to her cousin, Mr. George Jemison, to whom she referred us for information on that subject generally. The thoughts of his deeds, probably chilled her old heart, and made her dread to rehearse them, and at the same time she well knew they were no secret, for she had frequently heard him relate the whole, not only to her cousin, but to others.

Before she left us she was very sociable, and she resumed her naturally pleasant countenance, enlivened with a smile.

Her neighbors speak of her as possessing one of the happiest tempers and dispositions, and give her the name of never having done a censurable act to their knowledge.

Her habits, are those of the Indians—she sleeps on skins without a bedstead, sits upon the floor or on a bench, and holds her victuals on her lap, or in her hands.

Her ideas of religion, correspond in every respect with those of the great mass of the Senecas. She applauds virtue, and despises vice. She believes in a future state, in which the good will be happy, and the bad miserable; and that the acquisition of that happiness, depends primarily upon human volition, and the consequent good deeds of the happy recipient of blessedness. The doctrines taught in the Christian religion, she is a stranger to.

Her daughters are said to be active and enterprizing women, and her grandsons, who arrived to manhood, are considered able, decent and respectable men in their tribe.

Having in this cursory manner, introduced the subject of the following pages, I proceed to the narration of a life that has been viewed with attention, for a great number of years by a few, and which will be read by the public with the mixed sensations of pleasure and pain, and with interest, anxiety and satisfaction.

LIFE OF MARY JEMISON

Chapter I.

Nativity of her Parents.—Their removal to America.—Her Birth.—Parents settle in Pennsylvania.—Omen of her Captivity.

Although I may have frequently heard the history of my ancestry, my recollection is too imperfect to enable me to trace it further back than to my father and mother, whom I have often heard mention the families from whence they originated, as having possessed wealth and honorable stations under the government of the country in which they resided.

On the account of the great length of time that has elapsed since I was separated from my parents and friends, and having heard the story of their nativity only in the days of my childhood, I am not able to state positively, which of the two countries, Ireland or Scotland, was the land of my parents' birth and education. It, however, is my impression, that they were born and brought up in Ireland.

My Father's name was Thomas Jemison, and my mother's, before her marriage with him, was Jane Erwin. Their affection for each other was mutual, and of that happy kind which tends directly to sweeten the cup of life; to render connubial sorrows lighter; to assuage every discontentment; and to promote not only their own comfort, but that of all who come within the circle of their acquaintance. Of their happiness I recollect to have heard them speak; and the remembrance I yet retain of their mildness and perfect agreement in the government of their children, together with their mutual attention to our common education, manners, religious instruction and wants, renders it a fact in my mind, that they were ornaments to the married state, and examples of connubial love, worthy of imitation. After my remembrance, they were strict observers of religious duties; for it was the daily practice of my father, morning and evening, to attend, in his family, to the worship of God.

Resolved to leave the land of their nativity, they removed from their residence to a port in Ireland, where they lived but a short time before they set sail for this country, in the year 1742 or 3, on board the ship Mary William, bound to Philadelphia, in the state of Pennsylvania.

The intestine divisions, civil wars, and ecclesiastical rigidity and domination that prevailed in those days, were the causes of their leaving their mother country, to find a home in the American wilderness, under the mild and temperate government of the descendants of William Penn; where, without fear, they might worship God, and perform their usual avocations.

In Europe my parents had two sons and one daughter, whose names were John, Thomas and Betsey; with whom, after having put their effects on board, they embarked, leaving a large connexion of relatives and friends, under all those painful sensations, which are only felt when kindred souls give the parting hand and last farewell to those to whom they are endeared by every friendly tie.

In the course of their voyage I was born, to be the sport of fortune and almost an outcast to civil society; to stem the current of adversity through a long chain of vicissitudes, unsupported by the advice of tender parents, or the hand of an affectionate friend; and even without the enjoyment, from others, of any of those tender sympathies that are adapted to the sweetening of society, except such as naturally flow from uncultivated minds, that have been calloused by ferocity.

Excepting my birth, nothing remarkable occurred to my parents on their passage, and they were safely landed at Philadelphia. My father being fond of rural life, and having been bred to agricultural pursuits, soon left the city, and removed his family to the then frontier settlements of Pennsylvania, to a tract of excellent land lying on Marsh creek. At that place he cleared a large farm, and for seven or eight years enjoyed the fruits of his industry. Peace attended their labors; and they had nothing to alarm them, save the midnight howl of the prowling wolf, or the terrifying shriek of the ferocious panther, as they occasionally visited their improvements, to take a lamb or a calf to satisfy their hunger.

During this period my mother had two sons, between whose ages there was a difference of about three years: the oldest was named Matthew, and the other Robert.

Health presided on every countenance, and vigor and strength characterized every exertion. Our mansion was a little paradise. The morning of my childish, happy days, will ever stand fresh in my remembrance, notwithstanding the many severe trials through which I have passed, in arriving at my present situation, at so advanced an age. Even at this remote period, the recollection of my pleasant home at my father's, of my parents, of my brothers and sister, and of the manner in which I was deprived of them all at once, affects me so powerfully, that I am almost overwhelmed with grief, that is seemingly insupportable. Frequently I dream of those happy days: but, alas! they are gone: they have left me to be carried through a long life, dependent for the little pleasures of nearly seventy years, upon the tender mercies of the Indians! In the spring of 1752, and through the succeeding seasons, the stories of Indian barbarities inflicted upon the whites in those days, frequently excited in my parents the most serious alarm for our safety.

The next year the storm gathered faster; many murders were committed; and many captives were exposed to meet death in its most frightful form, by having their bodies stuck full of pine splinters, which were immediately set on fire, while their tormentors, exulting in their distress, would rejoice at their agony!

In 1754, an army for the protection of the settlers, and to drive back the French and Indians, was raised from the militia of the colonial governments, and placed (secondarily) under the command of Col. George Washington. In that army I had an uncle, whose name was John Jemison, who was killed at the battle at the Great Meadows, or Fort Necessity.

His wife had died some time before this, and left a young child, which my mother nursed in the most tender manner, till its mother's sister took it away, a few months after my uncle's death. The French and Indians, after the surrender of Fort Necessity by Col. Washington (which happened the same season, and soon after his victory over them at that place,) grew more and more terrible. The death of the whites, and plundering and burning their property, was apparently their only object: But as yet we had not heard the death-yell, nor seen the smoke of a dwelling that had been lit by an Indian's hand.

The return of a new-year's day found us unmolested; and though we knew that the enemy was at no great distance from us, my father concluded that he would continue to occupy his land another season: expecting (probably from the great exertions which the government was then making) that as soon as the troops could commence their operations in the spring, the enemy would be conquered and compelled to agree to a treaty of peace.

In the preceding autumn my father either moved to another part of his farm, or to another neighborhood, a short distance from our former abode. I well recollect moving, and that the barn that was on the place we moved to was built of logs, though the house was a good one.

The winter of 1754-5 was as mild as a common fall season, and the spring presented a pleasant seed time, and indicated a plenteous harvest. My father, with the assistance of his oldest sons, repaired his farm as usual, and was daily preparing the soil for the reception of the seed. His cattle and sheep were numerous, and according to the best idea of wealth that I can now form, he was wealthy.

But alas! how transitory are all human affairs! how fleeting are riches! how brittle the invisible thread on which all earthly comforts are suspended! Peace in a moment can take an immeasurable flight; health can lose its rosy cheeks; and life will vanish like a vapor at the appearance of the sun! In one fatal day our prospects were all blasted; and death, by cruel hands, inflicted upon almost the whole of the family.

On a pleasant day in the spring of 1755, when my father was sowing flax-seed, and my brothers driving the teams, I was sent to a neighbor's house, a distance of perhaps a mile, to procure a horse and return with it the next morning. I went as I was directed. I was out of the house in the beginning of the evening, and saw a sheet wide spread approaching towards me, in which I was caught (as I have ever since believed) and deprived of my senses! The family soon found me on the ground, almost lifeless (as they said,) took me in, and made use of every remedy in their power for my recovery, but without effect till day-break, when my senses returned, and I soon found myself in good health, so that I went home with the horse very early in the morning.

The appearance of that sheet, I have ever considered as a forerunner of the melancholy catastrophe that so soon afterwards happened to our family: and my being caught in it, I believe, was ominous of my preservation from death at the time we were captured.

Chapter II.

Her Education.—Captivity.—Journey to Fort Pitt.—Mother's Farewell Address.—Murder of her Family.—Preparation of the Scalps.—Indian Precautions.—Arrival at Fort Pitt, &c.

My education had received as much attention from my parents, as their situation in a new country would admit of. I had been at school some, where I learned to read in a book that was about half as large as a Bible; and in the Bible I had read a little. I had also learned the Catechism, which I used frequently to repeat to my parents, and every night, before I went to bed, I was obliged to stand up before my mother and repeat some words that I suppose was a prayer.

My reading, Catechism and prayers, I have long since forgotten; though for a number of the first years that I lived with the Indians, I repeated the prayers as often as I had an opportunity. After the revolutionary war, I remembered the names of some of the letters when I saw them, but have never read a word since I was taken prisoner. It is but a few years since a Missionary kindly gave me a Bible, which I am very fond of hearing my neighbors read to me, and should be pleased to learn to read it myself; but my sight has been for a number of years, so dim that I have not been able to distinguish one letter from another.

As I before observed, I got home with the horse very early in the morning, where I found a man that lived in our neighborhood, and his sister-in-law who had three children, one son and two daughters. I soon learned that they had come there to live a short time; but for what purpose I cannot say. The woman's husband, however, was at that time in Washington's army, fighting for his country; and as her brother-in-law had a house she had lived with him in his absence. Their names I have forgotten.

Immediately after I got home, the man took the horse to go to his house after a bag of grain, and took his gun in his hand for the purpose of killing game, if he should chance to see any.—Our family, as usual, was busily employed about their common business. Father was shaving an axe-helve at the side of the house; mother was making preparations for breakfast;—my two oldest brothers were at work near the barn; and the little ones, with myself, and the woman and her three children, were in the house.

Breakfast was not yet ready, when we were alarmed by the discharge of a number of guns, that seemed to be near. Mother and the women before mentioned, almost fainted at the report, and every one trembled with fear. On opening the door, the man and horse lay dead near the house, having just been shot by the Indians.

I was afterwards informed, that the Indians discovered him at his own house with his gun, and pursued him to father's, where they shot him as I have related. They first secured my father, and then rushed into the house, and without the least resistance made prisoners of my mother, Robert, Matthew, Betsey, the woman and her three children, and myself, and then commenced plundering.

My two brothers, Thomas and John, being at the barn, escaped and went to Virginia, where my grandfather Erwin then lived, as I was informed by a Mr. Fields, who was at my house about the close of the revolutionary war.

The party that took us consisted of six Indians and four Frenchmen, who immediately commenced plundering, as I just observed, and took what they considered most valuable; consisting principally of bread, meal and meat. Having taken as much provision as they could carry, they set out with their prisoners in great haste, for fear of detection, and soon entered the woods. On our march that day, an Indian went behind us with a whip, with which he frequently lashed the children to make them keep up. In this manner we travelled till dark without a mouthful of food or a drop of water; although we had not eaten since the night before. Whenever the little children cried for water, the Indians would make them drink urine or go thirsty. At night they encamped in the woods without fire and without shelter, where we were watched with the greatest vigilance. Extremely fatigued, and very hungry, we were compelled to lie upon the ground supperless and without a drop of water to satisfy the cravings of our appetites. As in the day time, so the little ones were made to drink urine in the night if they cried for water. Fatigue alone brought us a little sleep for the refreshment of our weary limbs; and at the dawn of day we were again started on our march in the same order that we had proceeded on the day before. About sunrise we were halted, and the Indians gave us a full breakfast of provision that they had brought from my father's house. Each of us being very hungry, partook of this bounty of the Indians, except father, who was so much overcome with his situation—so much exhausted by anxiety and grief, that silent despair seemed fastened upon his countenance, and he could not be prevailed upon to refresh his sinking nature by the use of a morsel of food. Our repast being finished, we again resumed our march, and before noon passed a small fort that I heard my father say was called Fort Canagojigge.

That was the only time that I heard him speak from the time we were taken till we were finally separated the following night.

Towards evening we arrived at the border of a dark and dismal swamp, which was covered with small hemlocks, or some other evergreen, and other bushes, into which we were conducted; and having gone a short distance we stopped to encamp for the night.

Here we had some bread and meat for supper: but the dreariness of our situation, together with the uncertainty under which we all labored, as to our future destiny, almost deprived us of the sense of hunger, and destroyed our relish for food.

Mother, from the time we were taken, had manifested a great degree of fortitude, and encouraged us to support our troubles without complaining; and by her conversation seemed to make the distance and time shorter, and the way more smooth. But father lost all his ambition in the beginning of our trouble, and continued apparently lost to every care—absorbed in melancholy. Here, as before, she insisted on the necessity of our eating; and we obeyed her, but it was done with heavy hearts.

As soon as I had finished my supper, an Indian took off my shoes and stockings and put a pair of moccasins on my feet, which my mother observed; and believing that they would spare my life, even if they should destroy the other captives, addressed me as near as I can remember in the following words:—

"My dear little Mary, I fear that the time has arrived when we must be parted forever Your life, my child, I think will be spared; but we shall probably be tomahawked here in this lonesome place by the Indians. O! how can I part with you my darling? What will become of my sweet little Mary? Oh! how can I think of your being continued in captivity without a hope of your being rescued? O that death had snatched you from my embraces in your infancy; the pain of parting then would have been pleasing to what it now is; and I should have seen the end of your troubles!—Alas, my dear! my heart bleeds at the thoughts of what awaits you; but, if you leave us, remember my child your own name, and the name of your father and mother. Be careful and not forget your English tongue. If you shall have an opportunity to get away from the Indians, don't try to escape; for if you do they will find and destroy you. Don't forget, my little daughter, the prayers that I have learned you—say them often; be a good child, and God will bless you. May God bless you my child, and make you comfortable and happy."

During this time, the Indians stripped the shoes and stockings from the little boy that belonged to the woman who was taken with us, and put moccasins on his feet, as they had done before on mine. I was crying. An Indian took the little boy and myself by the hand, to lead us off from the company, when my mother exclaimed, "Don't cry Mary— don't cry my child. God will bless you! Farewell—farewell!"

The Indian led us some distance into the bushes, or woods, and there lay down with us to spend the night. The recollection of parting with my tender mother kept me awake, while the tears constantly flowed from my eyes. A number of times in the night the little boy begged of me earnestly to run away with him and get clear of the Indians; but remembering the advice I had so lately received, and knowing the dangers to which we should be exposed, in travelling without a path and without a guide, through a wilderness unknown to us, I told him that I would not go, and persuaded him to lie still till morning.

Early the next morning the Indians and Frenchmen that we had left the night before, came to us; but our friends were left behind. It is impossible for any one to form a correct idea of what my feelings were at the sight of those savages, whom I supposed had murdered my parents and brothers, sister, and friends, and left them in the swamp to be devoured by wild beasts! But what could I do? A poor little defenceless girl; without the power or means of escaping; without a home to go to, even if I could be liberated; without a knowledge of the direction or distance to my former place of residence; and without a living friend to whom to fly for protection, I felt a kind of horror, anxiety, and dread, that, to me, seemed insupportable. I durst not cry—I durst not complain; and to inquire of them the fate of my friends (even if I could have mustered resolution) was beyond my ability, as I could not speak their language, nor they understand mine. My only relief was in silent stifled sobs.

My suspicions as to the fate of my parents proved too true; for soon after I left them they were killed and scalped, together with Robert, Matthew, Betsey, and the woman and her two children, and mangled in the most shocking manner.

Having given the little boy and myself some bread and meat for breakfast, they led us on as fast as we could travel, and one of them went behind and with a long staff, picked up all the grass and weeds that we trailed down by going over them. By taking that precaution they avoided detection; for each weed was so nicely placed in its natural position that no one would have suspected that we had passed that way. It is the custom of Indians when scouting, or on private expeditions, to step carefully and where no impression of their feet can be left—shunning wet or muddy ground. They seldom take hold of a bush or limb, and never break one; and by observing those precautions and that of setting up the weeds and grass which they necessarily lop, they completely elude the sagacity of their pursuers, and escape that punishment which they are conscious they merit from the hand of justice.

After a hard day's march we encamped in a thicket, where the Indians made a shelter of boughs, and then built a good fire to warm and dry our benumbed limbs and clothing; for it had rained some through the day. Here we were again fed as before. When the Indians had finished their supper they took from their baggage a number of scalps and went about preparing them for the market, or to keep without spoiling, by straining them over small hoops which they prepared for that purpose, and then drying and scraping them by the fire. Having put the scalps, yet wet and bloody, upon the hoops, and stretched them to their full extent, they held them to the fire till they were partly dried and then with their knives commenced scraping off the flesh; and in that way they continued to work, alternately drying and scraping them, till they were dry and clean. That being done they combed the hair in the neatest manner, and then painted it and the edges of the scalps yet on the hoops, red. Those scalps I knew at the time must have been taken from our family by the color of the hair. My mother's hair was red; and I could easily distinguish my father's and the children's from each other. That sight was most appalling; yet, I was obliged to endure it without complaining.

In the course of the night they made me to understand that they should not have killed the family if the whites had not pursued them.

Mr. Fields, whom I have before mentioned, informed me that at the time we were taken, he lived in the vicinity of my father; and that on hearing of our captivity, the whole neighborhood turned out in pursuit of the enemy, and to deliver us if possible: but that their efforts were unavailing. They however pursued us to the dark swamp, where they found my father, his family and companions, stripped and mangled in the most inhuman manner: That from thence the march of the cruel monsters could not be traced in any direction; and that they returned to their homes with the melancholy tidings of our misfortunes, supposing that we had all shared in the massacre.

The next morning we went on; the Indian going behind us and setting up the weeds as on the day before. At night we encamped on the ground in the open air, without a shelter or fire.

In the morning we again set out early, and travelled as on the two former days, though the weather was extremely uncomfortable, from the continual falling of rain and snow.

At night the snow fell fast, and the Indians built a shelter of boughs, and a fire, where we rested tolerably dry through that and the two succeeding nights.

When we stopped, and before the fire was kindled, I was so much fatigued from running, and so far benumbed by the wet and cold, that I expected that I must fail and die before I could get warm and comfortable. The fire, however, soon restored the circulation, and after I had taken my supper I felt so that I rested well through the night.

On account of the storm, we were two days at that place. On one of those days, a party consisting of six Indians who had been to the frontier settlements, came to where we were, and brought with them one prisoner, a young white man who was very tired and dejected. His name I have forgotten.

Misery certainly loves company. I was extremely glad to see him, though I knew from his appearance, that his situation was as deplorable as mine, and that he could afford me no kind of assistance. In the afternoon the Indians killed a deer, which they dressed, and then roasted it whole; which made them a full meal. We were each allowed a share of their venison, and some bread, so that we made a good meal also.

Having spent three nights and two days at that place, and the storm having ceased, early in the morning the whole company, consisting of twelve Indians, four Frenchmen, the young man, the little boy and myself, moved on at a moderate pace without an Indian behind us to deceive our pursuers.

In the afternoon we came in sight of Fort Pitt (as it is now called,) where we were halted while the Indians performed some customs upon their prisoners which they deemed necessary. That fort was then occupied by the French and Indians, and was called Fort Du Quesne. It

stood at the junction of the Monongahela, which is said to signify, in
some of the Indian languages, the Falling-in-Banks,[1] and the Alleghany[2]
rivers, where the Ohio river begins to take its name. The word O-hi-o,
signifies bloody.

At the place where we halted, the Indians combed the hair of the
young man, the boy and myself, and then painted our faces and hair
red, in the finest Indian style. We were then conducted into the fort,
where we received a little bread, and were then shut up and left to tarry
alone through the night.

Chapter III.

She is given to two Squaws.—Her journey down the Ohio.—Passes a
Shawanee town where white men had just been burnt.—Arrives at the
Seneca town.—Her Reception.—She is adopted.—Ceremony of Adoption.—
Indian Custom.—Address.—She receives a new name.—Her Employment.—
Retains her own and learns the Seneca Language.—Situation of the Town,
&c.—Indians go on a Hunting Tour to Sciota and take her with them.—
Returns.—She is taken to Fort Pitt, and then hurried back by her Indian
Sisters.—Her hopes of Liberty destroyed.—Second Tour to Sciota.—Return
to Wiishto, &c—Arrival of Prisoners.—Priscilla Ramsay.—Her Chain.—Mary
marries a Delaware.—Her Affection for him.—Birth and Death of her first
Child.—Her Sickness and Recovery.—Birth of Thomas Jemison.

The night was spent in gloomy forebodings. What the result of our captivity would be, it was out of our power to determine or even imagine.—
At times we could almost realize the approach of our masters to butcher
and scalp us;—again we could nearly see the pile of wood kindled on
which we were to be roasted; and then we would imagine ourselves at
liberty: alone and defenceless in the forest, surrounded by wild beasts
that were ready to devour us. The anxiety of our minds drove sleep
from our eyelids; and it was with a dreadful hope and painful impatience that we waited for the morning to determine our fate.

The morning at length arrived, and our masters came early and let
us out of the house, and gave the young man and boy to the French,

1. Navigator.

2. The word Alleghenny, was derived from an ancient race of Indians called
"Tallegawe." The Delaware Indians, instead of saying "Alleghenny," say "Allegawe," or
"Allegawenink." (*Western Tour*-p. 455)

who immediately took them away. Their fate I never learned; as I have not seen nor heard of them since.

I was now left alone in the fort, deprived of my former companions, and of every thing that was near or dear to me but life. But it was not long before I was in some measure relieved by the appearance of two pleasant looking squaws of the Seneca tribe, who came and examined me attentively for a short time, and then went out. After a few minutes absence they returned with my former masters, who gave me to them to dispose of as they pleased.

The Indians by whom I was taken were a party of Shawanees, if I re-member right, that lived, when at home, a long distance down the Ohio.

My former Indian masters, and the two squaws, were soon ready to leave the fort, and accordingly embarked; the Indians in a large canoe, and the two squaws and myself in a small one, and went down the Ohio.

When we set off, an Indian in the forward canoe took the scalps of my former friends, strung them on a pole that he placed upon his shoulder, and in that manner carried them, standing in the stern of the canoe, directly before us as we sailed down the river, to the town where the two squaws resided.

On our way we passed a Shawanee town, where I saw a number of heads, arms, legs, and other fragments of the bodies of some white people who had just been burnt. The parts that remained were hanging on a pole which was supported at each end by a crotch stuck in the ground, and were roasted or burnt black as a coal. The fire was yet burning; and the whole appearances afforded a spectacle so shocking, that, even to this day, my blood almost curdles in my veins when I think of them!

At night we arrived at a small Seneca Indian town, at the mouth of a small river, that was called by the Indians, in the Seneca language, She-nan-jee,[3] where the two Squaws to whom I belonged resided. There we landed, and the Indians went on; which was the last I ever saw of them.

Having made fast to the shore, the Squaws left me in the canoe while they went to their wigwam or house in the town, and returned with a suit of Indian clothing, all new, and very clean and nice. My clothes,

---

3. That town, according to the geographical description given by Mrs. Jemison, must have stood at the mouth of Indian Cross creek, which is about 76 miles by water, below Pittsburgh; or at the mouth of Indian Short creek, 87 miles below Pittsburgh, where the town of Warren now stands: But at which of those places I am unable to determine.
Author.

though whole and good when I was taken, were now torn in pieces, so that I was almost naked. They first undressed me and threw my rags into the river; then washed me clean and dressed me in the new suit they had just brought, in complete Indian style; and then led me home and seated me in the center of their wigwam.

I had been in that situation but a few minutes, before all the Squaws in the town came in to see me. I was soon surrounded by them, and they immediately set up a most dismal howling, crying bitterly, and wringing their hands in all the agonies of grief for a deceased relative.

Their tears flowed freely, and they exhibited all the signs of real mourning. At the commencement of this scene, one of their number began, in a voice somewhat between speaking and singing, to recite some words to the following purport, and continued the recitation till the ceremony was ended; the company at the same time varying the appearance of their countenances, gestures and tone of voice, so as to correspond with the sentiments expressed by their leader:

"Oh our brother! Alas! He is dead—he has gone; he will never re-turn! Friendless he died on the field of the slain, where his bones are yet lying unburied! Oh, who will not mourn his sad fate? No tears dropped around him; oh, no! No tears of his sisters were there! He fell in his prime, when his arm was most needed to keep us from danger! Alas! he has gone! and left us in sorrow, his loss to bewail: Oh where is his spirit? His spirit went naked, and hungry it wanders, and thirsty and wounded it groans to return! Oh helpless and wretched, our brother has gone! No blanket nor food to nourish and warm him; nor candles to light him, nor weapons of war:—Oh, none of those comforts had he! But well we remember his deeds!—The deer he could take on the chase! The panther shrunk back at the sight of his strength! His enemies fell at his feet! He was brave and courageous in war! As the fawn he was harmless: his friendship was ardent: his temper was gentle: his pity was great! Oh! our friend, our companion is dead! Our brother, our brother, alas! he is gone! But why do we grieve for his loss? In the strength of a warrior, un-daunted he left us, to fight by the side of the Chiefs! His war-whoop was shrill! His rifle well aimed laid his enemies low: his tomahawk drank of their blood: and his knife flayed their scalps while yet covered with gore! And why do we mourn? Though he fell on the field of the slain, with glory he fell, and his spirit went up to the land of his fathers in war! Then why do we mourn? With transports of joy they received him, and fed him, and clothed him, and welcomed him there! Oh friends, he is happy; then dry up your tears! His spirit has seen our distress, and sent us a helper whom with pleasure we greet. Dickewamis has come: then let us receive her with joy! She is handsome and pleasant! Oh! she is our sister, and gladly we welcome her here. In the place of our brother she stands in our tribe. With care we will guard her from trouble; and may she be happy till her spirit shall leave us."

In the course of that ceremony, from mourning they became serene— joy sparkled in their countenances, and they seemed to rejoice over me as over a long lost child. I was made welcome amongst them as a sister to the two Squaws before mentioned, and was called Dickewamis; which being interpreted, signifies a pretty girl, a handsome girl, or a pleasant, good thing. That is the name by which I have ever since been called by the Indians.

I afterwards learned that the ceremony I at that time passed through, was that of adoption. The two squaws had lost a brother in Washington's war, sometime in the year before, and in consequence of his death went up to Fort Pitt, on the day on which I arrived there, in order to receive a prisoner or an enemy's scalp, to supply their loss.

It is a custom of the Indians, when one of their number is slain or taken prisoner in battle, to give to the nearest relative to the dead or absent, a prisoner, if they have chanced to take one, and if not, to give him the scalp of an enemy. On the return of the Indians from conquest, which is always announced by peculiar shoutings, demonstrations of joy, and the exhibition of some trophy of victory, the mourners come forward and make their claims. If they receive a prisoner, it is at their option either to satiate their vengeance by taking his life in the most cruel manner they can conceive of; or, to receive and adopt him into the family, in the place of him whom they have lost. All the prisoners that are taken in battle and carried to the encampment or town by the Indians, are given to the bereaved families, till their number is made good. And unless the mourners have but just received the news of their bereavement, and are under the operation of a paroxysm of grief, anger and revenge; or, unless the prisoner is very old, sickly, or homely, they generally save him, and treat him kindly. But if their mental wound is fresh, their loss so great that they deem it irreparable, or if their prisoner or prisoners do not meet their approbation, no torture, let it be ever so cruel, seems sufficient to make them satisfaction. It is family, and not national, sacrifices amongst the Indians, that has given them an indelible stamp as barbarians, and identified their character with the idea which is generally formed of unfeeling ferocity, and the most abandoned cruelty.

It was my happy lot to be accepted for adoption; and at the time of the ceremony I was received by the two squaws, to supply the place of their brother in the family; and I was ever considered and treated by them as a real sister, the same as though I had been born of their mother.

During my adoption, I sat motionless, nearly terrified to death at the appearance and actions of the company, expecting every moment to feel their vengeance, and suffer death on the spot. I was, however, happily disappointed, when at the close of the ceremony the company retired, and my sisters went about employing every means for my consolation and comfort.

Being now settled and provided with a home, I was employed in nursing the children, and doing light work about the house. Occasionally I was sent out with the Indian hunters, when they went but a short distance, to help them carry their game. My situation was easy; I had no particular hardships to endure. But still, the recollection of my parents, my brothers and sisters, my home, and my own captivity, destroyed my happiness, and made me constantly solitary, lonesome and gloomy.

My sisters would not allow me to speak English in their hearing; but remembering the charge that my dear mother gave me at the time I left her, whenever I chanced to be alone I made a business of repeating my prayer, catechism, or something I had learned in order that I might not forget my own language. By practising in that way I retained it till I came to Genesee flats, where I soon became acquainted with English people with whom I have been almost daily in the habit of conversing.

My sisters were diligent in teaching me their language; and to their great satisfaction I soon learned so that I could understand it readily, and speak it fluently. I was very fortunate in falling into their hands; for they were kind good natured women; peaceable and mild in their dispositions; temperate and decent in their habits, and very tender and gentle towards me. I have great reason to respect them, though they have been dead a great number of years.

The town where they lived was pleasantly situated on the Ohio, at the mouth of the Shenanjee: the land produced good corn; the woods furnished a plenty of game, and the waters abounded with fish. Another river emptied itself into the Ohio, directly opposite the mouth of the Shenanjee. We spent the summer at that place, where we planted, hoed, and harvested a large crop of corn, of an excellent quality.

About the time of corn harvest, Fort Pitt was taken from the French by the English.[4]

The corn being harvested, the Indians took it on horses and in canoes, and proceeded down the Ohio, occasionally stopping to hunt a few days, till we arrived at the mouth of Sciota river; where they established their winter quarters, and continued hunting till the ensuing spring, in the adjacent wilderness. While at that place I went with the other children to assist the hunters to bring in their game. The forests on the Sciota were well stocked with elk, deer, and other large animals; and the marshes contained large numbers of beaver, muskrat, &c. which made excellent hunting for the Indians; who depended, for their meat, upon their success in taking elk and deer; and for ammunition and clothing, upon the beaver, muskrat, and other furs that they could take in addition to their peltry.

The season for hunting being passed, we all returned in the spring to the mouth of the river Shenanjee, to the houses and fields we had left in the fall before. There we again planted our corn, squashes, and beans, on the fields that we occupied the preceding summer.

About planting time, our Indians all went up to Fort Pitt, to make peace with the British, and took me with them.[5] We landed on the opposite side of the river from the fort, and encamped for the night. Early the next morning the Indians took me over to the fort to see the white people that were there. It was then that my heart bounded to be liberated from the Indians and to be restored to my friends and my country. The white people were surprized to see me with the Indians, enduring the hardships of a savage life, at so early an age, and with so delicate a constitution as I appeared to possess. They asked me my name; where and when I was taken—and appeared very much interested on my behalf. They

4. The above statement is apparently in error; and is to be attributed solely to the treachery of the old lady's memory; though she is confident that that event took place at the time above mentioned. It is certain that Fort Pitt was not evacuated by the French and given up to the English, till sometime in November, 1758. It is possible, however, that an armistice was agreed upon, and that for a time, between the spring of 1755 and 1758, both nations visited that post without fear of molestation. As the succeeding part of the narrative corresponds with the true historical chain of events, the public will overlook this circumstance, which appears unsupported by history. AUTHOR.

5. History is silent as to any treaty having been made between the English, and French and Indians, at that time; though it is possible that a truce was agreed upon, and that the parties met for the purpose of concluding a treaty of peace.

were continuing their inquiries, when my sisters became alarmed, believing that I should be taken from them, hurried me into their canoe and recrossed the river—took their bread out of the fire and fled with me, without stopping, till they arrived at the river Shenanjee. So great was their fear of losing me, or of my being given up in the treaty, that they never once stopped rowing till they got home.

Shortly after we left the shore opposite the fort, as I was informed by one of my Indian brothers, the white people came over to take me back; but after considerable inquiry, and having made diligent search to find where I was hid, they returned with heavy hearts. Although I had then been with the Indians something over a year, and had become considerably habituated to their mode of living, and attached to my sisters, the sight of white people who could speak English inspired me with an unspeakable anxiety to go home with them, and share in the blessings of civilization. My sudden departure and escape from them, seemed like a second captivity, and for a long time I brooded the thoughts of my miserable situation with almost as much sorrow and dejection as I had done those of my first sufferings. Time, the destroyer of every affection, wore away my unpleasant feelings, and I became as contented as before.

We tended our cornfields through the summer; and after we had harvested the crop, we again went down the river to the hunting ground on the Sciota, where we spent the winter, as we had done the winter before.

Early in the spring we sailed up the Ohio river, to a place that the Indians called Wiishto,[6] where one river emptied into the Ohio on one side, and another on the other. At that place the Indians built a town, and we planted corn.

We lived three summers at Wiishto, and spent each winter on the Sciota.

The first summer of our living at Wiishto, a party of Delaware Indians came up the river, took up their residence, and lived in common with us. They brought five white prisoners with them, who by their conversation, made my situation much more agreeable, as they could all speak English. I have forgotten the names of all of them except one, which was Priscilla Ramsay. She was a very handsome, good natured girl, and was married soon after she came to Wiishto to Capt. Little

6. Wiishto I suppose was situated near the mouth of Indian Guyundat, 327 miles below Pittsburgh, and 73 above Big Sciota; or at the mouth of Swan creek, 307 miles below Pittsburgh.

Billy's uncle, who went with her on a visit to her friends in the states. Having tarried with them as long as she wished to, she returned with her husband to Can-a-ah-tua, where he died. She, after his death, married a white man by the name of Nettles, and now lives with him (if she is living) on Grand River, Upper Canada.

Not long after the Delawares came to live with us, at Wiishto, my sisters told me that I must go and live with one of them, whose name was She-nin-jee. Not daring to cross them, or disobey their commands, with a great degree of reluctance I went; and Sheninjee and I were married according to Indian custom.

Sheninjee was a noble man; large in stature; elegant in his appearance; generous in his conduct; courageous in war; a friend to peace, and a great lover of justice. He supported a degree of dignity far above his rank, and merited and received the confidence and friendship of all the tribes with whom he was acquainted. Yet, Sheninjee was an Indian. The idea of spending my days with him, at first seemed perfectly irreconcilable to my feelings: but his good nature, generosity, tenderness, and friendship towards me, soon gained my affection; and, strange as it may seem, I loved him!—To me he was ever kind in sickness, and always treated me with gentleness; in fact, he was an agreeable husband, and a comfortable companion. We lived happily together till the time of our final separation, which happened two or three years after our marriage, as I shall presently relate.

In the second summer of my living at Wiishto, I had a child at the time that the kernels of corn first appeared on the cob. When I was taken sick, Sheninjee was absent, and I was sent to a small shed, on the bank of the river, which was made of boughs, where I was obliged to stay till my husband returned. My two sisters, who were my only companions, attended me, and on the second day of my confinement my child was born; but it lived only two days. It was a girl: and notwithstanding the shortness of the time that I possessed it, it was a great grief to me to lose it.

After the birth of my child, I was very sick, but was not allowed to go into the house for two weeks; when, to my great joy, Sheninjee returned, and I was taken in and as comfortably provided for as our situation would admit of. My disease continued to increase for a number of days; and I became so far reduced that my recovery was despaired of by my friends, and I concluded that my troubles would soon be finished. At length, however, my complaint took a favorable turn, and by the time that the corn was ripe I was able to get about. I continued to gain my health, and in the fall was able to go to our winter quarters, on the Sciota, with the Indians.

From that time, nothing remarkable occurred to me till the fourth winter of my captivity, when I had a son born, while I was at Sciota: I had a quick recovery, and my child was healthy. To commemorate the name of my much lamented father, I called my son Thomas Jemison.

Chapter IV.

She leaves Wiishto for Fort Pitt, in company with her Husband.—Her feelings on setting out.—Contrast between the labor of the white and Indian Women.—Deficiency of Arts amongst the Indians.—Their former Happiness.—Baneful effects of Civilization, and the introduction of ardent Spirits amongst them, &c.—Journey up the River.—Murder of three Traders by the Shawnees.—Her Husband stops at a Trading House.—Wantonness of the Shawnees.—Moves up the Sandusky.—Meets her Brother from Ge-nish-a-u.—Her Husband goes to Wiishto, and she sets out for Genishau in company with her Brothers.—They arrive at Sandusky. Occurrences at that place.—Her journey to Genishau, and Reception by her Mother and Friends.

In the spring, when Thomas was three or four moons [months] old, we returned from Sciota to Wiishto, and soon after set out to go to Fort Pitt, to dispose of our fur and skins, that we had taken in the winter, and procure some necessary articles for the use of our family.

I had then been with the Indians four summers and four winters, and had become so far accustomed to their mode of living, habits and dispositions, that my anxiety to get away, to be set at liberty, and leave them, had almost subsided. With them was my home; my family was there, and there I had many friends to whom I was warmly attached in consideration of the favors, affection and friendship with which they had uniformly treated me, from the time of my adoption. Our labor was not severe; and that of one year was exactly similar, in almost every re-spect, to that of the others, without that endless variety that is to be ob-served in the common labor of the white people. Notwithstanding the Indian women have all the fuel and bread to procure, and the cooking to perform, their task is probably not harder than that of white women, who have those articles provided for them; and their cares certainly are not half as numerous, nor as great. In the summer season, we planted, tended and harvested our corn, and generally had all our children with us; but had no master to oversee or drive us, so that we could work as leisurely as we pleased. We had no ploughs on the Ohio; but performed the whole process of planting and hoeing with a small tool that resembled, in some respects, a hoe with a very short handle.

Our cooking consisted in pounding our corn into samp or hommany, boiling the hommany, making now and then a cake and baking it in the ashes, and in boiling or roasting our venison. As our cooking and eating utensils consisted of a hommany block and pestle, a small kettle, a knife or two, and a few vessels of bark or wood, it required but little time to keep them in order for use.

Spinning, weaving, sewing, stocking knitting, and the like, are arts which have never been practised in the Indian tribes generally. After the revolutionary war, I learned to sew, so that I could make my own clothing after a poor fashion; but the other domestic arts I have been wholly ignorant of the application of, since my captivity. In the season of hunting, it was our business, in addition to our cooking, to bring home the game that was taken by the Indians, dress it, and carefully preserve the eatable meat, and prepare or dress the skins. Our clothing was fastened together with strings of deer skin, and tied on with the same.

In that manner we lived, without any of those jealousies, quarrels, and revengeful battles between families and individuals, which have been common in the Indian tribes since the introduction of ardent spirits amongst them.

The use of ardent spirits amongst the Indians, and the attempts which have been made to civilize and christianize them by the white people, has constantly made them worse and worse; increased their vices, and robbed them of many of their virtues; and will ultimately produce their extermination. I have seen, in a number of instances, the effects of education upon some of our Indians, who were taken when young, from their families, and placed at school before they had had an opportunity to contract many Indian habits, and there kept till they arrived to manhood; but I have never seen one of those but what was an Indian in every respect after he returned. Indians must and will be Indians, in spite of all the means that can be used for their cultivation in the sciences and arts.

One thing only marred my happiness, while I lived with them on the Ohio; and that was the recollection that I had once had tender parents, and a home that I loved. Aside from that consideration, or, if I had been taken in infancy, I should have been contented in my situation. Notwithstanding all that has been said against the Indians, in consequence of their cruelties to their enemies—cruelties that I have witnessed, and had abundant proof of—it is a fact that they are naturally kind, tender and peaceable towards their friends, and strictly honest; and that those cruelties have been practised, only upon their enemies, according to their idea of justice.

At the time we left Wiishto, it was impossible for me to suppress a sigh of regret on parting with those who had truly been my friends—with those whom I had every reason to respect. On account of a part of our family living at Genishau, we thought it doubtful whether we should return directly from Pittsburgh, or go from thence on a visit to see them.

Our company consisted of my husband, my two Indian brothers, my little son and myself. We embarked in a canoe that was large enough to contain ourselves and our effects, and proceeded on our voyage up the river.

Nothing remarkable occurred to us on our way, till we arrived at the mouth of a creek which Sheninjee and my brothers said was the outlet of Sandusky lake; where, as they said, two or three English traders in fur and skins had kept a trading house but a short time before, though they were then absent. We had passed the trading house but a short distance, when we met three white men floating down the river, with the appearance of having been recently murdered by the Indians. We supposed them to be the bodies of the traders, whose store we had passed the same day. Sheninjee being alarmed for fear of being apprehended as one of the murderers, if he should go on, resolved to put about immediately, and we accordingly returned to where the traders had lived, and there landed.

At the trading house we found a party of Shawnee Indians, who had taken a young white man prisoner, and had just begun to torture him for the sole purpose of gratifying their curiosity in exulting at his distress. They at first made him stand up, while they slowly pared his ears and split them into strings; they then made a number of slight incisions in his face; and then bound him upon the ground, rolled him in the dirt, and rubbed it in his wounds: some of them at the same time whipping him with small rods! The poor fellow cried for mercy and yelled most piteously.

The sight of his distress seemed too much for me to endure: I begged of them to desist—I entreated them with tears to release him. At length they attended to my intercessions, and set him at liberty. He was shockingly disfigured, bled profusely, and appeared to be in great pain: but as soon as he was liberated he made off in haste, which was the last I saw of him.

We soon learned that the same party of Shawnees had, but a few hours before, massacred the three white traders whom we saw in the river, and had plundered their store. We, however, were not molested by them, and after a short stay at that place, moved up the creek about forty miles to a Shawnee town, which the Indians called Gaw-gush-shaw-ga (which being interpreted signifies a mask or a false face.) The creek that we went up was called Candusky.

It was now summer; and having tarried a few days at Gawgush-shawga, we moved on up the creek to a place that was called Yis-kah-wa-na (meaning in English open mouth.)

As I have before observed, the family to which I belonged was part of a tribe of Seneca Indians, who lived, at that time, at a place called Genishau, from the name of the tribe, that was situated on a river of the same name which is now called Genesee. The word Genishau signifies a shining, clear or open place. Those of us who lived on the Ohio, had frequently received invitations from those at Genishau, by one of my brothers, who usually went and returned every season, to come and live with them, and my two sisters had been gone almost two years.

While we were at Yiskahwana, my brother arrived there from Geni-shau, and insisted so strenuously upon our going home (as he called it) with him, that my two brothers concluded to go, and to take me with them.

By this time the summer was gone, and the time for harvesting corn had arrived. My brothers, for fear of the rainy season setting in early, thought it best to set out immediately that we might have good travel-ling. Sheninjee consented to have me go with my brothers; but con-cluded to go down the river himself with some fur and skins which he had on hand, spend the winter in hunting with his friends, and come to me in the spring following.

That was accordingly agreed upon, and he set out for Wiishto; and my three brothers and myself, with my little son on my back, at the same time set out for Genishau. We came on to Upper Sandusky, to an Indian town that we found deserted by its inhabitants, in consequence of their having recently murdered some English traders, who resided amongst them. That town was owned and had been occupied by Delaware In-dians, who, when they left it, buried their provision in the earth, in order to preserve it from their enemies, or to have a supply for themselves if they should chance to return. My brothers understood the customs of the Indians when they were obliged to fly from their enemies; and suspecting that their corn at least must have been hid, made diligent search, and at length found a large quantity of it, together with beans, sugar and honey, so carefully buried that it was completely dry and as good as when they left it. As our stock of provision was scanty, we considered ourselves extremely fortunate in finding so seasonable a supply, with so little trouble. Having caught two or three horses, that we found there, and furnished ourselves with a good store of food, we travelled on till we came to the mouth of French Creek, where we hunted two days, and from thence came on to Conowongo Creek, where we were obliged to stay seven or ten days, in consequence of our horses having left us and straying into the woods. The horses, however, were found, and we again prepared to resume our journey. During our stay at that place the rain fell fast, and had raised the creek to such a height that it was seemingly impossible for us to cross it. A number of times we ventured in, but were compelled to return, barely escaping with our lives. At length we succeeded in swimming our horses and reached the opposite shore; though I but just escaped with my little boy from being drowned. From Sandusky the path that we travelled was crooked and obscure; but was tolerably well understood by my oldest brother, who had travelled it a number of times, when going to and returning from the Cherokee wars. The fall by this time was considerably advanced, and the rains, attended with cold winds, continued daily to increase the difficulties of travelling. From Conowongo we came to a place, called by the Indians Che-ua-shung-gau-tau, and from that to U-na-waum-gwa (which means an eddy, not strong,) where the early frosts had destroyed the corn so that the Indians were in danger of starving for the want of bread. Having rested ourselves two days at that place, we came on to Caneadea and stayed one day, and then continued our march till we arrived at Genishau. Genishau at that time was a large Seneca town, thickly inhabited, lying on Genesee river, opposite what is now called the Free Ferry, adjoining Fall-Brook, and about south west of the present village of Geneseo, the county seat for the county of Livingston, in the state of New-York.

Those only who have travelled on foot the distance of five or six hundred miles, through an almost pathless wilderness, can form an idea of the fatigue and sufferings that I endured on that journey. My clothing was thin and illy calculated to defend me from the continually drenching rains with which I was daily completely wet, and at night with nothing but my wet blanket to cover me, I had to sleep on the naked ground, and generally without a shelter, save such as nature had provided. In addition to all that, I had to carry my child, then about nine months old, every step of the journey on my back, or in my arms, and provide for his comfort and prevent his suffering, as far as my poverty of means would admit. Such was the fatigue that I sometimes felt, that I thought it impossible for me to go through, and I would almost abandon the idea of even trying to proceed. My brothers were attentive, and at length, as I have stated, we reached our place of destination, in good health, and without having experienced a day's sickness from the time we left Yiskahwana.

We were kindly received by my Indian mother and the other members of the family, who appeared to make me welcome; and my two sisters, whom I had not seen in two years, received me with every expression of love and friendship, and that they really felt what they expressed, I have never had the least reason to doubt. The warmth of their feelings, the kind reception which I met with, and the continued favors that I received at their hands, rivetted my affection for them so strongly that I am constrained to believe that I loved them as I should have loved my own sister had she lived, and I had been brought up with her.

Chapter V.

Indians march to Niagara to fight the British.—Return with two Prisoners, &c—Sacrifice them at Fall-Brook.—Her Indian Mother's Address to her Daughter.—Death of her Husband.—Bounty offered for the Prisoners taken in the last war.—John Van Sice attempts to take her to procure her Ransom.—Her Escape.—Edict of the Chiefs.—Old King of the tribe determines to have her given up.—Her brother threatens her Life.—Her narrow Escape.—The old King goes off.—Her brother is informed of the place of her concealment, and conducts her home.—Marriage to her second Husband.—Names of her Children.

When we arrived at Genishau, the Indians of that tribe were making active preparations for joining the French, in order to assist them in retaking Fort Ne-a-gaw (as Fort Niagara was called in the Seneca language) from the British, who had taken it from the French in the month preceding. They marched off the next day after our arrival, painted and accoutred in all the habiliments of Indian warfare, determined on death or victory; and joined the army in season to assist in accomplishing a plan that had been previously concerted for the destruction of a part of the British army. The British feeling themselves secure in the possession of Fort Neagaw, and unwilling that their enemies should occupy any of the military posts in that quarter, determined to take Fort Schlosser, lying a few miles up the river from Neagaw, which they expected to effect with but little loss. Accordingly a detachment of soldiers, sufficiently numerous, as was supposed, was sent out to take it, leaving a strong garrison in the fort, and marched off, well prepared to effect their object. But on their way they were surrounded by the French and Indians, who lay in ambush to receive them, and were driven off the bank of the river into a place called the "Devil's Hole," together with their horses, carriages, artillery, and every thing pertaining to the army. Not a single man escaped being driven off, and of the whole number one only was fortunate enough to escape with his life.[7] Our Indians were absent but a few days, and returned in triumph, bringing with them two white prisoners, and a number of oxen. Those were the first neat cattle that were ever brought to the Genesee flats.

The next day after their return to Genishau, was set apart as a day of feasting and frolicing, at the expence of the lives of their two unfortunate prisoners, on whom they purposed to glut their revenge, and satisfy their love for retaliation upon their enemies. My sister was anxious to attend the execution, and to take me with her, to witness the customs of the warriors, as it was one of the highest kind of frolics ever celebrated in their tribe, and one that was not often attended with so much pomp and parade as it was expected that would be. I felt a kind of anxiety to witness the scene, having never attended an execution, and yet I felt a kind of horrid dread that made my heart revolt, and inclined me to step back rather than support the idea of advancing. On the morning of the execution she made her intention of going to the frolic, and taking me with her, known to our mother, who in the most feeling terms remonstrated against a step at once so rash and unbecoming the true dignity of our sex:

"How, my daughter (said she, addressing my sister,) how can you even think of attending the feast and seeing the unspeakable torments that those poor unfortunate prisoners must inevitably suffer from the hands of our warriors? How can you stand and see them writhing in the warriors' fire, in all the agonies of a slow, a lingering death? How can you think of enduring the sound of their groanings and prayers

7. For the particulars of that event, see Appendix, No. 1. [Not included in this selection.]

to the Great Spirit for sudden deliverance from their enemies, or from life? And how can you think of conducting to that melancholy spot your poor sister Dickewamis (meaning myself,) who has so lately been a prisoner, who has lost her parents and brothers by the hands of the bloody warriors, and who has felt all the horrors of the loss of her freedom, in lonesome captivity? Oh! how can you think of making her bleed at the wounds which now are but partially healed? The recollection of her former troubles would deprive us of Dickewamis, and she would depart to the fields of the blessed, where fighting has ceased, and the corn needs no tending—where hunting is easy, the forests delightful, the summers are pleasant, and the winters are mild!—O! think once, my daughter, how soon you may have a brave brother made prisoner in battle, and sacrificed to feast the ambition of the enemies of his kindred, and leave us to mourn for the loss of a friend, a son and a brother, whose bow brought us venison, and supplied us with blankets!—Our task is quite easy at home, and our business needs our attention. With war we have nothing to do: our husbands and brothers are proud to defend us, and their hearts beat with ardor to meet our proud foes. Oh! stay then, my daughter; let our warriors alone perform on their victims their customs of war!"

This speech of our mother had the desired effect; we stayed at home and attended to our domestic concerns. The prisoners, however, were executed by having their heads taken off, their bodies cut in pieces and shockingly mangled, and then burnt to ashes!—They were burnt on the north side of Fall-brook, directly opposite the town which was on the south side, some time in the month of November, 1759.

I spent the winter comfortably, and as agreeably as I could have expected to, in the absence of my kind husband. Spring at length appeared, but Sheninjee was yet away; summer came on, but my husband had not found me. Fearful forebodings haunted my imagination; yet I felt confident that his affection for me was so great that if he was alive he would follow me and I should again see him. In the course of the summer, however, I received intelligence that soon after he left me at Yiskahwana he was taken sick and died at Wiishto. This was a heavy and an unexpected blow. I was now in my youthful days left a widow, with one son, and entirely dependent on myself for his and my support. My mother and her family gave me all the consolation in their power, and in a few months my grief wore off and I became contented.

In a year or two after this, according to my best recollection of the time, the King of England offered a bounty to those who would bring in the prisoners that had been taken in the war, to some military post where they might be redeemed and set at liberty.

John Van Sice, a Dutchman, who had frequently been at our place, and was well acquainted with every prisoner at Genishau, resolved to take me to Niagara, that I might there receive my liberty and he the offered bounty. I was notified of his intention; but as I was fully determined not to be redeemed at that time, especially with his assistance, I carefully watched his movements in order to avoid falling into his hands. It so happened, however, that he saw me alone at work in a corn-field, and thinking probably that he could secure me easily, ran towards me in great haste. I espied him at some distance, and well knowing the amount of his errand, run from him with all the speed I was mistress of, and never once stopped till I reached Gardow.[8] He gave up the chase, and returned: but I, fearing that he might be lying in wait for me, stayed three days and three nights in an old cabin at Gardow, and then went back trembling at every step for fear of being apprehended. I got home without difficulty; and soon after, the chiefs in council having learned the cause of my elopement, gave orders that I should not be taken to any military post without my consent; and that as it was my choice to stay, I should live amongst them quietly and undisturbed. But, notwithstanding the will of the chiefs, it was but a few days before the old king of our tribe told one of my Indian brothers that I should be redeemed, and he would take me to Niagara himself. In reply to the old king, my brother said that I should not be given up; but that, as it was my wish, I should stay with the tribe as long as I was pleased to. Upon this a serious quarrel ensued between them, in which my brother frankly told him that sooner than I should be taken by force, he would kill me with his own hands!—Highly enraged at the old king, my brother came to my sister's house, where I resided, and informed her of all that had passed respecting me; and that, if the old king should attempt to take me, as he firmly believed he would, he would immediately take my life, and hazard the consequences. He returned to the old king. As soon as I came in, my sister told me what she had just heard, and what she expected without doubt would befal me. Full of pity, and anxious for my preservation, she then directed me to take my child and go into some high weeds at no great distance from the house, and there hide myself and lay still till all was silent in the house, for my brother,

8. I have given this orthography, because it corresponds with the popular pronunciation.

she said, would return at evening and let her know the final conclusion of the matter, of which she promised to inform me in the following manner: If I was to be killed, she said she would bake a small cake and lay it at the door, on the outside, in a place that she then pointed out to me. When all was silent in the house, I was to creep softly to the door, and if the cake could not be found in the place specified, I was to go in: but if the cake was there, I was to take my child and go as fast as I possibly could to a large spring on the south side of Samp's Creek (a place that I had often seen,) and there wait till I should by some means hear from her.

Alarmed for my own safety, I instantly followed her advice, and went into the weeds, where I lay in a state of the greatest anxiety, till all was silent in the house, when I crept to the door, and there found, to my great distress, the little cake! I knew my fate was fixed, unless I could keep secreted till the storm was over; and accordingly crept back to the weeds, where my little Thomas lay, took him on my back, and laid my course for the spring as fast as my legs would carry me. Thomas was nearly three years old, and very large and heavy. I got to the spring early in the morning, almost overcome with fatigue, and at the same time fearing that I might be pursued and taken, I felt my life an almost insupportable burthen. I sat down with my child at the spring, and he and I made a breakfast of the little cake, and water of the spring, which I dipped and supped with the only implement which I possessed, my hand.

In the morning after I fled, as was expected, the old King came to our house in search of me, and to take me off; but, as I was not to be found, he gave me up, and went to Niagara with the prisoners he had already got into his possession.

As soon as the old King was fairly out of the way, my sister told my brother where he could find me. He immediately set out for the spring, and found me about noon. The first sight of him made me tremble with the fear of death; but when he came near, so that I could discover his countenance, tears of joy flowed down my cheeks, and I felt such a kind of instant relief as no one can possibly experience, unless when under the absolute sentence of death he receives an unlimited pardon. We were both rejoiced at the event of the old King's project; and after staying at the spring through the night, set out together for home early in the morning. When we got to a cornfield near the town, my brother secreted me till he could go and ascertain how my case stood; and finding that the old King was absent, and that all was peaceable, he returned to me, and I went home joyfully.

Not long after this, my mother went to Johnstown, on the Mohawk river, with five prisoners, who were redeemed by Sir William Johnson, and set at liberty.

When my son Thomas was three or four years old, I was married to an Indian, whose name was Hiokatoo, commonly called Gardow, by whom I had four daughters and two sons. I named my children, principally, after my relatives, from whom I was parted, by calling my girls Jane, Nancy, Betsey and Polly, and the boys John and Jesse. Jane died about twenty-nine years ago, in the month of August, a little before the great Council at Big-Tree, aged about fifteen years. My other daughters are yet living, and have families.

Chapter VI.

Peace amongst the Indians.—Celebrations.—Worship.—Exercises.—
Business of the Tribes.—Former Happiness of the Indians in time of peace
extolled.—Their Morals; Fidelity; Honesty; Chastity; Temperance.—Indians
called to German Flats.—Treaty with Americans.—They are sent for by
the British Commissioners, and go to Oswego.—Promises made by those
Commissioners.—Greatness of the King of England.—Reward that was
paid them for joining the British.—They make a Treaty.—Bounty offered
for Scalps.—Return richly dressed and equipped.—In 1776 they kill a man
at Cautega to provoke the Americans.—Prisoners taken at Cherry Valley,
brought to Beard's-Town; redeemed, &c.—Battle at Fort Stanivix.—Indians
suffer a great loss.—Mourning at Beard's Town.—Mrs. Jemison's care of and
services rendered to Butler and Brandt.

After the conclusion of the French war, our tribe had nothing to trouble it till the commencement of the Revolution. For twelve or fifteen years the use of the implements of war was not known, nor the war-whoop heard, save on days of festivity, when the achievements of former times were commemorated in a kind of mimic warfare, in which the chiefs and warriors displayed their prowess, and illustrated their former adroitness, by laying the ambuscade, surprizing their enemies, and performing many accurate manoeuvres with the tomahawk and scalping knife; thereby preserving and handing to their children, the theory of Indian warfare. During that period they also pertinaciously observed the religious rites of their progenitors, by attending with the most scrupulous exactness and a great degree of enthusiasm to the sacrifices, at particular times, to appease the anger of the evil deity, or to excite the commisseration and friendship of the Great Good Spirit, whom they adored with reverence, as the author, governor, supporter and disposer of every good thing of which they participated.

They also practised in various athletic games, such as running, wrestling, leaping, and playing ball, with a view that their bodies might be more supple, or rather that they might not become enervated, and that they might be enabled to make a proper selection of Chiefs for the councils of the nation and leaders for war.

While the Indians were thus engaged in their round of traditionary performances, with the addition of hunting, their women attended to agriculture, their families, and a few domestic concerns of small consequence, and attended with but little labor.

No people can live more happy than the Indians did in times of peace, before the introduction of spirituous liquors amongst them. Their lives were a continual round of pleasures. Their wants were few, and easily satisfied; and their cares were only for to-day; the bounds of their calculations for future comfort not extending to the incalculable uncertainties of to-morrow. If peace ever dwelt with men, it was in former times, in the recesses from war, amongst what are now termed barbarians. The moral character of the Indians was (if I may be allowed the expression) uncontaminated. Their fidelity was perfect, and became proverbial; they were strictly honest; they despised deception and falsehood; and chastity was held in high veneration, and a violation of it was considered sacrilege. They were temperate in their desires, moderate in their passions, and candid and honorable in the expression of their sentiments on every subject of importance.

Thus, at peace amongst themselves, and with the neighboring whites, though there were none at that time very near, our Indians lived quietly and peaceably at home, till a little before the breaking out of the revolutionary war, when they were sent for, together with the Chiefs and members of the Six Nations generally, by the people of the States, to go to the German Flats, and there hold a general council, in order that the people of the states might ascertain, in good season, who they should esteem and treat as enemies, and who as friends, in the great war which was then upon the point of breaking out between them and the King of England.

Our Indians obeyed the call, and the council was holden, at which the pipe of peace was smoked, and a treaty made, in which the Six Nations solemnly agreed that if a war should eventually break out, they would not take up arms on either side; but that they would observe a strict neutrality. With that the people of the states were satisfied, as they had not asked their assistance, nor did not wish it. The Indians returned to their homes well pleased that they could live on neutral ground, surrounded by the din of war, without being engaged in it.

About a year passed off, and we, as usual, were enjoying ourselves in the employments of peaceable times, when a messenger arrived from the British Commissioners, requesting all the Indians of our tribe to attend a general council which was soon to be held at Oswego. The council convened, and being opened, the British Commissioners informed the Chiefs that the object of calling a council of the Six Nations, was, to engage their assistance in subduing the rebels, the people of the states, who had risen up against the good King, their master, and were about to rob him of a great part of his possessions and wealth, and added that they would amply reward them for all their services.

The Chiefs then arose, and informed the Commissioners of the nature and extent of the treaty which they had entered into with the people of the states, the year before, and that they should not violate it by taking up the hatchet against them.

The Commissioners continued their entreaties without success, till they addressed their avarice, by telling our people that the people of the states were few in number, and easily subdued; and that on the account of their disobedience to the King, they justly merited all the punishment that it was possible for white men and Indians to inflict upon them; and added, that the King was rich and powerful, both in money and subjects: That his rum was as plenty as the water in lake Ontario: that his men were as numerous as the sands upon the lake shore:—and that the Indians, if they would assist in the war, and persevere in their friendship to the King, till it was closed, should never want for money or goods. Upon this the Chiefs concluded a treaty with the British Commissioners, in which they agreed to take up arms against the rebels, and continue in the service of his Majesty till they were subdued, in consideration of certain conditions which were stipulated in the treaty to be performed by the British government and its agents.

As soon as the treaty was finished, the Commissioners made a present to each Indian of a suit of clothes, a brass kettle, a gun and tomahawk, a scalping knife, a quantity of powder and lead, a piece of gold, and promised a bounty on every scalp that should be brought in. Thus richly clad and equipped, they returned home, after an absence of about two weeks, full of the fire of war, and anxious to encounter their enemies. Many of the kettles which the Indians received at that time are now in use on the Genesee Flats.

Hired to commit depredations upon the whites, who had given them no offence, they waited impatiently to commence their labor, till sometime in the spring of 1776, when a convenient opportunity offered for them to make an attack. At that time, a party of our Indians were at Cau-te-ga, who shot a man that was looking after his horse, for the sole purpose, as I was informed by my Indian brother, who was present, of commencing hostilities.

In May following, our Indians were in their first battle with the Americans; but at what place I am unable to determine. While they were absent at that time, my daughter Nancy was born.

The same year, at Cherry Valley, our Indians took a woman and her three daughters prisoners, and brought them on, leaving one at Canandaigua, one at Honeoy, one at Cattaraugus, and one (the woman) at Little Beard's Town, where I resided. The woman told me that she and her daughters might have escaped, but that they expected the British army only, and therefore made no effort. Her husband and sons got away. Sometime having elapsed, they were redeemed at Fort Niagara by Col. Butler, who clothed them well, and sent them home.

In the same expedition, Joseph Smith was taken prisoner at or near Cherry Valley, brought to Genesee, and detained till after the revolutionary war. He was then liberated, and the Indians made him a present, in company with Horatio Jones, of 6000 acres of land lying in the present town of Leicester, in the county of Livingston.

One of the girls just mentioned, was married to a British officer at Fort Niagara, by the name of Johnson, who at the time she was taken, took a gold ring from her finger, without any compliments or ceremonies. When he saw her at Niagara he recognized her features, restored the ring that he had so impolitely borrowed, and courted and married her.

Previous to the battle at Fort Stanwix, the British sent for the Indians to come and see them whip the rebels; and, at the same time stated that they did not wish to have them fight, but wanted to have them just sit down, smoke their pipes, and look on. Our Indians went, to a man; but contrary to their expectation, instead of smoking and looking on, they were obliged to fight for their lives, and in the end of the battle were completely beaten, with a great loss in killed and wounded. Our Indians alone had thirty-six killed, and a great number wounded. Our town exhibited a scene of real sorrow and distress, when our warriors returned and recounted their misfortunes, and stated the real loss they had sustained in the engagement. The mourning was excessive, and was expressed by the most doleful yells, shrieks, and howlings, and by inimitable gesticulations.

During the revolution, my house was the home of Col's Butler and Brandt, whenever they chanced to come into our neighborhood as they passed to and from Fort Niagara, which was the seat of their military operations. Many and many a night I have pounded samp for them from sun-set till sun-rise, and furnished them with necessary provision and clean clothing for their journey.

Chapter VII.

Gen. Sullivan with a large army arrives at Canandaigua.—Indians' troubles.—Determine to stop their march.—Skirmish at Connessius Lake.—Circumstances attending the Execution of an Oneida warrior.— Escape of an Indian Prisoner.—Lieut. Boyd and another man taken Prisoners.—Cruelty of Boyd's Execution.—Indians retreat to the woods.— Sullivan comes on to Genesee Flats and destroys the property of the Indians.—Returns.—Indians return.—Mrs. Jemison goes to Gardow.—Her Employment there.—Attention of an old Negro to her safety, &c.—Severe Winter.—Sufferings of the Indians.—Destruction of Game.—Indians Expedition to the Mohawk.—Capture old John O'Bail, &c.—Other Prisoners taken, &c.

For four or five years we sustained no loss in the war, except in the few who had been killed in distant battles; and our tribe, because of the re-moteness of its situation from the enemy, felt secure from an attack. At length, in the fall of 1779, intelligence was received that a large and powerful army of the rebels, under the command of General Sullivan, was making rapid progress towards our settlement, burning and de-stroying the huts and corn-fields; killing the cattle, hogs and horses, and cutting down the fruit trees belonging to the Indians throughout the country.

Our Indians immediately became alarmed, and suffered every thing but death from fear that they should be taken by surprize, and totally destroyed at a single blow. But in order to prevent so great a catas-trophe, they sent out a few spies who were to keep themselves at a short distance in front of the invading army, in order to watch its operations, and give information of its advances and success.

Sullivan arrived at Canandaigua Lake, and had finished his work of destruction there, and it was ascertained that he was about to march to our flats, when our Indians resolved to give him battle on the way, and prevent, if possible, the distresses to which they knew we should be subjected, if he should succeed in reaching our town. Accordingly they sent all their women and children into the woods a little west of Little Beard's Town, in order that we might make a good retreat if it should be necessary, and then, well armed, set out to face the conquering enemy. The place which they fixed upon for their battle ground lay between Honeoy Creek and the head of Connessius Lake.

At length a scouting party from Sullivan's army arrived at the spot selected, when the Indians arose from their ambush with all the fierceness and terror that it was possible for them to exercise, and directly put the party upon a retreat. Two Oneida Indians were all the prisoners that were taken in that skirmish. One of them was a pilot of Gen. Sullivan, and had been very active in the war, rendering to the people of the states essential services. At the commencement of the revolution he had a brother older than himself, who resolved to join the British service, and endeavored by all the art that he was capable of using to persuade his brother to accompany him; but his arguments proved abortive This went to the British, and that joined the American army. At this critical juncture they met, one in the capacity of a conqueror, the other in that of a prisoner; and as an Indian seldom forgets a countenance that he has seen, they recognized each other at sight. Envy and revenge glared in the features of the conquering savage, as he advanced to his brother (the prisoner) in all the haughtiness of Indian pride, heightened by a sense of power, and addressed him in the following manner:

"Brother, you have merited death! The hatchet or the war-club shall finish your career!—When I begged of you to follow me in the fortunes of war, you was deaf to my cries—you spurned my entreaties!

"Brother! you have merited death and shall have your deserts! When the rebels raised their hatchets to fight their good master, you sharpened your knife, you brightened your rifle and led on our foes to the fields of our fathers!—You have merited death and shall die by our hands! When those rebels had drove us from the fields of our fathers to seek out new homes, it was you who could dare to step forth as their pilot, and conduct them even to the doors of our wigwams, to butcher our children and put us to death! No crime can be greater!—But though you have merited death and shall die on this spot, my hands shall not be stained in the blood of a brother! *Who will strike?*"

Little Beard, who was standing by, as soon as the speech was ended, struck the prisoner on the head with his tomahawk, and despatched him at once!

Little Beard then informed the other Indian prisoner that as they were at war with the whites only, and not with the Indians, they would spare his life, and after a while give him his liberty in an honorable manner. The Oneida warrior, however, was jealous of Little Beard's fidelity; and suspecting that he should soon fall by his hands, watched for a favorable opportunity to make his escape; which he soon effected. Two Indians were leading him, one on each side, when he made a violent effort, threw them upon the ground, and run for his life towards where the main body of the American army was encamped. The Indians pursued him without success; but in their absence they fell in with a small detachment of Sullivan's men, with whom they had a short but severe skirmish, in which they killed a number of the enemy, took Capt. or Lieut. William Boyd and one private, prisoners, and brought them to Little Beard's Town, where they were soon after put to death in the most shocking and cruel manner. Little Beard, in this, as in all other scenes of cruelty that happened at his town, was master of ceremonies, and principal actor. Poor Boyd was stripped of his clothing, and then tied to a sapling, where the Indians menaced his life by throwing their tomahawks at the tree, directly over his head, brandishing their scalping knives around him in the most frightful manner, and accompanying their ceremonies with terrific shouts of joy. Having punished him sufficiently in this way, they made a small opening in his abdomen, took out an intestine, which they tied to the sapling, and then unbound him from the tree, and drove him round it till he had drawn out the whole of his intestines. He was then beheaded, his head was stuck upon a pole, and his body left on the ground unburied. Thus ended the life of poor William Boyd, who, it was said, had every appearance of being an active and enterprizing officer, of the first talents. The other prisoner was (if I remember distinctly) only beheaded and left near Boyd.

This tragedy being finished, our Indians again held a short council on the expediency of giving Sullivan battle, if he should continue to advance, and finally came to the conclusion that they were not strong enough to drive him, nor to prevent his taking possession of their fields: but that if it was possible they would escape with their own lives, preserve their families, and leave their possessions to be overrun by the invading army.

The women and children were then sent on still further towards Buffalo, to a large creek that was called by the Indians Catawba, accompanied by a part of the Indians, while the remainder secreted themselves in the woods back of Beard's Town, to watch the movements of the army.

At that time I had three children who went with me on foot, one who rode on horse back, and one whom I carried on my back.

Our corn was good that year; a part of which we had gathered and secured for winter.

In one or two days after the skirmish at Connissius lake, Sullivan and his army arrived at Genesee river, where they destroyed every article of the food kind that they could lay their hands on. A part of our corn they burnt, and threw the remainder into the river. They burnt our houses, killed what few cattle and horses they could find, destroyed our fruit trees, and left nothing but the bare soil and timber. But the Indians had eloped and were not to be found.

Having crossed and recrossed the river, and finished the work of destruction, the army marched off to the east. Our Indians saw them move off, but suspecting that it was Sullivan's intention to watch our return, and then to take us by surprize, resolved that the main body of our tribe should hunt where we then were, till Sullivan had gone so far that there would be no danger of his returning to molest us.

This being agreed to, we hunted continually till the Indians concluded that there could be no risk in our once more taking possession of our lands. Accordingly we all returned; but what were our feelings when we found that there was not a mouthful of any kind of sustenance left, not even enough to keep a child one day from perishing with hunger.

The weather by this time had become cold and stormy; and as we were destitute of houses and food too, I immediately resolved to take my children and look out for myself, without delay. With this intention I took two of my little ones on my back, bade the other three follow, and the same night arrived on the Gardow flats, where I have ever since resided.

At that time, two negroes, who had run away from their masters sometime before, were the only inhabitants of those flats. They lived in a small cabin and had planted and raised a large field of corn, which they had not yet harvested. As they were in want of help to secure their crop, I hired to them to husk corn till the whole was harvested.

I have laughed a thousand times to myself when I have thought of the good old negro, who hired me, who fearing that I should get taken or injured by the Indians, stood by me constantly when I was husking, with a loaded gun in his hand, in order to keep off the enemy, and thereby lost as much labor of his own as he received from me, by paying good wages. I, however, was not displeased with his attention; for I knew that I should need all the corn that I could earn, even if I should husk the whole. I husked enough for them, to gain for myself, at every tenth string, one hundred strings of ears, which were equal to twenty-five bushels of shelled corn. This seasonable supply made my family comfortable for samp and cakes through the succeeding winter, which was the most severe that I have witnessed since my remembrance. The snow fell about five feet deep, and remained so for a long time, and the weather was extremely cold; so much so indeed, that almost all the game upon which the Indians depended for subsistence, perished, and reduced them almost to a state of starvation through that and three or four succeeding years. When the snow melted in the spring, deer were found dead upon the ground in vast numbers; and other animals, of every description, perished from the cold also, and were found dead, in multitudes. Many of our people barely escaped with their lives, and some actually died of hunger and freezing.

But to return from this digression: Having been completely routed at Little Beard's Town, deprived of a house, and without the means of building one in season, after I had finished my husking, and having found from the short acquaintance which I had had with the negroes, that they were kind and friendly, I concluded, at their request, to take up my residence with them for a while in their cabin, till I should be able to provide a hut for myself. I lived more comfortable than I expected to through the winter, and the next season made a shelter for myself.

The negroes continued on my flats two or three years after this, and then left them for a place that they expected would suit them much better. But as that land became my own in a few years, by virtue of a deed from the Chiefs of the Six Nations, I have lived there from that to the present time.

My flats were cleared before I saw them; and it was the opinion of the oldest Indians that were at Genishau, at the time that I first went there, that all the flats on the Genesee river were improved before any of the Indian tribes ever saw them. I well remember that soon after I went to Little Beard's Town, the banks of Fall-Brook were washed off, which left a large number of human bones uncovered. The Indians then said that those were not the bones of Indians, because they had never heard of any of their dead being buried there; but that they were the bones of a race of men who a great many moons before, cleared that land and lived on the flats.

The next summer after Sullivan's campaign, our Indians, highly incensed at the whites for the treatment they had received, and the sufferings which they had consequently endured, determined to obtain some redress by destroying their frontier settlements. Corn Planter, otherwise called John O'Bail, led the Indians, and an officer by the name of Johnston commanded the British in the expedition. The force was large, and so strongly bent upon revenge and vengeance, that seemingly nothing could avert its march, nor prevent its depredations. After leaving Genesee they marched directly to some of the head waters of the Susquehannah river, and Schoharie Creek, went down that creek to the Mohawk river, thence up that river to Fort Stanwix, and from thence came home. In their route they burnt a number of places; destroyed all the cattle and other property that fell in their way; killed a number of white people, and brought home a few prisoners.

In that expedition, when they came to Fort Plain, on the Mohawk river, Corn Planter and a party of his Indians took old John O'Bail, a white man, and made him a prisoner. Old John O'Bail, in his younger days had frequently passed through the Indian settlements that lay between the Hudson and Fort Niagara, and in some of his excursions had become enamored with a squaw, by whom he had a son that was called Corn Planter.

Corn Planter, was a chief of considerable eminence; and having been informed of his parentage and of the place of his father's residence, took the old man at this time, in order that he might make an introduction leisurely, and become acquainted with a man to whom, though a stranger, he was satisfied that he owed his existence.

After he had taken the old man, his father, he led him as a prisoner ten or twelve miles up the river, and then stepped before him, faced about, and addressed him in the following terms:—

"My name is John O'Bail, commonly called Corn Planter. I am your son! you are my father! You are now my prisoner, and subject to the customs of Indian warfare: but you shall not be harmed; you need not fear. I am a warrior! Many are the scalps which I have taken! Many prisoners I have tortured to death! I am your son! I am a warrior! I was anxious to see you, and to greet you in friendship! I went to your cabin and took you by force! But your life shall be spared. Indians love their friends and their kindred, and treat them with kindness. If now you choose to follow the fortune of your yellow son, and to live with our people, I will cherish your old age with plenty of venison, and you shall live easy: But if it is your choice to return to your fields and live with your white children, I will send a party of my trusty young men to conduct you back in safety. I respect you, my father; you have been friendly to Indians, and they are your friends."

Old John chose to return. Corn Planter, as good as his word, ordered an escort to attend him home, which they did with the greatest care.

Amongst the prisoners that were brought to Genesee, was William Newkirk, a man by the name of Price, and two negroes.

Price lived a while with Little Beard, and afterwards with Jack Berry, an Indian. When he left Jack Berry he went to Niagara, where he now resides.

Newkirk was brought to Beard's Town, and lived with Little Beard and at Fort Niagara about one year, and then enlisted under Butler, and went with him on an expedition to the Monongahela.

Chapter VIII.

Life of Ebenezer Allen, a Tory.—He comes to Gardow.—His intimacy with a Nanticoke Squaw.—She gives him a Cap.—Her Husband's jealousy.—Cruelty to his Wife.—Hiokatoo's Mandate.—Allen supports her.—Her Husband is received into favor.—Allen labors.—Purchases Goods.—Stops the Indian War.—His troubles with the Indians.—Marries a Squaw.—Is taken and carried to Quebec.—Acquitted.—Goes to Philadelphia.—Returns to Genesee with a Store of Goods, &c.—Goes to Farming.—Moves to Allen's Creek.—Builds Mills at Rochester.—Drowns a Dutchman.—Marries a white Wife.—Kills an old Man.—Gets a Concubine.—Moves to Mt. Morris.—Marries a third Wife and gets another Concubine.—Receives a tract of Land.—Sends his Children to other States, &c.—Disposes of his Land.—Moves to Grand River, where he dies.—His Cruelties.

Sometime near the close of the revolutionary war, a white man by the name of Ebenezer Allen, left his people in the state of Pennsylvania on the account of some disaffection towards his countrymen, and came to the Genesee river, to reside with the Indians. He tarried at Genishau a few days, and came up to Gardow, where I then resided.—He was, apparently, without any business that would support him; but he soon became acquainted with my son Thomas, with whom he hunted for a long time, and made his home with him at my house; winter came on, and he continued his stay.

When Allen came to my house, I had a white man living on my land, who had a Nanticoke squaw for his wife, with whom he had lived very peaceably; for he was a moderate man commonly, and she was a kind, gentle, cunning creature. It so happened that he had no hay for his cattle; so that in the winter he was obliged to drive them every day, perhaps half a mile from his house, to let them feed on rushes, which in those days were so numerous as to nearly cover the ground.

Allen having frequently seen the squaw in the fall, took the opportunity when her husband was absent with his cows, daily to make her a visit; and in return for his kindnesses she made and gave him a red cap finished and decorated in the highest Indian style.

The husband had for some considerable length of time felt a degree of jealousy that Allen was trespassing upon him with the consent of his squaw; but when he saw Allen dressed in so fine an Indian cap, and found that his dear Nanticoke had presented it to him, his doubts all left him, and he became so violently enraged that he caught her by the hair of her head, dragged her on the ground to my house, a distance of forty rods, and threw her in at the door. Hiokatoo, my husband, exasperated at the sight of so much inhumanity, hastily took down his old tomahawk, which for awhile had lain idle, shook it over the cuckold's head, and bade him jogo (i.e. go off.) The enraged husband, well knowing that he should feel a blow if he waited to hear the order repeated, instantly retreated, and went down the river to his cattle. We protected the poor Nanticoke woman, and gave her victuals; and Allen sympathized with her in her misfortunes till spring, when her husband came to her, acknowledged his former errors, and that he had abused her without a cause, promised a reformation, and she received him with every mark of a renewal of her affection. They went home lovingly, and soon after removed to Niagara.

The same spring, Allen commenced working my flats, and continued to labor there till after the peace in 1783. He then went to Philadelphia on some business that detained him but a few days, and returned with a horse and some dry goods, which he carried to a place that is now called Mount Morris, where he built or bought a small house.

The British and Indians on the Niagara frontier, dissatisfied with the treaty of peace, were determined, at all hazards, to continue their depredations upon the white settlements which lay between them and Albany. They actually made ready, and were about setting out on an expedition to that effect, when Allen (who by this time understood their customs of war) took a belt of wampum, which he had fraudulently procured, and carried it as a token of peace from the Indians to the commander of the nearest American military post.

The Indians were soon answered by the American officer that the wampum was cordially accepted; and, that a continuance of peace was ardently wished for. The Indians, at this, were chagrined and disappointed beyond measure; but as they held the wampum to be a sacred thing, they dared not to go against the import of its meaning, and immediately buried the hatchet as it respected the people of the United States; and smoked the pipe of peace. They, however, resolved to punish Allen for his officiousness in meddling with their national affairs, by presenting the sacred wampum without their knowledge, and went about devising means for his detection. A party was accordingly despatched from Fort Niagara to apprehend him; with orders to conduct him to that post for trial, or for safe keeping, till such time as his fate should be determined upon in a legal manner.

The party came on; but before it arrived at Gardow, Allen got news of its approach, and fled for safety, leaving the horse and goods that he had brought from Philadelphia, an easy prey to his enemies. He had not been long absent when they arrived at Gardow, where they made diligent search for him till they were satisfied that they could not find him, and then seized the effects which he had left, and returned to Niagara. My son Thomas, went with them, with Allen's horse, and carried the goods.

Allen, on finding that his enemies had gone, came back to my house, where he lived as before; but of his return they were soon notified at Niagara, and Nettles (who married Priscilla Ramsay) with a small party of Indians came on to take him. He, however, by some means found that they were near, and gave me his box of money and trinkets to keep safely, till he called for it, and again took to the woods.

Nettles came on determined at all events to take him before he went back; and, in order to accomplish his design, he, with his Indians, hunted in the day time and lay by at night at my house, and in that way they practised for a number of days. Allen watched the motion of his pursuers, and every night after they had gone to rest, came home and got some food, and then returned to his retreat. It was in the fall, and the weather was cold and rainy, so that he suffered extremely. Some nights he sat in my chamber till nearly daybreak, while his enemies were below, and when the time arrived I assisted him to escape unnoticed.

Nettles at length abandoned the chase—went home, and Allen, all in tatters, came in. By running in the woods his clothing had become torn into rags, so that he was in a suffering condition, almost naked.

Hiokatoo gave him a blanket, and a piece of broadcloth for a pair of trowsers. Allen made his trowsers himself, and then built a raft, on which he went down the river to his own place at Mount Morris.

About that time he married a squaw, whose name was Sally.

The Niagara people finding that he was at his own house, came and took him by surprize when he least expected them, and carried him to Niagara. Fortunately for him, it so happened that just as they arrived at the fort, a house took fire and his keepers all left him to save the building, if possible. Allen had supposed his doom to be nearly sealed; but finding himself at liberty he took to his heels, left his escort to put out the fire, and ran to Tonnawanta. There an Indian gave him some refreshment, and a good gun, with which he hastened on to Little Beard's Town, where he found his squaw. Not daring to risk himself at that place for fear of being given up, he made her but a short visit, and came immediately to Gardow.

Just as he got to the top of the hill above the Gardow flats, he discovered a party of British soldiers and Indians in pursuit of him; and in fact they were so near that he was satisfied that they saw him, and concluded that it would be impossible for him to escape. The love of liberty, however, added to his natural swiftness, gave him sufficient strength to make his escape to his former castle of safety. His pursuers came immediately to my house, where they expected to have found him secreted, and under my protection. They told me where they had seen him but a few moments before, and that they were confident that it was within my power to put him into their hands. As I was perfectly clear of having had any hand in his escape, I told them plainly that I had not seen him since he was taken to Niagara, and that I could give them no information at all respecting him. Still unsatisfied, and doubting my veracity, they advised my Indian brother to use his influence to draw from me the secret of his concealment, which they had an idea that I considered of great importance, not only to him but to myself. I persisted in my ignorance of his situation, and finally they left me.

Although I had not seen Allen, I knew his place of security, and was well aware that if I told them the place where he had formerly hid himself, they would have no difficulty in making him a prisoner.

He came to my house in the night, and awoke me with the greatest caution, fearing that some of his enemies might be watching to take him at a time when, and in a place where it would be impossible for him to make his escape. I got up and assured him that he was then safe; but that his enemies would return early in the morning and search him out if it should be possible. Having given him some victuals, which he received thankfully, I told him to go, but to return the next night to a certain corner of the fence near my house where he would find a quantity of meal that I would have well prepared and deposited there for his use.

Early the next morning, Nettles and his company came in while I was pounding the meal for Allen, and insisted upon my giving him up. I again told them that I did not know where he was, and that I could not, neither would I, tell them any thing about him. I well knew that Allen considered his life in my hands; and although it was my intention not to lie, I was fully determined to keep his situation a profound secret. They continued their labor and examined (as they supposed) every crevice, gully, tree and hollow log in the neighboring woods, and at last concluded that he had left the country, and gave him up for lost, and went home.

At that time Allen lay in a secret place in the gulph a short distance above my flats, in a hole that he accidentally found in the rock near the river. At night he came and got the meal at the corner of the fence as I had directed him, and afterwards lived in the gulph two weeks. Each night he came to the pasture and milked one of my cows, without any other vessel in which to receive the milk than his hat, out of which he drank it. I supplied him with meal, but fearing to build a fire he was obliged to eat it raw and wash it down with the milk. Nettles having left our neighborhood, and Allen considering himself safe, left his little cave and came home. I gave him his box of money and trinkets, and he went to his own house at Mount Morris. It was generally considered by the Indians of our tribe, that Allen was an innocent man, and that the Niagara people were persecuting him without a just cause. Little Beard, then about to go to the eastward on public business, charged his Indians not to meddle with Allen, but to let him live amongst them peaceably, and enjoy himself with his family and property if he could. Having the protection of the chief, he felt himself safe, and let his situation be known to the whites from whom he suspected no harm. They, however, were more inimical than our Indians and were easily bribed by Nettles to assist in bringing him to justice. Nettles came on, and the whites, as they had agreed, gave poor Allen up to him. He was bound and carried to Niagara, where he was confined in prison through the winter. In the spring he was taken to Montreal or Quebec for trial, and was honorably acquitted. The crime for which he was tried was, for his having carried the wampum to the Americans, and thereby putting too sudden a stop to their war.

From the place of his trial he went directly to Philadelphia, and purchased on credit, a boat load of goods which he brought by water to Conhocton, where he left them and came to Mount Morris for assistance to get them brought on. The Indians readily went with horses and brought them to his house, where he disposed of his dry goods; but not daring to let the Indians begin to drink strong liquor, for fear of the quarrels which would naturally follow, he sent his spirits to my place and we sold them. For his goods he received ginseng roots, principally, and a few skins. Ginseng at that time was plenty, and commanded a high price. We prepared the whole that he received for the market, expecting that he would carry them to Philadelphia. In that I was disappointed; for when he had disposed of, and got pay for all his goods, he took the ginseng and skins to Niagara, and there sold them and came home.

Tired of dealing in goods, he planted a large field of corn on or near his own land, attended to it faithfully, and succeeded in raising a large crop, which he harvested, loaded into canoes and carried down the river to the mouth of Allen's Creek, then called by the Indians Gin-is-a-ga, where he unloaded it, built him a house, and lived with his family.

The next season he planted corn at that place and built a grist and saw mill on Genesee Falls, now called Rochester.

At the time Allen built the mills, he had an old German living with him by the name of Andrews, whom he sent in a canoe down the river with his mill irons. Allen went down at the same time; but before they got to the mills Allen threw the old man overboard and drowned him, as it was then generally believed, for he was never seen or heard of afterwards.

In the course of the season in which Allen built his mills, he became acquainted with the daughter of a white man, who was moving to Niagara. She was handsome, and Allen soon got into her good graces, so that he married and took her home, to be a joint partner with Sally, the squaw, whom she had never heard of till she got home and found her in full possession; but it was too late for her to retrace the hasty steps she had taken, for her father had left her in the care of a tender husband and gone on. She, however, found that she enjoyed at least an equal half of her husband's affections, and made herself contented. Her father's name I have forgotten, but her's was Lucy.

Allen was not contented with two wives, for in a short time after he had married Lucy he came up to my house, where he found a young woman who had an old husband with her. They had been on a long journey, and called at my place to recruit and rest themselves. She filled

Allen's eye, and he accordingly fixed upon a plan to get her into his possession. He praised his situation, enumerated his advantages, and finally persuaded them to go home and tarry with him a few days at least, and partake of a part of his comforts. They accepted his generous invitation and went home with him. But they had been there but two or three days when Allen took the old gentleman out to view his flats; and as they were deliberately walking on the bank of the river, pushed him into the water. The old man, almost strangled, succeeded in getting out; but his fall and exertions had so powerful an effect upon his system that he died in two or three days, and left his young widow to the protection of his murderer. She lived with him about one year in a state of concubinage and then left him.

How long Allen lived at Allen's Creek I am unable to state; but soon after the young widow left him, he removed to his old place at Mount Morris, and built a house, where he made Sally, his squaw, by whom he had two daughters, a slave to Lucy, by whom he had had one son; still, however, he considered Sally to be his wife.

After Allen came to Mt. Morris at that time, he married a girl by the name of Morilla Gregory, whose father at the time lived on Genesee Flats. The ceremony being over, he took her home to live in common with his other wives; but his house was too small for his family; for Sally and Lucy, conceiving that their lawful privileges would be abridged if they received a partner, united their strength and whipped poor Morilla so cruelly that he was obliged to keep her in a small Indian house a short distance from his own, or lose her entirely. Morilla, before she left Mt. Morris, had four children.

One of Morilla's sisters lived with Allen about a year after Morilla was married, and then quit him.

A short time after they all got to living at Mt. Morris, Allen prevailed upon the Chiefs to give to his Indian children, a tract of land four miles square, where he then resided. The Chiefs gave them the land, but he so artfully contrived the conveyance, that he could apply it to his own use, and by alienating his right, destroy the claim of his children.

Having secured the land, in that way, to himself, he sent his two Indian girls to Trenton (N. J.) and his white son to Philadelphia, for the purpose of giving each of them a respectable English education.

While his children were at school, he went to Philadelphia, and sold his right to the land which he had begged of the Indians for his children to Robert Morris. After that, he sent for his daughters to come home, which they did.

Having disposed of the whole of his property on the Genesee river, he took his two white wives and their children, together with his effects, and removed to a Delaware town on the river De Trench, in Upper Canada. When he left Mt. Morris, Sally, his squaw, insisted upon going with him, and actually followed him, crying bitterly, and praying for his protection some two or three miles, till he absolutely bade her leave him, or he would punish her with severity.

At length, finding her case hopeless, she returned to the Indians.

At the great treaty at Big Tree, one of Allen's daughters claimed the land which he had sold to Morris. The claim was examined and decided against her in favor of Ogden, Trumbull, Rogers and others, who were the creditors of Robert Morris. Allen yet believed that his daughter had an indisputable right to the land in question, and got me to go with mother Farly, a half Indian woman, to assist him by interceding with Morris for it, and to urge the propriety of her claim. We went to Thomas Morris, and having stated to him our business, he told us plainly that he had no land to give away, and that as the title was good, he never would allow Allen, nor his heirs, one foot, or words to that effect. We returned to Allen the answer we had received, and he, conceiving all further attempts to be useless, went home.

He died at the Delaware town, on the river De Trench, in the year 1814 or 15, and left two white widows and one squaw, with a number of children, to lament his loss.

By his last will he gave all his property to his last wife (Morilla,) and her children, without providing in the least for the support of Lucy, or any of the other members of his family. Lucy, soon after his death, went with her children down the Ohio river, to receive assistance from her friends.

In the revolutionary war, Allen was a tory, and by that means became acquainted with our Indians, when they were in the neighborhood of his native place, desolating the settlements on the Susquehannah. In those predatory battles, he joined them, and (as I have often heard the Indians say,) for cruelty was not exceeded by any of his Indian comrades!

At one time, when he was scouting with the Indians in the Susquehannah country, he entered a house very early in the morning, where he found a man, his wife, and one child, in bed. The man, as he entered the door, instantly sprang on the floor, for the purpose of defending himself and little family; but Allen dispatched him at one blow. He then cut off his head and threw it bleeding into the bed with the terrified woman; took the little infant from its mother's breast, and holding it by its legs, dashed its head against the jamb, and left the unhappy widow and mother to mourn alone over her murdered family. It has been said by some, that after he had killed the child, he opened the fire and buried it under the coals and embers: But of that I am not certain. I have often heard him speak of that transaction with a great degree of sorrow, and as the foulest crime he had ever committed—one for which I have no doubt he repented.

Chapter IX.

Mrs. Jemison has liberty to go to her Friends.—Chooses to stay.—Her Reasons, &c.—Her Indian Brother makes provision for her Settlement.— He goes to Grand River and dies.—Her Love for him, &c.—She is presented with the Gardow Reservation.—Is troubled by Speculators.—Description of the Soil, &c. of her Flats.—Indian notions of the ancient Inhabitants of this Country.

Soon after the close of the revolutionary war, my Indian brother, Kau-jises-tau-ge-au (which being interpreted signifies Black Coals,) offered me my liberty, and told me that if it was my choice I might go to my friends.

My son, Thomas, was anxious that I should go; and offered to go with me and assist me on the journey, by taking care of the younger children, and providing food as we travelled through the wilderness. But the Chiefs of our tribe, suspecting from his appearance, actions, and a few warlike exploits, that Thomas would be a great warrior, or a good counsellor, refused to let him leave them on any account whatever.

To go myself, and leave him, was more than I felt able to do; for he had been kind to me, and was one on whom I placed great dependence. The Chiefs refusing to let him go, was one reason for my resolving to stay; but another, more powerful, if possible, was, that I had got a large family of Indian children, that I must take with me; and that if I should be so fortunate as to find my relatives, they would despise them, if not myself; and treat us as enemies; or, at least with a degree of cold indifference, which I thought I could not endure.

Accordingly, after I had duly considered the matter, I told my brother that it was my choice to stay and spend the remainder of my days with my Indian friends, and live with my family as I had heretofore done. He appeared well pleased with my resolution, and informed me, that as that was my choice, I should have a piece of land that I could call my own, where I could live unmolested, and have something at my decease to leave for the benefit of my children.

In a short time he made himself ready to go to Upper Canada; but before he left us, he told me that he would speak to some of the Chiefs at Buffalo, to attend the great Council, which he expected would convene in a few years at farthest, and convey to me such a tract of land as I should select. My brother left us, as he had proposed, and soon after died at Grand River.

Kaujisestaugeau, was an excellent man, and ever treated me with kindness. Perhaps no one of his tribe at any time exceeded him in natural mildness of temper, and warmth and tenderness of affection. If he had taken my life at the time when the avarice of the old King inclined him to procure my emancipation, it would have been done with a pure heart and from good motives. He loved his friends; and was generally beloved. During the time that I lived in the family with him, he never offered the most trifling abuse; on the contrary, his whole conduct towards me was strictly honorable. I mourned his loss as that of a tender brother, and shall recollect him through life with emotions of friendship and gratitude.

I lived undisturbed, without hearing a word on the subject of my land, till the great Council was held at Big Tree, in 1797, when Farmer's Brother, whose Indian name is Ho-na-ye-wus, sent for me to attend the council. When I got there, he told me that my brother had spoken to him to see that I had a piece of land reserved for my use; and that then was the time for me to receive it.—He requested that I would choose for myself and describe the bounds of a piece that would suit me. I accordingly told him the place of beginning, and then went round a tract that I judged would be sufficient for my purpose (knowing that it would include the Gardow Flats,) by stating certain bounds with which I was acquainted.

When the Council was opened, and the business afforded a proper opportunity, Farmer's Brother presented my claim, and rehearsed the request of my brother. Red Jacket, whose Indian name is Sagu-yu-what-hah, which interpreted, is Keeper-awake, opposed me or my claim with all his influence and eloquence. Farmer's Brother insisted upon the necessity, propriety and expediency of his proposition, and got the land granted. The deed was made and signed, securing to me the title to all the land I had described; under the same restrictions and regulations that other Indian lands are subject to.

That land has ever since been known by the name of the Gardow Tract.

Red Jacket not only opposed my claim at the Council, but he withheld my money two or three years, on the account of my lands having been granted without his consent. Parrish and Jones at length convinced him that it was the white people, and not the Indians who had given me the land, and compelled him to pay over all the money which he had retained on my account.

My land derived its name, Gardow, from a hill that is within its limits, which is called in the Seneca language Kau-tam. Kautam when interpreted signifies up and down, or down and up, and is applied to a hill that you will ascend and descend in passing it; or to a valley. It has been said that Gardow was the name of my husband Hiokatoo, and that my land derived its name from him; that however was a mistake, for the old man always considered Gardow a nickname, and was uniformly offended when called by it.

About three hundred acres of my land, when I first saw it, was open flats, lying on the Genesee River, which it is supposed was cleared by a race of inhabitants who preceded the first Indian settlements in this part of the country. The Indians are confident that many parts of this country were settled and for a number of years occupied by people of whom their fathers never had any tradition, as they never had seen them. Whence those people originated, and whither they went, I have never heard one of our oldest and wisest Indians pretend to guess. When I first came to Genishau, the bank of Fall Brook had just slid off and exposed a large number of human bones, which the Indians said were buried there long before their fathers ever saw the place; and that they did not know what kind of people they were. It however was and is believed by our people, that they were not Indians.

My flats were extremely fertile; but needed more labor than my daughters and myself were able to perform, to produce a sufficient quantity of grain and other necessary productions of the earth, for the consumption of our family. The land had lain uncultivated so long that it was thickly covered with weeds of almost every description. In order that we might live more easy, Mr. Parrish, with the consent of the chiefs, gave me liberty to lease or let my land to white people to till on shares. I accordingly let it out, and have continued to do so, which makes my task less burthensome, while at the same time I am more comfortably supplied with the means of support.

Chapter X.

Happy situation of her Family.—Disagreement between her sons Thomas and John.—Her Advice to them, &c.—John kills Thomas.—Her Affliction.—Council. Decision of the Chiefs, &c.—Life of Thomas.—His Wives, Children, &c.—Cause of his Death, &c.

I have frequently heard it asserted by white people, and can truly say from my own experience, that the time at which parents take the most satisfaction and comfort with their families is when their children are young, incapable of providing for their own wants, and are about the fireside, where they can be daily observed and instructed.

Few mothers, perhaps, have had less trouble with their children during their minority than myself. In general, my children were friendly to each other, and it was very seldom that I knew them to have the least difference or quarrel: so far, indeed, were they from rendering themselves or me uncomfortable, that I considered myself happy—more so than commonly falls to the lot of parents, especially to women.

My happiness in this respect, however, was not without alloy; for my son Thomas, from some cause unknown to me, from the time he was a small lad, always called his brother John, a witch, which was the cause, as they grew towards manhood, of frequent and severe quarrels between them, and gave me much trouble and anxiety for their safety. After Thomas and John arrived to manhood, in addition to the former charge, John got two wives, with whom he lived till the time of his death. Although polygamy was tolerated in our tribe, Thomas considered it a violation of good and wholesome rules in society, and tending directly to destroy that friendly social intercourse and love, that ought to be the happy result of matrimony and chastity. Consequently, he frequently reprimanded John, by telling him that his conduct was beneath the dignity, and inconsistent with the principles of good Indians; indecent and unbecoming a gentleman; and, as he never could reconcile himself to it, he was frequently, almost constantly, when they were together, talking to him on the same subject. John always resented such reprimand, and reproof, with a great degree of passion, though they never quarrelled, unless Thomas was intoxicated.

In his fits of drunkenness, Thomas seemed to lose all his natural reason, and to conduct like a wild or crazy man, without regard to relatives, decency or propriety. At such times he often threatened to take my life for having raised a witch (as he called John,) and has gone so far as to raise his tomahawk to split my head. He, however, never struck me; but on John's account he struck Hiokatoo, and thereby excited in John a high degree of indignation, which was extinguished only by blood.

For a number of years their difficulties, and consequent unhappiness, continued and rather increased, continually exciting in my breast the most fearful apprehensions, and greatest anxiety for their safety. With tears in my eyes, I advised them to become reconciled to each other, and to be friendly; told them the consequences of their continuing to cherish so much malignity and malice, that it would end in their destruction, the disgrace of their families, and bring me down to the grave. No one can conceive of the constant trouble that I daily endured on their account—on the account of my two oldest sons, whom I loved equally, and with all the feelings and affection of a tender mother, stimulated by an anxious concern for their fate. Parents, mothers especially, will love their children, though ever so unkind and disobedient. Their eyes of compassion, of real sentimental affection, will be involuntarily extended after them, in their greatest excesses of iniquity; and those fine filaments of consanguinity, which gently entwine themselves around the heart where filial love and parental care is equal, will be lengthened, and enlarged to cords seemingly of sufficient strength to reach and reclaim the wanderer. I know that such exercises are frequently unavailing; but, notwithstanding their ultimate failure, it still remains true, and ever will, that the love of a parent for a disobedient child, will increase, and grow more and more ardent, so long as a hope of its reformation is capable of stimulating a disappointed breast.

My advice and expostulations with my sons were abortive; and year after year their disaffection for each other increased. At length, Thomas came to my house on the 1st day of July, 1811, in my absence, somewhat intoxicated, where he found John, with whom he immediately commenced a quarrel on their old subjects of difference.—John's anger became desperate. He caught Thomas by the hair of his head, dragged him out at the door and there killed him, by a blow which he gave him on the head with his tomahawk!

I returned soon after, and found my son lifeless at the door, on the spot where he was killed! No one can judge of my feelings on seeing this mournful spectacle; and what greatly added to my distress, was the fact that he had fallen by the murderous hand of his brother! I felt my situation unsupportable. Having passed through various scenes of trouble of the most cruel and trying kind, I had hoped to spend my few remaining days in quietude, and to die in peace, surrounded by my family. This fatal event, however, seemed to be a stream of woe poured into my cup of afflictions, filling it even to overflowing, and blasting all my prospects.

As soon as I had recovered a little from the shock which I felt at the sight of my departed son, and some of my neighbors had come in to assist in taking care of the corpse, I hired Shanks, an Indian, to go to Buffalo, and carry the sorrowful news of Thomas' death, to our friends at that place, and request the Chiefs to hold a Council, and dispose of John as they should think proper. Shanks set out on his errand immediately, and John, fearing that he should be apprehended and punished for the crime he had committed, at the same time went off towards Caneadea.

Thomas was decently interred in a style corresponding with his rank.

The Chiefs soon assembled in council on the trial of John, and after having seriously examined the matter according to their laws, justified his conduct, and acquitted him. They considered Thomas to have been the first transgressor, and that for the abuses which he had offered, he had merited from John the treatment that he had received.

John, on learning the decision of the council, returned to his family.

Thomas (except when intoxicated, which was not frequent,) was a kind and tender child, willing to assist me in my labor, and to remove every obstacle to my comfort. His natural abilities were said to be of a superior cast, and he soared above the trifling subjects of revenge, which are common amongst Indians, as being far beneath his attention. In his childish and boyish days, his natural turn was to practise in the art of war, though he despised the cruelties that the warriors inflicted upon their subjugated enemies. He was manly in his deportment, courageous and active; and commanded respect. Though he appeared well pleased with peace, he was cunning in Indian warfare, and succeeded to admiration in the execution of his plans.

At the age of fourteen or fifteen years, he went into the war with manly fortitude, armed with a tomahawk and scalping knife; and when he returned, brought one white man a prisoner, whom he had taken with his own hands, on the west branch of the Susquehannah river. It so happened, that as he was looking out for his enemies, he discovered two men boiling sap in the woods. He watched them unperceived, till dark when he advanced with a noiseless step to where they were standing, caught one of them before they were apprized of danger, and conducted him to the camp. He was well treated while a prisoner, and redeemed at the close of the war.

At the time Kaujisestaugeau gave me my liberty to go to my friends, Thomas was anxious to go with me; but as I have before observed, the Chiefs would not suffer him to leave them on the account of his courage and skill in war: expecting that they should need his assistance. He was a great Counsellor and a Chief when quite young; and in the last capacity, went two or three times to Philadelphia to assist in making treaties with the people of the states.

Thomas had four wives, by whom he had eight children. Jacob Jemison, his second son by his last wife, who is at this time twenty-seven or twenty-eight years of age, went to Dartmouth college, in the spring of 1816, for the purpose of receiving a good education, where it was said that he was an industrious scholar, and made great proficiency in the study of the different branches to which he attended. Having spent two years at that Institution, he returned in the winter of 1818, and is now at Buffalo; where I have understood that he contemplates commencing the study of medicine, as a profession.

Thomas, at the time he was killed, was a few moons over fifty-two years old, and John was forty-eight. As he was naturally good natured, and possessed a friendly disposition, he would not have come to so untimely an end, had it not been for his intemperance. He fell a victim to the use of ardent spirits—a poison that will soon exterminate the Indian tribes in this part of the country, and leave their names without a root or branch. The thought is melancholy; but no arguments, no examples, however persuasive or impressive, are sufficient to deter an Indian for an hour from taking the potent draught, which he knows at the time will derange his faculties, reduce him to a level with the beasts, or deprive him of life!

Chapter XI.

Death of Hiokatoo.—Biography.—His Birth—Education.—Goes against the Cherokees, &c.—Bloody Battle, &c.—His success and cruelties in the French War.—Battle at Fort Freeland.—Capts. Dougherty and Boon killed.— His Cruelties in the neighborhood of Cherry Valley, &c.—Indians remove their general Encampment.—In 1782, Col. Crawford is sent to destroy them, &c.—Is met by a Traitor,—Battle.—Crawford's Men surprized.— Irregular Retreat.—Crawford and Doct. Night taken.—Council.—Crawford Condemned and Burnt.—Aggravating Circumstances.—Night is sentenced to be Burnt.—Is Painted by Hiokatoo.—Is conducted off, &c.—His fortunate Escape.—Hiokatoo in the French War takes Col. Canton.—His Sentence.—Is bound on a wild Colt that runs loose three days.—Returns Alive.—Is made to run the Gauntlet.—Gets knocked down, &c.—Is Redeemed and sent Home.—Hiokatoo's Enmity to the Cherokees, &c.—His Height.—Strength—Speed, &c.

In the month of November 1811, my husband Hiokatoo, who had been sick four years of the consumption, died at the advanced age of one hundred and three years, as nearly as the time could be estimated. He was the last that remained to me of our family connection, or rather of my old friends with whom I was adopted, except a part of one family, which now lives at Tonewanta.

Hiokatoo was buried decently, and had all the insignia of a veteran warrior buried with him; consisting of a war club, tomahawk and scalping knife, a powder-flask, flint, a piece of spunk, a small cake and a cup; and in his best clothing.

Hiokatoo was an old man when I first saw him; but he was by no means enervated. During the term of nearly fifty years that I lived with him, I received, according to Indian customs, all the kindness and attention that was my due as his wife.—Although war was his trade from his youth till old age and decrepitude stopt his career, he uniformly treated me with tenderness, and never offered an insult.

I have frequently heard him repeat the history of his life from his childhood; and when he came to that part which related to his actions, his bravery and his valor in war; when he spoke of the ambush, the combat, the spoiling of his enemies and the sacrifice of the victims, his nerves seemed strung with youthful ardor, the warmth of the able warrior seemed to animate his frame, and to produce the heated gestures which he had practised in middle age. He was a man of tender feelings to his friends, ready and willing to assist them in distress, yet, as a warrior, his cruelties to his enemies perhaps were unparalleled, and will not admit a word of palliation.

Hiokatoo, was born in one of the tribes of the Six Nations that inhabited the banks of the Susquehannah; or, rather he belonged to a tribe of the Senecas that made, at the time of the great Indian treaty, a part of those nations. He was own cousin to Farmer's Brother, a Chief who has been justly celebrated for his worth. Their mothers were sisters, and it was through the influence of Farmer's Brother, that I became Hiokatoo's wife.

In early life, Hiokatoo showed signs of thirst for blood, by attending only to the art of war, in the use of the tomahawk and scalping knife; and in practising cruelties upon every thing that chanced to fall into his hands, which was susceptible of pain. In that way he learned to use his implements of war effectually, and at the same time blunted all those fine feelings and tender sympathies that are naturally excited, by hearing or seeing, a fellow being in distress. He could inflict the most excruciating tortures upon his enemies, and prided himself upon his fortitude, in having performed the most barbarous ceremonies and tortures, without the least degree of pity or remorse. Thus qualified, when very young he was initiated into scenes of carnage, by being engaged in the wars that prevailed amongst the Indian tribes.

In the year 1731, he was appointed a runner, to assist in collecting an army to go against the Cotawpes, Cherokees and other southern Indians. A large army was collected, and after a long and fatiguing march, met its enemies in what was then called the "low, dark and bloody lands," near the mouth of Red River, in what is now called the state of Kentucky.[9] The Cotawpes[10] and their associates, had, by some means, been apprized of their approach, and lay in ambush to take them at once, when they should come within their reach, and destroy the whole army. The northern Indians, with their usual sagacity, discovered the situation of their enemies, rushed upon the ambuscade and massacred 1200 on the spot. The battle continued for two days and two nights, with the utmost severity, in which the northern Indians were victorious, and so far succeeded in destroying the Cotawpes that they at that time ceased to be a nation. The victors suffered an immense loss in killed; but gained the hunting ground, which was their grand object, though the Cherokees would not give it up in a treaty, or consent to make peace. Bows and arrows, at that time, were in general use, though a few guns were employed.

From that time he was engaged in a number of battles in which Indians only were engaged, and made fighting his business, till the commencement of the French war. In those battles he took a number of Indians prisoners, whom he killed by tying them to trees and then setting

9. Those powerful armies met near the place that is now called Clarksville, which is situated at the fork where Red River joins the Cumberland, a few miles above the line between Kentucky and Tennessee.

10. The Author acknowledges himself unacquainted, from Indian history, with a nation of this name; but as 90 years have elapsed since the date of this occurrence, it is highly probable that such a nation did exist, and that it was absolutely exterminated at that eventful period.

small Indian boys to shooting at them with arrows, till death finished the misery of the sufferers; a process that frequently took two days for its completion!

During the French war he was in every battle that was fought on the Susquehannah and Ohio rivers; and was so fortunate as never to have been taken prisoner.

At Braddock's defeat he took two white prisoners, and burnt them alive in a fire of his own kindling.

In 1777, he was in the battle at Fort Freeland, in Northumberland county, Penn. The fort contained a great number of women and children, and was defended only by a small garrison. The force that went against it consisted of 100 British regulars, commanded by a Col. McDonald, and 300 Indians under Hiokatoo. After a short but bloody engagement, the fort was surrendered; the women and children were sent under an escort to the next fort below, and the men and boys taken off by a party of British to the general Indian encampment. As soon as the fort had capitulated and the firing had ceased, Hiokatoo with the help of a few Indians tomahawked every wounded American while earnestly begging with uplifted hands for quarters.

The massacre was but just finished when Capts. Dougherty and Boon arrived with a reinforcement to assist the garrison. On their arriving in sight of the fort they saw that it had surrendered, and that an Indian was holding the flag. This so much inflamed Capt. Dougherty that he left his command, stept forward and shot the Indian at the first fire. Another took the flag, and had no sooner got it erected than Dougherty dropt him as he had the first. A third presumed to hold it, who was also shot down by Dougherty. Hiokatoo, exasperated at the sight of such bravery, sallied out with a party of his Indians, and killed Capts. Dougherty, Boon, and fourteen men, at the first fire. The remainder of the two companies escaped by taking to flight, and soon arrived at the fort which they had left but a few hours before.

In an expedition that went out against Cherry Valley and the neighboring settlements, Captain David, a Mohawk Indian, was first, and Hiokatoo the second in command. The force consisted of several hundred Indians, who were determined on mischief, and the destruction of the whites. A continued series of wantonness and barbarity characterized their career, for they plundered and burnt every thing that came in their way, and killed a number of persons, among whom were several infants, whom Hiokatoo butchered or dashed upon the stones with his own hands. Besides the instances which have been mentioned, he was in a number of parties during the revolutionary war, where he ever acted a conspicuous part.

The Indians having removed the seat of their depredations and war to the frontiers of Pennsylvania, Ohio, Kentucky and the neighboring territories, assembled a large force at Upper Sandusky, their place of general rendezvous, from whence they went out to the various places which they designed to sacrifice.

Tired of the desolating scenes that were so often witnessed, and feeling a confidence that the savages might be subdued, and an end put to their crimes, the American government raised a regiment, consisting of 300 volunteers, for the purpose of dislodging them from their cantonment and preventing further barbarities. Col. William Crawford and Lieut. Col. David Williamson, men who had been thoroughly tried and approved, were commissioned by Gen. Washington to take the command of a service that seemed all-important to the welfare of the country. In the month of July, 1782, well armed and provided with a sufficient quantity of provision, this regiment made an expeditious march through the wilderness to Upper Sandusky, where, as had been anticipated, they found the Indians assembled in full force at their encampment, prepared to receive an attack.

As Col. Crawford and his brave band advanced, and when they had got within a short distance from the town, they were met by a white man, with a flag of truce from the Indians, who proposed to Col. Crawford that if he would surrender himself and his men to the Indians, their lives should be spared; but, that if they persisted in their undertaking, and attacked the town, they should all be massacred to a man.

Crawford, while hearing the proposition, attentively surveyed its bearer, and recognized in his features one of his former schoolmates and companions, with whom he was perfectly acquainted, by the name of Simon Gurty. Gurty, but a short time before this, had been a soldier in the American army, in the same regiment with Crawford; but on the account of his not having received the promotion that he expected, he became disaffected—swore an eternal war with his countrymen, fled to the Indians, and joined them, as a leader well qualified to conduct them to where they could annoint their thirst for blood, upon the innocent, unoffending and defenceless settlers.

Crawford sternly inquired of the traitor if his name was not Simon Gurty; and being answered in the affirmative, he informed him that he despised the offer which he had made; and that he should not surrender his army unless he should be compelled to do so, by a superior force.

Gurty returned, and Crawford immediately commenced an engagement that lasted till night, without the appearance of victory on either side, when the firing ceased, and the combatants on both sides retired to take refreshment, and to rest through the night. Crawford encamped in the woods near half a mile from the town, where, after the centinels were placed, and each had taken his ration, they slept on their arms, that they might be instantly ready in case they should be attacked. The stillness of death hovered over the little army, and sleep relieved the whole, except the wakeful centinels who vigilantly attended to their duty.—But what was their surprise, when they found late in the night, that they were surrounded by the Indians on every side, except a narrow space between them and the town? Every man was under arms, and the officers instantly consulted each other on the best method of escaping; for they saw that to fight, would be useless, and that to surrender, would be death.

Crawford proposed to retreat through the ranks of the enemy in an opposite direction from the town, as being the most sure course to take. Lt. Col. Williamson advised to march directly through the town, where there appeared to be no Indians, and the fires were yet burning.

There was no time or place for debates: Col. Crawford, with sixty followers retreated on the route that he had proposed by attempting to rush through the enemy; but they had no sooner got amongst the Indians, than every man was killed or taken prisoner! Amongst the prisoners, were Col. Crawford, and Doct. Night, surgeon of the regiment.

Lt. Col. Williamson, with the remainder of the regiment, together with the wounded, set out at the same time that Crawford did, went through the town without losing a man, and by the help of good guides arrived at their homes in safety.

The next day after the engagement the Indians disposed of all their prisoners to the different tribes, except Col. Crawford and Doct. Night; but those unfortunate men were reserved for a more cruel destiny. A council was immediately held on Sandusky plains, consisting of all the Chiefs and warriors, ranged in their customary order, in a circular form; and Crawford and Night were brought forward and seated in the centre of the circle.

The council being opened, the Chiefs began to examine Crawford on various subjects relative to the war. At length they enquired who conducted the military operations of the American army on the Ohio and Susquehannah rivers, during the year before; and who had led that army against them with so much skill, and so uniform success? Crawford very honestly and without suspecting any harm from his reply, promptly answered that he was the man who had led his countrymen to victory, who had driven the enemy from the settlements, and by that means had procured a great degree of happiness to many of his fellow-citizens. Upon hearing this, a Chief, who had lost a son in the year before, in a battle where Colonel Crawford commanded, left his station in the council, stepped to Crawford, blacked his face, and at the same time told him that the next day he should be burnt.

The council was immediately dissolved on its hearing the sentence from the Chief, and the prisoners were taken off the ground, and kept in custody through the night. Crawford now viewed his fate as sealed; and despairing of ever returning to his home or his country, only dreaded the tediousness of death, as commonly inflicted by the savages, and earnestly hoped that he might be despatched at a single blow.

Early the next morning, the Indians assembled at the place of execution, and Crawford was led to the post—the goal of savage torture, to which he was fastened. The post was a stick of timber placed firmly in the ground, having an arm framed in at the top, and extending some six or eight feet from it, like the arm of a sign post. A pile of wood containing about two cords, lay a few feet from the place where he stood, which he was informed was to be kindled into a fire that would burn him alive, as many had been burnt on the same spot, who had been much less deserving than himself.

Gurty stood and composedly looked on the preparations that were making for the funeral of one his former playmates; a hero by whose side he had fought; of a man whose valor had won laurels which, if he could have returned, would have been strewed upon his grave, by his grateful countrymen. Dreading the agony that he saw he was about to feel, Crawford used every argument which his perilous situation could suggest to prevail upon Gurty to ransom him at any price, and deliver him (as it was in his power,) from the savages, and their torments. Gurty heard his prayers, and expostulations, and saw his tears with indifference, and finally told the forsaken victim that he would not procure him a moment's respite, nor afford him the most trifling assistance.

The Col. was then bound, stripped naked and tied by his wrists to the arm, which extended horizontally from the post, in such a manner that his arms were extended over his head, with his feet just standing upon the ground. This being done, the savages placed the wood in a circle around him at the distance of a few feet, in order that his misery might be protracted to the greatest length, and then kindled it in a number of places at the same time. The flames arose and the scorching heat became almost insupportable. Again he prayed to Gurty in all the anguish of his torment, to rescue him from the fire, or shoot him dead upon the spot. A demoniac smile suffused the countenance of Gurty, while he calmly replied to the dying suppliant, that he had no pity for his sufferings; but that he was then satisfying that spirit of revenge, which for a long time he had hoped to have an opportunity to wreak upon him. Nature now almost exhausted from the intensity of the heat, he settled down a little, when a squaw threw coals of fire and embers upon him, which made him groan most piteously, while the whole camp rung with exultation. During the execution they manifested all the exstacy of a complete triumph. Poor Crawford soon died and was entirely consumed.

Thus ended the life of a patriot and hero, who had been an intimate with Gen. Washington, and who shared in an eminent degree the confidence of that great, good man, to whom, in the time of revolutionary perils, the sons of legitimate freedom looked with a degree of faith in his mental resources, unequalled in the history of the world.

That tragedy being ended, Doct. Night was informed that on the next day he should be burnt in the same manner that his comrade Crawford had been, at Lower Sandusky. Hiokatoo, who had been a leading chief in the battle with, and in the execution of Crawford, painted Doct. Night's face black, and then bound and gave him up to two able bodied Indians to conduct to the place of execution.

They set off with him immediately, and travelled till towards evening, when they halted to encamp till morning. The afternoon had been very rainy, and the storm still continued, which rendered it very difficult for the Indians to kindle a fire. Night observing the difficulty under which they labored, made them to understand by signs, that if they would unbind him, he would assist them.—They accordingly unloosed him, and he soon succeeded in making a fire by the application of small dry stuff which he was at considerable trouble to procure. While the Indians were warming themselves, the Doct. continued to gather wood to last through the night, and in doing this, he found a club which he placed in a situation from whence he could take it conveniently whenever an opportunity should present itself, in which he could use it effectually. The Indians continued warming, till at length the Doct. saw that they had placed themselves in a favorable position for the execution of his design, when, stimulated by the love of life, he cautiously took his club and at two blows knocked them both down. Determined to finish the work of death which he had so well begun, he drew one of their scalping knives, with which he beheaded and scalped them both! He then took a rifle, tomahawk, and some ammunition, and directed his course for home, where he arrived without having experienced any difficulty on his journey.

The next morning, the Indians took the track of their victim and his attendants, to go to Lower Sandusky, and there execute the sentence which they had pronounced upon him. But what was their surprise and disappointment, when they arrived at the place of encampment, where they found their trusty friends scalped and decapitated, and that their prisoner had made his escape?—Chagrined beyond measure, they immediately separated, and went in every direction in pursuit of their prey; but after having spent a number of days unsuccessfully, they gave up the chase, and returned to their encampment.[11]

In the time of the French war, in an engagement that took place on the Ohio river, Hiokatoo took a British Col. by the name of Simon Canton, whom he carried to the Indian encampment. A council was held, and the Col. was sentenced to suffer death, by being tied on a wild colt, with his face towards its tail, and then having the colt turned loose to run where it pleased. He was accordingly tied on, and the colt let loose, agreeable to the sentence. The colt run two days and then returned with its rider yet alive. The Indians, thinking that he would never die in that way, took him off, and made him run the gauntlet three times; but in the last race a squaw knocked him down, and he was supposed to have

11. I have understood (from unauthenticated sources however,) that soon after the revolutionary war, Doct. Night published a pamphlet, containing an account of the battle at Sandusky, and of his own sufferings. My information on this subject, was derived from a different quarter.

The subject of this narrative in giving the account of her last husband, Hiokatoo, referred us to Mr. George Jemison, who (as it will be noticed) lived on her land a number of years, and who had frequently heard the old Chief relate the story of his life; particularly that part which related to his military career. Mr. Jemison, on being enquired of, gave the foregoing account, partly from his own personal knowledge, and the remainder, from the account given by Hiokatoo.

Mr. Jemison was in the battle, was personally acquainted with Col. Crawford, and one that escaped with Lt. Col. Williamson. We have no doubt of the truth of the statement, and have therefore inserted the whole account, as an addition to the historical facts which are daily coming into a state of preservation, in relation to the American Revolution.

AUTHOR.

been dead. He, however, recovered, and was sold for fifty dollars to a Frenchman, who sent him as a prisoner to Detroit. On the return of the Frenchman to Detroit, the Col. besought him to ransom him, and give, or set him at liberty, with so much warmth, and promised with so much solemnity, to reward him as one of the best of benefactors, if he would let him go, that the Frenchman took his word, and sent him home to his family. The Col. remembered his promise, and in a short time sent his deliverer one hundred and fifty dollars, as a reward for his generosity.

Since the commencement of the revolutionary war, Hiokatoo has been in seventeen campaigns, four of which were in the Cherokee war. He was so great an enemy to the Cherokees, and so fully determined upon their subjugation, that on his march to their country, he raised his own army for those four campaigns, and commanded it; and also superintended its subsistence. In one of those campaigns, which continued two whole years without intermission, he attacked his enemies on the Mobile, drove them to the country of the Creek Nation, where he continued to harrass them, till being tired of war, he returned to his family. He brought home a great number of scalps, which he had taken from the enemy, and ever seemed to possess an unconquerable will that the Cherokees might be utterly destroyed. Towards the close of his last fighting in that country, he took two squaws, whom he sold on his way home for money to defray the expense of his journey.

Hiokatoo was about six feet four or five inches high, large boned, and rather inclined to leanness. He was very stout and active, for a man of his size, for it was said by himself and others, that he had never found an Indian who could keep up with him on a race, or throw him at wrestling. His eye was quick and penetrating; and his voice was of that harsh and powerful kind, which, amongst Indians, always commands attention. His health had been uniformly good. He never was confined by sickness, till he was attacked with the consumption, four years before his death. And, although he had, from his earliest days, been inured to almost constant fatigue, and exposure to the inclemency of the weather, in the open air, he seemed to lose the vigor of the prime of life only by the natural decay occasioned by old age.

Chapter XII.

Her Troubles Renewed.—John's jealousy towards his brother Jesse.—
Circumstances attending the Murder of Jesse Jemison.—Her Grief.—His
Funeral—Age—Filial Kindness, &c.

Being now left a widow in my old age, to mourn the loss of a husband, who had treated me well, and with whom I had raised five children, and having suffered the loss of an affectionate son, I fondly fostered the hope that my melancholy vicissitudes had ended, and that the remainder of my time would be characterized by nothing unpropitious. My children, dutiful and kind, lived near me, and apparently nothing obstructed our happiness.

But a short time, however, elapsed after my husband's death, before my troubles were renewed with redoubled severity.

John's hands having been once stained in the blood of a brother, it was not strange that after his acquital, every person of his acquaintance should shun him, from a fear of his repeating upon them the same ceremony that he had practised upon Thomas. My son Jesse, went to Mt. Morris, a few miles from home, on business, in the winter after the death of his father; and it so happened that his brother John was there, who requested Jesse to come home with him. Jesse, fearing that John would commence a quarrel with him on the way, declined the invitation, and tarried over night.

From that time John conceived himself despised by Jesse, and was highly enraged at the treatment which he had received. Very little was said, however, and it all passed off, apparently, till sometime in the month of May, 1812, at which time Mr. Robert Whaley, who lived in the town of Castile, within four miles of me, came to my house early on Monday morning, to hire George Chongo, my son-in-law, and John and Jesse, to go that day and help him slide a quantity of boards from the top of the hill to the river, where he calculated to build a raft of them for market.

They all concluded to go with Mr. Whaley, and made ready as soon as possible. But before they set out I charged them not to drink any whiskey; for I was confident that if they did, they would surely have a quarrel in consequence of it. They went and worked till almost night, when a quarrel ensued between Chongo and Jesse, in consequence of the whiskey that they had drank through the day, which terminated in a battle, and Chongo got whipped.

When Jesse had got through with Chongo, he told Mr. Whaley that he would go home, and directly went off. He, however, went but a few rods before he stopped and lay down by the side of a log to wait (as was supposed,) for company. John, as soon as Jesse was gone, went to Mr. Whaley, with his knife in his hand, and bade him jogo; (i.e. be gone,) at the same time telling him that Jesse was a bad man. Mr.

Whaley, seeing that his countenance was changed, and that he was determined upon something desperate, was alarmed for his own safety, and turned towards home, leaving Chongo on the ground drunk, near to where Jesse had lain, who by this time had got up, and was advancing towards John. Mr. Whaley was soon out of hearing of them; but some of his workmen staid till it was dark. Jesse came up to John, and said to him, you want more whiskey, and more fighting, and after a few words went at him, to try in the first place to get away his knife. In this he did not succeed, and they parted. By this time the night had come on, and it was dark. Again they clenched and at length in their struggle they both fell. John, having his knife in his hand, came under, and in that situation gave Jesse a fatal stab with his knife, and repeated the blows till Jesse cried out, brother, you have killed me, quit his hold and settled back upon the ground.—Upon hearing this, John left him and came to Thomas' widow's house, told them that he had been fighting with their uncle, whom he had killed, and showed them his knife.

Next morning as soon as it was light, Thomas' and John's children came and told me that Jesse was dead in the woods, and also informed me how he came by his death. John soon followed them and informed me himself of all that had taken place between him and his brother, and seemed to be somewhat sorrowful for his conduct. You can better imagine what my feelings were than I can describe them. My darling son, my youngest child, him on whom I depended, was dead; and I in my old age left destitute of a helping hand!

As soon as it was consistent for me, I got Mr. George Jemison (of whom I shall have occasion to speak,) to go with his sleigh to where Jesse was, and bring him home, a distance of 3 or 4 miles. My daughter Polly arrived at the fatal spot first: we got there soon after her; though I went the whole distance on foot. By this time, Chongo (who was left on the ground drunk the night before,) had become sober and sensible of the great misfortune which had happened to our family.

I was overcome with grief at the sight of my murdered son, and so far lost the command of myself as to be almost frantic; and those who were present were obliged to hold me from going near him.

On examining the body it was found that it had received eighteen wounds so deep and large that it was believed that either of them would have proved mortal. The corpse was carried to my house, and kept till the Thursday following, when it was buried after the manner of burying white people.

Jesse was twenty-seven or eight years old when he was killed. His temper had been uniformly very mild and friendly; and he was inclined to copy after the white people; both in his manners and dress. Although he was naturally temperate, he occasionally became intoxicated; but never was quarrelsome or mischievous. With the white people he was intimate, and learned from them their habits of industry, which he was fond of practising, especially when my comfort demanded his labor. As I have observed, it is the custom amongst the Indians, for the women to perform all the labor in, and out of doors, and I had the whole to do, with the help of my daughters, till Jesse arrived to a sufficient age to assist us. He was disposed to labor in the cornfield, to chop my wood, milk my cows, and attend to any kind of business that would make my task the lighter. On the account of his having been my youngest child, and so willing to help me, I am sensible that I loved him better than I did either of my other children. After he began to understand my situation, and the means of rendering it more easy, I never wanted for any thing that was in his power to bestow; but since his death, as I have had all my labor to perform alone, I have constantly seen hard times.

Jesse shunned the company of his brothers, and the Indians generally, and never attended their frolics; and it was supposed that this, together with my partiality for him, were the causes which excited in John so great a degree of envy, that nothing short of death would satisfy it.

Chapter XIII.

Mrs. Jemison is informed that she has a Cousin in the Neighborhood, by the name of George Jemison.—His Poverty.—Her Kindness.—His Ingratitude.—Her Trouble from Land Speculation.—Her Cousin moves off.

A year or two before the death of my husband, Capt. H. Jones sent me word, that a cousin of mine was then living in Leicester (a few miles from Gardow,) by the name of George Jemison, and as he was very poor, thought it advisable for me to go and see him, and take him home to live with me on my land. My Indian friends were pleased to hear that one of my relatives was so near, and also advised me to send for him and his family immediately. I accordingly had him and his family moved into one of my houses, in the month of March, 1810.

He said that he was my father's brother's son—that his father did not leave Europe, till after the French war in America, and that when he did come over, he settled in Pennsylvania, where he died. George had no personal knowledge of my father; but from information, was confident that the relationship which he claimed between himself and me, actually existed. Although I had never before heard of my father having had but one brother (him who was killed at Fort Necessity,) yet I knew that he might have had others, and, as the story of George carried with it a probability that it was true, I received him as a kinsman, and treated him with every degree of friendship which his situation demanded.[12]

I found that he was destitute of the means of subsistence, and in debt to the amount of seventy dollars, without the ability to pay one cent. He had no cow, and finally, was completely poor. I paid his debts to the amount of seventy-two dollars, and bought him a cow, for which I paid twenty dollars, and a sow and pigs, that I paid eight dollars for. I also paid sixteen dollars for pork that I gave him, and furnished him with other provisions and furniture; so that his family was comfortable. As he was destitute of a team, I furnished him with one, and also supplied him with tools for farming. In addition to all this, I let him have one of Thomas' cows, for two seasons.

My only object in mentioning his poverty, and the articles with which I supplied him, is to show how ungrateful a person can be for favors, and how soon a kind benefactor will, to all appearance, be forgotten.

Thus furnished with the necessary implements of husbandry, a good team, and as much land as he could till, he commenced farming on my flats, and for some time labored well. At length, however, he got an idea that if he could become the owner of a part of my reservation, he could live more easy, and certainly be more rich, and accordingly set himself about laying a plan to obtain it, in the easiest manner possible.

I supported Jemison and his family eight years, and probably should have continued to have done so to this day, had it not been for the occurrence of the following circumstance.

When he had lived with me some six or seven years, a friend of mine told me that as Jemison was my Cousin, and very poor, I ought to give him a piece of land that he might have something whereon to live, that he would call his own. My friend and Jemison were then together at my house, prepared to complete a bargain. I asked how much land

12. Mrs. Jemison is now confident that George Jemison is not her cousin, and thinks that he claimed the relationship, only to gain assistance: But the old gentleman, who is now living, is certain that his and her father were brothers, as before stated.

he wanted? Jemison said that he should be glad to receive his old field (as he called it) containing about fourteen acres, and a new one that contained twenty-six.

I observed to them that as I was incapable of transacting business of that nature, I would wait till Mr. Thomas Clute (a neighbor on whom I depended,) should return from Albany, before I should do any thing about it. To this Jemison replied that if I waited till Mr. Clute returned, he should not get the land at all, and appeared very anxious to have the business closed without delay. On my part, I felt disposed to give him some land, but knowing my ignorance of writing, feared to do it alone, lest they might include as much land as they pleased, without my knowledge.

They then read the deed which my friend had prepared before he came from home, describing a piece of land by certain bounds that were a specified number of chains and links from each other. Not understanding the length of a chain or link, I described the bounds of a piece of land that I intended Jemison should have, which they said was just the same that the deed contained and no more. I told them that the deed must not include a lot that was called the Steele place, and they assured me that it did not. Upon this, putting confidence in them both, I signed the deed to George Jemison, containing, and conveying to him as I supposed, forty acres of land. The deed being completed they charged me never to mention the bargain which I had then made to any person; because if I did, they said it would spoil the contract. The whole matter was afterwards disclosed; when it was found that that deed instead of containing only forty acres, contained four hundred, and that one half of it actually belonged to my friend, as it had been given to him by Jemison as a reward for his trouble in procuring the deed, in the fraudulent manner above mentioned.

My friend, however, by the advice of some well disposed people, awhile afterwards gave up his claim; but Jemison held his till he sold it for a trifle to a gentleman in the south part of Genesee County.

Sometime after the death of my son Thomas, one of his sons went to Jemison to get the cow that I had let him have two years; but Jemison refused to let her go, and struck the boy so violent a blow as to almost kill him. Jemison then run to Jellis Clute, Esq. to procure a warrant to take the boy; but Young King, an Indian Chief, went down to Squawky hill to Esq. Clute's, and settled the affair by Jemison's agreeing never to use that club again. Having satisfactorily found out the friendly disposition of my cousin towards me, I got him off my premises as soon as possible.

Chapter XIV.

Another Family Affliction.—Her son John's Occupation.—He goes to
Buffalo—Returns.—Great Slide by him considered Ominous—Trouble, &c.—
He goes to Squawky Hill—Quarrels—Is murdered by two Indians.—His
Funeral—Mourners, &c.—His Disposition.—Ominous Dream.—Black Chief's
Advice, &c.—His Widows and Family.—His Age.—His Murderers flee.—
Her Advice to them.—They set out to leave their Country.—Their Uncle's
Speech to them on parting.—They return.—Jack proposes to Doctor to kill
each other.—Doctor's Speech in Reply.—Jack's Suicide.—Doctor's Death.

Trouble seldom comes single. While George Jemison was busily engaged in his pursuit of wealth at my expence, another event of a much
more serious nature occurred, which added greatly to my afflictions,
and consequently destroyed, at least a part of the happiness that I had
anticipated was laid up in the archives of Providence, to be dispensed
on my old age.

My son John, was a doctor, considerably celebrated amongst the
Indians of various tribes, for his skill in curing their diseases, by the
administration of roots and herbs, which he gathered in the forests, and
other places where they had been planted by the hand of nature.

In the month of April, or first of May, 1817, he was called upon to
go to Buffalo, Cattaraugus and Allegany, to cure some who were sick.
He went, and was absent about two months. When he returned, he observed the Great Slide of the bank of Genesee river, a short distance
above my house, which had taken place during his absence; and conceiving that circumstance to be ominous of his own death, called at his
sister Nancy's, told her that he should live but a few days, and wept
bitterly at the near approach of his dissolution. Nancy endeavored to
persuade him that his trouble was imaginary, and that he ought not
to be affected by a fancy which was visionary. Her arguments were ineffectual, and afforded no alleviation to his mental sufferings. From his
sister's, he went to his own house, where he stayed only two nights,
and then went to Squawky Hill to procure money, with which to purchase flour for the use of his family.

While at Squawky Hill he got into the company of two Squawky Hill
Indians, whose names were Doctor and Jack, with whom he drank
freely, and in the afternoon had a desperate quarrel, in which his opponents (as it was afterwards understood,) agreed to kill him. The quarrel
ended, and each appeared to be friendly. John bought some spirits, of

which they all drank, and then set out for home. John and an Allegany Indian were on horseback, and Doctor and Jack were on foot. It was dark when they set out. They had not proceeded far, when Doctor and Jack commenced another quarrel with John, clenched and dragged him off his horse, and then with a stone gave him so severe a blow on his head, that some of his brains were discharged from the wound. The Allegany Indian, fearing that his turn would come next, fled for safety as fast as possible.

John recovered a little from the shock he had received, and endeavored to get to an old hut that stood near; but they caught him, and with an axe cut his throat, and beat out his brains, so that when he was found the contents of his skull were lying on his arms.

Some squaws, who heard the uproar, ran to find out the cause of it; but before they had time to offer their assistance, the murderers drove them into a house, and threatened to take their lives if they did not stay there, or if they made any noise.

Next morning, Esq. Clute sent me word that John was dead, and also informed me of the means by which his life was taken. A number of people went from Gardow to where the body lay, and Doct. Levi Brundridge brought it up home, where the funeral was attended after the manner of the white people. Mr. Benjamin Luther, and Mr. William Wiles, preached a sermon, and performed the funeral services; and myself and family followed the corpse to the grave as mourners. I had now buried my three sons, who had been snatched from me by the hands of violence, when I least expected it.

Although John had taken the life of his two brothers, and caused me unspeakable trouble and grief, his death made a solemn impression upon my mind, and seemed, in addition to my former misfortunes, enough to bring down my grey hairs with sorrow to the grave. Yet, on a second thought, I could not mourn for him as I had for my other sons, because I knew that his death was just, and what he had deserved for a long time, from the hand of justice.

John's vices were so great and so aggravated, that I have nothing to say in his favor: yet, as a mother, I pitied him while he lived, and have ever felt a great degree of sorrow for him, because of his bad conduct.

From his childhood, he carried something in his features indicative of an evil disposition, that would result in the perpetration of enormities of some kind; and it was the opinion and saying of Ebenezer Allen, that he would be a bad man, and be guilty of some crime deserving of death. There is no doubt but what the thoughts of murder rankled in his breast, and disturbed his mind even in his sleep; for he dreamed that he had killed Thomas for a trifling offence, and thereby forfeited his own life. Alarmed at the revelation, and fearing that he might in some unguarded moment destroy his brother, he went to the Black Chief, to whom he told the dream, and expressed his fears that the vision would be verified. Having related the dream, together with his feelings on the subject, he asked for the best advice that his old friend was capable of giving, to prevent so sad an event. The Black Chief, with his usual promptitude, told him, that from the nature of the dream, he was fearful that something serious would take place between him and Thomas; and advised him by all means to govern his temper, and avoid any quarrel which in future he might see arising, especially if Thomas was a party. John, however, did not keep the good counsel of the Chief; for soon after he killed Thomas, as I have related.

John left two wives with whom he had lived at the same time, and raised nine children. His widows are now living at Caneadea with their father, and keep their children with, and near them. His children are tolerably white, and have got light colored hair. John died about the last day of June, 1817, aged 54 years.

Doctor and Jack, having finished their murderous design, fled before they could be apprehended, and lay six weeks in the woods back of Canisteo. They then returned and sent me some wampum by Chongo (my son-in-law,) and Sun-ge-waw (that is Big Kettle) expecting that I would pardon them, and suffer them to live as they had done with their tribe. I however, would not accept their wampum, but returned it with a request, that, rather than have them killed, they would run away and keep out of danger.

On their receiving back the wampum, they took my advice, and prepared to leave their country and people immediately. Their relatives accompanied them a short distance on their journey, and when about to part, their old uncle, the Tall Chief, addressed them in the following pathetic and sentimental speech:

"Friends, hear my voice!—When the Great Spirit made Indians, he made them all good, and gave them good corn-fields; good rivers, well stored with fish; good forests, filled with game and good bows and arrows. But very soon each wanted more than his share, and Indians quarrelled with Indians, and some were killed, and others were wounded. Then the Great Spirit made a very good word, and put it in every Indians breast, to tell us when we have done good, or when we have done bad; and that word has never told a lie.

"Friends! whenever you have stole, or got drunk, or lied, that good word has told you that you were bad Indians, and made you afraid of good Indians; and made you ashamed and look down.

"Friends! your crime is greater than all those:—you have killed an Indian in a time of peace; and made the wind hear his groans, and the earth drink his blood. You are bad Indians! Yes, you are very bad Indians; and what can you do? If you go into the woods to live alone, the ghost of John Jemison will follow you, crying, blood! blood! and will give you no peace! If you go to the land of your nation, there that ghost will attend you, and say to your relatives, see my murderers! If you plant, it will blast your corn; if you hunt, it will scare your game; and when you are asleep, its groans, and the sight of an avenging toma-hawk, will awake you! What can you do? Deserving of death, you can-not live here; and to fly from your country, to leave all your relatives, and to abandon all that you have known to be pleasant and dear, must be keener than an arrow, more bitter than gall, more terrible than death! And how must we feel?—Your path will be muddy; the woods will be dark; the lightnings will glance down the trees by your side, and you will start at every sound! peace has left you, and you must be wretched.

"Friends, hear me, and take my advice. Return with us to your homes. Offer to the Great Spirit your best wampum, and try to be good Indians! And, if those whom you have bereaved shall claim your lives as their only satisfaction, surrender them cheerfully, and die like good Indians. And—" Here Jack, highly incensed, interrupted the old man, and bade him stop speaking or he would take his life. Affrighted at the appearance of so much desperation, the company hastened towards home, and left Doctor and Jack to consult their own feelings.

As soon as they were alone, Jack said to Doctor, "I had rather die here, than leave my country and friends! Put the muzzle of your rifle into my mouth, and I will put the muzzle of mine into yours, and at a given signal we will discharge them, and rid ourselves at once of all the troubles under which we now labor, and satisfy the claims which jus-tice holds against us."

Doctor heard the proposition, and after a moment's pause, made the following reply:—"I am as sensible as you can be of the unhappy situa-tion in which we have placed ourselves. We are bad Indians. We have forfeited our lives, and must expect in some way to atone for our crime: but, because we are bad and miserable, shall we make ourselves worse? If we were now innocent, and in a calm reflecting moment should kill ourselves, that act would make us bad, and deprive us of our share of the good hunting in the land where our fathers have gone! What would Little Beard[13] say to us on our arrival at his cabin? He would say, 'Bad Indians! Cowards! You were afraid to wait till we wanted your help! Go (Jogo) to where snakes will lie in your path; where the panthers will starve you, by devouring the venison; and where you will be naked and suffer with the cold! Jogo (go,) none but the brave and good Indians live here!' I cannot think of performing an act that will add to my wretchedness. It is hard enough for me to suffer here, and have good hunting hereafter—worse to lose the whole."

Upon this, Jack withdrew his proposal. They went on about two miles, and then turned about and came home. Guilty and uneasy, they lurked about Squawky Hill near a fortnight, and then went to Cattaraugus, and were gone six weeks. When they came back, Jack's wife earnestly requested him to remove his family to Tonnewonta; but he remonstrated against her project, and utterly declined going. His wife and family, however, tired of the tumult by which they were surrounded, packed up their effects in spite of what he could say, and went off.

Jack deliberated a short time upon the proper course for himself to pursue, and finally, rather than leave his old home, he ate a large quantity of muskrat root, and died in 10 or 12 hours. His family being immediately notified of his death, returned to attend the burial, and is yet living at Squawky Hill.

Nothing was ever done with Doctor, who continued to live quietly at Squawky Hill till sometime in the year 1819, when he died of Consumption.

Chapter XV.

Micah Brooks, Esq. volunteers to get the Title to her Land confirmed to herself.—She is Naturalized.—Great Council of Chiefs, &c. in Sept. 1823.— She Disposes of her Reservation.—Reserves a Tract 2 miles long, and 1 mile wide, &c.—The Consideration how Paid, &c.

In 1816, Micah Brooks, Esq. of Bloomfield, Ontario county, was recommended to me (as it was said) by a Mr. Ingles, to be a man of candor, honesty and integrity, who would by no means cheat me out of a cent. Mr. Brooks soon after, came to my house and informed me that he was

13. Little Beard was a Chief who died in 1806.

disposed to assist me in regard to my land, by procuring a legislative act that would invest me with full power to dispose of it for my own benefit, and give as simple a title as could be given by any citizen of the state. He observed that as it was then situated, it was of but little value, because it was not in my power to dispose of it, let my necessities be ever so great. He then proposed to take the agency of the business upon himself, and to get the title of one half of my reservation vested in me personally, upon the condition that, as a reward for his services, I would give him the other half.

I sent for my son John, who on being consulted, objected to my going into any bargain with Mr. Brooks, without the advice and consent of Mr. Thomas Clute, who then lived on my land and near me. Mr. Clute was accordingly called on, to whom Mr. Brooks repeated his former statement, and added, that he would get an act passed in the Congress of the United States, that would invest me with all the rights and immunities of a citizen, so far as it respected my property. Mr. Clute, suspecting that some plan was in operation that would deprive me of my possessions, advised me to have nothing to say on the subject to Mr. Brooks, till I had seen Esquire Clute, of Squawky Hill. Soon after this Thomas Clute saw Esq. Clute, who informed him that the petition for my naturalization would be presented to the Legislature of this State, instead of being sent to Congress; and that the object would succeed to his and my satisfaction. Mr. Clute then observed to his brother, Esq. Clute, that as the sale of Indian lands, which had been reserved, belonged exclusively to the United States, an act of the Legislature of New-York could have no effect in securing to me a title to my reservation, or in depriving me of my property. They finally agreed that I should sign a petition to Congress, praying for my naturalization, and for the confirmation of the title of my land to me, my heirs, &c.

Mr. Brooks came with the petition: I signed it, and it was witnessed by Thomas Clute, and two others, and then returned to Mr. Brooks, who presented it to the Legislature of this state at its session in the winter of 1816–17. On the 19th of April, 1817, an act was passed for my naturalization, and ratifying and confirming the title of my land, agreeable to the tenor of the petition, which act Mr. Brooks presented to me on the first day of May following.

Thomas Clute having examined the law, told me that it would probably answer, though it was not according to the agreement made by Mr. Brooks, and Esq. Clute and himself, for me. I then executed to Micah

Brooks and Jellis Clute, a deed of all my land lying east of the picket line on the Gardow reservation, containing about 7000 acres.

It is proper in this place to observe, in relation to Mr. Thomas Clute, that my son John, a few months before his death, advised me to take him for my guardian (as I had become old and incapable of managing my property,) and to compensate him for his trouble by giving him a lot of land on the west side of my reservation where he should choose it. I accordingly took my son's advice, and Mr. Clute has ever since been faithful and honest in all his advice and dealings with, and for, myself and family.

In the month of August, 1817, Mr. Brooks and Esq. Clute again came to me with a request that I would give them a lease of the land which I had already deeded to them, together with the other part of my reservation, excepting and reserving to myself only about 4000 acres.

At this time I informed Thomas Clute of what John had advised, and recommended me to do, and that I had consulted my daughters on the subject, who had approved of the measure. He readily agreed to assist me; whereupon I told him he was entitled to a lot of land, and might select as John had mentioned. He accordingly at that time took such a piece as he chose, and the same has ever since been reserved for him in all the land contracts which I have made.

On the 24th of August, 1817, I leased to Micah Brooks and Jellis Clute, the whole of my original reservation, except 4000 acres, and Thomas Clute's lot. Finding their title still incomplete, on account of the United States government and Seneca Chiefs not having sanctioned my acts, they solicited me to renew the contract, and have the conveyance made to them in such a manner as that they should thereby be constituted sole proprietors of the soil.

In the winter of 1822–3, I agreed with them, that if they would get the chiefs of our nation, and a United States Commissioner of Indian Lands, to meet in council at Moscow, Livingston county, N. Y. and there concur in my agreement, that I would sell to them all my right and title to the Gardow reservation, with the exception of a tract for my own benefit, two miles long, and one mile wide, lying on the river where I should choose it; and also reserving Thomas Clute's lot. This arrangement was agreed upon, and the council assembled at the place appointed, on the 3d or 4th day of September, 1823.

That council consisted of Major Carrol, who had been appointed by the President to dispose of my lands, Judge Howell and N. Gorham, of

Canandaigua (who acted in concert with Maj. Carrol,) Jasper Parrish, Indian Agent, Horatio Jones, Interpreter, and a great number of Chiefs.

The bargain was assented to unanimously, and a deed given to H. B. Gibson, Micah Brooks and Jellis Clute, of the whole Gardow tract, excepting the last mentioned reservations, which was signed by myself and upwards of twenty Chiefs.

The land which I now own, is bounded as follows:—Beginning at the center of the Great Slide[14] and running west one mile, thence north two miles, thence east about one mile to Genesee river, thence south on the west bank of Genesee river to the place of beginning.

In consideration of the above sale, the purchasers have bound themselves, their heirs, assigns, &c. to pay to me, my heirs or successors, three hundred dollars a year forever.

Whenever the land which I have reserved, shall be sold, the income of it is to be equally divided amongst the members of the Seneca nation, without any reference to tribes or families.

Chapter XVI.

Conclusion.—Review of her Life.—Reflections on the loss of Liberty.—
Care she took to preserve her Health.—Indians' abstemiousness in Drinking, after the French War.—Care of their Lives, &c.—General use of Spirits.—
Her natural Strength.—Purchase of her first Cow.—Means by which she has been supplied with Food.—Suspicions of her having been a Witch.—Her Constancy.—Number of Children.—Number Living.—Their Residence.—
Closing Reflection.

When I review my life, the privations that I have suffered, the hardships I have endured, the vicissitudes I have passed, and the complete revolution that I have experienced in my manner of living; when I consider my reduction from a civilized to a savage state, and the various steps by which that process has been effected, and that my life has been

14. The Great Slide of the bank of Genesee river is a curiosity worthy of the attention of the traveller. In the month of May, 1817, a portion of land thickly covered with timber, situated at the upper end of the Gardow flats, on the west side of the river, all of a sudden gave way, and with a tremendous crash, slid into the bed of the river, which it so completely filled, that the stream formed a new passage on the east side of it, where it continues to run, without overflowing the slide. This slide, as it now lies, contains 22 acres, and has a considerable share of the timber that formerly covered it, still standing erect upon it, and growing.

prolonged, and my health and reason spared, it seems a miracle that I am unable to account for, and is a tragical medley that I hope will never be repeated.

The bare loss of liberty is but a mere trifle when compared with the circumstances that necessarily attend, and are inseparably connected with it. It is the recollection of what we once were, of the friends, the home, and the pleasures that we have left or lost; the anticipation of misery, the appearance of wretchedness, the anxiety for freedom, the hope of release, the devising of means of escaping, and the vigilance with which we watch our keepers, that constitute the nauseous dregs of the bitter cup of slavery. I am sensible, however, that no one can pass from a state of freedom to that of slavery, and in the last situation rest perfectly contented; but as every one knows that great exertions of the mind tend directly to debilitate the body, it will appear obvious that we ought, when confined, to exert all our faculties to promote our present comfort, and let future days provide their own sacrifices. In regard to ourselves, just as we feel, we are.

For the preservation of my life to the present time I am indebted to an excellent constitution, with which I have been blessed in as great a degree as any other person. After I arrived to years of understanding, the care of my own health was one of my principal studies; and by avoiding exposures to wet and cold, by temperance in eating, abstaining from the use of spirits, and shunning the excesses to which I was frequently exposed, I effected my object beyond what I expected. I have never once been sick till within a year or two, only as I have related.

Spirits and tobacco I have never used, and I have never once attended an Indian frolic. When I was taken prisoner, and for sometime after that, spirits was not known; and when it was first introduced, it was in small quantities, and used only by the Indians; so that it was a long time before the Indian women begun to even taste it.

After the French war, for a number of years, it was the practice of the Indians of our tribe to send to Niagara and get two or three kegs of rum (in all six or eight gallons,) and hold a frolic as long as it lasted. When the rum was brought to the town, all the Indians collected, and before a drop was drank, gave all their knives, tomahawks, guns, and other instruments of war, to one Indian, whose business it was to bury them in a private place, keep them concealed, and remain perfectly sober till the frolic was ended. Having thus divested themselves, they commenced drinking, and continued their frolic till every drop was consumed. If any of them became quarrelsome, or got to fighting, those who were sober enough bound them upon the ground, where they were obliged to lie till they got sober, and then were unbound. When the fumes of the spirits had left the company, the sober Indian returned to each the instruments with which they had entrusted him, and all went home satisfied. A frolic of that kind was held but once a year, and that at the time the Indians quit their hunting, and come in with their deer-skins.

In those frolics the women never participated. Soon after the revolutionary war, however, spirits became common in our tribe, and has been used indiscriminately by both sexes; though there are not so frequent instances of intoxication amongst the squaws as amongst the Indians.

To the introduction and use of that baneful article, which has made such devastation in our tribes, and threatens the extinction of our people (the Indians,) I can with the greatest propriety impute the whole of my misfortune in losing my three sons. But as I have before observed, not even the love of life will restrain an Indian from sipping the poison that he knows will destroy him. The voice of nature, the rebukes of reason, the advice of parents, the expostulations of friends, and the numerous instances of sudden death, are all insufficient to reclaim an Indian, who has once experienced the exhilarating and inebriating effects of spirits, from seeking his grave in the bottom of his bottle!

My strength has been great for a woman of my size, otherwise I must long ago have died under the burdens which I was obliged to carry. I learned to carry loads on my back, in a strap placed across my forehead, soon after my captivity; and continue to carry in the same way. Upwards of thirty years ago, with the help of my young children, I backed all the boards that were used about my house from Allen's mill at the outlet of Silver Lake, a distance of five miles. I have planted, hoed, and harvested corn every season but one since I was taken prisoner. Even this present fall (1823) I have husked my corn and backed it into the house.

The first cow that I ever owned, I bought of a squaw sometime after the revolution. It had been stolen from the enemy. I had owned it but a few days when it fell into a hole, and almost died before we could get it out. After this, the squaw wanted to be recanted, but as I would not give up the cow, I gave her money enough to make, when added to the sum which I paid her at first, thirty-five dollars. Cows were plenty on the Ohio, when I lived there, and of good quality.

For provisions I have never suffered since I came upon the flats; nor have I ever been in debt to any other hands than my own for the plenty that I have shared.

My vices, that have been suspected, have been but few. It was believed for a long time, by some of our people, that I was a great witch; but they were unable to prove my guilt, and consequently I escaped the certain doom of those who are convicted of that crime, which, by Indians, is considered as heinous as murder. Some of my children had light brown hair, and tolerable fair skin, which used to make some say that I stole them; yet as I was ever conscious of my own constancy, I never thought that any one really believed that I was guilty of adultery.

I have been the mother of eight children; three of whom are now living, and I have at this time thirty-nine grand children, and fourteen great-grand children, all living in the neighborhood of Genesee River, and at Buffalo.

I live in my own house, and on my own land, with my youngest daughter, Polly, who is married to George Chongo, and has three children.

My daughter Nancy, who is married to Billy Green, lives about 80 rods south of my house, and has seven children.

My other daughter, Betsey, is married to John Green, has seven children, and resides 80 rods north of my house:

Thus situated in the midst of my children, I expect I shall soon leave the world, and make room for the rising generation. I feel the weight of years with which I am loaded, and am sensible of my daily failure in seeing, hearing and strength; but my only anxiety is for my family. If my family will live happily, and I can be exempted from trouble while I have to stay, I feel as though I could lay down in peace a life that has been checked in almost every hour, with troubles of a deeper dye, than are commonly experienced by mortals.

3

The Life and Religious Experience of Jarena Lee (1836)

Jarena Lee

JARENA LEE (1783–?) was born in Cape May, New Jersey, to free parents of modest means. At seven she was hired out as a servant. In 1811 she married Joseph Lee, a pastor at a black church in a town called Snow Hill, outside Philadelphia. In the next six years, Lee suffered five family deaths, including that of her husband. Not much is known of Jarena Lee's childhood or her life after 1849.

Lee attests that her life truly began at the age of 21 in 1804 with a dramatic conversion to Christianity as she was listening to a sermon at the Bethel African Methodist Episcopal Church in Philadelphia, of which she had been a member for three weeks. Although Lee's conversion was sudden, she struggled with periods of doubt and anguish, some suicidal, for the next four years. William Scott, another African American believer, became her mentor, teaching her about Methodist founder John Wesley's doctrine of sanctification and persuading her that her conversion was not yet complete. Years later, married and living in Snow Hill, Lee felt a call to begin preaching and consulted her pastor, Richard Allen, founder of the Bethel Church. Allen refused her request, insisting that Methodism did not allow female ministers.

In 1818 Lee returned to Philadelphia with her two remaining children. There, Allen, who since Lee's departure had become bishop of the African Methodist Episcopal Church, the first African American denomination in the United States, granted her permission to hold prayer meetings in her home. A year later Lee convinced Allen of her calling when she spontaneously interrupted a sermon and began preaching on the theme and passage that the minister had been exploring. Astonished, Allen authorized her to continue. With the unprecedented approval of the church, Lee traveled in the northern states and as far west as Dayton, Ohio, to preach to white and black audiences, giving almost seven hundred sermons in 1835, and traveling at least as many miles, mostly on foot. In 1833 she contacted an editor about publishing her journal of religious activities to inspire others with the publication of her conversion story and her self-depiction as an early female preacher of the first African Methodist Episcopal Church. In 1836 Lee paid thirty-eight dollars for one thousand copies of *The Life and Religious Experience of Jarena Lee, a Colored Lady, Giving an Account of Her Call to Preach the Gospel,* which she distributed at church meetings. In western Pennsylvania in 1839, Lee met African American evangelist, Zilpha Elaw, who had been born and raised on the outskirts of Philadelphia. The two women spent several months preaching together. During this time she also distributed another thousand copies of her narrative. Convinced that abolition might spread Christianity, Lee became a member of the American Antislavery Society in 1840. Four years later Lee's request to the African Episcopal Church's Book Committee to publish her newly extended autobiography was denied; in 1849, however, she published a second, much longer edition containing the original 1836 narrative and new journal entries up to 1843.

Little else is known about Lee's activities. She may have participated in a spontaneous gathering of female preachers at the 1850 Philadelphia Conference of the African Methodist Episcopal Church. There women proclaimed that they had been ordained by God to preach despite the church's refusal to authorize them, sparking continuing debates about women's rights to work as evangelists.

Lee's narrative has received considerable critical attention in both its original and expanded versions. The introduction to it by William L. Andrews is indispensable, as is his discussion in *To Tell a Free Story* (69–70) of Lee's "radical challenge to systems of naming" in moving from "lady" to androgynous preacher. Sue E. Houchins contrasts the scope of the two editions of Lee's narrative in *Spiritual Narratives* (1988). More recent inquiries include Richard J. Douglass-Chin's 2001 work on autobiographies by nineteenth-century African American women evangelists, and Chanta M. Haywood's *Prophesying Daughters: Black Women Preachers and the Word, 1823–1913* (2003).

Revised and corrected from the Original Mss., written by herself.
Second Edition.
Cincinnati:
Printed and Published for the Author.
1839.

The Life and Religious Experience of Jarena Lee, a Colored Lady, Giving an Account of Her Call to Preach the Gospel.

Life of Jarena Lee.

And it shall come to pass . . . that I will pour out my Spirit upon all flesh; and your sons, and your *daughters* shall prophecy.
        Joel ii. 28

I was born February 11th, 1783, at Cape May, state of New Jersey. At the age of seven years I was parted from my parents, and went to live as a servant maid, with a Mr. Sharp, at the distance of about sixty miles from the place of my birth.

My parents being wholly ignorant of the knowledge of God, had not therefore instructed me in any degree in this great matter. Not long after the commencement of my attendance on this lady, she had bid me do something respecting my work, which in a little while after, she asked me if I had done, when I replied, Yes—but this was not true.

At this awful point, in my early history, the spirit of God moved in power through my conscience, and told me I was a wretched sinner. On this account so great was the impression, and so strong were the feelings of guilt, that I promised in my heart that I would not tell another lie.

But notwithstanding this promise my heart grew harder, after a while, yet the spirit of the Lord never entirely forsook me, but continued mercifully striving with me, until his gracious power converted my soul.

The manner of this great accomplishment, was as follows: In the year 1804, it so happened that I went with others to hear a missionary of the Presbyterian order preach. It was an afternoon meeting, but few were there, the place was a school room; but the preacher was solemn, and in his countenance the earnestness of his master's business appeared equally strong, as though he were about to speak to a multitude.

At the reading of the Psalms, a ray of renewed conviction darted into my soul. These were the words, composing the first verse of the Psalms for the service:

> Lord, I am vile, conceived in sin,
> Born unholy and unclean,
> Sprung from men, whose guilty fall
> Corrupts the race, and taints us all.

This description of my condition struck me to the heart, and made me to feel in some measure, the weight of my sins, and sinful nature. But not knowing how to run immediately to the Lord for Help, I was driven of Satan, in the course of a few days, and tempted to destroy myself.

There was a brook about a quarter of a mile from the house, in which there was a deep hole, where the water whirled about among the rocks; to this place it was suggested, I must go and drown myself.

At the time I had a book in my hand; it was on a Sabbath morning, about ten o'clock; to this place I resorted where on coming to the water I sat down on the bank, and on my looking into it, it was suggested, that drowning would be an easy death. It seemed as if some one was speaking to me, saying put your head under, it will not distress you. But by some means, of which I can give no recount, my thoughts were taken entirely from this purpose, when I went from the place to the house again. It was the unseen arm of God which saved me from self murder.

But notwithstanding this escape from death, my mind was not at rest—but so great was the labour of my spirit and the fearful oppressions of a judgment to come, that I was reduced to one extremely ill. On which account, a physician was called to attend me, from which illness I recovered in about three months.

But as yet I had not found him of whom Moses and the prophets did write, being extremely ignorant; there being no one to instruct me in the way of life and salvation as yet. After my recovery, I left the lady, who during my sickness, was exceedingly kind, and went to Philadelphia. From this place I soon went a few miles into the country, where I resided in the family of a Roman Catholic. But my anxiety still continued respecting my poor soul, on which account, I used to watch my opportunity to read in the Bible; and this lady observing this, took the Bible from me and hid it, giving me a novel in its stead—which when I perceived, I refused to read.

Soon after this I again went to the city of Philadelphia; and commenced going to the English Church, the pastor of which was an Englishman, by the name of Pilmore, one of the number, who at first preached Methodism in America, in the city of New York.

But while sitting under the ministration of this man which was about three months, and at the last time, it appeared that there was a wall between me and a communion with that people, which was higher than I could possibly see over, and seemed to make this impression upon my mind, *this is not the people for you.*

But on returning home at noon I inquired of the head cook of the house respecting the rules of the Methodists, as I knew she belonged to that society, who told me what they were; on which account I replied, that I should not be able to abide by such strict rules not even one year;—however, I told her that I would go with her and hear what they had to say.

The man who was to speak in the afternoon of that day, was the Rev. Richard Allen, since bishop of the African Episcopal Methodists in America. During the labors of this man that afternoon, I had come to the conclusion that this is the people to which my heart unites, and it so happened, that as soon as the service closed, he invited such as felt a desire to flee the wrath to come, to unite on trial with them—I embraced the opportunity. Three weeks from that day, my soul was gloriously converted to God, under preaching, at the very outset of the sermon. The text was barely pronounced, which was: "I perceive thy heart is not right in the sight of God," when there appeared to *my* view, in the centre of the heart *one* sin; this was *malice* against one particular individual, who had strove deeply to injure me, which I resented. At this discovery I said, *Lord,* I forgive *every* creature.

That instant, it appeared to me, as if a garment, which had entirely enveloped my whole person, even to my fingers ends, split at the crown of my head, and was stripped away from me, passing like a shadow, from my sight when the glory of God seemed to cover me in its stead.

That moment, though hundreds were present, I did leap to my feet, and declare that God, for Christ's sake, had pardoned the sins of my soul. Great was the ecstasy of my mind, for I felt that not only the sin of malice was pardoned, but all other sins were, swept away together. That day was the first when my heart had believed, and my tongue had made confession unto salvation—the first words uttered, a part of that song, which shall fill eternity with its sound, was *glory to God*. For a few moments, I had power to exhort sinners, and to tell of the wonders and of the goodness of Him who had clothed me with his salvation. During this, the minister was silent, until my soul felt its duty had been performed, when he declared another witness of the power of Christ to forgive sins on earth, was manifest in my conversion.

From the day on which I first went to the Methodist church, until the hour of my deliverance, I was strangely buffeted by that enemy of all righteousness—the devil.

I was naturally of a lively turn of disposition; and during the space of time from my first awakening until I knew my peace was made with God, I rejoiced in the vanities of this life, and then again sunk back into sorrow.

For four years I had continued in this way, frequently laboring under the awful apprehension, that I could never be happy in this life. This persuasion was greatly strengthened, during the three weeks, which was the last of Satan's power over me, in this peculiar manner: on which account, I had come to the conclusion that I had better be dead then alive. Here I was again tempted to destroy my life by drowning; but suddenly this mode was changed—and while in the dusk of the evening, as I was walking to and fro in the yard of the house, I was beset to hang myself, with a cord suspended from the wall enclosing the secluded spot.

But no sooner was the intention resolved on in my mind, than an awful dread came over me, when I ran into the house; still the tempter pursued me. There was standing a vessel of water—into this I was strongly impressed to plunge my head, so as to extinguish the life which God had given me. Had I done this, I have been always of the opinion that I should have been unable to have released myself; although the vessel was scarcely large enough to hold a gallon of water. Of me, it may not be said, as written by Isaiah (chap. 65. verses 1, 2.) "I am sought of them that asked not for me: I am found of them that sought me not." Glory be to God for his redeeming power, which saved me from the violence of my own hands, from the malice of Satan, and from eternal death; for had I have killed myself, a great ransom could not have delivered me; for it is written—"No murderer hath eternal life abiding in him." How appropriately can I sing—

> Jesus sought me, when a stranger,
> Wandering from the fold of God;
> He to rescue me from danger,
> Interposed his precious blood.

But notwithstanding the terror which seized upon me, when about to end my life, I had no view of the precipice on the edge of which I was tottering, until it was over, and my eyes were opened. Then the awful gulf of hell seemed to be open beneath me, covered only, as it were, by a spider's web, on which I stood. I seemed to hear the howling of the damned, to see the smoke of the bottomless pit, and to hear the rattling of those chains, which hold the impenitent under clouds of darkness of the judgment of the great day.

I trembled like Belshazzar, and cried out in the horror of my spirit. "God be merciful to me a sinner." That night I formed a resolution to pray; which, when resolved upon, there appeared, sitting in one corner of the room, Satan, in the form of a monstrous dog, and in a rave, as if in pursuit, his tongue protruding from his month to a great length, and his eyes looked like two balls of fire; it soon, however, vanished out of my sight. From this state of terror and dismay, I was happily delivered under the preaching of the Gospel as before related.

This view, which I was permitted to have of Satan, in the form of a dog, is evidence, which corroborates in my estimation, the Bible account of a hell of fire, which burneth with brimstone, called in Scripture the bottomless pit; the place where all liars, who repent not, shall have their portion; as also the Sabbath breaker, the adulterer, the fornicator, with the fearful, the abominable, and the unbelieving, this shall be the portion of their cup.

This language is too strong and expressive to be applied to any state of suffering in *time*. Were it to be thus applied, the reality could no where be found in human life; the consequence would be, that *this* scripture would be found a false testimony. But when made to apply to an endless state of perdition, in eternity, beyond the bounds of human life, then this language is found not to exceed our views of a state of eternal damnation.

During the latter part of my state of conviction, I can now apply to my case, as it then was, the beautiful words of the poet:

> The more I strove against its power,
> I felt its weight and guilt the more;
> 'Till late I heard my Saviour say,
> Come hither soul, I am the way.

This I found to be true, to the joy of my disconsolate and despairing heart, in the hour of my conversion to God.

During this state of mind, while sitting near the fire one evening, after I had heard Rev. Richard Allen, as before related, a view of my distressed condition so affected my heart, that I could not refrain from weeping and crying aloud; which caused the lady with whom I then lived, to inquire, with surprise, what ailed me; to which I answered, that I knew not what ailed me. She replied that I ought to pray. I arose from where I was sitting, being in an agony, and weeping convulsively, requested her to pray for me; but at the very moment when she would have done so, some person wrapped heavily at the door for admittance; it was but a person of the house, but this occurrence was sufficient to interrupt us in our intentions; and I believe to this day, I should have found salvation to my soul. This interruption was, doubtless, also the work of Satan.

Although at this time, when my conviction was so great, yet I knew not that Jesus Christ was the Son of God, the second person in the adorable trinity. I knew him not in the pardon of my sins, yet I felt a consciousness that if I died without pardon, that my lot must inevitably be damnation. If I would pray—I knew not how. I could form no connexion of ideas into words; but I knew the Lord's prayer; this I uttered with a loud voice, and with all my might and strength. I was the most ignorant creature in the world; I did not even know that Christ had died for the sins of the world, and to save sinners. Every circumstance, however, was so directed as still to continue and increase the sorrows of my heart, which I now know to have been a godly sorrow which wrought repentance, which is not to be repented of. Even the falling of the dead leaves from the forests, and the dried spires of the mown grass, showed me that I too must die, in like manner, But my case was awfully different from that of the grass of the field, or the wide spread decay of a thousand forests, as I felt within me a living principle, an immortal spirit, which cannot die, and must forever either enjoy the smiles of its Creator, or feel the pangs of ceaseless damnation.

But the Lord led me on; being gracious, he took pity on my ignorance; he heard my wailings, which had entered into the ear of the Lord of Sabaoth. Circumstances so transpired, that I soon came to a knowledge of the being and character of the Son of God, of whom I knew nothing.

My strength had left me. I had become feverish and sickly through the violence of my feelings, on which account, I left my place of service to spend a week with a colored physician, who was a member of the Methodist society, and also to spend this week in going to places where prayer and supplication was statedly made for such as me.

Through this means I had learned much, so as to be able in some degree to comprehend the spiritual meaning of the text, which the minister took on the Sabbath morning, as before related, which was, "I perceive thy heart is not right in the sight of God." Acts, chap. 8, verse 21.

This text, as already related, became the power of God unto salvation to me, because I believed. I was baptized according to the direction of our Lord, who said, as he was about to ascend from the mount, to his disciples, "Go ye into all the world and preach my gospel to every creature, he that believeth and is baptized shall be saved."

I have now passed through the account of my conviction, and also of my conversion to God; and shall next speak of the blessing of sanctification.

A time after I had received forgiveness flowed sweetly on; day and night my joy was full, no temptation was permitted to molest me. I could say continually with the Psalmist, that "God had separated my sins from me, as far as the east is from the west." I was ready continually to cry,

> Come all the world, come sinner thou,
> All things in Christ are ready now.

I continued in this happy state of mind for almost three months, when a certain colored man, by name William Scott, came to pay me a religious visit. He had been for many years a faithful follower of the Lamb; and he had also taken much time in visiting the sick and distressed of our color, and understood well the great things belonging to a man of full stature in Christ Jesus.

In the course of our conversation, he inquired if the Lord had justified my soul. I answered, yes. He then asked me if he had sanctified me. I answered, no and that I did not know what that was. He then undertook to instruct me further in the knowledge of the Lord respecting this blessing.

He told me the progress of the soul from a state of darkness, or of nature, was three-fold or consisted in three degrees, as follows:—First, conviction for sin. Second, justification from sin. Third, the entire sanctification of the soul to God. I thought this description was beautiful, and immediately believed in it. He then inquired if I would promise to pray for this in my secret devotions. I told him, yes. Very soon I began to call upon the Lord to show me all that was in my heart, which was not according to his will. Now there appeared to be a new struggle commencing in my soul, not accompanied with fear, guilt, and bitter distress, as while under my first conviction for sin, but a laboring of mind to know more of the right way of the Lord. I began now to feel that my heart was not clean in his sight; that there yet remained the roots of bitterness, which if not destroyed, would ere long sprout up from these roots, and overwhelm me in a new growth of the brambles and brushwood of sin.

By the increased light of the Spirit, I had found there yet remained the root of pride, anger, self-will, with many evils, the result of fallen nature. I now became alarmed at this discovery, and began to fear that I had been deceived in my experience. I was now greatly alarmed, lest I should fall away from what I knew I had enjoyed; and to guard against this I prayed almost incessantly, without acting faith on the power and promises of God to keep me from falling. I had not yet learned how to war against temptation of this kind. Satan well knew that if he could succeed in making me disbelieve my conversion, that he would catch me either on the ground of complete despair, or on the ground of infidelity. For if all I had passed through was to go for nothing, and was but a fiction, the mere ravings of a disordered mind, that I would be naturally led to believe that there is nothing in religion at all.

From this snare I was mercifully preserved, and led to believe that there was yet a greater work than that of pardon to be wrought in me. I retired to a secret place (after having sought his blessing, as well as I could, for nearly three months, from the time brother Scott had instructed me respecting it,) for prayer, about four o'clock in the afternoon. I had struggled long and hard, but found not the desire of my heart. When I rose from my knees, there seemed a voice speaking to me, as I yet stood in a leaning posture—"Ask for sanctification." When to my surprise, I recollected that I had not even thought of it in my whole prayer. It would seem Satan had hidden the very object from my mind, for which I had purposely kneeled to pray. But when this voice whispered in my heart, saying, "Pray for sanctification," I again bowed in the same place, at the same time, and said, "Lord, *sanctify* my soul for Christ's sake." That very instant, as if lightning had darted through me, I sprang to my feet, and cried, "The Lord has sanctified my soul!" There was none to hear this but the angels who stood around to witness my joy—and Satan, whose malice raged the more. That Satan was there, I knew; for no sooner had I cried out "The Lord has sanctified my soul," than there seemed another voice behind me, saying, "No, it is too great a work to be done." But another spirit said, "Bow down for the witness—I received it—*thou* art *sanctified!*" The first I knew of myself after that, I was standing in the yard with my hands spread out, and looking with my face toward heaven.

I now ran into the house and told them what had happened to me, when, as it were, a new rush of the same ecstasy came upon me, and caused me to feel as if I were in an ocean of light and bliss.

During this, I stood perfectly still, the tears rolling in a flood from my eyes. So great was the joy, that it is past description. There is no language that can describe it, except that which was heard by St. Paul, when he was caught up to the third heaven, and heard words which it was not lawful to utter.

My Call to Preach the Gospel.

Between four and five years after my sanctification, on a certain time, an impressive silence fell upon me, and I stood as if some one was about to speak to me, yet I had no such thought in my heart. But to my utter surprise, there seemed to sound a voice which I thought I distinctly heard, and most certainly understood, which said to me, "Go preach the Gospel!" I immediately replied aloud, "No one will believe me." Again I listened, and again the same voice seemed to say— "Preach the Gospel; I will put words in your mouth, and will turn your enemies to become your friends."

At first I suppose that Satan had spoken to me, for I had read that he could transform himself into an angel of light, for the purpose of deception. Immediately I went into a secret place, and called upon the Lord to know if he had called me to preach, and whether I was deceived or not; when there appeared to my view the form and figure of a pulpit, with a Bible lying thereon, the back of which was presented to me as plainly as if it had been a literal fact.

In consequence of this, my mind became so exercised that during the night following, I took a text, and preached in my sleep. I thought there stood before me a great multitude, while I expounded to them the things of religion. So violent were my exertions, and so loud were my exclamations, that I awoke from the sound of my own voice, which also awoke the family of the house where I resided. Two days after, I went to see the preacher in charge of the African Society, who was the Rev. Richard Allen, the same before named in these pages, to tell him that I felt it my duty to preach the gospel. But as I drew near the street in which his house was, which was in the city of Philadelphia, my courage began to fail me; so terrible did the cross appear, it seemed that I should not be able to bear it. Previous to my setting out to go to see him, so agitated was my mind, that my appetite for my daily food failed me entirely. Several times on my way there, I turned back again; but as often I felt my strength again renewed, and I soon found that the nearer I approached to the house of the minister, the less was my fear. Accordingly, as soon as I came to the door, my fears subsided, the cross was removed, all things appeared pleasant—I was tranquil.

I now told him that the Lord had revealed it to me; that I must preach the gospel. He replied, by asking, in what sphere I wished to move in? I said, among the Methodists. He then replied, that a Mrs. Cook, a Methodist lady, had also some time before requested the same privilege; who it was believed, had done much good in the way of exhortation, and holding prayer meetings; and who had been permitted to do so by the verbal license of the preacher in charge at the time. But as to women preaching, he said that our Discipline knew nothing at all about it—that it did not call for women preachers. This I was glad to hear, because it removed the fear of the cross—but no sooner did this feeling cross my mind, than I found that a love of souls had in a measure departed from me; that holy energy which burned within me, as a fire, began to be smothered. This I soon perceived.

O how careful ought we to be, lest through our by-laws of church government and discipline, we bring into disrepute even the word of life. For as unseemly as it may appear now-a-days for a woman to preach, it should be remembered that nothing is impossible with God. And why should it be thought impossible, heterodox, or improper, for a woman to preach? seeing the Savior died for the woman as well as the man.

If the man may preach, because the Saviour died for him, why not the woman? seeing he died for her also. Is he not a whole Saviour, instead of a half one as those who told it wrong for a woman to preach, would seem to make it appear.

Did not Mary *first* preach the risen Saviour, and is not the doctrine of the resurrection the very climax of Christianity—hangs not all our hope on this, as argued by St. Paul? Then did not Mary, a woman, preach the gospel? for she preached the resurrection of the crucified Son of God.

But some will say, that Mary did not expound the Scripture, therefore, she did not preach, in the proper sense of the term. To this I reply, it may be that the term *preach*, in those primitive times, did not mean exactly what it is now *made* to mean; perhaps it was a great deal more simple then, than it is now:—if it were not, the unlearned fishermen could not have preached the gospel at all, as they had no learning.

To this it may be replied, by those who are determined not to believe that it is right for a woman to preach, that the disciples, though they were fishermen, and ignorant of letters too, were inspired so to do. To which I would reply, that though they were inspired, yet that inspiration did not save them from showing their ignorance of letters, and of man's wisdom; this the multitude soon found out, by listening to the remarks of the envious Jewish priests. If then, to preach the gospel, by the gift of heaven, comes by inspiration solely, is God straitened? must he take the man exclusively? May he not, did he not, and can he not inspire a female to preach the simple story of the birth, life, death, and resurrection of our Lord, and accompany it too, with power to the sinner's heart. As for me, I am fully persuaded that the Lord called me to labour according to what I have received, in his vineyard. If he has not, how could he consistently bear testimony in favor of my poor labors, in awakening and converting sinners?

In my wanderings up and down among men, preaching according to my ability, I have frequently found families who told me that they had not for several years been to a meeting, and yet, while listening to hear what God would say by his poor colored female instrument, have believed with trembling—tears rolling down their cheeks, the signs of contrition and repentance towards God. I firmly believe that I have sown seed, in the name of the Lord, which shall appear with its increase at the great day of accounts, when Christ shall come to make up his jewels.

At a certain time, I was beset with the idea, that soon or late I should fall from grace, and lose my soul at last. I was frequently called to the throne of grace about this matter, but found no relief; the temptation pursued me still. Being more and more afflicted with it, till at a certain time when the spirit strongly impressed it on my mind to enter into my closet, and carry my case once more to the Lord; the Lord enabled me to draw nigh to him, and to his mercy seat, at this time, in an extraordinary manner; for while I wrestled with him for the victory over this disposition to doubt whether I should persevere, there appeared a form of fire, about the size of a man's hand, as I was on my knees; at the same moment, there appeared to the eye of faith a man robed in a white garment, from the shoulders down to the feet ; from him a voice proceeded, saying: "Thou shalt never return from the cross" Since that time I have never doubted, but believe that God will keep me until the day of redemption. Now I could adopt the very language of St. Paul, and say that nothing could have separated my soul from the love of God, which is in Christ Jesus. From that time, 1807, until the present, 1833, I have not yet doubted the power and goodness of God to keep me from falling, through sanctification of the spirit and belief of the truth.

My Marriage.

In the year 1811, I changed my situation in life, having married Mr. Joseph Lee, Pastor of a Colored Society at Snow Hill, about six miles from the city of Philadelphia. It became necessary, therefore, for me to remove. This was a great trial at first, as I knew no person at Snow Hill, except my husband; and to leave my associates in the society, and especially those who composed the *band* of which I was one. Not but those who have been in sweet fellowship with such as really love God, and have together drank bliss and happiness from the same fountain, can tell how dear such company is, and how hard it is to part from them.

At Snow Hill, as was feared, I never found that agreement and closeness in communion and fellowship, that I had in Philadelphia, among my young companions, nor ought I to have expected it. The manners and customs at this place were somewhat different, on which account I became discontented in the course of a year, and began to importune my husband to remove to the city. But this plan did not suit him, as he was the Pastor of the Society, he could not bring his mind to leave them. This afflicted me a little. But the Lord soon showed me in a dream what his will was concerning this matter.

I dreamed that as I was walking on the summit of a beautiful hill, that I saw near me a flock of sheep, fair and white, as if but newly washed; when there came walking toward me, a man of a grave and dignified countenance, dressed entirely in white, as it were in a robe, and looking at me, said emphatically, "Joseph Lee must take care of these sheep, or the wolf will come and devour them." When I awoke, I was convinced of my error, and immediately, with a glad heart, yielded to the right way of the Lord. This also greatly strengthened my husband in his care over them, for fear the wolf should by some means take any of them away. The following verse was beautifully suited to our condition, as well as to all the little flocks of God scattered up and down this land:

Us into Thy protection take,
And gather with Thine arm;
Unless the fold we first forsake,
The wolf can never harm.

After this, I fell into a state of general debility, and in an ill state of health, so much so, that I could not sit up; but a desire to warn sinners to flee the wrath to come, burned vehemently in my heart, when the Lord would send sinners into the house to see me. Such opportunities I embraced to press home on their consciences the things of eternity, and so effectual was the word of exhortation made through the Spirit, that I have seen them fall to the floor crying aloud for mercy.

From this sickness I did not expect to recover, and there was but one thing which bound me to earth, and this was, that I had not as yet preached the gospel to the fallen sons and daughters of Adam's race, to the satisfaction of my mind. I wished to go from one end of the card to the other, crying, Behold, behold the Lamb! To this end I earnestly prayed the Lord to raise me up, if consistent with his will. He condescended to hear my prayer, and to give me a token in a dream, that in due time I should recover my health. The dream was as follows: I thought I saw the sun rise in the morning, and ascend to an altitude of about half an hour high, and then become obscured by a dense black cloud, which continued to hide its rays for about one third part of the day, and then it burst forth again with renewed strength.

This dream I interpreted to signify my early life, my conversion to God, and this sickness, which was a great affliction, as it hindered me, and I feared would forever hinder me from preaching the gospel, was signified by the cloud; and the bursting forth of the sun, again, was the recovery of my health, and being permitted to preach.

I went to the throne of grace on this subject, where the Lord made this impressive reply in my heart, while on my knees "Ye shall be restored to thy health again, and worship God in full purpose of heart."

This manifestation was so impressive, that I could but hide my face, as if some one was gazing upon me, to think of the great goodness of the Almighty God to my poor soul and body. From that very time I began to gain strength of body and mind, glory to God in the highest, until tiny health was fully recovered.

For six years from this time I continued to receive from above, such baptisms of the Spirit as mortality could scarcely bear. About that time I was called to suffer in my family by, death—five, in the course of about six years, fell by his hand; my husband being one of the number, which was the greatest affliction of all.

I was now left alone in the world, with two infant children, one of the age of about two years, the other six months, with no other dependence than the promise of Him who hath said—I will be the widow's God, and a father to the fatherless. Accordingly, he raised me up friends, whose liberality comforted and solaced me in my state of widowhood and sorrows. I could sing with the greatest propriety the words of the poet.

> He helps the stranger in distress,
> The widow and the fatherless,
> And grants the prisoner sweet release.

I can say even now, with the Psalmist, " Once I was young, but now I am old, yet I have never seen the righteous forsaken, nor his seed begging bread." I have ever been fed by his bounty, clothed by his mercy, comforted and healed when sick, succored when tempted, and everywhere upheld by his hand.

The Subject of My Call to Preach Renewed.

It was now eight years since I had made application to be permitted to preach the gospel, during which time I had only been allowed to exhort, and even this privilege but seldom. This subject now was renewed afresh in my mind; it was as a fire shut up in my bones. About thirteen months passed on, while under this renewed impression. During this time, I had solicited of the Rev. Bishop Richard Allen, who at this time had become Bishop of the African Episcopal Methodists in America, to be permitted the liberty of holding prayer meetings in my own hired house, and of exhorting as I found liberty, which was granted me. By this means, my mind was relieved, as the house was soon filled when the hour appointed for prayer had arrived.

I cannot but relate in this place, before I proceed further with the above subject, the singular conversion of a very wicked young man. He was a colored man, who had generally attended our meetings, but not for any good purpose; but rather to disturb and to ridicule our denomination. He openly and uniformly declared that he neither believed in religion, nor wanted any thing to do with it. He was of a Gallio disposition, and took the lead among the young people of color. But after a while he fell sick, and lay about three months in a state of ill health; his disease was a consumption. Toward the close of his, his sister who was a member of the society, came and desired me to go and see her brother, as she had no hopes of his recovery, perhaps the Lord might break into his mind. I went alone, and found him very low. I soon commenced to inquire respecting his state of feeling, and how he found mind. His answer was, "O, tolerable well," with an air of indifference. I asked him if I should pray for him. He answered in a sluggish and careless manner, "O yes, if you have time." I then sung a hymn, kneeled down and prayed for him, and then went my way.

Three days after this, I went again to visit the young man. At this time, there went with me two of the sisters in Christ. We found the Rev. Mr. Cornish, of our denomination, laboring with him. But he said he received but little satisfaction from him. Pretty soon, however, brother Cornish took his leave; when myself, with the two sisters, one of which was an elderly woman named Jane Hutt, the other was younger, both colored, commenced conversing with him, respecting his eternal interest, and of his hope of a happy eternity, if any he had, He said but little; we then kneeled down together and besought the Lord in his behalf, praying that if mercy were not clear gone for ever, to shed a ray of softening grace upon the hardness of his heart. He appeared now to be somewhat more tender, and we thought we could perceive some tokens of conviction, as he wished us to visit him again, in a tone of voice not quite as indifferent as he had hitherto manifested.

But two days had elapsed after this visit, when his sister came for me in haste, saying, that site believed her brother was then dying, and that he had *sent* for me. I immediately called on Jane Hutt, who was still among us as a mother in Israel, to go with me. When we arrived there, we found him sitting up in his bed, very restless and uneasy, but he soon laid down again. He now wished me to come to him, by the side of his bed. I asked him how he was. He said, "Very well;" and added, "Pray for me, quick!" We now perceived his time in this world to be short. I took up the hymn-book, and opened to a hymn suitable to his case, and commenced to sing. But there seemed to be a *horror* in the room—a darkness of a mental kind, which was felt by us all; there being five persons, except the sick young man and his nurse. We had sung but one verse, when they all gave over singing, on account of this unearthly sensation, but myself. I continued to sing on alone, but in a dull and heavy manner, though looking up to God all the while for help. Suddenly, I felt a spring of energy awake in my heart, when darkness gave way in some degree. It was but a glimmer from above. When the hymn was finished, we all kneeled down to pray for him. While calling on the name of the Lord, to have mercy on his soul, and to grant his repentance unto life, it came suddenly into my mind never to rise from lay knees until God should hear prayer in his behalf, until he should convert and save his soul.

Now, while I thus continued importuning heaven, as I felt I was led, a ray of light, more abundant, broke forth among us. There appeared to my view, though my eyes were closed, the Saviour in full stature, nailed to the cross, just over the head of the young man, against the ceiling of the room. I cried out, brother look up, the Saviour is come, he will pardon you, your sins he will forgive. My sorrow for the soul of the young man was gone; I could no longer pray—joy and rapture made it impossible.—We rose from our knees, when lo, his eyes were gazing with ecstasy upward; over his face there was an expression of joy; his lips were clothed in a sweet and holy smile; but no sound came from his tongue; it was heard in its stillness of bliss; full of hope and immortality. Thus, as I held him by the hand, his happy and purified soul soared away, without a sigh or a groan, to its eternal rest.

I now closed his eyes, straightened out his limbs, and left him to be dressed for the grave. But as for me, I was filled with the power of the Holy Ghost, the very room seemed filled with glory. His sister and all that were in the room rejoiced, nothing doubting but he had entered into Paradise; and I believe I shall see him at the last and great day, safe on the shores of salvation.

But to return to the subject of my call to preach. Soon after this, as above related, the Rev. Richard Williams was to preach at Bethel Church, where I with others were as assembled. He entered the pulpit, gave out the hymn, which was sung, and then addressed the throne of grace; took his text, passed through the exordium, and commenced to expound it. The text he took is in Jonah, 2d chap., 9th verse—"Salvation is of the Lord." But as he proceeded to explain, he seemed to have lost the spirit; when in the same instant, I sprang; as by an altogether supernatural impulse, to my feet, when I was aided from above to give an exhortation on the very text which my brother Williams had taken.

I told them that I was like Jonah; for it had been then nearly eight years since the Lord had called me to preach his gospel to the fallen sons and daughters of Adam's race, but that I had lingered like him, and delayed to do so at the bidding of the Lord, and warn those who are as deeply guilty as were the people of Ninevah.

During the exhortation, God made manifest his power in a manner sufficient to show the world that I was called to labor according to my ability, and the grace given unto ire, in the vineyard of the good husbandman.

I now sat down, scarcely knowing what I had done, being frightened. I imagined, that for this indecorum, as I feared it might be called, I should be expelled from the church. But instead of this, the Bishop rose up in the assembly, and related that I had called upon him eight years before, asking to be permitted to preach, and that he had put me off; but that he now as much believed that I was called to that work, as any of the preachers present.—These remarks greatly strengthened me, so that my fears of having given an offence, and made myself liable as an offender, subsided, giving place to a sweet serenity, a holy joy of a peculiar kind, untasted in my bosom until then.

The next Sabbath day, while sitting under the word of the gospel, I felt moved to attempt to speak to the people in a public manner, but I could not bring my mind to attempt it in the church. I said, Lord, any where but here. Accordingly, there was a house not far off which was pointed out to me, to this I went. It was the house of a sister belonging to the same society with myself. Her name was Anderson. I told her I had come to hold meeting in her house, if she would call in her neighbors. With this request she immediately complied. My congregation consisted of but five persons. I commenced by reading and singing a hymn, when I dropped to my knees by the side of a table to pray. When I arose I found my, hand resting on the Bible, which I had not noticed till that moment. It now occurred to me to take a text. I opened the Scripture, as it happened, at the 141st Psalm, fixing my eye on the 3d verse, which reads: "Set a watch, O Lord, before my mouth, keep the door of my lips." My sermon, such as it was, I applied wholly to myself; and added an exhortation. Two of my congregation wept much, as the fruit of my labor this time. In closing, I said to the few, that if any one would open a door, I would hold a meeting the next sixth-day evening; when one answered that her house was at my service. Accordingly I went, and God made manifest his power among the people. Some wept, while others shouted for joy. One whole seat of females, by the power of God, as the rushing of a wind, were all bowed to the floor at once, and screamed out. Also a sick man and woman in one house, the Lord convicted them both; one lived, and the other died. God wrought a judgment—some were well at night, and died next morning. At this place I continued to hold meetings about six months. During that time I kept house with my little son, who was very sickly. About this time I had a call to preach at a place about thirty miles distant, among the

Methodists, with whom I remained one week, and during the whole time, not a thought of my little son came into my mind; it was hid from me, lest I should have been diverted from the work I had to do, to look after my son. Here by the instrumentality of a poor colored woman, the Lord poured forth his spirit among the people. Though, as I was told, there were lawyers, doctors, and magistrates present, to hear me speak, yet there was mourning and crying among sinners, for the Lord scattered fire among them of his own kindling. The Lord gave his handmaiden power to speak for his great name, for he arrested the hearts of the people, and caused a shaking amongst the multitude, for God was in the midst.

I now returned home, found all well; no harm had come to my child although I left him very sick. Friends had taken care of it which was of the Lord. I now began to think seriously of breaking up housekeeping, and forsaking all, to preach the everlasting Gospel. I felt a strong desire to return to the place of my nativity, at Cape May, after an absence of about fourteen years. To this place, where the heaviest cross was to be met with, the Lord sent me, as Saul of Tarsus was sent to Jerusalem, to preach the same gospel which he had neglected and despised before his conversion. I went by water, and on my passage was much distressed by sea sickness, so much so that I expected to have died, but such was not the will of the Lord respecting me. After I had disembarked, proceeded on as opportunities offered, toward where my mother lived. When within ten miles of that place, I appointed an evening meeting. There were a goodly number came out to hear. The Lord was pleased to give me light and liberty among the people. After meeting, there came an elderly lady to me and said, she believed the Lord had sent me among them; she then appointed me another meeting there two weeks from that night. The next day I hastened forward to the place of my mother, who was happy to see me, and the happiness was mutual between us. With her, I left my poor sickly boy, while I departed to do my Master's will. In this neighborhood I had an uncle, who was a Methodist, and who gladly threw open his door for meetings to be held there. At the first meeting which I held at my uncle's house, there was, with others who had come from curiosity to hear the colored woman preacher, an old man, who was a deist, and who said he did not believe the colored people had any souls—he was sure they had none. He took a seat very near where I was standing, and boldly tried to look me out of countenance. But as I labored on in the best manner I was able, looking to God all the while, though it seemed to me I had but little liberty, yet there went an arrow from the bent bow of the gospel, and fastened in his till then obdurate heart. After I had done speaking, he went out, and called the people around him, said that my preaching might seem a small thing, yet he believed I had the worth of souls at heart. This language was different from what it was a little time before, as he now seemed to admit that colored people had souls, as it was to these I was chiefly speaking; and unless they had souls, whose good I find in view, his remark must have been without meaning. He now came into the house, and in the most friendly manner shook hands with me, saying, he hoped God had spared him to some good purpose. This man was a great slave holder, and had been very cruel; thinking nothing of knocking down a slave with a fence stake, or whatever might come to hand. From this time it was said of him, that he became greatly altered in his ways for the better. At that time he was about seventy years old, his head as white as snow; but whether he became a converted man or not, I never heard.

The week following, I had an invitation to hold a meeting at the Court House of the County, when I spoke from the 53d chap, of Isaiah, 3d verse. It was a solemn time, and the Lord attended the word; I had life and liberty, though there were people there of various denominations. Here again I saw the aged slaveholder, who notwithstanding his age, walked about three miles to hear me. This day I spoke twice, and walked six miles to the place appointed. There was a magistrate present, who showed his friendship, by saying in a friendly manner, that he had heard of me; he handed me a hymn book, pointing to a hymn which he had selected. When the meeting was over, he invited me to preach in a schoolhouse in his neighborhood, about three miles distant from where I then was. During this meeting one backslider was reclaimed. This day I walked six miles, and preached twice to large congregations, both in the morning and evening. The Lord was with me, glory be to his holy name. I next went six miles and held a meeting in a colored friend's house, at eleven o'clock in the morning, and preached to a well behaved congregation of both colored and white. After service I again walked back, which was in all twelve miles in the same day. This was on Sabbath, or as I sometimes call it, seventh-day: for after my conversion, I preferred the plain language of the quakers. On fourth day, after this, in compliance with an invitation received by note, from the same magistrate who had heard me at the above place, I preached to a large congregation, where we had a precious time: much weeping was heard among the people. The same gentleman, now at the close of the meeting, gave out another appointment at the same place that day week. Here again I had liberty, there was a move among the people. Ten years from that time, in the neighborhood of Cape May, I held a prayer meeting in a school house, which was then the regular place of preaching for the Episcopal Methodists; after service, there came a white lady of the first distinction, a member of the Methodist Society, and told me that at the some school house, ten years before, under my preaching, the Lord first awakened her. She rejoiced much to see me, and invited me home with her; where I staid till the next day. This was bread cast on the waters, seen after many days.

From this place I next went to Dennis Creek meeting house, where at the invitation of an cider, I spoke to a large congregation of various and conflicting sentiments, when a wonderful shock of God's power was felt, shown every where by groans, by sighs, and loud and happy omens. I felt as if aided from above. My tongue was cut loose, the stammerer spoke freely; the love of God, and of his service, burned with a vehement flame within me—his name was glorified among the people.

But here I feel myself constrained to give over, as from the smallness of this pamphlet I cannot go through with the whole of my, journal, as it would probably make a volume of two hundred pages; which, if the Lord be willing, may at some future day be published. But for the satisfaction of such as may follow after me, when I am no more, I have recorded how the Lord called me to his work, and how he has kept me from falling from grace, as I feared I should. In all things he has proved himself a God of truth to me; and in his service I am now as much determined to spend and be spent, as at the very first.—My ardor for the progress of his cause abates not a whit, so far as I am able to judge, though I am now more than fifty years of age.

As to the nature of uncommon impressions, not but have noticed, and possibly sneered at in the course of these pages, they may be accounted for in this way: It is known that the blind have the sense of hearing in a manner much more acute than those who can see: also their sense of feeling is exceedingly fine, and is found to detect any roughness on the smoothest surface, where those who can see can find none. So it may be with such as *I* am, who has never had more than three months schooling: and wishing to know much of the way and law of God, have therefore watched the more closely, the operations of the Spirit, and have in consequence been led thereby. But let it be remarked that *I* have never found that Spirit to lead me contrary to the Scriptures of truth, as *I* understand them. For as many as are led by the *Spirit* of God are the sons of God."—Rom: viii. 14.

I have now only to say, May the blessing of the Father, and of the Son, and of the Holy Ghost, accompany the reading of this poor effort to speak well of his name, wherever it may be read. AMEN.

4

Selections from *Journal of a Residence on a Georgian Plantation in 1838–1839* (1863)

FANNY KEMBLE

FRANCES ANNE "FANNY" KEMBLE (1809–1893) was born into a family of acclaimed Shakespearean actors in London on November 27, 1809. Raised primarily by an aunt, she was educated for several years in France. While in Paris, she studied French, Italian, and the Bible and was introduced to the poetry of Lord Byron and Dante, who influenced her early writing career. Kemble went on to become a prolific woman of letters in the Victorian era, writing plays, poetry, letters, journals, and memoirs.

Kemble first gained notoriety at the age of twenty as Juliet in a Covent Garden Theater production of *Romeo and Juliet*. In 1832, in debt, the Kembles left England for America, hoping for a profitable American tour. After successfully opening in New York, Philadelphia, Washington, Baltimore, and Boston, Kemble began to socialize with such luminaries as Andrew Jackson, Catharine Maria Sedgwick (then America's most famous woman novelist), and Dr. William Ellery Channing (proponent of New England liberalism), and performed for Dolly Madison and John Quincy Adams. She became a sensation, even inspiring "Fanny Kemble curls," and kept a journal published as *Journal of a Residence in America* in 1835. In 1834 she married a member of her devoted entourage, Pierce Meese Butler, enabling her to leave theater life and return to England, where she gained time to write.

Kemble's marriage, however, changed her life in other ways. Shortly after their marriage, Butler inherited two plantations in Georgia (Butler Island and Hampton Point), becoming one of the state's premier slaveholders. Already committed to abolitionism as a result of her English upbringing, Kemble began reading and writing abolitionist tracts. After moving to Georgia in 1839, she became increasingly disturbed by the conditions of slavery and started writing an epistolary journal addressed to her friend Elizabeth Dwight Sedgwick (sister-in-law of novelist Catharine Maria Sedgwick); she kept the journal for almost four months (until the family moved north). In it she recorded her horrified responses to the treatment of slaves, especially women after childbirth. Kemble's political differences with her husband grew, and she gave up her abolitionist writing for the sake of her family, despite an 1842 appeal by Lydia Maria Child to publish it. The couple finally divorced in 1848. Butler was awarded custody of their daughters and prevented Fanny from seeing them until they were married. Alone, she returned to her maiden name, to the stage, and to London.

In 1863 Kemble, dismayed by proslavery sentiments and criticism of the North, decided to revise and publish her journal to discourage British support of the Confederacy. Kemble distributed *Journal of a Residence on a Georgia Plantation in 1838–1839* in England and America. Her narrative, appearing in the year of the Emancipation Proclamation, enjoyed much popularity, evidenced by two sizeable printings in the United States.

In 1867 Butler died in debt and disgrace (due to his alleged gambling and infidelities, as well as Northern distrust of his Confederate sympathies), and Kemble moved back to Butler Island, living on various Butler properties until her return to London. In Rome in 1872, she met Henry James, who became a close friend. Kemble died in London on January 15, 1893, at the age of 84. Critics have discussed her journals primarily as historical evidence of a white woman's awareness of the harsh lives of enslaved women and as a critique of repressive gender strictures (see biographies by John A. Scott and J. C. Furnas and Eleanor

Boyle's introduction to *The Terrific Kemble*). A sustained analysis of her journals as autobiographical writing has yet to be done.

New York:
Harper & Brothers, Publishers,
Franklin Square.
1863.

To
Elizabeth Dwight Sedgwick,
this journal,
originally kept for her,
is
most affectionately
Dedicated.

Journal of a Residence on a Georgian Plantation in 1838-1839

SLAVERY THE CHIEF CORNER STONE
This stone (Slavery), which was rejected by the first builders, is become the chief stone of the corner of our new edifice.
> Speech of Alexander H. Stephens, Vice-President of
> the Confederate States: delivered March 21, 1861.

Preface

The following diary was kept in the winter and spring of 1838-9, on an estate consisting of rice and cotton plantations, in the islands at the entrance of the Altamaha, on the coast of Georgia.

The slaves in whom I then had an unfortunate interest were sold some years ago. The islands themselves are at present in the power of the Northern troops. The record contained in the following pages is a picture of conditions of human existence which I hope and believe have passed away.

London, January 16, 1863.

Darien, Georgia.

Dear E——, —Minuteness of detail, and fidelity in the account of my daily doings, will hardly, I fear, render my letters very interesting to you now; but cut off as I am here from all the usual resources and amusements of civilized existence, I shall find but little to communicate to you that is not furnished by my observations on the novel appearance of external nature, and the moral and physical condition of Mr. ——'s people. The latter subject is, I know, one sufficiently interesting in itself to you, and I shall not scruple to impart all the reflections which may occur to me relative to their state during my stay here, where inquiry into their mode of existence will form my chief occupation, and, necessarily also, the staple commodity of my letters. I purpose, while I reside here, keeping a sort of journal, such as Monk Lewis wrote during his visit to his West India plantations. I wish I had any prospect of rendering my diary as interesting and amusing to you as his was to me.

In taking my first walk on the island, I directed my steps toward the rice mill, a large building on the banks of the river, within a few yards of the house we occupy. Is it not rather curious that Miss Martineau should have mentioned the erection of a steam mill for threshing rice somewhere in the vicinity of Charleston as a singular novelty, likely to form an era in Southern agriculture, and to produce the most desirable changes in the system of labor by which it is carried on? Now on this estate alone there are three threshing mills—one worked by steam, one by the tide, and one by horses; there are two private steam mills on plantations adjacent to ours, and a public one at Savannah, where the planters who have none on their own estates are in the habit of sending their rice to be threshed at a certain percentage; these have been in operation for some years, and I therefore am at a loss to understand what made her hail the erection of the one at Charleston as likely to produce such immediate and happy results. By-the-by—of the misstatements, or rather mistakes, for they are such, in her books, with regard to certain facts— her only disadvantage in acquiring information was not by any means that natural infirmity on which the periodical press, both here and in England, has commented with so much brutality. She had the misfortune to possess, too, that unsuspecting reliance upon the truth of others which they are apt to feel who themselves hold truth most sacred; and this was a sore disadvantage to her in a country where I have heard it myself repeatedly asserted—and, what is more, much gloried in—that she was purposely misled by the persons to whom she addressed her inquiries, who did not scruple to disgrace themselves by imposing in

the grossest manner upon her credulity and anxiety to obtain information. It is a knowledge of this very shameful proceeding which has
made me most especially anxious to avoid *fact hunting.* I might fill my
letters to you with accounts received from others, but, as I am aware of
the risk which I run in so doing, I shall furnish you with no details but
those which come under my own immediate observation. To return to
the rice mill: it is worked by a steam-engine of thirty horse power, and,
besides threshing great part of our own rice, is kept constantly employed by the neighboring planters, who send their grain to it in prefer-
ence to the more distant mill at Savannah, paying, of course, the same
percentage, which makes it a very profitable addition to the estate. Immediately opposite to this building is a small shed, which they call the
cook's shop, and where the daily allowance of rice and corn grits of the
people is boiled and distributed to them by an old woman, whose special business this is. There are four settlements or villages (or, as the negroes call them, camps) on the island, consisting of from ten to twenty
houses, and to each settlement is annexed a cook's shop with capacious
caldrons, and the oldest wife of the settlement for officiating priestess.
Pursuing my walk along the river's bank, upon an artificial dike, sufficiently high and broad to protect the fields from inundation by the
ordinary rising of the tide—for the whole island is below high-water
mark—I passed the blacksmith's and cooper's shops. At the first all the
common iron implements of husbandry or household use for the estate
are made, and at the latter all the rice barrels necessary for the crop,
besides tubs and buckets, large and small, for the use of the people, and
cedar tubs, of noble dimensions and exceedingly neat workmanship,
for our own household purposes. The fragrance of these when they are
first made, as well as their ample size, renders them preferable as
dressing-room furniture, in my opinion, to all the china foot-tubs that
ever came out of Staffordshire. After this I got out of the vicinity of the
settlement, and pursued my way along a narrow dike—the river on the
one hand, and, on the other, a slimy, poisonous-looking swamp, all
rattling with sedges of enormous height, in which one might lose one's
way as effectually as in a forest of oaks. Beyond this, the low rice-fields,
all clothed in their rugged stubble, divided by dikes into monotonous
squares, a species of prospect by no means beautiful to the mere lover
of the picturesque. The only thing that I met with to attract my attention
was a most beautiful species of ivy, the leaf longer and more graceful
than that of the common English creeper, glittering with the highest
varnish, delicately veined, and of a rich brown-green, growing in

profuse garlands from branch to branch of some stunted evergreen bushes which border the dike, and which the people call salt-water bush. My walks are rather circumscribed, inasmuch as the dikes are the only promenades. On all sides of these lie either the marshy rice-fields, the brimming river, or the swampy patches of yet unreclaimed forest, where the hugh [sic] cypress-trees and exquisite evergreen undergrowth spring up from a stagnant sweltering pool, that effectually forbids the foot of the explorer.

As I skirted one of these thickets to-day, I stood still to admire the beauty of the shrubbery. Every shade of green, every variety of form, every degree of varnish, and all in full leaf and beauty in the very depth of winter. The stunted dark-colored oak; the magnolia bay (like our own culinary and fragrant bay), which grows to a very great size; the wild myrtle, a beautiful and profuse shrub, rising to a height of six, eight, and ten feet, and branching on all sides in luxuriant tufted fullness; most beautiful of all, that pride of the South, the magnolia grandiflora, whose lustrous dark green perfect foliage would alone render it an object of admiration, without the queenly blossom whose color, size, and perfume are unrivaled in the whole vegetable kingdom. This last magnificent creature grows to the size of a forest tree in these swamps, but seldom adorns a high or dry soil, or suffers itself to be successfully transplanted. Under all these the spiked palmetto forms an impenetrable covert, and from glittering graceful branch to branch hang garlands of evergreen creepers, on which the mocking-birds are swinging and singing even now; while I, bethinking me of the pinching cold that is at this hour tyrannizing over your region, look round on this strange scene—on these green woods, this unfettered river, and sunny sky— and feel very much like one in another planet from yourself.

The profusion of birds here is one thing that strikes me as curious, coming from the vicinity of Philadelphia, where even the robin red-breast, held sacred by the humanity of all other Christian people, is not safe from the *gunning* prowess of the unlicensed sportsmen of your free country. The negroes (of course) are not allowed the use of firearms, and their very simply constructed traps do not do much havoc among the feathered hordes that haunt their rice-fields. Their case is rather a hard one, as partridges, snipes, and the most delicious wild ducks abound here, and their allowance of rice and Indian meal would not be the worse for such additions. No day passes that I do not, in the course of my walk, put up a number of the land birds, and startle from among the gigantic sedges the long-necked water-fowl by dozens. It arouses the killing propensity in me most dreadfully, and I really entertain serious thoughts of learning to use a gun, for the mere pleasure of destroying these pretty birds as they whirr from their secret coverts close beside my path. How strong an instinct of animal *humanity* this is, and how strange if one be more strange than another. Reflection rebukes it almost instantaneously, and yet for the life of me I can not help wishing I had a fowling-piece whenever I put up a covey of these creatures; though I suppose, if one were brought bleeding and maimed to me, I should begin to cry, and be very pathetic, after the fashion of Jacques. However, one must live, you know; and here our living consists very mainly of wild ducks, wild geese, wild turkeys, and venison. Now, perhaps, can one imagine the universal doom overtaking a creature with less misery than in the case of the bird who, in the very moment of his triumphant soaring, is brought dead to the ground. I should like to bargain for such a finis myself amazingly, I know, and have always thought that the death I should prefer would be to break my neck off the back of my horse at a full gallop on a fine day. Of course a bad shot should be hung—a man who shatters his birds' wings and legs; if I undertook the trade, I would learn of some Southern duelist, and always shoot my bird through the head or heart—as an expert murderer knows how. Besides these birds of which we make our prey, there are others that prey upon their own fraternity. Hawks of every sort and size wheel their steady rounds above the rice-fields; and the great, turkey-buzzards—those most unsightly carrion birds—spread their broad black wings, and soar over the river like so many mock eagles. I do not know that I ever saw any winged creature of so forbidding an aspect as these same turkey-buzzards; their heavy flight, their awkward gait, their bald-looking head and neck, and their devotion to every species of foul and detestable food, render them almost abhorrent to me. They abound in the South, and in Charleston are held in especial veneration for their scavenger-like propensities, killing one of them being, I believe, a finable offense by the city police regulations. Among the Brobdignagian sedges that in some parts of the island fringe the Altamaha, the nightshade (apparently the same as the European creeper) weaves a perfect matting of its poisonous garlands, and in my remembrance of its prevalence in the woods and hedges of England did not reconcile me to its appearance here. How much of this is mere association I can not tell; but, whether the wild duck makes its nest under its green arches, or the alligators and snakes of the Altamaha have their secret bowers there, it is an evil-looking weed, and I shall have every leaf of it cleared away.

I must inform you of a curious conversation which took place between my little girl and the woman who performs for us the offices of chambermaid here—of course one of Mr. ——'s slaves. What suggested it to the child, or whence indeed she gathered her information, I know not; but children are made of eyes and ears, and nothing, however minute, escapes their microscopic observation. She suddenly began addressing this woman. "Mary, some persons are free and some are not (the woman made no reply). I am a free person (of a little more than three years old). I say, I am a free person, Mary—do you know that?" "Yes, missis." "Some persons are free and some are not—do you know that, Mary?" "Yes, missis, *here*," was the reply; "I know it is so here, in this world." Here my child's white nurse, my dear Margery, who had hitherto been silent, interfered, saying, "Oh, then you think it will not always be so?" "Me hope not, missis." I am afraid, E——, this woman actually imagines that there will be no slaves in heaven; isn't that preposterous, now, when, by the account of most of the Southerners, slavery itself must be heaven, or something uncommonly like it? Oh, if you could imagine how this title "Missis," addressed to me and to my children, shocks all my feelings! Several times I have exclaimed, "For God's sake do not call me that!" and only been awakened, by the stupid amazement of the poor creatures I was addressing, to the perfect uselessness of my thus expostulating with them; once or twice, indeed, I have done more—I have explained to them, and they appeared to comprehend me well, that I had no ownership over them, for that I held such ownership sinful, and that, though I was the wife of the man who pretends to own them, I was, in truth, no more their mistress than they were mine. Some of them I know understood me, more of them did not.

Our servants—those who have been selected to wait upon us in the house—consist of a man, who is quite a tolerable cook (I believe this is a natural gift with them, as with Frenchmen); a dairy-woman, who churns for us; a laundry-woman; her daughter, our housemaid, the aforesaid Mary; and two young lads of from fifteen to twenty, who wait upon us in the capacity of footmen. As, however, the latter are perfectly filthy in their persons and clothes—their faces, hands, and naked feet being literally incrusted with dirt—their attendance at our meals is not, as you may suppose, particularly agreeable to me, and I dispense with it as often as possible. Mary, too, is so intolerably offensive in her person that it is impossible to endure her proximity, and the consequence is that, among Mr. ——'s slaves, I wait upon myself more than I have ever done in my life before. About this same personal offensiveness, the

Southerners, you know, insist that it is inherent with the race, and it is one of their most cogent reasons for keeping them as slaves. But, as this very disagreeable peculiarity does not prevent Southern women from hanging their infants at the breasts of negresses, nor almost every planter's wife and daughter from having one or more little pet blacks sleeping like puppy-dogs in their very bedchamber, nor almost every planter from admitting one or several of his female slaves to the still closer intimacy of his bed, it seems to me that this objection to doing them right is not very valid. I can not imagine that they would smell much worse if they were free, or come in much closer contact with the delicate organs of their white fellow-countrymen; indeed, inasmuch as good deeds are spoken of as having a sweet savor before God, it might be supposed that the freeing of the blacks might prove rather an odoriferous process than the contrary. However this may be, I must tell you that this potent reason for enslaving a whole race of people is no more potent with me than most of the others adduced to support the system, inasmuch as, from observation and some experience, I am strongly inclined to believe that peculiar ignorance of the laws of health and the habits of decent cleanliness are the real and only causes of this disagreeable characteristic of the race, thorough ablutions and change of linen, when tried, having been perfectly successful in removing all such objections; and if ever you have come into any thing like neighborly proximity with a low Irishman or woman, I think you will allow that the same causes produce very nearly the same effects. The stench in an Irish, Scotch, Italian, or French hovel are quite as intolerable as any I ever found in our negro houses, and the filth and vermin which abound about the clothes and persons of the lower peasantry of any of those countries as abominable as the same conditions in the black population of the United States. A total absence of self-respect begets these hateful physical results, and in proportion as moral influences are remote, physical evils will abound. Well-being, freedom, and industry induce self-respect, self-respect induces cleanliness and personal attention, so that slavery is answerable for all the evils that exhibit themselves where it exists—from lying, thieving, and adultery, to dirty houses, ragged clothes, and foul smells.

But to return to our Ganymedes. One of them—the eldest son of our laundry-woman, and Mary's brother, a boy of the name of Aleck (Alexander)—is uncommonly bright and intelligent; he performs all the offices of a well-instructed waiter with great efficiency, and any where out of slave land would be able to earn fourteen or fifteen dollars a month for himself; he is remarkably good tempered and well disposed. The other poor boy is so stupid that he appears sullen from absolute darkness of intellect; instead of being a little lower than the angels, he is scarcely a little higher than the brutes, and to this condition are reduced the majority of his kind by the institutions under which they live. I should tell you that Aleck's parents and kindred have always been about the house of the overseer, and in daily habits of intercourse with him and his wife; and wherever this is the case the effect of involuntary education is evident in the improved intelligence of the degraded race. In a conversation which Mr. ——— had this evening with Mr. O———, the overseer, the latter mentioned that two of our carpenters had in their leisure time made a boat, which they had disposed of to some neighboring planter for sixty dollars.

Now E———, I have no intention of telling you a one-sided story, or concealing from you what are cited as the advantages which these poor people possess; you, who know that no indulgence is worth simple justice, either to him who gives or him who receives, will not thence conclude that their situation thus mitigated is, therefore, what it should be. On this matter of the sixty dollars earned by Mr. ———'s two men much stress was laid by him and his overseer. I look at it thus: If these men were industrious enough, out of their scanty leisure, to earn sixty dollars, how much more of remuneration, of comfort, of improvement might they not have achieved were the price of their daily labor duly paid them, instead of being unjustly withheld to support an idle young man and his idle family—i.e., myself and my children.

And here it may be well to inform you that the slaves on this plantation are divided into field-hands and mechanics or artisans. The former, the great majority, are the more stupid and brutish of the tribe; the others, who are regularly taught their trades, are not only exceedingly expert at them, but exhibit a greater general activity of intellect, which must necessarily result from even a partial degree of cultivation. There are here a gang (for that is the honorable term) of coopers, of blacksmiths, of bricklayers, of carpenters, all well acquainted with their peculiar trades. The latter constructed the wash-hand stands, clothespresses, sofas, tables, etc., with which our house is furnished, and they are very neat pieces of workmanship—neither veneered or polished indeed, nor of very costly materials, but of the white pine wood planed as smooth as marble—a species of furniture not very luxurious perhaps, but all the better adapted therefore to the house itself, which is certainly rather more devoid of the conveniences and adornments of modern existence than anything I ever took up my abode in before. It consists of three small rooms, and three still smaller, which would be more appropriately designated as closets, a wooden recess by way of pantry, and a kitchen detached from the dwelling—a mere wooden out-house, with no floor but the bare earth, and for furniture a congregation of filthy negroes, who lounge in and out of it like hungry hounds at all hours of the day and night, picking up such scraps of food as they can find about, which they discuss squatting down upon their hams, in which interesting position and occupation I generally find a number of them whenever I have sufficient hardihood to venture within those precincts, the sight of which and its tenants is enough to slacken the appetite of the hungriest hunter that ever lost all nice regards in the mere animal desire for food. Of our three apartments, one is our sitting, eating, and *living* room, and is sixteen feet by fifteen. The walls are plastered indeed, but neither painted nor papered; it is divided from our bedroom (a similarly elegant and comfortable chamber) by a dingy wooden partition covered all over with hooks, pegs, and nails, to which hats, caps, keys, etc., etc., are suspended in graceful irregularity. The doors open by wooden latches, raised by means of small bits of pack-thread—I imagine, the same primitive order of fastening celebrated in the touching chronicle of Red Riding Hood; how they shut I will not attempt to describe, as the shutting of a door is a process of extremely rare occurrence throughout the whole Southern country. The third room, a chamber with sloping ceiling, immediately over our sitting-room and under the roof, is appropriated to the nurse and my two babies. Of the closets, one is Mr. ———, the overseer's, bedroom, the other his office or place of business; and the third, adjoining our bedroom, and opening immediately out of doors, is Mr. ———'s dressing-room and cabinet d'affaires, where he gives audiences to the negroes, redresses grievances, distributes red woolen caps (a singular gratification to a slave), shaves himself, and performs the other offices of his toilet. Such being our abode, I think you will allow there is little danger of my being dazzled by the luxurious splendors of a Southern slave residence. Our sole mode of summoning our attendants is by a pack-thread bell-rope suspended in the sitting-room. From the bedrooms we have to raise the windows and our voices, and bring them by power of lungs, or help ourselves— which, I thank God, was never yet a hardship to me.

I mentioned to you just now that two of the carpenters had made a boat in their leisure time. I must explain this to you, and this will involve the mention of another of Miss Martineau's mistakes with regard to slave labor, at least in many parts of the Southern States. She mentions that on one estate of which she knew, the proprietor had made the experiment, and very successfully of appointing to each of his slaves a certain task to be performed in the day, which once accomplished, no matter how early, the rest of the four-and-twenty hours were allowed to the laborer to employ as he pleased. She mentions this as a single experiment and rejoices over it as a decided amelioration in the condition of the slave, and one deserving of general adoption. But in the part of Georgia where this estate is situated, the custom of task labor is universal, and it prevails, I believe, throughout Georgia, South Carolina, and parts of North Carolina; in other parts of the latter state, however—as I was informed by our overseer, who is a native of that state—the estates are small, rather deserving the name of farms, and the laborers are much upon the same footing as the laboring men at the North, working from sunrise to sunset in the fields with the farmer and his sons, and coming in with them to their meals, which they take immediately after the rest of the family. In Louisiana and the new southwestern slave states, I believe, task labor does not prevail; but it is in those that the condition of the poor human cattle is most deplorable, as you know it was there that the humane calculation was not only made, but openly and unhesitatingly avowed, that the planters found it, upon the whole, their most profitable plan to work off (kill with labor) their whole number of slaves about once in seven years, and renew the whole stock. By-the-by, the Jewish institution of slavery is much insisted upon by the Southern upholders of the system; perhaps this is their notion of the Jewish jubilee, when the slaves were by Moses's strict enactment to be all set free. Well, this task system is pursued on this estate; and thus it is that the two carpenters were enabled to make the boat they sold for sixty dollars. These tasks, of course, profess to be graduated according to the sex, age, and strength of the laborer; but in many instances this is not the case, as I think you will agree when I tell you that on Mr. ———'s first visit to his estates he found that the men and the women who labored in the fields had the same task to perform. This was a noble admission of female equality, was it not?—and thus it had been on the estate for many years past. Mr. ———, of course, altered the distribution of the work, diminishing the quantity done by the women.

I had a most ludicrous visit this morning from the midwife of the estate—rather an important personage both to master and slave, as to her unassisted skill and science the ushering of all the young negroes into their existence of bondage is intrusted. I heard a great deal of conversation in the dressing-room adjoining mine while performing my own toilet, and presently Mr. —— opened my room door, ushering in a dirty, fat, good-humored looking old negress, saying, "The midwife, Rose, wants to make your acquaintance." "Oh massa!" shrieked out the old creature, in a paroxysm of admiration, "where you get this lilly alabaster baby!" For a moment I looked round to see if she was speaking of my baby; but no, my dear, this superlative apostrophe was elicited by the fairness of *my skin:* so much for degrees of comparison. Now I suppose that if I chose to walk arm in arm with the dingiest mulatto through the streets of Philadelphia, nobody could possibly tell by my complexion that I was not his sister, so that the mere quality of mistress must have had a most miraculous effect upon my skin in the eyes of poor Rose. But this species of outrageous flattery is as usual with these people as with the low Irish, and arises from the ignorant desire, common to both the races, of propitiating at all costs the fellow-creature who is to them as a Providence—or rather, I should say, a fate—for 'tis a heathen and no Christian relationship. Soon after this visit, I was summoned into the wooden porch or piazza of the house, to see a poor woman who desired to speak to me. This was none other than the tall, emaciated-looking negress who, on the day of our arrival, had embraced me and my nurse with such irresistible zeal. She appeared very ill to-day, and presently unfolded to me a most distressing history of bodily afflictions. She was the mother of a very large family, and complained to me that, what with childbearing and hard field labor, her back was almost broken in two. With an almost savage vehemence of gesticulation, she suddenly tore up her scanty clothing, and exhibited a spectacle with which I was inconceivably shocked and sickened. The facts, without any of her corroborating statements, bore tolerable witness to the hardships of her existence. I promised to attend to her ailments and give her proper remedies; but these are natural results, inevitable and irremediable ones, of improper treatment of the female frame; and, though there may be alleviation, there can not be any cure when once the beautiful and wonderful structure has been thus made the victim of ignorance, folly, and wickedness.

After the departure of this poor woman, I walked down the settlement toward the Infirmary or hospital, calling in at one or two of the houses along the row. These cabins consist of one room, about twelve feet by fifteen, with a couple of closets smaller and closer than the state-rooms of a ship, divided off from the main room and each other by rough wooden partitions, in which the inhabitants sleep. They have almost

all of them a rude bedstead, with the gray moss of the forests for mattress, and filthy, pestilential-looking blankets for covering. Two families
(sometimes eight and ten in number) reside in one of these huts, which
are mere wooden frames pinned, as it were, to the earth by a brick chimney outside, whose enormous aperture within pours down a flood of
air, but little counteracted by the miserable spark of fire, which hardly
sends an attenuated thread of lingering smoke up its huge throat. A
wide ditch runs immediately at the back of these dwellings, which is
filled and emptied daily by the tide. Attached to each hovel is a small
scrap of ground for a garden, which, however, is for the most part un-
tended and uncultivated. Such of these dwellings as I visited to-day
were filthy and wretched in the extreme, and exhibited that most deplorable consequence of ignorance and an abject condition, the inability
of the inhabitants to secure and improve even such pitiful comfort as
might yet be achieved by them. Instead of the order, neatness, and ingenuity which might convert even these miserable hovels into tolerable
residences, there was the careless, reckless, filthy indolence which even
the brutes do not exhibit in their lairs and nests, and which seemed incapable of applying to the uses of existence the few miserable means of
comfort yet within their reach. Firewood and shavings lay littered about
the floors, while the half-naked children were cowering round two or
three smouldering cinders. The moss with which the chinks and cran-
nies of their ill-protecting dwellings might have been stuffed was trailing in dirt and dust about the ground, while the back door of the huts,
opening upon a most unsightly ditch, was left wide open for the fowls
and ducks, which they are allowed to raise, to travel in and out, increasing the filth of the cabin by what they brought and left in every direction. In the midst of the floor, or squatting round the cold hearth, would
be four or five little children from four to ten years old, the latter all
with babies in their arms, the care of the infants being taken from the
mothers (who are driven afield as soon as they recover from child
labor), and devolved upon these poor little nurses, as they are called,
whose business it is to watch the infant, and carry it to its mother whenever it may require nourishment. To these hardly human little beings I
addressed my remonstrances about the filth, cold, and unnecessary
wretchedness of their room, bidding the elder boys and girls kindle up
the fire, sweep the floor, and expel the poultry. For a long time my very
words seemed unintelligible to them, till, when I began to sweep and
make up the fire, etc., they first fell to laughing, and then imitating
me. The incrustations of dirt on their hands, feet, and faces were my

next object of attack, and the stupid negro practice (by-the-by, but a short time since nearly universal in enlightened Europe) of keeping the babies with their feet bare, and their heads, already well capped by nature with their woolly hair, wrapped in half a dozen hot, filthy coverings. Thus I traveled down the "street," in every dwelling endeavoring to awaken a new perception, that of cleanliness, sighing, as I went, over the futility of my own exertions, for how can slaves be improved? Nathless, thought I, let what can be done; for it may be that, the two being incompatible, improvement may yet expel slavery; and so it might, and surely would, if, instead of beginning at the end, I could but begin at the beginning of my task. If the mind and soul were awakened, instead of mere physical good attempted, the physical good would result, and the great curse vanish away; but my hands are tied fast, and this corner of the work is all that I may do. Yet it can not be but, from my words and actions, some revelations should reach these poor people; and going in and out among them perpetually, I shall teach, and they learn involuntarily a thousand things of deepest import. They must learn, and who can tell the fruit of that knowledge alone, that there are beings in the world, even with skins of a different color from their own, who have sympathy for their misfortunes, love for their virtues, and respect for their common nature—but oh! my heart is full almost to bursting as I walk among these most poor creatures.

The Infirmary is a large two-story building, terminating the broad orange-planted space between the two rows of houses which form the first settlement; it is built of whitewashed wood, and contains four large-sized rooms. But how shall I describe to you the spectacle which was presented to me on entering the first of these? But half the casements, of which there were six, were glazed, and these were obscured with dirt, almost as much as the other windowless ones were darkened by the dingy shutters, which the shivering inmates had fastened to in order to protect themselves from the cold. In the enormous chimney glimmered the powerless embers of a few sticks of wood, round which, however, as many of the sick women as could approach were cowering, some on wooden settles, most of them on the ground, excluding those who were too ill to rise; and these last poor wretches lay prostrate on the floor, without bed, mattress, or pillow, buried in tattered and filthy blankets, which, huddled round them as they lay strewed about, left hardly space to move upon the floor. And here, in their hour of sickness and suffering, lay those whose health and strength are spent in unrequited labor for us—those who, perhaps even yesterday, were being

urged on to their unpaid task—those whose husbands, fathers, brothers, and sons were even at that hour sweating over the earth, whose produce was to buy for us all the luxuries which health can revel in, all the
comforts which can alleviate sickness. I stood in the midst of them, perfectly unable to speak, the tears pouring from my eyes at this sad spectacle of their misery, myself and my emotion alike strange and incom-
prehensible to them. Here lay women expecting every hour the terrors
and agonies of childbirth, others who had just brought their doomed
offspring into the world, others who were groaning over the anguish
and bitter disappointment of miscarriages—here lay some burning
with fever, others chilled with cold and aching with rheumatism, upon
the hard cold ground, the draughts and dampness of the atmosphere increasing their sufferings, and dirt, noise, and stench, and every aggravation of which sickness is capable, combined in their condition—here
they lay like brute beasts, absorbed in physical suffering; unvisited by
any of those Divine influences which may ennoble the dispensations of
pain and illness, forsaken, as it seemed to me, of all good; and yet, O
God, Thou surely hadst not forsaken them! Now pray take notice that
this is the hospital of an estate where the owners are supposed to be humane, the overseer efficient and kind, and the negroes remarkably well
cared for and comfortable. As soon as I recovered from my dismay, I addressed old Rose the midwife, who had charge of this room, bidding
her open the shutters of such windows as were glazed, and let in the
light. I next proceeded to make up the fire; but, upon my lifting a log for
that purpose, there was one universal outcry of horror, and old Rose,
attempting to snatch it from me, exclaimed, "Let alone, missis—let be;
what for you lift wood? you have nigger enough, missis, to do it!" I
hereupon had to explain to them my view of the purposes for which
hands and arms were appended to our bodies, and forthwith began
making Rose tidy up the miserable apartment, removing all the filth
and rubbish from the floor that could be removed, folding up in piles
the blankets of the patients who were not using them, and placing, in
rather more sheltered and comfortable positions, those who were unable to rise. It was all that I could do, and having enforced upon them
all my earnest desire that they should keep their room swept, and as
tidy as possible, I passed on to the other room on the ground floor, and
to the two above, one of which is appropriated to the use of the men
who are ill. They were all in the same deplorable condition, the upper
rooms being rather the more miserable, inasmuch as none of the windows were glazed at all, and they had, therefore, only the alternative of

utter darkness, or killing draughts of air from the unsheltered casements. In all, filth, disorder, and misery abounded; the floor was the
only bed, and scanty begrimed rags of blankets the only covering. I left
this refuge for Mrs. ———'s sick dependents with my clothes covered
with dust, and full of vermin, and with a heart heavy enough, as you
will well believe. My morning's work had fatigued me not a little, and I
was glad to return to the house, where I gave vent to my indignation
and regret at the scene I had just witnessed to Mr. ——— and his overseer,
who, here, is a member of our family. The latter told me that the condition of the hospital had appeared to him, from his first entering upon his
situation (only within the last year), to require a reform, and that he had
proposed it to the former manager, Mr. K———, and Mr. ———'s brother,
who is part proprietor of the estate, but, receiving no encouragement
from them, had supposed that it was a matter of indifference to the owners, and had left it, in the condition in which he had found it, in which
condition it has been for the last nineteen years and upward.

This new overseer of ours has lived fourteen years with an old
Scotch gentleman, who owns an estate adjoining Mr. ———'s, on the island of St. Simon's, upon which estate, from every thing I can gather,
and from what I know of the proprietor's character, the slaves are probably treated with as much humanity as is consistent with slavery at all,
and where the management and comfort of the hospital in particular
had been most carefully and judiciously attended to. With regard to the
indifference of our former manager upon the subject of the accommodation for the sick, he was an excellent overseer, *videlicet* the estate returned a full income under his management, and such men have nothing to do with sick slaves: they are tools, to be mended only if they can
be made available again; if not, to be flung by as useless, without farther expense of money, time, or trouble.

I am learning to row here, for circumscribed, as my walks necessarily
are, impossible as it is to resort to my favorite exercise on horseback
upon these narrow dikes, I must do something to prevent my blood
from stagnating; and this broad brimming river, and the beautiful light
canoes which lie moored at the steps, are very inviting persuaders to
this species of exercise. My first attempt was confined to pulling an oar
across the stream, for which I rejoiced in sundry aches and pains altogether novel, letting alone a delightful row of blisters on each of my
hands. I forgot to tell you that in the hospital were several sick babies,
whose mothers were permitted to suspend their field labor in order to
nurse them. Upon addressing some remonstrances to one of these,

who, besides having a sick child, was ill herself, about the horribly dirty condition of her baby, she assured me that it was impossible for them to keep their children clean; that they went out to work at daybreak, and did not get their tasks done till evening, and that then they were too tired and worn out to do any thing but throw themselves down and sleep. This statement of hers I mentioned on my return from the hospital, and the overseer appeared extremely annoyed by it, and assured me repeatedly that it was not true.

In the evening Mr. ——, who had been over to Darien, mentioned that one of the storekeepers there had told him that, in the course of a few years, he had paid the negroes of this estate several thousand dollars for moss, which is a very profitable article of traffic with them: they collect it from the trees, dry and pick it, and then sell it to the people in Darien for mattresses, sofas, and all sorts of stuffing purposes, which, in my opinion, it answers better than any other material whatever that I am acquainted with, being as light as horse-hair, as springy and elastic, and a great deal less harsh and rigid. It is now bedtime, dear E——, and I doubt not it has been sleepy time with you over this letter long ere you came thus far. There is a preliminary to my repose, however, in this agreeable residence, which I rather dread, namely, the hunting for, or discovering without hunting, in fine relief upon the whitewashed walls of my bedroom, a most hideous and detestable species of *reptile* called centipedes, which come out of the cracks and crevices of the walls, and fill my very heart with dismay. They are from an inch to two inches long, and appear to have not a hundred, but a thousand legs. I can not ascertain very certainly from the negroes whether they sting or not, but they look exceedingly as if they might, and I visit my babies every night in fear and trembling, lest I should find one or more of these hateful creatures mounting guard over them. Good-night; you are well to be free from centipedes—better to be free from slaves.

Dear E——, —This morning I paid my second visit to the Infirmary, and found there had been some faint attempt at sweeping and cleaning, in compliance with my entreaties. The poor woman Harriet, however, whose statement with regard to the impossibility of their attending properly to their children had been so vehemently denied by the overseer, was crying bitterly. I asked her what ailed her, when, more by signs and dumb show than words, she and old Rose informed me that Mr. O—— had flogged her that morning for having told me that the women had not time to keep their children clean. It is part of the regular duty of every overseer to visit the Infirmary at least once a day, which he generally does in the morning, and Mr. O———'s visit had preceded mine but a short time only, or I might have been edified by seeing a man horsewhip a woman. I again and again made her repeat her story, and she again and again affirmed that she had been flogged for what she told me, none of the whole company in the room denying it or contradicting her. I left the room because I was so disgusted and indignant that I could hardly restrain my feelings, and to express them could have produced no single good result. In the next ward, stretched upon the ground, apparently either asleep or so overcome with sickness as to be incapable of moving, lay an immense woman; her stature, as she cumbered the earth, must have been, I should think, five feet seven or eight, and her bulk enormous. She was wrapped in filthy rags, and lay with her face on the floor. As I approached, and stooped to see what ailed her, she suddenly threw out her arms, and, seized with violent convulsions, rolled over and over upon the floor, beating her head violently upon the ground, and throwing her enormous limbs about in a horrible manner. Immediately upon the occurrence of this fit, four or five women threw themselves literally upon her, and held her down by main force; they even proceeded to bind her legs and arms together, to prevent her dashing herself about; but this violent coercion and tight bandaging seemed to me, in my profound ignorance, more likely to increase her illness by impeding her breathing and the circulation of her blood, and I bade them desist, and unfasten all the strings and ligatures not only that they had put round her limbs, but which, by tightening her clothes round her body, caused any obstruction. How much I wished that, instead of music, and dancing, and such stuff, I had learned something of sickness and health, of the conditions and liabilities of the human body, that I might have known how to assist this poor creature, and to direct her ignorant and helpless nurses! The fit presently subsided, and was succeeded by the most deplorable prostration and weakness of nerves, the tears streaming down the poor woman's cheeks in showers, without, however, her uttering a single word, though she moaned incessantly. After bathing her forehead, hands, and chest with vinegar, we raised her up and I sent to the house for a chair with a back (there was no such thing in the hospital), and we contrived to place her in it. I have seldom seen finer women than this poor creature and her younger sister, an immense strapping lass called Chloe—tall, straight, and extremely well made—who was assisting her sister, and whom I had remarked, for the extreme delight and merriment which my cleansing propensities seemed to give her, on my last visit to the hospital. She was here taking care of a sick baby, and helping to nurse her sister Molly, who, it seems, is subject to those fits, about which I spoke to our physician here—an intelligent man residing in Darien, who visits the estate whenever medical assistance is required. He seemed to attribute them to nervous disorder, brought on by frequent childbearing. This woman is young, I suppose at the outside not thirty, and her sister informed me that she had had ten children—ten children, E——! Fits and hard labor in the fields, unpaid labor, labor exacted with stripes—how do you fancy that? I wonder if my mere narration can make your blood boil as the facts did mine? Among the patients in this room was a young girl, apparently from fourteen to fifteen, whose hands and feet were literally rotting away piecemeal, from the effect of a horrible disease, to which the negroes are subject here, and I believe in the West Indies, and when it attacks the joints of the toes and fingers, the pieces absolutely decay and come off, leaving the limb a maimed and horrible stump! I believe no cure is known for this disgusting malady, which seems confined to these poor creatures. Another disease, of which they complained much, and which, of course, I was utterly incapable of accounting for, was a species of lock-jaw, to which their babies very frequently fall victims in the first or second week after their birth, refusing the breast, and the mouth gradually losing the power of opening itself. The horrible diseased state of head, common among their babies, is a mere result of filth and confinement, and therefore, though I never any where saw such distressing and disgusting objects as some of these poor little woolly skulls presented, the cause was sufficiently obvious. Pleurisy, or a tendency to it, seems very common among them; also peri-pneumonia, or inflammation of the lungs, which is terribly prevalent, and generally fatal. Rheumatism is almost universal; and as it proceeds from exposure, and want of knowledge and care, attacks indiscriminately the young and old. A great number of the women are victims to falling of the womb and weakness in the spine; but these are necessary results of their laborious existence, and do not belong either to climate or constitution.

I have ingeniously contrived to introduce bribery, corruption, and pauperism, all in a breath, upon this island, which, until my advent, was as innocent of these pollutions, I suppose, as Prospero's isle of refuge. Wishing, however, to appeal to some perception, perhaps a little less dim in their minds than the abstract loveliness of cleanliness, I have proclaimed to all the little baby nurses that I will give a cent to every little boy or girl whose baby's face shall be clean, and one to every individual

with clean face and hands of their own. My appeal was fully comprehended by the majority, it seems, for this morning I was surrounded, as
soon as I came out, by a swarm of children carrying their little charges
on their backs and in their arms, the shining, and, in many instances,
wet faces and hands of the latter bearing ample testimony to the ablutions which had been inflicted upon them. How they will curse me and
the copper cause of all their woes in their baby bosoms! Do you know
that, little as grown negroes are admirable for their personal beauty (in
my opinion, at least), the black babies of a year or two old are very
pretty; they have, for the most part, beautiful eyes and eyelashes, the
pearly perfect teeth, which they retain after their other juvenile graces
have left them; their skins are all (I mean of blacks generally) infinitely
finer and softer than the skins of white people. Perhaps you are not
aware that among the white race the *finest grained* skins generally belong to persons of dark complexion. This, as a characteristic of the black
race, I think might be accepted as some compensation for the coarse
woolly hair. The nose and mouth, which are so peculiarly displeasing
in their conformation in the face of a negro man or woman, being the
features least developed in a baby's countenance, do not at first present
the ugliness which they assume as they become more marked; and
when the very unusual operation of washing has been performed, the
blood shines through the fine texture of the skin, giving life and richness to the dingy color, and displaying a species of beauty which I think
scarcely any body who observed it would fail to acknowledge. I have
seen many babies on this plantation who were quite as pretty as white
children, and this very day stooped to kiss a little sleeping creature that
lay on its mother's knees in the Infirmary—as beautiful a specimen of a
sleeping infant as I ever saw. The caress excited the irrepressible delight
of all the women present—poor creatures! who seemed to forget that I
was a woman, and had children myself, and bore a woman's and a
mother's heart toward them and theirs; but, indeed, the Honorable Mr.
Slumkey could not have achieved more popularity by his performances
in that line than I by this exhibition of feeling; and, had the question
been my election, I am very sure nobody else would have had a chance
of a vote through the island. But wisely is it said that use is second nature, and the contempt and neglect to which these poor people are used
make the commonest expression of human sympathy appear a boon
and gracious condescension. While I am speaking of the negro countenance, there is another beauty which is not at all unfrequent among
those I see here—a finely-shaped oval face—and those who know (as

all painters and sculptors, all who understand beauty do) how much expression there is in the outline of the head, and how very rare it is to see a well-formed face, will be apt to consider this a higher matter than any coloring, of which, indeed, the red and white one so often admired is by no means the most rich, picturesque, or expressive. At first the dark color confounded all features to my eye and I could hardly tell one face from another. Becoming, however, accustomed to the complexion, I now perceive all the variety among these black countenances that there is among our own race, and as much difference in features and in expression as among the same number of whites. There is another peculiarity which I have remarked among the women here—very considerable beauty in the make of the hands; their feet are very generally ill made, which must be a natural, and not an acquired defect, as they seldom injure their feet by wearing shoes. The figures of some of the women are handsome, and their carriage, from the absence of any confining or tightening clothing, and the habit they have of balancing great weights on their heads, erect and good.

At the upper end of the row of houses, and nearest to our overseer's residence, is the hut of the head driver. Let me explain, by the way, his office. The negroes, as I before told you, are divided into troops or gangs, as they are called; at the head of each gang is a driver, who stands over them, whip in hand, while they perform their daily task, who renders an account of each individual slave and his work every evening to the overseer, and receives from him directions for their next day's tasks. Each driver is allowed to inflict a dozen lashes upon any refractory slave in the field, and at the time of the offense; they may not, however, extend the chastisement, and if it is found ineffectual, their remedy lies in reporting the unmanageable individual either to the head driver or the overseer, the former of whom has power to inflict three dozen lashes at his own discretion, and the latter as many as he himself sees fit, within the number of fifty; which limit, however, I must tell you, is an arbitrary one on this plantation, appointed by the founder of the estate, Major ——, Mr. ——'s grandfather, many of whose regulations, indeed I believe most of them, are still observed in the government of the plantation. Limits of this sort, however, to the power of either driver, head driver, or overseer, may or may not exist elsewhere; they are, to a certain degree, a check upon the power of these individuals; but in the absence of the master, the overseer may confine himself within the limit or not, as he chooses; and as for the master himself, where is his limit? He may, if he likes, flog a slave to death, for the laws which pretend that he may not are a mere pretense, inasmuch as the testimony of a black is never taken against a white; and upon this plantation of ours, and a thousand more, the overseer is the *only* white man, so whence should come the testimony to any crime of his? With regard to the oft-repeated statement that it is not the owner's interest to destroy his human property, it answers nothing; the instances in which men, to gratify the immediate impulse of passion, sacrifice not only their eternal, but their evident, palpable, positive worldly interest, are infinite. Nothing is commoner than for a man under the transient influence of anger to disregard his worldly advantage; and the black slave, whose preservation is indeed supposed to be his owner's interest may be, will be, and is occasionally sacrificed to the blind impulse of passion.

To return to our head driver, or, as he is familiarly called, head man, Frank—he is second in authority only to the overseer, and exercises rule alike over the drivers and the gangs in the absence of the sovereign white man from the estate, which happens whenever Mr. O—— visits the other two plantations at Woodville and St. Simon's. He is sole master and governor of the island, appoints the work, pronounces punishments, gives permission to the men to leave the island (without it they never may do so), and exercises all functions of undisputed mastery over his fellow-slaves, for you will observe that all this while he is just as much a slave as any of the rest. Trustworthy, upright, intelligent, he may be flogged to-morrow if Mr. O—— or Mr. —— so please it, and sold the next day, like a cart-horse, at the will of the latter. Besides his various other responsibilities, he has the key of all the stores, and gives out the people's rations weekly; nor is it only the people's provisions that are put under his charge—meat, which is only given out to them occasionally, and provisions for the use of the family, are also intrusted to his care. Thus you see, among these *inferior* creatures, their own masters yet look to find, surviving all their best efforts to destroy them, good sense, honesty, self-denial, and all the qualities, mental and moral, that make one man worthy to be trusted by another. From the imperceptible but inevitable effect of the sympathies and influences of human creatures toward and over each other, Frank's intelligence has become uncommonly developed by intimate communion in the discharge of his duty with the former overseer, a very intelligent man, who has only just left the estate, after managing it for nineteen years; the effect of this intercourse, and of the trust and responsibility laid upon the man, are that he is clear-headed, well judging, active, intelligent, extremely well mannered, and, being respected, he respects himself. He is as ignorant as the rest of the slaves; but he is always clean and tidy in his person, with a courteousness of demeanor far removed from servility, and exhibits a strong instance of the intolerable and wicked injustice of the system under which he lives, having advanced thus far toward improvement, in spite of all the bars it puts to progress; and here being arrested, not by want of energy, want of sense, or any want of his own, but by being held as another man's property, who can only thus hold him by forbidding him farther improvement. When I see that man, who keeps himself a good aloof from the rest, in his leisure hours looking, with a countenance of deep thought, as I did to-day, over the broad river, which is to him as a prison wall, to the fields and forest beyond, not one inch or branch of which his utmost industry can conquer as his own, or acquire and leave an independent heritage to his children, I marvel what the thoughts of such a man may be. I was in his house to-day, and the same superiority in cleanliness, comfort, and propriety exhibited itself in his dwelling as in his own personal appearance and that of his wife—a most active, trustworthy, excellent woman, daughter of the oldest, and probably most highly respected of all Mr. ———'s slaves. To the excellent conduct of this woman, and, indeed, every member of her family, both the present and the last overseer bear unqualified testimony.

As I was returning toward the house after my long morning's lounge, a man rushed out of the blacksmith's shop, and, catching me by the skirt of my gown, poured forth a torrent of self-gratulations on having at length found the "right misses." They have no idea, of course, of a white person performing any of the offices of a servant, and as throughout the whole Southern country the owner's children are nursed and tended, and sometimes *suckled* by their slaves (I wonder how this inferior milk agrees with the lordly *white* babies?), the appearance of M——— with my two children had immediately suggested the idea that she must be the misses. Many of the poor negroes flocked to her, paying their profound homage under this impression; and when she explained to them that she was not their owner's wife, the confusion in their minds seemed very great—Heaven only knows whether they did not conclude that they had two mistresses, and Mr. ———s two wives; for the privileged race must seem, in their eyes, to have such absolute masterdom on earth, that perhaps they thought polygamy might be one of the sovereign white men's numerous indulgences. The ecstasy of the blacksmith on discovering the "right missis" at last was very funny, and was expressed with such extraordinary grimaces, contortions, and gesticulations, that I thought I should have died of laughing at this rapturous identification of my most melancholy relation to the poor fellow.

Having at length extricated myself from the group which forms round me whenever I stop but for a few minutes, I pursued my voyage of discovery by peeping into the kitchen garden. I dared do no more; the aspect of the place would have rejoiced the very soul of Solomon's sluggard of old—a few cabbages and weeds innumerable filled the neglected-looking inclosure, and I ventured no farther than the entrance into its most uninviting precincts. You are to understand that upon this swamp island of ours we have quite a large stock of cattle, cows, sheep, pigs, and poultry in the most enormous and inconvenient abundance. The cows are pretty miserably off for pasture, the banks and pathways of the dikes being their only grazing ground, which the sheep perambulate also, in earnest search of a nibble of fresh herbage; both the cows and sheep are fed with rice flour in great abundance, and are pretty often carried down for change of air and more sufficient grazing to Hampton, Mr. ———'s estate, on the island of St Simon's, fifteen miles from this place, farther down the river—or rather, indeed, I should say in the sea, for 'tis salt water all round, and one end of the island has a noble beach open to the vast Atlantic. The pigs thrive admirably here, and attain very great perfection of size and flavor, the rice flour upon which they are chiefly fed tending to make them very delicate. As for the poultry, it being one of the few privileges of the poor blacks to raise as many they can, their abundance is literally a nuisance—ducks, fowls, pigeons, turkeys (the two latter species, by-the-by, are exclusively the master's property), cluck, scream, gabble, gobble, crow, cackle, fight, fly, and flutter in all directions, and to their immense concourse, and the perfect freedom with which they intrude themselves even into the piazza of the house, the pantry, and kitchen, I partly attribute the swarms of fleas, and other still less agreeable vermin, with which we are most horribly pestered.

My walk lay to-day along the bank of a canal, which has been dug through nearly the whole length of the island, to render more direct and easy the transportation of the rice from one end of the estate to another, or from the various distant fields to the principal mill at Settlement No. 1. It is of considerable width and depth, and opens by various locks into the river. It has, unfortunately, no trees on its banks, but a good foot-path renders it, in spite of that deficiency, about the best walk on the island. I passed again to-day one of those beautiful evergreen thickets, which I described to you in my last letter; it is called a reserve, and is kept uncleared and uncultivated in its natural swampy condition, to allow of the people's procuring their firewood from it. I can not get accustomed, so as to be indifferent to this exquisite natural ornamental growth, and think, as I contemplate the various and beautiful foliage of these watery woods, how many of our finest English parks and gardens owe their chiefest adornments to plantations of these shrubs, procured at immense cost, reared with infinite pain and care, which are here basking in the winter's sunshine, waiting to be cut down for firewood! These little groves are peopled with wild pigeons and birds, which they designate here as blackbirds. These sometimes rise from the rice fields with a whirr of multitudinous wings that is almost startling, and positively overshadow the ground beneath like a cloud.

I had a conversation that interested me a good deal, during my walk to-day, with my peculiar slave Jack. This lad, whom Mr. ―― has appointed to attend me in my roamings about the island, and rowing expeditions on the river, is the son of the last head driver, a man of very extraordinary intelligence and faithfulness—such, at least, is the account given of him by his employers (in the burial-ground of the negroes is a stone dedicated to his memory, a mark of distinction accorded by his masters, which his son never failed to point out to me when we passed that way). Jack appears to inherit his quickness of apprehension; his questions, like those of an intelligent child, are absolutely inexhaustible; his curiosity about all things beyond this island, the prison-house of his existence, is perfectly intense; his countenance is very pleasing, mild, and not otherwise than thoughtful; he is, in common with the rest of them, a stupendous flatterer, and, like the rest of them, also seems devoid of physical and moral courage. To-day, in the midst of his torrent of inquiries about places and things, I suddenly asked him if he would like to be free. A gleam of light absolutely shot over his whole countenance, like the vivid and instantaneous lightning; he stammered, hesitated, became excessively confused, and at length replied, "Free, missis! what for me wish to be free? Oh no, missis, me no wish to be free, if massa only let we keep pig!" The fear of offending by uttering that forbidden wish—the dread of admitting, by its expression, the slightest discontent with his present situation—the desire to conciliate my favor, even at the expense of strangling the intense natural longing that absolutely glowed in his every feature—it was a sad spectacle, and I repented my question. As for the pitiful request, which he reiterated several times, adding, "No, missis, me no want to be free; me work till me die for missis and massa," with increased emphasis; it amounted only to this, that negroes once were, but no longer are, permitted to keep pigs. The increase of filth and foul smells consequent upon their being raised is, of course, very great; and, moreover, Mr. —— told me, when I preferred poor Jack's request to him, that their allowance was no more than would suffice their own necessity, and that they had not the means of feeding the animals. With a little good management they might very easily obtain them, however; their little "kail-yard" alone would suffice to it, and the pork and bacon would prove a most welcome addition to their farinaceous diet. You perceive at once (or, if you could have seen the boy's face, you would have perceived at once) that his situation was no mystery to him; that his value to Mr. ——, and, as he supposed, to me, was perfectly well known to him, and that he comprehended immediately that his expressing even the desire to be free might be construed by me into an offense, and sought, by eager protestations of his delighted acquiescence in slavery, to conceal his soul's natural yearning, lest I should resent it. 'Twas a sad passage between us, and sent me home full of the most painful thoughts. I told Mr. ——, with much indignation, of poor Harriet's flogging, and represented that if the people were to be chastised for any thing they said to me, I must leave the place, as I could not but hear their complaints, and endeavor, by all my miserable limited means, to better their condition while I was here. He said he would ask Mr. O—— about it, assuring me, at the same time; that it was impossible to believe a single word any of these people said. At dinner, accordingly, the inquiry was made as to the cause of her punishment, and Mr. O—— then said it was not at all for what she had told me that he had flogged her, but for having answered him impertinently; that he had ordered her into the field, whereupon she had said she was ill and could not work; that he retorted he knew better, and bade her get up and go to work; she replied, "Very well, I'll go, but I shall just come back again!" meaning that when in the field she would be unable to work, and obliged to return to the hospital. "For this reply," Mr. O—— said, "I gave her a good lashing; it was her business to have gone into the field without answering me, and then we should have soon seen whether she could work or not; I gave it to Chloe too for some such impudence." I give you the words of the conversation, which was prolonged to a great length, the overseer complaining of the sham sicknesses of the slaves, and detailing the most disgusting struggle which is going on the whole time, on the one hand to inflict, and on the other to evade oppression and injustice. With this sauce I ate my dinner, and truly it tasted bitter.

Toward sunset I went on the river to take my rowing lesson. A darling little canoe, which carries two oars and a steersman, and rejoices in the appropriate title of the "Dolphin," is my especial vessel; and with Jack's help and instructions, I contrived this evening to row upward of half a mile, coasting the reed-crowned edge of the island and to another very large rice mill, the enormous wheel of which is turned by the tide. A small bank of mud and sand, covered with reedy coarse grass, divides the river into two arms on this side of the island; the deep channel is on the outside of this bank, and as we rowed home this evening, the tide having fallen, we scraped sand almost the whole way. Mr. ———'s domain, it seems to me, will presently fill up this shallow stream, and join itself to the above-mentioned mud-bank. The whole course of this most noble river is full of shoals, banks, mud, and sand-bars, and the navigation, which is difficult to those who know it well, is utterly baffling to the inexperienced. The fact is, that the two elements are so fused hereabouts that there are hardly such things as earth or water proper; that which styles itself the former is a fat, muddy, slimy sponge, that, floating half under the turbid river, looks yet saturated with the thick waves which every now and then reclaim their late dominion, and cover it almost entirely; the water, again, cloudy and yellow, like pea-soup, seems but a solution of such islands, rolling turbid and thick with alluvium, which it both gathers and deposits as it sweeps along with a swollen, smooth rapidity, that almost deceives the eye. Amphibious creatures, alligators, serpents, and wild-fowl haunt these yet but half-formed regions, where land and water are of the consistency of hasty-pudding—the one seeming too unstable to walk on, the other almost too thick to float in. But then the sky—if no human chisel ever yet cut breath, neither did any human pen ever write light; if it did, mine should spread out before you the unspeakable glories of these Southern heavens, the saffron brightness of morning, the blue intense brilliancy of noon, the golden splendor and the rosy softness of sunset. Italy and Claude Lorraine may go hang themselves together! Heaven itself does not seem brighter or more beautiful to the imagination than these surpassing pageants of fiery rays, and piled-up beds of orange, golden clouds, with edges too bright to look on, scattered wreaths of faintest rosy bloom, amber streaks and pale green lakes between, and amid sky all mingled blue and rose tints, a spectacle to make one fall over the side of the boat, with one's head broken off with looking adoringly upward, but which, on paper, means nothing.

At six o'clock our little canoe grazed the steps at the landing. These were covered with young women, and boys, and girls, drawing water for their various household purposes. A very small cedar pail—a piggin as they termed it—serves to scoops up the river water; and having, by this means, filled a large bucket, they transfer this to their heads, and, thus laden, march home with the purifying element—what to do with it I can not imagine, for evidence of its ever having been introduced into their dwellings I saw none. As I ascended the stairs, they surrounded me with shrieks and yells of joy, uttering exclamations of delight and amazement at my rowing. Considering that they dig, delve, carry burdens, and perform many more athletic exercises than pulling a light oar, I was rather amused at this; but it was the singular fact of seeing a white woman stretch her sinews in any toilsome exercise which astounded them, accustomed as they are to see both men and women of the privileged skin eschew the slightest shadow of labor as a thing not only painful, but degrading. They will learn another lesson from me, however, whose idea of heaven was pronounced by a friend of mine, to whom I once communicated it, to be "devilish hard work!" It was only just six o'clock, and these women had all done all their tasks. I exhorted them to go home and wash their children, and clean their houses and themselves, which they professed themselves ready to do, but said they had no soap. Then began a chorus of mingled requests for soap, for summer clothing, and a variety of things, which, if "Missis only give we, we be so clean forever!"

This request for summer clothing, by-the-by, I think a very reasonable one. The allowance of clothes made yearly to each slave by the present regulations of the estate is a certain number of yards of flannel, and as much more of what they call plains—an extremely stout, thick, heavy woolen cloth, of a dark gray or blue color, which resembles the species of carpet we call drugget. This, and two pair of shoes, is the regular ration of clothing; but these plains would be intolerable to any but negroes, even in winter, in this climate, and are intolerable to them in the summer. A far better arrangement, in my opinion, would be to increase their allowance of flannel and under clothing, and to give them dark chintzes instead of these thick carpets, which are very often the only covering they wear at all. I did not impart all this to my petitioners, but, disengaging myself from them, for they held my hands and clothes, I conjured them to offer us some encouragement to better their condition by bettering it as much as they could themselves—enforced the virtue of washing themselves and all belonging to them, and at length made good my retreat. As there is no particular reason why such a letter as this should ever come to an end, I had better spare you for the present. You shall have a faithful journal, I promise you, henceforward, as hitherto, from yours ever.

5

Transcription of Speech Given at the Akron Women's Rights Convention, from the *Anti-Slavery Bugle* (June 21, 1851)

Sojourner Truth

SOJOURNER TRUTH (1797–1883) was born Isabella Baumfree, a slave on the Hardenbergh estate in Ulster County, New York. Sold several times, her last master was John Dumont of Hurley in Ulster County, New York. In slavery she bore five children. When New York law prohibited slavery in 1827, she gained her legal freedom and became active in various organizations and religious communities. Then in 1843 Isabella took the sobriquet Sojourner Truth as she responded to a call from God to broadcast the truth. Although non-literate, she spoke English and Dutch and was a popular orator at antislavery and women's rights meetings. Jeffrey C. Stewart notes that in taking the name Sojourner Truth, the ex-slave "broke with two traditions at once—the tradition of former slaves taking their masters' names and that of married women taking their husbands' names" (xiii).

In a famous speech lodged to counter the attack on women's rights by the male ministers in attendance at the Women's Rights Convention in Akron in 1851, Truth emphasizes the ennobling rather than degrading value of women's, and specifically African women's, labor as a basis for claims of equality. The version of the speech included here is the transcription that appeared in the *Anti-Slavery Bugle* in Salem, Ohio, on June 21, 1851.

As Truth's reputation as an activist spread, the white anti-slavery activist Olive Gilbert took down Truth's dictated life narrative for publication in 1851 as *Narrative of Sojourner Truth*. Scholars such as Santamarina and Stewart have analyzed the ways in which Truth's agency as a narrator, activist, and moralist manages to emerge despite Gilbert's controlling transcription and her embedding of Truth's voice, words, and narration in her own version of the black woman's story. Santamarina has also explored in detail how Truth's self-presentation as a physically laboring woman contests stereotypes of black women as degraded laborers.

At the end of the Civil War, Truth worked in the Freedman's Hospital in Washington, D.C. In the late 1860s she established her home in Battle Creek, Michigan, though she continued to travel widely, speaking on behalf of various causes. She lived in Michigan until her death in 1883. Nell Irvin Painter has written a definitive biography of Truth (1996).

Transcription of Speech Given at the Akron Women's Rights Convention

"May I say a few words?" Receiving an affirmative answer, she proceeded: "I want to say a few words about this matter. I am a woman's rights. I have as much muscle as any man, and can do as much work as any man. I have plowed and reaped and husked and chopped and mowed, and can any man do more than that? I have heard much about the sexes being equal; I can carry as much as any man, and can eat as much too, if I can get it. I am as strong as any man that is now. As for intellect, all I can say is, if woman have a pint and man a quart—why can't she have her little pint full? You need not be afraid to give us our rights for fear we will take too much, for we can't take more than our pint'll hold. The poor men seem to be all in confusion, and don't know what to do. Why children, if you have woman's rights give it to her and you will feel better. You will have your own rights, and they won't be so much trouble. I can't read, but I can hear. I have heard the bible and have learned that Eve caused man to sin. Well if woman upset the world, do give her a chance to set it right side up again. The Lady has spoken about Jesus, how he never spurned woman from him, and she was right. When Lazarus died, Mary and Martha came to him with faith and love and besought him to raise their brother. And Jesus wept—and Lazarus came forth. And how came Jesus into the world? Through God who created him and woman who bore him. Man, where is your part? But the women are coming up, blessed be God, and a few of the men are coming with them. But man is in a tight place, the poor slave is on him, woman is coming on him, and he is surely between a hawk and a buzzard."

6

Selections from "Youth," from *Memoirs of Margaret Fuller Ossoli* (1852)

Margaret Fuller

SARAH MARGARET FULLER (1810–1850) was born in Cambridgeport, Massachusetts, in 1810. Her father, Timothy Fuller, a lawyer and later a congressman, encouraged her education, enabling her to learn Greek, Latin, German, French, and Italian. Fuller's educational accomplishments were so impressive that Harvard University admitted her to its men-only library to facilitate her studies. When her father's death forced the family into financial difficulties, Fuller taught school for two years but abandoned teaching to dedicate herself to writing and the life of Boston's intellectual circles.

As a civic intellectual, Fuller instituted a series of formal conversations for women, each dedicated to a philosophical question. She became friends with Henry David Thoreau, the Peabody sisters, the Alcotts, Horace Greeley, and Thomas Carlyle, and served with Ralph Waldo Emerson as editor of *The Dial* from 1840 to 1842. In 1843 *The Dial* published Fuller's essay calling for women's equality, which she justified by appeal to Transcendentalist philosophy.

A trip to the Great Lakes region in 1843 inspired her to write *Summer on the Lakes,* a travel narrative that included reflections on the treatment of women and Native Americans. She was then invited to join the *New York Tribune* as editor of book reviews and a commentator on arts and cultural events. In 1845 she published a manifesto, *Woman in the Nineteenth Century*, that has become a foundational feminist text.

In 1846 Fuller moved to Europe as a foreign correspondent for the paper, touring England and France before taking up residence in Italy. Caught up in the 1847 Roman revolution against the Papal State, she met a young revolutionary, the Marchese Giovanni Angelo d'Ossoli, with whom she had a son. Upon the failure of the revolution, Fuller and her family set sail for the United States, carrying a book that she had written on the Italian revolution. During the voyage the captain died of smallpox and his inadequate replacement ran the ship aground during a storm near Fire Island, New York. Margaret, her partner, and her son were all drowned. Apparently Henry David Thoreau visited the wreckage in search of Fuller's manuscript, but it was never found.

Since the 1970s, feminist literary scholars have written extensively on Margaret Fuller's work and her role as an early advocate of women's equality. The selections included here are taken from "Youth," sketches of her childhood that she wrote in her thirties. "Youth" is drawn from the *Memoirs of Margaret Fuller Ossoli*, an 1852 publication compiled by William Henry Channing, Ralph Waldo Emerson, and James Freeman Clarke. Mary Kelley, who included "Youth" under the title "Autobiographical Sketch," helpfully contextualizes Fuller's life and career in *The Portable Margaret Fuller*.

Compiled and edited by William Henry Channing, Ralph Waldo Emerson,
James Freeman Clark.

2 vols,

Boston: Phillips, Sampson & Co.

I. Youth.

Autobiography.

"Tieck, who has embodied so many Runic secrets, explained to me
what I have often felt toward myself, when he tells of the poor changeling, who, turned from the door of her adopted home, sat down on a
stone and so pitied herself that she wept. Yet me also, the wonderful
bird, singing in the wild forest, has tempted on, and not in vain."

Thus wrote Margaret in the noon of life, when looking back through
youth to the "dewy dawn of memory." She was the eldest child of Timothy Fuller and Margaret Crane, and was born in Cambridge-Port,
Massachusetts, on the 23d of May, 1810.

Among her papers fortunately remains this unfinished sketch of
youth, prepared by her own hand, in 1840, as the introductory chapter
to an autobiographical romance.

PARENTS.

My father was a lawyer and a politician. He was a man largely
endowed with that sagacious energy, which the state of New England
society, for the last half century, has been so well fitted to develop. His
father was a clergyman, settled as pastor in Princeton, Massachusetts,
within the bounds of whose parish-farm was Wachuset. His means
were small, and the great object of his ambition was to send his sons
to college. As a boy, my father was taught to think only of preparing
himself for Harvard University, and when there of preparing himself
for the profession of Law. As a Lawyer, again, the ends constantly presented were to work for distinction in the community, and for the means
of supporting a family. To be an honored citizen, and to have a home
on earth, were made the great aims of existence. To open the deeper
fountains of the soul, to regard life here as the prophetic entrance to
immortality, to develop his spirit to perfection,—motives like these had
never been suggested to him, either by fellow-beings or by outward

circumstances. The result was a character, in its social aspect, of quite the common sort. A good son and brother, a kind neighbor, an active man of business—in all these outward relations he was but one of a class, which surrounding conditions have made the majority among us. In the more delicate and individual relations, he never approached but two mortals, my mother and myself.

His love for my mother was the green spot on which he stood apart from the common-places of a mere bread-winning, bread-bestowing existence. She was one of those fair and flower-like natures, which sometimes spring up even beside the most dusty high ways of life—a creature not to be shaped into a merely useful instrument, but bound by one law with the blue sky, the dew, and the frolic birds. Of all persons whom I have known, she had in her most of the angelic—of that spontaneous love for every living thing, for man, and beast, and tree, which restores the golden age.

DEATH IN THE HOUSE.

My earliest recollection is of a death,—the death of a sister, two years younger than myself. Probably there is a sense of childish endearments, such as belong to this tie, mingled with that of loss, of wonder, and mystery; but these last are prominent in memory. I remember coming home and meeting our nursery-maid, her face streaming with tears. That strange sight of tears made an indelible impression. I realize how little I was of stature, in that I looked up to this weeping face;—and it has often seemed since, that—full-grown for the life of this earth, I have looked up just so, at times of threatening, of doubt, and distress, and that just so has some being of the next higher order of existences looked down, aware of a law unknown to me, and tenderly commiserating the pain I must endure in emerging from my ignorance.

She took me by the hand and led me into a still and dark chamber,—then drew aside the curtain and showed my sister. I see yet that beauty of death! The highest achievements of sculpture are only the reminder of its severe sweetness. Then I remember the house all still and dark,—the people in their black clothes and dreary faces,—the scent of the newly-made coffin,—my being set up in a chair and detained by a gentle hand to hear the clergyman,—the carriages slowly going, the procession slowly doling out their steps to the grave. But I have no remembrance of what I have since been told I did,—insisting, with loud cries, that they should not put the body in the ground. I suppose that my emotion was spent at the time, and so there was nothing to fix that moment in my memory.

I did not then, nor do I now, find any beauty in these ceremonies. What had they to do with the sweet playful child? Her life and death were alike beautiful, but all this sad parade was not. Thus my first experience of life was one of death. She who would have been the companion of my life was severed from me, and I was left alone. This has made a vast difference in my lot. Her character, if that fair face promised right, would have been soft, graceful and lively; it would have tempered mine to a gentler and more gradual course.

OVERWORK.

My father,—all whose feelings were now concentred on me,—instructed me himself. The effect of this was so far good that, not passing through the hands of many ignorant and weak persons as so many do at preparatory schools, I was put at once under discipline of considerable severity, and, at the same time, had a more than ordinarily high standard presented to me. My father was a man of business, even in literature; he had been a high scholar at college, and was warmly attached to all he had learned there, both from the pleasure he had derived in the exercise of his faculties and the associated memories of success and good repute. He was, beside, well read in French literature, and in English, a Queen Anne's man. He hoped to make me the heir of all he knew, and of as much more as the income of his profession enabled him to give me means of acquiring. At the very beginning, he made one great mistake, more common, it is to be hoped, in the last generation, than the warnings of physiologists will permit it to be with the next. He thought to gain time, by bringing forward the intellect as early as possible. Thus I had tasks given me, as many and various as the hours would allow, and on subjects beyond my age; with the additional disadvantage of reciting to him in the evening, after he returned from his office. As he was subject to many interruptions, I was often kept up till very late; and as he was a severe teacher, both from his habits of mind and his ambition for me, my feelings were kept on the stretch till the recitations were over. Thus frequently, I was sent to bed several hours too late, with nerves unnaturally stimulated. The consequence was a premature development of the brain, that made me a "youthful prodigy" by day, and by night a victim of spectral illusions, nightmare, and somnambulism, which at the time prevented the harmonious development of my bodily powers and checked my growth, while, later, they induced continual headache, weakness and nervous affections, of all kinds. As these again re-acted on the brain, giving undue force to every thought and every feeling, there was finally produced a state of being both too active and too intense, which wasted my constitution, and will bring me,—even although I have learned to understand and regulate my now morbid temperament,—to a premature grave.

No one understood this subject of health then. No one knew why this child, already kept up so late, was still unwilling to retire. My aunts cried out upon the "spoiled child, the most unreasonable child that ever was,—if brother could but open his eyes to see it,—who was never willing to go to bed." They did not know that, so soon as the light was taken away, she seemed to see colossal faces advancing slowly towards her, the eyes dilating, and each feature swelling loathsomely as they came; till at last, when they were about to close upon her, she started up with a shriek which drove them away, but only to return when she lay down again. They did not know that, when at last she went to sleep, it was to dream of horses trampling over her, and to awake once more in fright; or, as she had just read in her Virgil, of being among trees that dripped with blood, where she walked and walked and could not get out, while the blood became a pool and plashed over her feet, and rose higher and higher, till soon she dreamed it would reach her lips. No wonder the child arose and walked in her sleep, moaning all over the house, till once, when they heard her, and came and waked her, and she told what she had dreamed, her father sharply bid her "leave off thinking of such nonsense, or she would be crazy,"—never knowing that he was himself the cause of all these horrors of the night. Often she dreamed of following to the grave the body of her mother, as she had done that of her sister, and woke to find the pillow drenched in tears. These dreams softened her heart too much, and cast a deep shadow over her young days; for then, and later, the life of dreams,—probably because there was in it less to distract the mind from its own earnestness,—has often seemed to her more real, and been remembered with more interest, than that of waking hours.

Poor child! Far remote in time, in thought, from that period, I look back on these glooms and terrors, wherein I was enveloped, and perceive that I had no 'natural childhood.'

BOOKS.

Thus passed my first years. My mother was in delicate health, and much absorbed in the care of her younger children. In the house was neither dog nor bird, nor any graceful animated form of existence. I saw no persons who took my fancy, and real life offered no attraction. Thus my already over-excited mind found no relief from without, and was driven for refuge from itself to the world of books. I was taught Latin and English grammar at the same time, and began to read Latin at six years old, after which, for some years, I read it daily. In this branch of study, first by my father, and afterwards by a tutor, I was trained to quite a high degree of precision. I was expected to understand the mechanism of the language thoroughly, and in translating to give the thoughts in as few well-arranged words as possible, and without breaks or hesitation,—for with these my father had absolutely no patience.

Indeed, he demanded accuracy and clearness in everything: you must not speak, unless you can make your meaning perfectly intelligible to the person addressed; must not express a thought, unless you can give a reason for it, if required; must not make a statement, unless sure of all particulars—such were his rules. "But," "if," "unless," "I am mistaken," and "it may be so," were words and phrases excluded from the province where he held sway. Trained to great dexterity in artificial methods, accurate, ready, with entire command of his resources, he had no belief in minds that listen, wait, and receive. He had no conception of the subtle and indirect motions of imagination and feeling. His influence on me was great, and opposed to the natural unfolding of my character, which was fervent, of strong grasp, and disposed to infatuation, and self-forgetfulness. He made the common prose world so present to me, that my natural bias was controlled. I did not go mad, as many would do, at being continually roused from my dreams. I had too much strength to be crushed,—and since I must put on the fetters, could not submit to let them impede my motions. My own world sank deep within, away from the surface of my life; in what I did and said I learned to have reference to other minds. But my true life was only the dearer that it was secluded and veiled over by a thick curtain of available intellect, and that coarse, but wearable stuff woven by the ages,—Common Sense.

In accordance with this discipline in heroic common sense, was the influence of those great Romans, whose thoughts and lives were my daily food during those plastic years. The genius of Rome displayed itself in Character, and scarcely needed an occasional wave of the torch of thought to show its lineaments, so marble strong they gleamed in every light. Who, that has lived with those men, but admires the plain force of fact, of thought passed into action? They take up things with their naked hands. There is just the man, and the block he casts before you,—no divinity, no demon, no unfulfilled aim, but just the man and Rome, and what he did for Rome. Everything turns your attention to what a man can become, not by yielding himself freely to impressions, not by letting nature play freely through him, but by a single thought, an earnest purpose, an indomitable will, by hardihood, self-command, and force of expression. Architecture was the art in which Rome excelled, and this corresponds with the feeling these men of Rome excite. They did not grow,—they built themselves up, or were built up by the fate of Rome, as a temple for Jupiter Stator. The ruined Roman sits among the ruins; he flies to no green garden; he does not look to heaven; if his intent is defeated, if he is less than he meant to be, he lives no more. The names which end in "us," seem to speak with lyric cadence. That measured cadence,—that tramp and march,—which are not stilted, because they indicate real force, yet which seem so when compared with any other language,—make Latin a study in itself of mighty influence. The language alone, without the literature, would give one the *thought* of Rome. Man present in nature, commanding nature too sternly to be inspired by it, standing like the rock amid the sea, or moving like the fire over the land, either impassive, or irresistible; knowing not the soft mediums or fine flights of life, but by the force which he expresses, piercing to the centre.

We are never better understood than when we speak of a "Roman virtue," a "Roman outline." There is somewhat indefinite, somewhat yet unfulfilled in the thought of Greece, of Spain, of modern Italy; but ROME! it stands by itself, a clear Word. The power of will, the dignity of a fixed purpose is what it utters. Every Roman was an emperor. It is well that the infallible church should have been founded on this rock, that the presumptuous Peter should hold the keys, as the conquering Jove did before his thunderbolts, to be seen of all the world. The Apollo tends flocks with Admetus; Christ teaches by the lonely lake, or plucks wheat as he wanders through the fields some Sabbath morning. They never come to this stronghold; they could not have breathed freely where all became stone as soon as spoken, where divine youth found no horizon for its all-promising glance, but every thought put on, before it dared issue to the day in action, its *toga virilis*.

Suckled by this wolf, man gains a different complexion from that which is fed by the Greek honey. He takes a noble bronze in camps and battle-fields; the wrinkles of council well beseem his brow, and the eye cuts its way like the sword. The Eagle should never have been used as a symbol by any other nation: it belonged to Rome.

The history of Rome abides in mind, of course, more than the litera-ture. It was degeneracy for a Roman to use the pen; his life was in the day. The "vaunting" of Rome, like that of the North American Indians, is her proper literature. A man rises; he tells who he is, and what he has done; he speaks of his country and her brave men; he knows that a con-quering god is there, whose agent is his own right hand; and he should end like the Indian, "I have no more to say."

It never shocks us that the Roman is self-conscious. One wants no universal truths from him, no philosophy, no creation, but only his life, his Roman life felt in every pulse, realized in every gesture. The univer-sal heaven takes in the Roman only to make us feel his individuality the more. The Will, the Resolve of Man!—it has been expressed,—fully expressed!

I steadily loved this ideal in my childhood, and this is the cause, probably, why I have always felt that man must know how to stand firm on the ground, before he can fly. In vain for me are men more, if they are less, than Romans. Dante was far greater than any Roman, yet I feel he was right to take the Mantuan as his guide through hell, and to heaven.

Horace was a great deal to me then, and is so still. Though his words do not abide in memory, his presence does: serene, courtly, of darting hazel eye, a self-sufficient grace, and an appreciation of the world of stern realities, sometimes pathetic, never tragic. He is the natural man of the world; he is what he ought to be, and his darts never fail of their aim. There is a perfume and raciness, too, which makes life a banquet, where the wit sparkles no less that the viands were bought with blood.

Ovid gave me not Rome, nor himself, but a view into the enchanted gardens of the Greek mythology. This path I followed, have been fol-lowing ever since; and now, life half over, it seems to me, as in my child-hood, that every thought of which man is susceptible, is intimated there. In those young years, indeed, I did not see what I now see, but loved to creep from amid the Roman pikes to lie beneath this great vine, and see the smiling and serene shapes go by, woven from the finest fibres of all the elements. I knew not why, at that time,—but I loved to get away from the hum of the forum, and the mailed clang of Roman speech, to these shifting shows of nature, these Gods and Nymphs born of the sunbeam, the wave, the shadows on the hill.

As with Rome I antedated the world of deeds, so I lived in those Greek forms the true faith of a refined and intense childhood. So great was the force of reality with which these forms impressed me, that I prayed earnestly for a sign,—that it would lighten in some particular region of the heavens, or that I might find a bunch of grapes in the path, when I went forth in the morning. But no sign was given, and I was left a waif stranded upon the shores of modern life!

Of the Greek language, I knew only enough to feel that the sounds told the same story as the mythology;—that the law of life in that land was beauty, as in Rome it was a stern composure. I wish I had learned as much of Greece as of Rome,—so freely does the mind play in her sunny waters, where there is no chill, and the restraint is from within out; for these Greeks, in an atmosphere of ample grace, could not be impetuous, or stern, but loved moderation as equable life always must, for it is the law of beauty.

With these books I passed my days. The great amount of study exacted of me soon ceased to be a burden, and reading became a habit and a passion. The force of feeling, which, under other circumstances, might have ripened thought, was turned to learn the thoughts of others. This was not a tame state, for the energies brought out by rapid acquisition gave glow enough. I thought with rapture of the all-accomplished man, him of the many talents, wide resources, clear sight, and omnipotent will. A Caesar seemed great enough. I did not then know that such men impoverish the treasury to build the palace. I kept their statues as belonging to the hall of my ancestors, and loved to conquer obstacles, and fed my youth and strength for their sake.

Still, though this bias was so great that in earliest years I learned, in these ways, how the world takes hold of a powerful nature, I had yet other experiences. None of these were deeper than what I found in the happiest haunt of my childish years,—our little garden. Our house, though comfortable, was very ugly, and in a neighborhood which I detested,—every dwelling and its appurtenances having a *mesquin* and huddled look. I liked nothing about us except the tall graceful elms before the house, and the dear little garden behind. Our back door opened on a high flight of steps, by which I went down to a green plot, much injured in my ambitious eyes by the presence of the pump and toolhouse. This opened into a little garden, full of choice flowers and fruit-trees, which was my mother's delight, and was carefully kept. Here I felt at home. A gate opened thence into the fields,—a wooden gate made of boards, in a high, unpainted board wall, and embowered in the clematis creeper. This gate I used to open to see the sunset heaven; beyond this black frame I did not step; for I liked to look at the deep gold behind it. How exquisitely happy I was in its beauty, and how I loved the silvery wreaths of my protecting vine! I never would pluck one of its flowers at that time, I was so jealous of its beauty, but often since I carry off wreaths of it from the wild-wood, and it stands in nature to my mind as the emblem of domestic love.

Of late I have thankfully felt what I owe to that garden, where the best hours of my lonely childhood were spent. Within the house everything was socially utilitarian; my books told of a proud world, but in another temper were the teachings of the little garden. There my thoughts could lie callow in the nest, and only be fed and kept warm, not called to fly or sing before the time. I loved to gaze on the roses, the violets, the lilies, the pinks; my mother's hand had planted them, and they bloomed for me. I culled the most beautiful. I looked at them on every side. I kissed them, I pressed them to my bosom with passionate emotions, such as I have never dared express to any human being. An ambition swelled my heart to be as beautiful, as perfect as they. I have not kept my vow. Yet, forgive, ye wild asters, which gleam so sadly amid the fading grass; forgive me, ye golden autumn flowers, which so strive to reflect the glories of the departing distant sun; and ye silvery flowers, whose moonlight eyes I knew so well, forgive! Living and blooming in your unchecked law, ye know nothing of the blights, the distortions, which beset the human being; and which at such hours it would seem that no glories of free agency could ever repay!

There was, in the house, no apartment appropriated to the purpose of a library, but there was in my father's room a large closet filled with books, and to these I had free access when the task-work of the day was done. Its window overlooked wide fields, gentle slopes, a rich and smiling country, whose aspect pleased without much occupying the eye, while a range of blue hills, rising at about twelve miles distance, allured to reverie. "Distant mountains," says Tieck, "excite the fancy, for beyond them we place the scene of our Paradise." Thus, in the poems of fairy adventure, we climb the rocky barrier, pass fearless its dragon caves, and dark pine forests, and find the scene of enchantment in the vale behind. My hopes were never so definite, but my eye was constantly allured to that distant blue range, and I would sit, lost in fancies, till tears fell on my cheek. I loved this sadness; but only in later years, when the realities of life had taught me moderation, did the passionate emotions excited by seeing them again teach how glorious were the hopes that swelled my heart while gazing on them in those early days.

Melancholy attends on the best joys of a merely ideal life, else I should call most happy the hours in the garden, the hours in the book closet. Here were the best French writers of the last century; for my father had been more than half a Jacobin, in the time when the French Republic cast its glare of promise over the world. Here, too, were the Queen Anne authors, his models, and the English novelists; but among them I found none that charmed me. Smollett, Fielding, and the like, deal too broadly with the coarse actualities of life. The best of their men and women—so merely natural, with the nature found every day—do not meet our hopes. Sometimes the simple picture, warm with life and the light of the common sun, cannot fail to charm,—as in the wedded love of Fielding's Amelia,—but it is at a later day, when the mind is trained to comparison, that we learn to prize excellence like this as it deserves. Early youth is prince-like: it will bend only to "the king, my father." Various kinds of excellence please, and leave their impression, but the most commanding, alone, is duly acknowledged at that all-exacting age.

Three great authors it was my fortune to meet at this important period,—all, though of unequal, yet congenial powers,—all of rich and wide, rather than aspiring genius,—all free to the extent of the horizon their eye took in,—all fresh with impulse, racy with experience; never to be lost sight of, or superseded, but always to be apprehended more and more.

Ever memorable is the day on which I first took a volume of Shakespeare in my hand to read. It was on a Sunday.

—This day was punctiliously set apart in our house. We had family prayers, for which there was not time on other days. Our dinners were different, and our clothes. We went to church. My father put some limitations on my reading, but—bless him for the gentleness which has left me a pleasant feeling for the day!—he did not prescribe what was, but only what was *not*, to be done. And the liberty this left was a large one. "You must not read a novel, or a play;" but all other books, the worst or best were open to me. The distinction was merely technical. The day was pleasing to me, as relieving me from the routine of tasks and recitations; it gave me freer play than usual, and there were fewer things occurred in its course, which reminded me of the divisions of time; still the church-going, where I heard nothing that had any connection with my inward life, and these rules, gave me associations with the day of empty formalities, and arbitrary restrictions; but though the forbidden book or walk always seemed more charming then, I was seldom attempted to disobey.

This Sunday—I was only eight years old—I took from the book-shelf a volume lettered Shakespeare. It was not the first time I had looked at it, but before I had been deterred from attempting to read, by the broken appearance along the page, and preferred smooth narrative. But this time I held in my hand "Romeo and Juliet" long enough to get my eye fastened to the page. It was a cold winter afternoon. I took the book to the parlor fire, and had there been seated an hour or two, when my father looked up and asked what I was reading so intently. "Shakespeare," replied the child, merely raising her eye from the page. "Shakespeare,—that won't do; that's no book for Sunday; go put it away and take another." I went as I was bid, but took no other. Returning to my seat, the unfinished story, the personages to whom I was but just introduced, thronged and burnt my brain. I could not bear it long; such a lure it was impossible to resist. I went and brought the book again. There were several guests present, and I had got half through the play before I again attracted attention. "What is that child about that she don't hear a word that's said to her?" quoth my aunt. "What are you reading?" said my father. "Shakespeare" was again the reply, in a clear, though somewhat impatient, tone. "How?" said my father angrily,—then restraining himself before his guests,—"Give me the book and go directly to bed."

Into my little room no care of his anger followed me. Alone, in the dark, I thought only of the scene placed by the poet before my eye, where the free flow of life, sudden and graceful dialogue, and forms, whether grotesque or fair, seen in the broad lustre of his imagination, gave just what I wanted, and brought home the life I seemed born to live. My fancies swarmed like bees, as I contrived the rest of the story;—what all would do, what say, where go. My confinement tortured me. I could not go forth from this prison to ask after these friends; I could not make my pillow of the dreams about them which yet I could not forbear to frame. Thus was I absorbed when my father entered. He felt it right, before going to rest, to reason with me about my disobedience, shown in a way, as he considered, so insolent. I listened, but could not feel interested in what he said, nor turn my mind from what engaged it. He went away really grieved at my impenitence, and quite at a loss to understand conduct in me so unusual.

—Often since I have seen the same misunderstanding between parent and child,—the parent thrusting the morale, the discipline, of life upon the child, when just engrossed by some game of real importance an great leadings to it. That is only a wooden horse to the father,—the child was careering to distant scenes of conquest and crusade, through a country of elsewhere unimagined beauty. None but poets remember their youth; but the father who does not retain poetical apprehension of the world, free and splendid as it stretches out before the child, who cannot read his natural history, and follow out its intimations with reverence, must be a tyrant in his home, and the purest intentions will not prevent his doing much to cramp him. Each new child is a new Thought, and has bearings and discernings, which the Thoughts older in date know not yet, but must learn.—

My attention thus fixed on Shakespeare, I returned to him at every hour I could command. Here was a counterpoise to my Romans, still more forcible than the little garden. My author could read the Roman nature too,—read it in the sternness of Coriolanus, and in the varied wealth of Caesar. But he viewed these men of will as only one kind of men; he kept them in their place, and I found that he, who could understand the Roman, yet expressed in Hamlet a deeper thought.

In Cervantes, I found far less productive talent,—indeed, a far less powerful genius,—but the same wide wisdom, a discernment piercing the shows and symbols of existence, yet rejoicing in them all, both for their own life, and as signs of the unseen reality. Not that Cervantes philosophized,—his genius was too deeply philosophical for that; he took things as they came before him, and saw their actual relations and bearings. Thus the work he produced was of deep meaning, though he might never have expressed that meaning to himself. It was left implied in the whole. A Coleridge comes and calls Don Quixote the pure Reason, and Sancho the Understanding. Cervantes made no such distinctions in his own mind; but he had seen and suffered enough to bring out all his faculties, and to make him comprehend the higher as well as the lower part of our nature. Sancho is too amusing and sagacious to be contemptible; the Don too noble and clear-sighted towards absolute truth, to be ridiculous. And we are pleased to see manifested in this way, how the lower must follow and serve the higher, despite its jeering mistrust and the stubborn realities which break up the plans of this pure-minded champion.

The effect produced on the mind is nowise that described by Byron:—

"Cervantes smiled Spain's chivalry away," &c.

On the contrary, who is not conscious of a sincere reverence for the Don, prancing forth on his gaunt steed? Who would not rather be he than any of the persons who laugh at him?—Yet the one we would wish to be is thyself, Cervantes, unconquerable spirit! gaining flavor and color like wine from every change, while being carried round the world; in whose eye the serene sagacious laughter could not be dimmed by poverty, slavery, or unsuccessful authorship. Thou art to us still more the Man, though less the Genius, than Shakespeare; thou dost not evade our sight, but, holding the lamp to thine own magic shows, dost enjoy them with us.

My third friend was Moliére, one very much lower, both in range and depth, than the others, but, as far as he goes, of the same character. Nothing secluded or partial is there about his genius,—a man of the world, and a man by himself, as he is. It was, indeed, only the poor social world of Paris that he saw, but he viewed it from the firm foundations of his manhood, and every lightest laugh rings from a clear perception, and teaches life anew.

These men were all alike in this,—they loved the *natural history* of man. Not what he should be, but what he is, was the favorite subject of their thought. Whenever a noble leading opened to the eye new paths of light, they rejoiced; but it was never fancy, but always fact, that inspired them. They loved a thorough penetration of the murkiest dens, and most tangled paths of nature; they did not spin from the desires of their own special natures, but reconstructed the world from materials which they collected on every side. Thus their influence upon me was not to prompt me to follow out thought in myself so much as to detect it everywhere, for each of these men is not only a nature, but a happy interpreter of many natures. They taught me to distrust all invention which is not based on a wide experience. Perhaps, too, they taught me to overvalue an outward experience at the expense of inward growth; but all this I did not appreciate till later.

It will be seen that my youth was not unfriended, since those great minds came to me in kindness. A moment of action in one's self, however, is worth an age of apprehension through others; not that our deeds are better, but that they produce a renewal of our being. I have had more productive moments and of deeper joy, but never hours of more tranquil pleasure than those in which these demi-gods visited me,—and with a smile so familiar, that I imagined the world to be full of such. They did me good, for by them a standard was early given of sight and thought, from which I could never go back, and beneath which I cannot suffer patiently my own life or that of any friend to fall. They did me harm, too, for the child fed with meat instead of milk becomes too soon mature. Expectations and desires were thus early raised, after which I must long toil before they can be realized. How poor the scene around, how tame ones own existence, how meagre and faint every power, with these beings in my mind! Often I must cast them quite aside in order to grow in my small way, and not sink into despair. Certainly I do not wish that instead of these masters I had read baby books, written down to children, and with such ignorant dullness that they blunt the senses and corrupt the tastes of the still plastic human being. But I do wish that I had read no books at all till later,—that I had lived with toys, and played in the open air. Children should not cull the fruits of reflection and observation early, but expand in the sun, and let thoughts come to them. They should not through books antedate their actual experiences, but should take them gradually, as sympathy and interpretation are needed. With me, much of life was devoured in the bud.

FIRST FRIEND.

For a few months, this bookish and solitary life was invaded by interest in a living, breathing figure. At church, I used to look around with a feeling of coldness and disdain, which, though I now well understand its causes, seems to my wiser mind as odious as it was unnatural. The puny child sought everywhere for the Roman or Shakespeare figures, and she was met by the shrewd, honest eye, the homely decency, or the smartness of a New England village on Sunday. There was beauty, but I could not see it then; it was not of the kind I longed for. In the next pew sat a family who were my especial aversion. There were five daughters, the eldest not above four-and-twenty,—yet they had the old fairy knowing look, hard, dry, dwarfed, strangers to the All-Fair,—were working-day residents in this beautiful planet. They looked as if their thoughts had never strayed beyond the jobs of the day, and they were glad of it. Their mother was one of those shrunken, faded patterns of woman who have never done anything to keep smooth the cheek and dignify the brow. The father had a Scotch look of shrewd narrowness, and entire self-complacency. I could not endure this family, whose existence contradicted all my visions; yet I could not forbear looking at them.

As my eye one day was ranging about with its accustomed coldness, and the proudly foolish sense of being in a shroud of thoughts that were not their thoughts, it was arrested by a face most fair, and well-known as it seemed at first glance,—for surely I had met her before and waited for her long. But soon I saw that she was a new apparition foreign to that scene, if not to me. Her dress,—the arrangement of her hair, which had the graceful pliancy of races highly cultivated for long,—the intelligent and full picture of her eye, whose reserve was in its self-possession, not in timidity,—all combined to make up a whole impression, which, though too young to understand, I was well prepared to feel.

How wearisome now appears that thorough-bred *millefleur* beauty, the distilled result of ages of European culture! Give me rather the wild heath on the lonely hill-side, than such a rose-tree from the daintily clipped garden. But, then, I had but tasted the cup, and knew not how little it could satisfy; more, more, was all my cry; continued through years, till I had been at the very fountain. Indeed, it was a ruby-red, a perfumed draught, and I need not abuse the wine because I prefer water, but merely say I have had enough of it. Then, the first sight, the first knowledge of such a person was intoxication.

She was an English lady, who, by a singular chance, was cast upon this region for a few months. Elegant and captivating, her every look and gesture was tuned to a different pitch from anything I had ever known. She was in various ways "accomplished," as it is called, though to what degree I cannot now judge. She painted in oils;—I had never before seen any one use the brush, and days would not have been too long for me to watch the pictures growing beneath her hand. She played the harp; and its tones are still to me the heralds of the promised land I saw before me then. She rose, she looked, she spoke; and the gentle swaying motion she made all through life has gladdened memory, as the stream does the woods and meadows.

As she was often at the house of one of our neighbors, and afterwards at our own, my thoughts were fixed on her with all the force of my nature. It was my first real interest in my kind, and it engrossed me wholly. I had seen her,—I should see her,—and my mind lay steeped in the visions that flowed from this source. My task-work I went through with, as I have done on similar occasions all my life, aided by pride that could not bear to fail, or to be questioned. Could I cease from doing the work of the day, and hear the reason sneeringly given,—"Her head is so completely taken up with—that she can do nothing?" Impossible.

Should the first love be blighted, they say, the mind loses its sense of eternity. All forms of existence seem fragile, the prison of time real, for a god is dead. Equally true is this of friendship. I thank Heaven that this first feeling was permitted its free flow. The years that lay between the woman and the girl only brought her beauty into perspective, and enabled me to see her as I did the mountains from my window, and made her presence to me a gate of Paradise. That which she was, that which she brought, that which she might have brought, were mine, and over a whole region of new life I ruled proprietor of the soil in my own right.

Her mind was sufficiently unoccupied to delight in my warm devotion. She could not know what it was to me, but the light cast by the flame through so delicate a vase cheered and charmed her. All who saw admired her in their way; but she would lightly turn her head from their hard or oppressive looks, and fix a glance of full-eyed sweetness on the child, who, from a distance, watched all her looks and motions. She did not say much to me—not much to any one; she spoke in her whole being rather than by chosen words. Indeed, her proper speech was dance or song, and what was less expressive did not greatly interest her. But she saw much, having in its perfection the woman's delicate sense for sympathies and attractions. We walked in the fields, alone. Though others were present, her eyes were gliding over all the field and plain for the objects of beauty to which she was of kin. She was not cold to her seeming companions; a sweet courtesy satisfied them, but it hung about her like her mantle that she wore without thinking of it; her thoughts were free, for these civilized beings call really live two lives at the same moment. With them she seemed to be, but her hand was given to the child at her side; others did not observe me, but to her I was the only human presence. Like a guardian spirit she led me through the fields and groves, and every tree, every bird greeted me, and said, what I felt, "She is the first angel of your life."

One time I had been passing the afternoon with her. She had been playing to me on the harp, and I sat listening in happiness almost unbearable. Some guests were announced. She went into another room to receive them, and I took up her book. It was Guy Mannering, then lately published, and the first of Scott's novels I had ever seen. I opened where her mark lay, and read merely with the feeling of continuing our mutual existence by passing my eyes over the same page where hers had been. It was the description of the rocks on the sea-coast where the little Harry Bertram was lost. I had never seen such places, and my mind was vividly stirred to imagine them. The scene rose before me, very unlike reality, doubtless, but majestic and wild. I was the little Harry Bertram, and had lost her,—all I had to lose,—and sought her vainly in long dark caves that had no end, plashing through the water; while the crags beetled above, threatening to fall and crush the poor child. Absorbed in the painful vision, tears rolled down my cheeks. Just then she entered with light step, and full-beaming eye. When she saw me thus, a soft cloud stole over her face, and clothed every feature with a lovelier tenderness than I had seen there before. She did not question, but fixed on me inquiring looks of beautiful love. I laid my head against her shoulder and wept,—dimly feeling that I must lose her and all,—all who spoke to me of the same things,—that the cold wave must rush over me. She waited till my tears were spent, then rising took from a little box a bunch of golden amaranths or everlasting flowers, and gave them to me. They were very fragrant. "They came," she said, "from Madeira," These flowers stayed with me seventeen years. "Madeira" seemed to me the fortunate isle, apart in the blue ocean from all of ill or dread. Whenever I saw a sail passing in the distance,—if it bore itself with fullness of beautiful certainty,—I felt that it was going to Madeira. Those thoughts are all gone now. No Madeira exists for me now,—no fortunate purple isle,—and all these hopes and fancies are lifted from the sea into the sky. Yet I thank the charms that fixed them here so long,—fixed there till perfumes like those of the golden flowers were drawn from the earth, teaching me to know my birth-place.

I can tell little else of this time,—indeed, I remember little, except the state of feeling in which I lived. For I *lived,* and when this is the case, there is little to tell in the form of thought. We meet—at least those who are true to their instincts meet—a succession of persons through our lives, all of whom have some peculiar errand to us. There is an outer circle, whose existence we perceive, but with whom we stand in no real relation. They tell us the news, they act on us in the offices of society, they show us kindness and aversion; but their influence does not penetrate; we are nothing to them, nor they to us, except as a part of the world's furniture. Another circle, within this, are dear and near to us. We know them and of what kind they are. They are to us not mere facts, but intelligible thoughts of the divine mind. We like to see how they are unfolded; we like to meet them and part from them; we like their action upon us and the pause that succeeds and enables us to appreciate its quality. Often we leave them on our path, and return no more, but we bear them in our memory, tales which have been told, and whose meaning has been felt.

But yet a nearer group there are, beings born under the same star, and bound with us in a common destiny. These are not mere acquaintances, mere friends, but, when we meet, are sharers of our very existence. There is no separation; the same thought is given at the same moment to both,—indeed, it is born of the meeting, and would not otherwise have been called into existence at all. These not only know themselves more, but *are* more for having met, and regions of their being, which would else have laid sealed in cold obstruction, burst into leaf and bloom and song.

The times of these meetings are fated, nor will either party be able ever to meet any other person in the same way. Both seem to rise at a glance into that part of the heavens where the word can be spoken, by which they are revealed to one another and to themselves. The step in being thus gained, can never be lost, nor can it be re-trod; for neither party will be again what the other wants. They are no longer fit to interchange mutual influence, for they do not really need it, and if they think they do, it is because they weakly pine after a past pleasure.

To this inmost circle of relations but few are admitted, because some prejudice or lack of courage has prevented the many from listening to their instincts the first time they manifested themselves. If the voice is once disregarded it becomes fainter each time, till, at last, it is wholly silenced, and the man lives in this world, a stranger to its real life, deluded like the maniac who fancies he has attained his throne, while in reality he is on a bed of musty straw. Yet, if the voice finds a listener and servant the first time of speaking, it is encouraged to more and more clearness. Thus it was with me,—from no merit of mine, but because I had the good fortune to be free enough to yield to my impressions. Common ties had not bound me; there were no traditionary notions in my mind; I believed in nothing merely because others believed in it; I had taken no feelings on trust. Thus my mind was open to their sway.

This woman came to me, a star from the east, a morning star, and I worshipped her. She too was elevated by that worship, and her fairest self called out. To the mind she brought assurance that there was a region congenial with its tendencies and tastes, a region of elegant culture and intercourse, whose object, fulfilled or not, was to gratify the sense of beauty, not the mere utilities of life. In our relation she was lifted to the top of her being. She had known many celebrities, had roused to passionate desire many hearts, and became afterwards a wife; but I do not believe she ever more truly realized her best self than towards the lonely child whose heaven she was, whose eye she met, and whose possibilities she predicted. "He raised me," said a woman inspired by love, "upon the pedestal of his own high thoughts, and wings came at once, but I did not fly away. I stood there with downcast eyes worthy of his love, for he had made me so."

Thus we do always for those who inspire us to expect from them the best. That which they are able to be, they become, because we demand it of them. "We expect the impossible—and find it."

My English friend went across the sea. She passed into her former life, and into ties that engrossed her days. But she has never ceased to think of me. Her thoughts turn forcibly back to the child who was to her all she saw of the really New World. On the promised coasts she had found only cities, careful men and women, the aims and habits of ordinary life in her own land, without that elegant culture which she, probably, over estimated, because it was her home. But in the mind of the child she found the fresh prairie, the untrodden forests for which she had longed. I saw in her the storied castles, the fair stately parks and the wind laden with tones from the past, which I desired to know. We wrote to one another for many years;—her shallow and delicate epistles did not disenchant me, nor did she fail to see something of the old poetry in my rude characters and stammering speech. But we must never meet again.

When this friend was withdrawn I fell into a profound depression. I knew not how to exert myself, but lay bound hand and foot. Melancholy enfolded me in an atmosphere, as joy had done. This suffering, too, was out of the gradual and natural course. Those who are really children could not know such love, or feel such sorrow. "I am to blame," said my father, "in keeping her at home so long merely to please myself. She needs to be with other girls, needs play and variety. She does not seem to me really sick, but dull rather. She eats nothing, you say. I see she grows thin. She ought to change the scene."

I was indeed *dull.* The books, the garden, had lost all charm. I had the excuse of headache, constantly, for not attending to my lessons. The light of life was set, and every leaf was withered. At such an early age there are no back or side scenes where the mind, weary and sorrowful, may retreat. Older, we realize the width of the world more, and it is not easy to despair on any point. The effort at thought to which we are compelled relieves and affords a dreary retreat, like hiding in a brick-kiln till the shower be over. But then all joy seemed to have departed with my friend, and the emptiness of our house stood revealed. This I had not felt while I every day expected to see or had seen her, or annoyance and dullness were unnoticed or swallowed up in the one thought that clothed my days with beauty. But now she was gone and I was roused from habits of reading or reverie to feel the fiery temper of the soul, and to learn that it must have vent, that it would not be pacified by shadows, neither meet without consuming what lay around it. I avoided the table as much as possible, took long walks and lay in bed, or on the floor of my room. I complained of my head, and it was not wrong to do so, for a sense of dullness and suffocation, if not pain, was there constantly.

But when it was proposed that I should go to school, that was a remedy I could not listen to with patience for a moment. The peculiarity of my education had separated me entirely from the girls around, except that when they were playing at active games, I would sometimes go out and join them. I liked violent bodily exercise, which always relieved my nerves. But I had no success in associating with them beyond the mere play. Not only I was not their school-mate, but my book-life and lonely habits had given a cold aloofness to my whole expression, and veiled my manner with a hauteur which turned all hearts away. Yet, as this reserve was superficial, and rather ignorance than arrogance, it produced no deep dislike. Besides, the girls supposed me really superior to themselves, and did not hate me for feeling it, but neither did they like me, nor wish to have me with them. Indeed, I had gradually given up all such wishes myself; for they seemed to me rude, tiresome, and childish, as I did to them dull and strange. This experience had been earlier, before I was admitted to any real friendship; but now that I had been lifted into the life of mature years, and into just that atmosphere of European life to which I had before been tending, the thought of sending me to school filled me with disgust.

Yet what could I tell my father of such feelings? I resisted all I could, but in vain. He had no faith in medical aid generally, and justly saw that this was no occasion for its use. He thought I needed change of scene, and to be roused to activity by other children. "I have kept you at home," he said, "because I took such pleasure in teaching you myself, and besides I knew that you would learn faster with one who is so desirous to aid you. But you will learn fast enough wherever you are, and you ought to be more with others of your own age. I shall soon hear that you are better, I trust."

7

"Testimony" Given in Canada (1855)

Harriet Tubman

HARRIET TUBMAN (c. 1820–1913) was born a plantation
slave in Maryland. Growing up in the southern slavery system, she
observed its brutality when two older sisters were taken away to a
chain gang. Married to John Tubman, but childless, she fled to the
North in 1849, possibly with the help of a white woman (Humez
16–18), and vowed to liberate her entire family through dangerous
trips back south for each of them. Sustained by her family's spiritual
practices and Christian beliefs, despite the hypocrisy of antebellum
churches, she affiliated with the abolitionist movement in Philadelphia
and began working with the Quaker community in the Underground
Railroad, earning the name "Moses."

Her success in bringing her entire family north to Auburn, New
York, after time in Canada won her acclaim in antislavery networks.
She encountered Frederick Douglass, John Brown, William Wells
Brown, and other black antislavery activists as she gave speeches
around the Northeast (Humez 29–37). Tubman also associated with
the growing women's rights movement, arguing for the importance
of the work done by women of African origin. During the Civil War
she served in the Union Army as a spy and scout in the South and
afterward, as a nurse, she aided newly freed women in the refugee
camps. Injured when a train conductor ejected her from a railroad car,

Tubman criticized the violence and inequities that persisted during Reconstruction. The violence included the murder of her estranged husband and the perpetrator's acquittal, which mobilized a drive for black male suffrage (Humez 76–77).

Living in Auburn, Tubman, who never learned to read or write, collaborated on a memoir with Sarah Hopkins Bradford as a fundraising project. While *Scenes in the Life of Harriet Tubman* (1869), telling her story as a former slave, depicts Tubman sentimentally as a "suffering saint," its reissue as *Harriet, the Moses of Her People* (1886) offers insight, if highly mediated, into her sense of being "a stranger in a strange land" (Humez 85, 94). In her later years Tubman spoke at gatherings around Auburn on behalf of women's suffrage, telling tales of women's brave deeds during the war. She was welcomed at the founding convention of the National Association of Colored Women (1896) and was hailed as a heroic figure. In 1908 the Tubman Home was dedicated in Auburn.

The first-person testimony from Tubman included here is a version of the oral storytelling of her life that Tubman performed at fundraisers, with eloquent gestures and scriptural references, to enthralled audiences. In this transcribed form it mixes the writer's perspective with Tubman's and is not her unmediated life narrative, although as a text dictated to Benjamin Drew (who published it in *The Refugee: or, a North-Side View of Slavery* [cited in Humez, 279–80]), it was closely under her control.

"Testimony"

I grew up like a neglected weed,—ignorant of liberty, having no experience of it. Then I was not happy or contented; every time I saw a white man I was afraid of being carried away.

I had two sisters carried away in a chain-gang,—one of them left two children. We were always uneasy.

Now I've been free, I know what a dreadful condition slavery is. I have seen hundreds of escaped slaves, but I never saw one who was willing to go back and be a slave.

I have no opportunity to see my friends in my native land. We would rather stay in our native land, if we could be as free there as we are here.

I think slavery is the next thing to hell. If a person would send another into bondage, he would, it appears to me, be bad enough to send him into hell, if he could.

8

"A Brief Narrative of the Life of Mrs. Adele M. Jewel" (1869)

ADELE M. JEWEL

ADELE M. JEWEL (née George; 1834–?) was born deaf in Cincinnati in 1834. At the age of three, she and her family moved to Michigan and bought a farm where they lived for nine years. At her father's death, she and her mother were forced to sell the farm to pay debts. Jewel and her mother then moved to Jackson, Michigan, where Jewel met and befriended Almena Knight. Knight became Jewel's mentor and encouraged her to attend the Michigan School for the Deaf in Flint. Shortly thereafter, Jewel had to withdraw from the school due to severe illness that left her disabled and partially blind. Left without means of support, Jewel and her invalid mother became homeless. In response to these hardships, Jewel was inspired to write a pamphlet about her life to raise money for herself and her mother. Jewel sold her story on the streets, generating enough money to provide a living for herself and her mother. Shortly after the publication of her pamphlet, Jewel married and subsequently had three children—two daughters and a deaf son. Not much is known about her marriage except that it was unhappy. When the marriage ended, Jewel, as a single mother, again used the pamphlet to support her family and to send her son to the Michigan School for the Deaf. While the exact date of the pamphlet's publication is unknown, it was probably published first in the mid-1850s. Over the years she expanded the work and sold revised editions. The following edition was published by Dr. Chase's Steam Printing House in 1869.

The emergence of disability studies in the last decade has led to reawakened interest in Jewel's narrative, an excerpt of which is published in *A Mighty Change: An Anthology of Deaf American Writing, 1816–1864*, edited by Christopher Krentz.

Please read this.

A Brief Narrative of the Life of Mrs. Adele M. Jewel (Being Deaf and Dumb.)

"As you would that others should do unto you, do ye even so unto them."

Mrs. Jewel presents this little sketch of her life, as a means of support, with the hope of meeting with friends, and some degree of sympathy from the benevolent and traveling public.

Ann Arbor, Mich:

Dr. Chase's Steam Printing House, 41 & 43 N. Main St.

1869.

"A Brief Narrative of the Life of Mrs. Adele M. Jewel"

Preface.

Many years ago, I first became acquainted with Adele M. George. She was at that time a lovely and intelligent little girl of ten summers, with bright, laughing eyes, and an artless, winning manner that quite charmed us, and we soon became very fond of her, for the dear child was a mute. As she was the only child of her doting parents, nothing that could impart pleasure, or make her comfortable and happy was denied, to make up as far as possible for the great blessing of which nature had deprived her. Indeed, she seemed hardly to have a wish ungratified. Such is the beautiful picture our memory presents of her childhood. At length her family moved westward, and we lost sight, for a time, of the little deaf and dumb girl. And when we met, nearly fourteen years after, we were surprised and pleased at her improvement, and yet grieved at the change in her circumstances. She had become a lovely and accomplished young lady. Having acquired an education at Flint, she was interesting and communicative. Conversing rapidly, in the sign language, to those who understood that method of speaking, or writing in a clear and graceful hand with a pencil, to others. But sorrows had fallen heavily upon herself and home. Sickness had deprived her of the use of one eye—and death had robbed her of an indulgent father, and left her solely to the care of an invalid mother. They had lost their property, and were now without even a home of their own. In their straightened circumstances, Adele conceived the idea of writing a little history of her life, and offering it to a sympathizing public as the only means afforded of supporting herself and mother. The plan succeeded, through the aid of a few interested friends, and for some years she thus secured a comfortable living, and might have continued in well-doing, but for an unfortunate marriage, which has left her again dependent upon her aged mother, with three little helpless children upon her hands, the eldest, a mute, like herself. Thus she is again thrown upon her own resources for support.

Friends of the unfortunate, I appeal to your sympathies and aid for this dear child of affliction. Let me assure you that she is *every way worthy* of your patronage and your kind wishes. By purchasing this little book, containing a brief history of her life, you may find something that will amuse or interest yourselves, and at the same time lighten the burden that lies so heavily upon her frail shoulders. Do not pass her coldly by. It is but a trifle in itself, but every purchaser lends a hand in making a sad heart happy; and that Heaven will bless and reward you is the sincere prayer of

A Friend.

[Part One]

The history of my life is made up more of thought and feeling than of incidents and events. It is brief and simple, and yet may be interesting to those who are curious enough to know how the world and its experiences are regarded by one who can neither hear nor speak. I know that there are many kind hearts ever open in sympathy for the sorrowful and afflicted, and those I am sure will give me hearing, as I am one of the afflicted. It is the will of God that some of his children should be forever excluded from the sweet sights and sounds of earth. Why, we know not, only that it *is* so; and it remains for us who are thus, to "Be still and know that he is God." And though we cannot understand it, we must believe that it is all for the best. I was born deaf, on the 15th of November, 1834, in the city of Cincinnati, though I do not remember much before our removal to Detroit, in the year 1838. Among my early acquaintances was a little girl nearly my own age, Charlotte Monroe. We became warm friends from the first, and were seldom separated from morning till night. Our plays, our toys, everything we had, was shared in common; and by the use of our own signs—a language taught by nature—we understood each other very well. They tell me that she ran in to her mother, saying, in a voice of gladness, "Ma, I can talk deaf and dumb as good as Dellie."

My father had a tame black bear chained up in the yard. He was harmless, at least, we believed him so, and were not afraid to play near him, and even sometimes to pat him on the head,—I and my little friend Lottie. But he soon taught us not to be quite so familiar. We used to feed him apples and cake, and were delighted when we could make him show his teeth, or climb the pole, or rear upon his hind legs. One day (I shall never forget that) I had a piece of cake in my hand, which I held temptingly before him, though I had no intention of dividing with him, and frequently disappointed him by drawing it back. He became enraged at last, and seizing me in his arms, he tore my clothes off in an instant, and would have killed me had not my shrieks brought me instant relief. My father dared not keep so dangerous a pet, and soon disposed of him.

Lottie and myself were up to a great many mischievous pranks, which caused our friends considerable troublesome times, I fear. I laugh now when I think of them; but I have not seen her in a good many years, and they tell me that she is married and the mother of four children. I can never think of her except as a little fun-loving girl.

When a few years older, my parents removed from Detroit to Grass Lake, on the Central Railroad. There I found myself among strangers, and longed for the friends of my other home. It seemed as if no one would ever understand me as Lottie did, and I missed her sadly. But I was not long left to pine in solitude. Dear Polly Ann Osgood, I soon learned to love her as well. We grew up together like sisters. How many delightful rambles we had about the fields and forest, gathering berries and other fruits, and weaving the sweet wild flowers into garlands to crown our heads; and although I could not hear the warbling of birds, my little friend did, and she tried to make me understand it.

I was always charmed with the scenes of nature, and have been out for hours alone watching with an exultant heart the skimming swallow, the green meadows, the rippling streams, the waving forest. The glad sunshine, the cooling breeze, and the flying clouds were all subjects to me of wonder and delight, and I longed to know more of them and their Author. Who made the beautiful world and who made *us*?

My young mind was filled with thoughts all unexpressed and inexpressible. Deep, fervent and glowing, I longed to worship *something*, I knew not who or what. My dear mother was constantly importuned with questions, who made the grass and the flowers and all the living creatures that throng the earth? The sky, with its shifting clouds, its glowing sun, its mild moon, and its myriad stars?

Oh how I yearned for the knowledge to illumine my darkened mind. My mother, as well as she was able, explained to me that One who dwells above made them all; and that I must kneel and raise my eyes, hands and heart in adoration. Oh, I thought "If I *could* only see him." But since I have been able to read His Holy Word, I have learned more of Him. I have learned to worship Him in spirit and in truth; the only true worship, for He is a Spirit and comprehends the language of the heart though the lips move not.

While dwelling in Grass Lake an event took place that I shall never forget, the remembrance of it even now fills me with horror. My father used sometimes to pour powder upon the hearth to make it flash for my amusement. I think he did not know what a mad-cap I was, or he would hardly have thought it prudent to set me such an example.

One day I was left at home alone, and I got the powder, and sprinkling it about the floor set it on fire. It flashed in earnest, setting fire to everything. I had on a flannel dress, fortunately, or I might have flashed with the rest. But I caught my little dog in my arms, and drew my father's trunk to the door. It was very heavy, and I could not lift it over the sill. So I was obliged to leave it and run more than a quarter of a mile to the house of the nearest neighbor to give the alarm.

When they reached the house the roof had fallen in, and the house with all its contents was consumed. When my mother and father came home, there was no home to receive them. My dear father had taught his foolish little dumb girl a trick that had robbed him of it; though they did not know it then. I could not explain the cause of the fire, and they were so happy to find that I had not also perished in the flames, they thought little of their great loss in the house, though many valuable papers and other articles were destroyed which were never replaced. After I learned to write, however, I gave my mother a faithful account of my part in the affair.

When about twelve years of age I was sent to a common school. I tried as hard as I could to learn, but it was a dry, tedious process, as my teacher was not qualified to instruct the dumb, and I gave it up in despair; feeling, oh how bitterly, that I was not like the rest and could never hope to acquire as much knowledge.

I had an uncle who wished to take me to the Deaf and Dumb Asylum in New York; but my father's health was fast failing, and as I am an only child, my mother could not endure the thought of separation, and that project was also relinquished. And I, much as I longed for a more enlarged and cultivated sphere, much as I hungered and thirsted for a high knowledge of the world in which I lived, was brought up wild and wayward, with no definite understanding of my relation to the world, or the duties required of me. My young heart was brimful of love and holy aspirations, and I fought and rebelled against the small compass of surrounding circumstances that hedged me about, yet knew not how the evil could be overcome.

About this time it became evident to all—all but me—that my father's days on earth were numbered. I had never seen a person die, and death to me was a subject upon which I had never thought. To *die*! what was it? I saw the change upon his face. I saw the last dying glance of his eyes as the film gathered o'er them. I felt the last grasp of his icy fingers—then he lay cold and motionless. It was a sight so terrible that I clung frightened to my mother. And yet I could not believe that I must give him up. I believed the change only temporary. It seemed to me that he would rise up again, and speak to us, and live as before. But long hours and days passed away and the change came not. Then they placed his rigid body in a long box, and screwed the lid down tightly, and buried him up in the earth.

What did it all mean? Was this death? Oh how terrible. How could people ever be happy when they knew that sometime they must die? They tried to explain to me that some part of him was still alive and gone to God. But I shook my head. No, God lives up in the sky, and I saw him buried in the ground, I said. They told me that it was "only the poor wasted body which was buried, that the part of man that *never* dies, the spirit, had gone to God." I thought it was cruel in God to deprive me of so beloved a parent, and I could not feel reconciled. That was my first sorrow. But after a little while my dearest friend, Polly

Ann, sickened and died also. She was taken away and buried, and I became so hopeless and disconsolate that I hardly cared to live myself. I was sullen, gloomy and resentful. I refused to look upon the lovely face of nature and take heart for the future. All things had ceased to charm me—"what are they all good for if we must die and leave them?" I thought. It seemed to me that if God could do as he pleased with all the world, he could not be good to deprive the poor little mute of some of her dearest friends, rendering her life so dark and cheerless. I visited the graves of my dead friends, mourned and wept over them with a sorrow that refused to be comforted.

A knowledge of God's love and what he has done for me was unknown to me then; but after I was taught to read his Holy Word, many things, once so dark and mysterious have been revealed to me. I have found it a fountain of living waters, from which I can drink deep draughts of light and truth, and my soul is satisfied. It fortifies my weak soul against the sins and sorrows of this life and enables me to do my duty with a cheerful heart.

I have confidence in God's love towards mankind, and in his wisdom and goodness which rules and directs all things. I have had many crosses in life to bear, but I will lean upon his Mighty Arm, so strong to save and he will save me. "Yes, though he *slay* me, yet will I trust in Him."

After my father's death, my mother and myself were left quite alone and found it hard to get along on the farm. So we sold it, and after paying all the debts contracted during his long sickness, there was little left for ourselves, and we moved to Jackson, where we endeavored to obtain sewing or any kind of work that would enable us to get an honest living. We lived in that city three years and during that time found several good, true friends who did all they could to aid us. Here I formed the acquaintance of a young lady also deaf and dumb, who had been educated at an Asylum in Ohio. She was the first mute I ever saw and the mysterious ties of sympathy immediately established a friendly feeling between us. I was surprised and delighted at her superior attainments.

She could write a beautiful hand on her slate to those who knew not the use of signs, and in a little while taught me the sign language by which we conversed very easily together. We enjoyed many pleasant seasons together, and I shall always count among my dearest friends, Miss Almena Knight, the name of this young lady. Many of our readers doubtless are already familiar with her little history.

After I saw Miss Knight I grew very anxious to become a pupil at Flint. Some friends who felt interested in my welfare, obtained my mother's consent and assisted me to go. Thanks for the instructions received of Miss Knight, I succeeded in making myself understood, and from being an entire stranger, soon became as a member of one large family. My instructors found me an "apt scholar," and when I had been there ten weeks, I sent home a written article of my own composition. My friends were surprised and pleased at the rapid progress I had made.

Elsie Fairbairn was my especial friend among the pupils; we became warmly attached and seldom separated. The parents of friend "Eppy," as I called her, were also true friends to me, and did many things to show their kindness to myself and mother. I shall always remember them with gratitude.

During my stay at Flint I was taken with inflammation in my eyes, causing me great suffering and destroying the sight of one. My health became poor, and I was obliged to withdraw from the school. I resigned my place with much regret, as I still felt greatly deficient in useful knowledge. The loss of my sight is a great loss to me, still I am thankful for the blessings I do enjoy; for though poor and with slender means of support, I have laid up my treasures in Heaven; looking forward to that glorious time when the mute tongue shall burst forth in strains of love and praise to its Creator in a world of peace and joy. When the lame can walk, the blind shall see, the deaf hear, and the dumb shall speak. All will be right there—no aching heart, no saddened countenance. What a comfort it is for me to believe thus!

> We speak of the realms of the blest
> Of that country so bright and so fair,
> And oft are its glories confest;
> But what must it be to be there?
>
> We speak of its pathway of gold,
> And its walls decked with jewels so rare
> Of its wonders and pleasures untold;
> But what must it be to be there?
>
> We speak of its freedom from sin,
> From sorrow, temptation and care,
> From trials without and within;
> But what must it be to be there?
>
> We speak of its service of love,
> Of the robes which the glorified wear,

Of the church of the first-born above
But what must it be to be there?

Then let us, midst pleasure and woe,
Still for heaven our spirits prepare;
And shortly we all shall know
And feel what it is to be there![1]

―――――――

Abide with me! Fast falls the eventide,
The darkness deepens—Lord with me abide!
When other helpers fail, and comforts flee
Help of the helpless, oh, abide with me!

Swift to its close ebbs out life's little day;
Earth's joys grow dim; its glories pass away;
Change and decay in all around I see;
Oh, Thou who changes not, abide with me!

I heed Thy presence every passing hour;
What but Thy grace can foil the tempter's power?
Who like Thyself my guide and stay can be?
On to the close, oh Lord abide with me![2]

Part Second.

Dear Reader:

Let me add a few more pages to the brief sketch you have just read of my life, which was written over four years ago. It was a great undertaking for me to publish for perusal by the public a history of my life, and then offer it for sale. I shrunk from it, and could never have done so, had it not been really necessary for me to do something for my own maintenance. But though sometimes chilled by averted looks and want of sympathy, I have found many ready and willing to extend the helping hand; many earnest, true friends who have aided and encouraged me. The son of Mr. Barns, my former publisher (who is a true gentleman, has also been afflicted with deafness, though not mute), and the

1. The first two stanzas of this hymn are taken from a popular hymn, "We speak of the realms of the blest," written by Elizabeth K. Mills in 1829.

2. Here Jewel quotes from the first, second, and sixth stanzas of a hymn by Henry F. Lyte written in 1847 entitled "Abide with me."

printers in the *Tribune* office, made me a present of the first thousand copies of my little book and a few dollars in money to help me on. Words fail to express my gratitude for this kindness, but I shall ever cherish for them the most grateful remembrance. By this means I was enabled to secure a home for myself and mother.

R. N. Rice, a gentleman widely known for his Christian virtues and his benevolence, has gained my gratitude by doing much to assist me.

And now I will tell you what I have seen in my travels. Many things very interesting and wonderful to me. Thank Heaven for sight, precious sight! To the deaf it is both hearing and speech. I have only the full enjoyment of one eye—the other is still so dim that I cannot distinguish objects with it. But the sight I do have is invaluable to me. Some of my blind friends seem very cheerful, and even happy. Yet pleasures which sight secures can never be theirs. The faces of beloved friends, beaming with smiles of affection—the green fields—the beautiful flowers—the trees waving in the summer winds, white with blossoms or laden with ripe fruits—the broad, winding river sparkling in the sun, while boats of every shape and size glide over its bosom. How endless are the objects presented to the eye of a traveler. How I love to watch the changes in the beautiful blue sky bending so lovingly over us; now so clear that scarcely the softest shadow of a cloud is seen; then covered with white, fast-sailing clouds or clouds at rest, tinted with the hues of the rainbow. Then we have the fierce dark rain clouds, with vivid lightning passing through them. Then at night when the sky is clear how all ablaze it seems with its millions of stars. These objects are familiar with all, but I am afraid we do not think as much as we should of Him who made them. Oh how we ought to love and adore One whose wisdom and goodness is so manifest in all His works. The most wonderful sight I ever beheld, a sight that made me tremble and worship God, was the Falls of Niagara. Such a great river, pouring over such a descent! It made me dizzy to look at it; and it shook the earth far and near. What a dreadful thing it must be to go over the Falls. As I stood upon the bank and watched the foaming spray, and heard its awful thunder—for even the deaf can hear that—my guide pointed out the log just above the falls, that Mr. Avery clung to in despair, out of reach of all human help. Thousands of spectators gathered on the shore anxious and eager to extend assistance, but in vain. The tide was so rapid it would have been madness to attempt to reach him with a boat; no ropes could be thrown far enough, and after remaining there for many hours, the strength of the unfortunate man failed, and he went over, down, into the foaming cataract many hundred feet, and was never seen more.

My guide told me, also, of the fate of the steamer Caroline. Fired by the Canadians and sent over the Falls. He said it was enveloped in flames and it looked grand as it was plunged into the foaming abyss.

We saw Fereni walk a tight-rope across the river while at the Falls. A great many people assembled to witness the feat. Fereni walked away steadily until half way across—then he fell! We all thought he was gone forever. But by a dexterous movement he caught by one hand and saved himself. Then he got upon his feet again and walked across. I could hardly breathe until he was safe upon the ground again. I do not like to see people get into such dangerous places. It seems to me as if they were defying death. But this man had walked across many times without accidents, and he had grown careless.

We saw many Indians and Squaws sitting about on the shore, with their little children playing about them. Many of them were nearly white and very pretty. They were employed with bead-work, which they wrought with great ingenuity, and offered for sale to visitors. I brought away several little relics which I prize highly.

The Suspension Bridge is a wonderful structure. In the distance it looked like a spider-web. It seems almost incredible that such a bridge could be built strong enough to bear up a heavily loaded train of cars. Yet it is true. It would be fearful to fall at such a time!

At the Suspension Bridge we found an Asylum for the deaf, dumb, and blind. It was a private school kept by Dr. Skinner and his wife. The Doctor had been blind two years—his wife, though she could see, was a mute. This worthy couple, though white themselves, were deeply interested in the poor colored children afflicted like themselves, and their pupils are all colored. Those who could see had bright sparkling eyes, and were quiet and respectful. The blind were very tidy and attentive. They all seemed very contented and happy, and it was interesting to see the dumb scholars converse with their blind associates.

The institution is supported partly by donations and contributions from those who sympathize in the good work, and partly by the publication of a paper—the work is done by the pupils who are printers and compositors.

We came away much pleased with our visit and praying for success and prosperity of the Asylum, and for the welfare of the generous instructors and founders.

At the Suspension Bridge we took the cars for Portage, passing, on our road, Perry, Wyoming and several other little villages. When we left the cars and took a carriage, our way lay along a high ridge of hills. The carriage track was very narrow, with scarcely a foot space between it and a frightful precipice on one side, and a high, steep bank on the other. I trembled and clung to the side of the carriage, fearing every moment to be dashed to destruction—a single mis-step of the horses, or mismanagement on the part of the driver, making such a result inevitable. But we passed over safely. Every now and then entering some densely wooded dingle or tangled wild, which made it seem as if we were hundreds of miles from any human habitation, and then a sudden turn in the road would reveal the most enchanting little village imaginable, nestled in a warm valley at our feet; we could look directly down upon the roofs of some of them. It seemed to me like fairy land. Thus we were several times surprised and delighted during our ride.

The Portage Falls, though much smaller than Niagara, looked very beautiful, flying and flashing in the sunlight, and pouring its sheet of white foam down the rocks.

Messenger's Hollow was another beautiful town, situated at the foot of the Alleghany Mountains. Indeed, I could fill a large book, describing what I saw through that country, but I can only briefly allude to them here. All along this delightful tour I found much pleasure in conversing with some of my fellow passengers, thanks to Monsieur Gallaudet, the noble benefactor of his race, who first became interested in the happiness of the poor mute and invented a language by which we can converse with others, and be cheerful and happy. Those who could not understand the sign language could write, and I also made frequent use of my pencil.

Leaving Nunda, we pursued our way to the village of Mount Morris—the early home of my mother. She was much surprised at the great improvement and the changes everywhere so apparent. It was almost a wilderness then, with here and there a solitary farm house. Now, thriving little villages are scattered all along our way; and the place called Mount Morris was now a town of considerable importance. Here the cars and the canal afforded opportunities for travel. We took the cars for Cayuga at this place, passing through Bloomfield, Canandaigua, Geneva, and in view of Seneca Falls—another cataract worthy of note. It looked very beautiful, and the scenery around it passes my power of description.

At Cayuga village we rested for the night, and the next morning went off on a steamer to Genoa, about twenty miles off. The Lake was only two miles wide, and we could very plainly see the shore on either side. On one side the shore was very near to us much of the way.

We passed a burial ground three miles above Cayuga Bridge. Its white monuments and tablets gleamed through the trees. It was a lovely, peaceful spot. Here, my mother told me, the body of my grandmother had slept for many years. She died when my mother was very young.

Arriving in Genoa, we went to visit uncle's family, who received us with much joy, and my young cousins did all they could to make our visit pleasant. We remained a week, and when we set out on our return my aged grandfather and his wife accompanied us and spent the winter with us. My beloved Aunt Lucy—my mother's only sister—was very ill, and the following spring, hoping she might be benefited by the change, we induced her to come to our home in Michigan. But she grew no better, and after watching and attending to her with great care and affection for several months, she died, and was buried but a little way from home, where I have visited her grave often. My grandfather returned home in the fall, and my young cousin joined the army. So my mother and myself are left alone again.

Two years ago the Principal of the Indiana Asylum sent me an invitation to visit the institution and remain a pupil.

Miss Almena Knight accompanied me. We had a very pleasant visit, and were treated with great respect by the teachers. The process of teaching is similar to that of Flint; and the exercises in the school were very interesting. We remained, however, but a few days, for I was not able to meet the expenses of tuition there.

And now for the present, dear readers, adieu. At some future time I may tell you more. My home is not yet free from incumbrance, and could I emerge from indebtedness, I shall be forever grateful to all who, by purchasing my little book, enable me to do so. It is still a great trial for me to offer my book for sale, for though on one hand I meet with sympathy and kindness, on the other, coldness, slight, and discouragement chill me. Still I will hope for the best. May the dear Lord, who was ever a friend to the poor, bless ever the tender, generous heart, is the sincere and constant prayer of

Adele M. George.

And now, again, after the lapse of five years, I present you with a continuation of my simple history. I have drank bitterly of the cup of sorrow, since my marriage; but I cannot here speak of the trials that have fallen to my lot. I am a member of the Baptist Church, and my home at present is in Ann Arbor, with my mother, who is still spared to me.

She is my good, faithful—my *only* friend; and were it not for her I know not what would become of me and my helpless little children. She has charge of them while I do what I can to support myself and them. Please do not regard me with coldness and distrust. As truly as I hope for the protection and blessing of my Heavenly Father, I have always striven to do right in his sight, and to be worthy of the love and respect of my fellow-beings. I have a little son, also a mute, and two darling little girls who can see and hear; and all who will aid me to secure a comfortable living for them, will make the burden lighter for the afflicted mother.

Mrs. Adele M. Jewel.

9

Selections from Her Journals (1874/78)

M. Carey Thomas

MARTHA CAREY THOMAS (1857–1935) was born in Baltimore in 1857, the eldest of ten children. Her father was a physician and a preacher, and her mother was an active member of the Women's Christian Temperance Union. Called "Minnie" as a child, she later preferred that her first name be dropped. At seven, Thomas was severely burned by a lamp, and the family felt the accident and her recovery signaled that she would become an important figure.

Thomas grew up an avid reader with an interest in women's rights and increasing skepticism about religion. Her father opposed her wish to attend Cornell University, but with her mother's support she graduated from Cornell in 1877. She did a year of graduate work at Johns Hopkins, where, as a woman, she could only have private tutoring. She then studied in Germany at the University of Leipzig but was required to sit separately from male students and was refused a doctoral degree. Thomas went on to the University of Zurich, where she graduated summa cum laude in 1882, the first woman to receive a PhD with such high honors. The next year, in a letter to the trustees (including her father) of the newly established

Bryn Mawr College, she nominated herself for its presidency. She was hired instead as dean and professor of English in 1884, the first dean of a women's college to hold a PhD. In 1894 she became president and served in that capacity until retiring in 1922. Bryn Mawr was the first women's college to have a graduate program and, under Thomas, the college established a progressive climate, admitting foreign exchange students, pioneering an innovative curriculum, and promoting freedom for its students and liberal hiring practices. Thomas also created the Summer School for Women Workers in Industry. Her love of architecture is evident in the beauty of campus buildings.

A staunch supporter of women's suffrage, Thomas left the National American Woman Suffrage Association (later the League of Women Voters) for the National Women's Party, which adopted a more radical agenda that proposed an Equal Rights Amendment. She supported birth control, decried marriage, and sustained lifelong relationships with two women. Leila Rupp contrasts Thomas's romantic friendship or "little love" with Mamie Gwinn, which both women considered a "marriage," to the intense passion she shared with Mary Garrett, noting that Thomas had to arrange the two women's alternating visits. For Rupp, Thomas is a woman who successfully bridged the nineteenth-century world of romantic friendship and the twentieth-century world of lesbian identities (90 and Ch. 4, passim).

In 1891 Thomas, Garrett (who became a dean at Bryn Mawr), and Gwinn assembled a Women's Fund for Johns Hopkins in exchange for an equal admissions policy to the Medical School. Like many intellectuals of her time, Thomas was a supporter of eugenics and the superiority of northern European "races," beliefs that are now repudiated. Thomas wrote an entry for the American Peace Prize (to provide a U.S. plan to maintain global peace) that was published with the top twenty entries. In 1915 Garrett had bequeathed her wealth to Thomas, who, upon retiring, rented a villa on the French Riviera where she planned to write an autobiography. Instead, she devoted herself to adventurous world travel.

After Thomas died on December 2, 1935, her letters and journals were stored for decades in four large trunks hidden on the Bryn Mawr campus. A fire led to their rediscovery, though it took Thomas's last living executor, Millicent McIntosh, to release them officially to Bryn Mawr. In 1979 Marjorie Housepian Dobkin, who sorted out the collection, published an anthology of Thomas's writings, *The Making of a Feminist: Early Journals and Letters of M. Carey Thomas*. The autobiographical sketch we include, drawn from this collection, suggests Thomas's struggle to define a gendered identity and sexuality in conflict with the religious orthodoxy of her youth. While to date Thomas has not been critically considered as an autobiographical writer, in 1994 Helen Lefkowitz Horowitz published a biography of her.

Early Journals

I am beginning to look forward to another summer and to think that last summer we were everything to each other and now—but I am no different only may be able to understand more what sorrow means.

I took up my journal today though with the intention of writing about a friendship of last term in case it should never be renewed that at least I may have *some* remembrance. It was with Libbie Conkey—we got acquainted, how I hardly know. The girls said we "smashed" on each other or "made love" I don't know—I only know it was elegant. She called me "her boy" her "liebe knabe" and she was my "Elsie." We used to see each other oftenest in Professor Satterthaite's room in the gallery of the gymnasium hall and there after supper we would sit and talk in the twilight. Then after all the classes I would wait for her and we would walk over together—we studied Latin—she was reading the Fifth book of Virgil and I read it with her for fun (I think we learnt something else except Latin, at least I learned to care for her more than I knew). Always in fact *every* Sunday evening last term, after tea, we would talk and at last I cared so much about her that my lessons were a secondary matter. Well, the end of the term came—I wrote her a piece of poetry—we said "Goodbye"—she went to Rochester, I home—that is all about the very pleasantest friendship that I have ever had. Of course she may come back next year and we have letters, but her "boy" is very lonely here. There is nobody I care about that *way* now—Oh Journal why is it that when you get to care so much about people life is nothing but Goodbyes, some longer, some shorter—But now my own "sweetheart" goodbye once more on paper, and if we should never meet again this page of my journal will always call up "Memories and Remembrance sweet" of my darling Elsie.

Thanksgiving, 1873

Howland—It is a cold snowy day—the girls are off somewhere and in the quiet of our room I have sat down to write a little for sometimes I think in after life it will be nice to look back and see a peep here and there of my life. I have entered the senior class and the long long summer has gone and I am here for my last year. Last night Alice Hicks and I sat up until a quarter to three and read Paly. . . . [1]

August 1, 1874

Atlantic City—This quiet Sunday afternoon with the noise of the breakers alone breaking the stillness I have sat down to write a little in my long forgotten journal. On the seventh of July our class graduated. Everything went off well and now that page of my life, the page Bessie and I were so anxious to turn, is closed. On the whole Howland has been an experience I would not have missed for much. It has been a first rate place to study and an elegant place for fun—My two pleasantest friendships almost, have been formed up here, the one with Libbie Conkey—we have written to each other and I visited her in Rochester, she was at school commencement and every time I have seen her our friendship has been nicer. The other with Carrie Ladd. When Libbie went home at the close of the winter term of '73 we began to know each other. We were in Astronomy together and almost every night would trace out the stars. Betelgeuse was my star and Rigel hers—both in Orion. We used to play and romp and discuss and argue and have such good times. In the summer we both got up to look at Orion, and from twelve till six as I sat on the porch and saw constellation after constellation pass by, I wrote her [a poem]. Last year was a busy one at school for us both. Carrie is as practical as a Yankee and has an original way of looking at things and we used to have the nicest talks. For a half an hour a day we used to read Emerson's *Essays* out loud. I hoped our intimacy helped us as I'm sure it gave us a great deal of pleasure. Bessie King from the first never approved of it entirely, I think, but I don't think she understands Carrie. Carrie is a dear darling friend and I love and admire her extremely.

1. Perhaps William Paley, English theologian (1743–1805), author of *A View of the Evidences of Christianity.*

Dr. Test has given us some noble lessons which we will remember forever, I think. He has given me a love for Latin and Greek which I will never lose. He has given us a glimpse of a grand and noble theology which will remain with us. He has my earnest love and gratitude for the many many helps he has given me. But there is one who stands higher than all—Miss Slocum. From the very beginning she seemed to like me and helped me in every way. She is a noble woman and lives an unselfish life. She said to me lately, "Minnie, I wish I had the chance you girls have—it is too late for me to begin to study now—all I can do is to give you what thoughts I have and help you all I can and then send you out to do what I might have done."

Sometimes I have thought she let me come closer to her than the other girls, for when I would go to bid her goodnight she would draw me to her and kiss me and tell me my love helped her more than I knew. It is a noble thing to help girls as she has helped us, to see her day after day talking to us, trying to show us the worth and importance of life. Our class was her favorite and she said to some one we were the smartest class that had ever graduated. While I was writing out my Political Economy examination she watched me in a very peculiar way and as soon as I went out she followed and asked me to come in her parlor as she wanted to speak to me. Then she said as nearly as I can remember these words—I want to put them down so that they may be an inspiration to me—

"I don't want to flatter you but I don't think it ever does harm to tell people the truth. I have watched you carefully ever since you came—I have been pleased with your recitations and with your examination papers. Both have showed that you go to the root of things and understand them. You would be surprised to know how few girls do. You have good habits of study and now I think I have found out what you can do. You are the only girl I have seen who has the power and mind to do this. What we want in the cause of women are not doctors and lawyers (there are plenty of those), we want scholars. You have, I think, as fair a start as any boy of seventeen in the country and now I want you to be a great scholar. I don't think you will be content to merely receive and not originate. You have a great deal of time and none of it is lost if you work steadily for your end. I want great things of you."

What could I say except that I cared more for her opinion than any one else's, that the thing she wanted was the one thing I had dreamed of—that I would try and show her that I was worthy of her confidence and trust. And so I will devote my life to study and try to work some

good from it. There is no use of saying any more—this book is filled
with enthusiastic rhapsodies but God help me to be true to what is best!
When I kissed Miss Slocum goodbye after commencement she put her
arms around me and said "Goodbye precious, remember I shan't ever
give you up."

[Journal] June 12, 1877
Sage College, Cornell University. It is almost two years since I have
made an entry. I have now finished all my senior examinations and
have nothing to do for the next nine days except wait for my degree. . . .

At last the object of my ambition—the one purpose that runs
through my journals has been attained. I have graduated at a university. I have a degree that represents more than a Vassar one.

I wish I had kept a slight, at least, record of my experience here and
now it is too late to recall it. The first two years I had a difficult time to get
into the new methods of study and especially in Latin I entered behind.

Altogether I have learned a great deal and it has been thoroughly
profitable to be here—it has given me a new outlook. Though I feel very
far from a good Latin and Greek scholar, yet I do see light somewhat.
My life here has been very hermit like, except seven girls. I have seen
very few people, half the men here are uncultivated and Cornell misses
all that glorious culture that one reads of in college books. The girls are
for the most part of a different social station and I have seen very little
of them as they have nothing to counterbalance that fact.

I want to write about my fifth friendship, for in spite of myself I have
one. When I came here I made up my mind that at Howland I had
wasted a great deal of time with friends and that it amounted to very
little except pleasure and that especially away from home the pain of
being separated more than overbalanced the other.

The first girl I saw was a young lady in Algebra examination—
lace-dressed, in gray with a brown hat with a wing in it. She was up at
Pres. White's to tea and we had a little talk. I thought she was smart and
well prepared in the examinations next day. I "rather hoped" I should
see her again next fall. Next fall came—she was the first person I saw as
I drove up to the Sage College. Her mother was with her and together
we chose our rooms on the same corridor third hall. Miss Mills was to
room with Miss Hicks and would not unpack until she had heard from
her examinations. Miss Putnam whom I had met at Prof. Russel's chose
a room on the same floor. It was lonely at first—my only consolation
was going down to Howland every other Friday and seeing Carrie

[Ladd]. At first I rather looked down on the girls in our hall. Miss Hicks, Miss Putnam, Miss Mills, Miss Head and Miss Mitchell—they seemed more interested in fun than anything else. And not one of them was smart except Miss Hicks; the other girls in the Sage were good enough students but not ladies, and the gentlemen, except Prof. Boyesen, were second rate, "half cut" Bessie would say.

Well, I began to see more and more of Miss Hicks. She got in the habit of coming and reading me her mother's letters and of bidding me good night. We used to go and study some time in Casquadilla woods and when it would get dark we would sit under her blue shawl and talk. Then we came across Swinburne's "Atalanta in Calydon" and Miss Hicks would come in her wrapper after I was in bed and we would read it out loud and we learned several of the choruses. One night we had stopped reading later than usual and obeying a sudden impulse I turned to her and asked, "Do you love me?" She threw her arms around me and whispered, "I love you passionately." She did not go home that night and we talked and talked. She told me she had been praying that I might care for her.

That was the beginning and from that time, it was the fall of '75, till June '77 we have been inseparable. I put this all down because I cannot understand it. I am sure it is not best for people to care about each other so much. In the first place it wasted my time—it was a pleasure to be with Miss Hicks and as I cared to be with no one else, I would have spent all that time in reading. It was different with her—as she likes a great many people and liked the other girls and would have wasted her time anyway. In the second place it was almost more pain than pleasure because we quarreled so. All our ideas were opposite. Miss Hicks' mother I think is rising in society and there is not the least bit of fastidiousness in Miss Hicks' nature. She likes everyone. She cares for everyone's opinion. She would do a great many things I did not think suitable. I would object and say more than I ought to and Miss Hicks would fling herself on the lounge in a passion of tears and sometimes we would both cry—altogether it was dreadful—yet all the time we cared about each other so much that we could not give up our friendship. Again and again we gave up in despair and then we would care and have such lovely times that we began again and the whole thing was over again. Often I prayed that I might stop loving her.

This high tragedy seems ridiculous written but I know I shall forget the possibility of such things unless I do. It seems rather too bad when one goes to college to study to be distracted by such things. It was not

Miss Hicks' fault but I know I did not study as well because of her, but I could not help it. I was mastered by it—one thing that made our friendship as unpleasant as it sometimes was was my feeling that I ought not to give way to it. Miss Hicks has no generous abandon in study—her companionship did not help me, I think, in an intellectual way. I tell her she ought to be obliged to me. I taught her to love passionately and to be passionately angry. Neither of which she had experienced before.

She is lovely in many ways. She has a sweet simplicity and straightforwardness about her, an utter faithfulness—I would trust her absolutely with any secret—she is naturally very smart but I think, at least until she came to Cornell, she studies because she had nothing else to do and because of her love of approbation. She wants to be an architect and seems very fond of it but I do not feel as if she would make a success. She seems to me to be easily turned aside by people. It is hard to talk to her—I never feel except when she is angry as if she were really saying what she feels with all her heart. In her manners she wants a certain quiet self assurance. I think she will probably get married. These are almost all unfavorable things but I leave out all her prettiness and her traits of character that attract me—in fact I just fell in love with her and I did it gradually too (not that adoring worship I had for Libbie [Conkey], nor the equal fun and earnest loving devoted friendship Carrie and I have) but, that Atalanta night I knew I did not care as much as she did and so it went on, I getting fonder and fonder of her until it was as I say—all the time against my better judgment and yet I cannot tell why it was. She is lovely, in many many ways much better than I am.

[Journal] January 20, 1878

Never did a New Year come in with such a want of resolutions—in an agony of sleepiness during the $\frac{1}{4}$ before 12.

I am also twenty-one and as you know studying for a second degree in the Johns Hopkins. Prof. Gilder[sleeve] has laid out my work for the ten weeks to April 1st . . . enough to keep me busy.

January 31

I am utterly discouraged. For the last week I have been trying to study ten hours a day—six in the morning and four after tea. But in my reading Greek it is dreadful to see how often I mistake the meaning and then the terrible thought comes again and again. After all can I possibly get any more infinite shades of meaning out of the Greek than the translator—is this trouble after all worth it? Is it not a waste of one's life? Then the amount of study necessary. I am absolutely at the threshold: inaccurate, badly trained, not able to write a sentence of correct Greek. To give myself all this without a teacher, without even a guide—it seems like a labor of Hercules. I have no time to read, no time to see people—not that that amounts to much but still it is a kind of living death; but then if I had my choice this moment I know I would choose nothing else . . . my precious Agamemnon—the one inspiration to study when I lose all heart! The pleasure I had from that, the sweet echoing of lines from it that fills the pauses of dressing and eating almost is worth it all— Perhaps my studying is all a mistake—if I *only* were more master of the subject I could tell better. . . .

February 2, 1878

Last night our Friday Evening [group] met here (Mary Garrett, Julia Rogers, Mamie Gwinn, Carrie, Bess and I meet every two weeks at each other's houses and write two chapters of a novel and an essay or two each night).

Miss Gwinn wrote a remarkable chapter which brought up the whole question of marriage. She believes in free love according to Godwin's view, but now in the Malthus theory and therefore refuses to consider the bringing up of children. Says that if a man cared enough for her to wish to be her intimate friend, she would consider him a beast if he did not agree.

This started the whole question and we discussed it till eleven o'clock. We all concluded there is something wrong about the present relations of marriage and yet none of us accepted Miss Gwinn's views. . . . I said and think that as for a few words in church or before a magistrate making all the difference between right and wrong, of course that is nonsense. But we must judge this question purely on grounds of expedience on what will lead to the best moral results. Now it *does* seem to me that free love will (and platonic friendship I think is not possible with men) degrade matters and above all women. . . . I do wonder what will become of us all. I really think that I personally do not know what to say about this matter and must wait till I see and know more to decide. I am afraid I could, if I let myself, be devoted to Miss Gwinn—she has a strong fascination for me. Have I time?

February 13, 1878

Last night I went to the theatre for the first time. Father and Mother of course disapproved but I was twenty-one last month and I went entirely on my own responsibility. Mary and Julia and Miss ——————[2] and three gentlemen and I. The play was *Camille* and Modjeska acted it. It came up and went beyond anything I had imagined. I utterly lost all idea of locality and just saw Camille in her magnificent longings after a better life. The play might have been made a disagreeable one but the whole thing was raised by the purity of the passion and I could see no imaginable harm in it and oh it is such a mighty pleasure! . . . I feel deprived all these years.

Mary and I talked till eleven o'clock and had an elegant time. I like her very much—there is a sort of sweet strength about her. There are so many points we have in common sympathy. There is something horrible about being separated by this thought life from other people. Mary says she feels it more and more. We discussed the whole question of women.

There seems no solution of the question of marriage, for it is difficult to conceive a woman who really feels her separate lifework to give it all up when she marries a man and yet I think—a fact which I used to ignore—that it is and must be a giving up. Then a man, I should think, would not care for that sort of a wife. Bessie asked me whether I would refuse a man I loved for that reason. . . . Oh, it is a real question and Julia and Mary and Bessie and I all feel it. Will the solution be that we will be four old maids?[3] If a woman has children I do not see but what she will have to, at least for some time, give up her work and of all terrible things taking care of children does seem the most utterly unintellectual. But then one talks of "doing" and "life work" and yet after all what is it to be! I *do* feel as if I could do something but then every young person feels so I suppose. And think if everything were given up and for *nothing*!

February 22, 1878

Libbie has been here since Monday. Before she came I read over what I wrote about her in my journal and my poem, and all my eager, passionate feelings of grief at parting with her came over me. The next day I waited as coolly for her to come and kissed her and etc. without one pulse beat the faster. How can such a thing go so utterly? I have been amusing her and giving up all study. . . .

2. Usually an indication that she could not remember a name or date.

3. Carey, Mary, and Julia never married. Bessie King in middle age married a cousin named Ellicott, an architect.

I have to put the wax in my ears and with my own hands keep myself to the mast—a living death—and do nothing but devote myself to Greek. But I have been putting it off too long and I shall fail—and I who care so much for women and their cause—will fail and do them more harm than if I had never tried. But it is so hard.

Well, about my girl friends: Mary Garrett I like more and more but Julia I am disappointed in. She is oh, I do not know, shallow and not soulful somehow. I cannot have deep confidence in her. Miss Gwinn I really like and trust and find a pleasure in her. If she would once break down the barriers and care for someone and be broad enough to comprehend another, the thing needful would come. She is now too self-centered. Bessie has something lacking for a perfect friend. She is not perfectly dependable. She sometimes defends a side unexpectedly which she does not believe. She cares too much for admiration and young men I think. She wants abandon and a largeness of vision. Who does not—I myself lack everything and am contemptible, but then we judge from an ideal standpoint. I have been thinking for some time about Friendship and analyzing my feeling toward it:

FRIENDSHIP

For the most part we go along on the level of every day affairs with a feeling as if we were, as it were, feeding our individualities. We are stirred out of ourselves by generous impulses but always falling back into loneliness. But there is one loop hole through which we escape into an upper region. A new breath seems to come into our life; a rare, intimate devoted friendship between man and man, woman and woman. We are carried out of self and see through another's eyes. We understand another's nature as we never can unless love unbars the way. Not of such a friendship as this can it be said, "Come down, oh maid." In love between a man and a woman there must be more or less of coming down. There is an element of selfishness, of self gratification in it; but girls know that they are each other's for only a little while, as long as each is worthy and love lasts. It has not the commonness that possession gives. . . .

I *worshipped* Libbie, she was lovely and far above me in my thought of her. I have been different ever since from the mere feeling. Of course now I see her as she is and all that passionate devotion has gone but I hate to miss it.

Carrie I loved too, though never quite that way. Now I see she was not what I thought her and everything except a calm liking and sense of obligation is gone.

Cornell is just full of Miss Hicks. The pine forests and the falls and glens and walks. . . . Our friendship was an absorbing one—everything we did or read together is impressed with her image, or rather my idea of her. She came to see me Christmas—thought I cared for her—yet now the feeling has gone. How perfectly unaccountable! I can give no reason for it. This does not speak well for perhaps the very thing I am longing to prove—friendship. . . .

Now, for the first time since I went to Howland in '72 do I feel perfectly free to give myself to study without the desire to see anyone except, of course, as an ordinary friendship requires, where companionship is an aid, pleasant but not necessary. But then I can never pour my very thought out to anyone now, when complete sympathy of love if not of abstract thought and clasped hands and loving eyes and close kisses and admiration, bowing before another's spirit . . . all join in making thought and your soul life a real thing and make you feel noble and generous living in another, not selfcentered. This is what I imagine friendship could be.

March 18, 1878

Just home from Meeting. As I said to Bessie afterwards are we fools or are we idiots that when we can't get time to go to really instructive lectures or to read splendid books we sit there and listen to a discourse about "cows and twenty-four Indian princes" prolonged anecdotes, mere exhortation to believe in Christ. I am in a perfect maze theologically. I cannot help thinking there is something in religion and yet upon my word, between dogma and narrowness it seems as if all the divine primal inspiration had escaped between the lines. . . .

Mamie Gwinn I do like very much. She is a terrible temptation to me as I tell her—she represents all that side of my nature I am trying to suppress, the roving through literature and study, seeking out whatever the bent of my fancy leads to—the dilettante spirit, the complete contradiction to the steady working spirit I am endeavoring to summon. . . . But life is so full, and Greek life after all is only a part.

My interest is now in the first part of present century; Godwin and Shelley, etc. Miss Gwinn introduced me to Godwin and his *Political Justice* has really changed my thought very much. How could I have been so blind to all the sufferings and miserable inequality of people around?

March 23, 1878

Have just come in from a ride with Mary Garrett. She is lovely. I do not
know when I have admired a girl so much—her fearlessness on horseback really gives me a sensation of real, warm admiration. I should so
like to have an earnest friendship with her.

10

"The Yakima Affair," from *Life Among the Piutes: Their Wrongs and Claims* (1883)

Sarah Winnemucca

SARAH WINNEMUCCA (1844-1891) was born Thocmetony ("shell flower") in 1844 in the Northern Paiute nation near what is now northern Nevada. Her father and grandfather, both tribal chiefs, promoted different relationships to whites—her grandfather established friendly relations, while her father endorsed a more distanced approach. Winnemucca's own relationship to the dominant white culture was often conflicted because of her various roles as activist, lobbyist, lecturer, and translator.

At the age of six she traveled with her grandfather to California where she was immersed in non-indigenous culture and began to learn English. She received a year of education in the home of Major Ormsby in Mormon Station (now Genoa), Nevada, becoming one of two Paiutes in Nevada who could read, write, and speak in English. By the age of fourteen she was also fluent in three Indian languages and Spanish. Heeding the deathbed request of her grandfather, she and her sister Elma unofficially attended school at St. Mary's Convent in San Jose, California, but were forced to leave because of white resistance to their presence.

As white westward expansion continued, Paiutes were forced onto reservations, from Pyramid Lake, Nevada, to Malheur Reservation, Oregon, and ultimately to Yakima, Washington. When violence erupted with white settlers at Pyramid Lake, Winnemucca became an interpreter and participated in negotiations to reduce the bloodshed. Angered by her intervention, white settlers murdered her mother, sister, and brother. Thereafter the U.S. Army hired Winnemucca, only a teenager, as a translator. This position, and her 1871 work as an interpreter for the Bureau of Indian Affairs, made her familiar with American bureaucracy. She came to see the persecution of the Paiutes as largely the fault of corrupt, government-appointed Indian agents, a conviction that motivated much of her activism and lobbying. Despite her efforts, however, her pleas met with no success.

In 1871 Winnemucca entered a short-lived marriage to Lieutenant E. C. Bartlett. A later marriage to an American Indian also failed due to his abusive treatment of her.

In 1878 Winnemucca participated in the Bannock War but laid down her arms to seek peace as an interpreter, convincing her father to withdraw from Idaho and return to Nevada. In 1880 she presented her case to President Hayes and received promises, later broken, that policies toward her people would be reformed and their treatment improved. As an activist, Winnemucca gave over four hundred speeches. Her supporters Elizabeth Palmer Peabody and Mary Peabody Mann (wife of educator, lawyer, and politician Horace Mann) encouraged her to write her life story as another way to reach a wider audience. Her 1883 *Life Among the Piutes: Their Wrongs and Claims* was the first known book-length life narrative published by a Native American woman. It was edited by Mary (Mrs. Horace) Mann. The following excerpt, from the last chapter of the book, narrates the difficult journey to the Yakima reservation, the abusive treatment of the Catholic priest heading it, and the complicity of the "civilized Indians." Winnemucca goes on to express fear that she has unintentionally sold out her people based on misrepresentations made to her by agents and soldiers: "I know I have told you more lies than I have hairs on my head" (236). She indicts official practice in both the United States and Canada: "My people have been signing papers for the last twenty-three years. They don't know what they sign." And she announces her determination now to resist by "talking against the government officials" (242). She implores General Howard to "hear our pitiful cry to you, sweep away the agency system; give us homes to live in" and declares the government policy is "driving us from place to place as if we were beasts" (243–44). Pointing out that "if we are treated by white savages as if we are savages, we are relentless and desperate," she argues that when the Paiute are treated like human beings "we will behave like a people" (244). Winnemucca's narrative concludes with regret that she could not intervene in Yakima, but announces her determination to speak and write on her people's behalf to Eastern officials.

Near the end of Winnemucca's life, when Paiutes began to leave the state of Washington for Nevada, they experienced relatively little harassment, due largely to her influence. She also returned to Nevada, where she founded Native schools statewide, including the Peabody Institute near Lovelock. After her last husband, Lieutenant L. H. Hopkins, died of tuberculosis, and the school subsequently closed, Winnemucca moved to Henry's Lake, Idaho, with her sister Elma. She died of tuberculosis on October 17, 1891.

Edited by Mrs. Horace Mann,
and
Printed for the Author.
Boston:
For Sale by Cupples, Upham & Co.
283 Washington Street;
G. P. Putnam's Sons, New York;
And by the Author.
1883.

Chapter VIII. The Yakima Affair.

One day the commanding officer sent for me. Oh, how my heart did jump! I said to Mattie, "There is bad news." Truly I had not felt like this since the night Egan was killed by the Umatillas. I got ready and went down to the office, trembling as if something fearful was waiting for me. I walked into the office. Then the officer said to me,—

"Sarah, I have some news to tell you and I want you to keep it still until we are sure if it will be true."

I then promised I would keep it still if it was not too awful bad news. He said, "It is pretty bad." He looked at me and said, "Sarah, you look as if you were ready to die. It is nothing about you; it is about your people. Sarah, an order is issued that your people are to be taken to Yakima Reservation, across the Columbia River."

I said, "All of my people?"

"No, not your father's, but all that are here." I asked, "What for?"

He said he did not know.

I said, "Major, my people have not done anything, and why should they be sent away from their own country? If there are any to be sent away, let it be Oytes and his men, numbering about twenty-five men in all, and the few Bannocks that are with them. Oh, Major! if you knew what I have promised my people, you would leave nothing undone but what you would try not to have them sent away. Oh, Major! my people will never believe me again."

"Well, Sarah, I will do all I can. I will write to the President and see what he thinks about it. I will tell him all you have said about your people."

I was crying. He told me to keep up a good heart, and he would do all he could for me.

I went home and told Mattie all, and she said, "Well, sister, we cannot help it if the white people won't keep their word. We can't help it. We have to work for them and if they get our people not to love us, by telling what is not true to them, what can we do? It is they, not us."

I said, "Our people won't think so because they will never know that it was they who told the lie. Oh! I know all our people will say we are working against them and are getting money for all this."

In the evening Mattie and I took a walk down to their camp. There they were so happy; singing here, singing there and everywhere. I thought to myself, "My poor, poor people, you will be happy to-day; to-morrow or next week your happiness will be turned to weeping." Oh, how sad I was for them! I could not sleep at night, for the sad thing that had come.

At last one evening I was sent for by the commanding officer. Oh! how can I tell it? My poor heart stood still. I said to Mattie, "Mattie, I wish this was my last day in this cruel world."

I came to myself and I said, "No, Mattie, I don't mean the world. I mean the cruel,—yes, the cruel, wicked, white people, who are going to drive us to some foreign country, away from our own. Mattie, I feel so badly I don't think I can walk down there." Mattie said, "I will go with you."

We then went down, and Major Cochran met us at the door and said, " Sarah, are you sick? You look so badly."

I said, "No."

He then replied, "Sarah, I am heartily sorry for you, but we cannot help it. We are ordered to take your people to Yakima Reservation."

It was just a little before Christmas. My people were only given one week to get ready in.

I said, "What! In this cold winter and in all this snow, and my people have so many little children? Why, they will all die. Oh, what can the President be thinking about? Oh, tell me, what is he? Is he man or beast? Yes, he must be a beast; if he has no feeling for my people, surely he ought to have some for the soldiers."

"I have never seen a president in my life and I want to know whether he is made of wood or rock, for I cannot for once think that he can be a human being. No human being would do such a thing as that,—send people across a fearful mountain in midwinter."

I was told not to say anything till three days before starting. Every night I imagined I could see the thing called President. He had long ears, he had big eyes and long legs, and a head like a bull-frog or something like that. I could not think of anything that could be so inhuman as to do such a thing,—send people across mountains with snow so deep.

Mattie and I got all the furs we could; we had fur caps, fur gloves, and fur overshoes.

At last the time arrived. The commanding-officer told me to tell Leggins to come to him. I did so. He came, and Major Cochrane told me to tell him that he wanted him to tell which of the Bannock men were the worst, or which was the leader in the war. Leggins told him, and counted out twelve men to him. After this talk, Major Cochrane asked me to go and tell these men to come up to the office. They were Oytes, Bannock Joe, Captain Bearskin, Paddy Cap, Boss, Big John, Eagle Eye, Charley, D. E. Johnson, Beads, and Oytes' son-in-law, called Surger. An officer was sent with me. I called out the men by their names. They all came out to me. I said to Oytes,—

"Your soldier-father wants you all to go up to see him." We went up, and Oytes asked me many things.

We had to go right by the guard-house. Just as we got near it, the soldier on guard came out and headed us off and took the men and put them into the guard-house. After they were put in there the soldiers told me to tell them they must not try to get away, or they would be shot.

"We put you in here for safe-keeping," they said. "The citizens are coming over here from Canyon City to arrest you-all, and we don't want them to take you; that is why we put you in here."

Ten soldiers were sent down to guard the whole encampment,—not Leggins' band, only Oytes' and the Bannocks. I was then ordered to tell them to get ready to go to Yakima Reservation.

Oh, how sad they were! Women cried and blamed their husbands for going with the Bannocks; but Leggins and his band were told they were not going with the prisoners of war, and that he was not going at all.

Then Leggins moved down the creek about two miles. At night some would get out and go off. Brother Lee and Leggins were sent out to bring them back again. One afternoon Mattie and I were sent out to get five women who got away during the night, and an officer was sent with us. We were riding very fast, and my sister Mattie's horse jumped on one side and threw her off and hurt her. The blood ran out of her mouth, and I thought she would die right off; but, poor dear, she went on, for an ambulance was at our command. She had great suffering during our journey.

Oh, for shame! You who are educated by a Christian government in the art of war; the practice of whose profession makes you natural enemies of the savages, so called by you. Yes, you, who call yourselves the great civilization; you who have knelt upon Plymouth Rock, covenanting with God to make this land the home of the free and the brave. Ah, then you rise from your bended knees and seizing the welcoming hands of those who are the owners of this land, which you are not, our carbines rise upon the bleak shore, and your so-called civilization sweeps inland from the ocean wave; but, oh, my God! leaving its pathway marked by crimson lines of blood; and strewed by the bones of two races, the inheritor and the invader; and I am crying out to you for justice,—yes, pleading for the far-off plains of the West, for the dusky mourner, whose tears of love are pleading for her husband, or for their children, who are sent far away from them. Your Christian minister will hold my people against their will; not because he loves them,—no, far from it,—but because it puts money in his pockets.

Now we are ready to start for Yakima. Fifty wagons were brought, and citizens were to take us there. Some of the wagons cost the government from ten dollars to fifteen dollars per day. We got to Canyon City, and while we camped there Captain Winters got a telegram from Washington, telling him he must take Leggins' band too. So we had to wait for them to overtake us. While we were waiting, our dear good father and mother, Mr. Charles W. Parrish, came with his wife and children to see us. My people threw their arms round him and his wife, crying, "Oh, our father and mother, if you had staid with us we would not suffer this."

Poor Mrs. Parrish could not stop her tears at seeing the people who once loved her, the children whom she had taught,—yes, the savage children who once called her their white-lily mother, the children who used to bring her wild flowers, with happy faces, now ragged, no clothes whatever. They all cried out to him and his wife, saying, "Oh, good father and mother, talk for us! Don't let them take us away; take us back to our home!" He told them he could do nothing for them. They asked him where his brother, Sam Parrish, was. He told them he was a long way off; and then they bade us good-by, and that was the last they saw of him.

While we were waiting for Leggins, it snowed all the time. In two days the rest of my people overtook us. It was so very cold some of them had to be left on the road; but they came in later. That night an old man was left in the road in a wagon. The next morning they went back to get the wagon,-and found the old man frozen to death. The citizen who owned the wagon did not bring him to the camp; but threw him out of his wagon and left him! I thought it was the most fearful thing I ever saw in my life.

Early the next morning, the captain sent me to tell Leggins that he wanted him to help the soldiers guard the prisoners and see that none of them got away. He said the Big Father in Washington wanted him to do this, and then he and his people could come back in the spring. I went to tell Leggins; but he would not speak to me, neither would my brother Lee. I told him all and went away. When I got back, the captain asked me what he said. I told him he would not speak to me.

"Did you tell him what I told you to?"

"I did."

"Go and tell the prisoners to be ready to march in half an hour."

We travelled all day. It snowed all day long. We camped, and that night a woman became a mother; and during the night the baby died, and was put under the snow. The next morning the mother was put into the wagon. She was almost dead when we went into camp. That night she too was gone, and left on the roadside, her poor body not even covered with the snow.

In five days three more children were frozen to death, and another woman became a mother. Her child lived three days, but the mother lived. We then crossed Columbia River.

All the time my poor dear little Mattie was dying little by little.

At last we arrived in Yakima on the last day of the month. Father Wilbur and the chief of the Yakima Indians came to meet us. We came into camp about thirty miles from where the agency buildings are, and staid at this place for ten days. Another one of my people died here, but oh, thanks be to the Good Father in the Spirit-land, he was buried as if he were a man. At the end of the ten days we were turned over to Father Wilbur and his civilized Indians, as he called them. Well, as I was saying, we were turned over to him as if we were so many horses or cattle. After he received us he had some of his civilized Indians come with their wagons to take us up to Fort Simcoe. They did not come because they loved us, or because they were Christians. No; they were just like all civilized people; they came to take us up there because they were to be paid for it. They had a kind of shed made to put us in. You know what kind of shed you make for your stock in winter time. It was of that kind. Oh, how we did suffer with cold. There was no wood, and the snow was waist-deep, and many died off just as cattle or horses do after travelling so long in the cold.

All my people were dressed well in soldiers' clothes. Almost all the men had beautiful blue overcoats; they looked like a company of soldiers, but we had not been with these civilized people long before they had won all my people's clothes from them. Some would give them one buckskin for an overcoat and pants, and some of them got little ponies for their clothes, but the ponies would disappear, and could not be found in the country afterwards. Leggins had a great many good horses, which were lost in the same way. My people would go and tell the agent, Wilbur, about the way his people were treating them, and the loss of their horses; but he would tell them their horses were all right on the reservation somewhere, only we could not find them. My people would ask him to tell his people to tell us if they saw our horses, so that we might go and get them. He told his Christian and civilized Indians, but none of them came to tell us where our horses were. The civilized Indians would tell my people not to go far away, for the white people would kill them; but my cousin, Frank Winnemucca, and his sister's son, who was named after our good agent, Samuel Parrish, were out hunting their horses. They were gone eight days. They travelled along the Yakima River, and saw an island between Yakima City and the reservation. They swam across to it, and there they found their horses, and two of the Christian Yakima Indians watching them. They brought them back. After that it was worse than ever. All our best horses were gone, which we never did find. My Meride was found three months afterwards. They were using my horse as a pack-horse. It was so lean the back was sore. I took it to Mrs. Wilbur to show her what the Yakima Indians were doing to our horses. I asked her if I could turn the horse into their lot. She told me I could, but the horse was gone again, and I have never seen it since.

We had another talk with Father Wilbur about our horses, but he kindly told us he did not wish to be troubled by us about our horses. Then my people said,—

"We have lost all our clothes and our horses, and our father says he does not want to be troubled by us." My people said everything that was bad about these people.

Now came the working time. My people were set to work clearing land; both men and women went to work, and boys too. They cleared sixty acres of land for wheat. They had it all cleared in about ten days. Father Wilbur hired six civilized Indians to plough it for them; these Indians got three dollars a day for their work, because they were civilized and Christian.

It was now about the last of April. I was told to tell my people that he had sent for clothes for them, and it was already at the Dalles. He was going to send seventeen wagons down, and have them brought right off. I told my people what he said, and I assure you they were very glad indeed, for they were almost naked. No money,—no, nothing. Now our clothing came; everything you could wish or think of came for my poor, dear people—blankets of all kinds, shawls, woollen goods, calicoes, and everything beautiful.

Issuing day came. It was in May. Poor Mattie was so sick, I had to go by myself to issue to my people. Oh, such a heart-sickening issue! There were twenty-eight little shawls given out, and dress-goods that you white people would sift flour through, from two to three yards to each woman. The largest issue was to a woman who had six children. It was six yards, and I was told to say to her she must make clothes for the children out of what was left after she had made her own! At this my people all laughed. Some of the men who worked hardest got blankets, some got nothing at all; a few of the hats were issued, and the good minister, Father Wilbur, told me to say he would issue again later in the fall, that is, blankets. After the issue was over, my people talked and said,—

"Another Reinhard!—don't you see he is the same? He looks up into the sky and says something, just like Reinhard." They said, "All white people like that are bad." Every night some of them would come and take blankets off from sleeping men and women until all were gone. All this was told to the agent, but he would not help my poor people, and Father Wilbur's civilized Indians would say most shameful things about my people. They would tell him that they were knocking their doors in, and killing their horses for food, and stealing clothes. At one time they said my people killed a little child. Their Indian minister, whose name was George Waters, told me one of my women had been seen killing the child. He said the child's head was cut to pieces. I said to brother Lee,—

"We will go and see the child."

I asked the white doctor to go with us to see it. I told him what had been said. They had him all wrapped up, and said they did not want anybody to see him. George was there. I said,—

"We must see him. You said our people had killed him, and that his head is cut in pieces." So the doctor took off all the blankets that were wound round him. There was no sign of anything on him. He had fallen into the river and had been drowned.

On May 29, my poor little sister Mattie died. Oh, how she did suffer before she died! And I was left all alone. During this time, all the goods that were brought for us were sold to whoever had money. All the civilized Indians bought the best of everything.

Father Wilbur said to my people the very same thing that Reinhard did. He told them he would pay them one dollar a day. My people worked the same, and they were paid in clothes, and little money was paid to them. They were told not to go anywhere else to buy but to this store. At this, my people asked him why he told them that the clothes were theirs. At this Mrs. Wilbur said they had to sell them in order to hold their position. This is the way all the agents issue clothing to the people. Every Indian on that reservation had to pay for everything.

For all the wagons they ever got they were to pay one hundred and twenty-five dollars, if it took ten years to pay it. I know this is true, because the agent told me to tell my brother Lee so, and he told Leggins the same if he wanted wagons, and that they could pay him little by little until they had paid it all.

We had the finest wheat that ever was raised on the reservation, for my people pulled out all the cockle and smut. The civilized Indians were so lazy they would not clean their field, and their wheat was so bad that after it was made into bread it was as black as dirt. I am sorry to say that Father Wilbur kept our wheat for his white friends, and gave us the bad wheat, and the bad wheat was ground just as you would grind it for your hogs. The bad flour made us all sick. My poor people died off very fast. At first Father Wilbur and his Christian Indians told us we could bury our dead in their graveyard; but they soon got tired of us, and said we could not bury them there any more.

Doctor Kuykendall could not cure any of my people, or he did not try. When I would go to him for medicine for them, he would say, "Well, Sarah, I will give you a little sugar and rice, or a little tea for him or her"; he would say laughing, "give them something good to eat before they die." This is the way the agent treated us, and then they dare to say that they are doing all they can for my people. I say, my dear friends, the minister who is called agent, says there will be or there is a time coming when every one is going to give an account of all he does in this life. I am a little afraid the agent will have to give an account of himself, and say, "I have filled my pockets with that worthless thing called money. I am not worthy to go to heaven." That is, if that book you civilized people call the Holy Bible is true. In that, it says he who steals and tells lies will go to hell. Well, I am afraid this book is true, as your agents say; and I am sure they will never see heaven, for I am sure there is hardly an agent but what steals a little, and, they all know that if there is a God above us, they can't deny it before Him who is called God. This was in July, 1879.

11

"An Old Woman and Her Recollections" (as recorded by Thomas Savage) (1877)

Eulalia Pérez

EULALIA PÉREZ (dates unknown) describes her life in this narrative she dictated to Thomas Savage in 1877. Hired as an assistant to the Western historian Hubert Howe Bancroft in 1873, Savage interviewed California pioneers and natives, collecting information and oral histories for Bancroft's *History of California*, published from 1884 to 1890. Though of New England stock, Savage, born in Havana, was a native Spanish speaker who had served as U.S. consulate to Havana for twenty-one years and had been U.S. consul to both Guatemala and El Salvador. In 1988 the Friends of the Bancroft Library published three of the transcriptions of oral interviews made by Savage, including that of Eulalia Pérez, as *Three Memoirs of Mexican California*.

Little is known about Pérez aside from the information her oral history provides. Beneath the dictation's title, Savage noted simply, "Dictated by Doña Eulalia Pérez, who lives at the San Gabriel Mission, at the advanced age of 139 years," though his account of the interview suggests her age was exaggerated. Perez's as-told-to narrative details the responsibility she assumed at the San Gabriel mission as supervisor for fourteen years of a large household with indigenous workers who were converting to Christianity. The story she tells suggests her "remarkable appropriation of authority" over men, in Genaro Padilla's phrase (133). Pérez seems to have become self-sufficient, far more than a wife and domestic.

Bancroft and his assistants collected at least twelve oral histories of women that, according to Rosaura Sánchez, are "doubly-voiced" (284) because they are mediated through both an interviewer's recording and translation into English. Sánchez characterizes early oral testimonies, archived and not published for nearly a hundred years, as part of the "silenced voice, the voice of the subaltern" in Mexican California (279). The recovery of Pérez's narrative has been important for scholars of Chicana/o history and culture such as Padilla, who is concerned with the relation of folklore and everyday life to autobiographical subjectivity and ethnic identity.

Dictated by Doña Eulalia Pérez
who lives at the San Gabriel Mission,
at the advanced age of 139 years

Thomas Savage, for the
Bancroft Library
1877

"An Old Woman and Her Recollections"

Eulalia Pérez, widow, first of Miguel Antonio Guillén, and next of Juan Mariné, lives in the San Isidro Ranch belonging to her son-in-law Michael C. White, who is upwards of seventy-five and his wife upwards of sixty-three years of age.

Whatever may be in the real age of Madame Eulalia Pérez, she is certainly a very ancient person; there can be no doubt, from her personal appearance that she is a centenarian. The accompanying photograph gives a very correct idea of her as I found her when I took from her lips the notes which appear on the annexed pages.

For a person of such an uncommon age, she is not entirely feeble or helpless, in as much as she can do some needle work, and walk about the house unsupported even by a staff.

She sat by me upon a chair a while yesterday; but her usual seat is on the floor, and when flies or mosquitoes annoy her, she slaps & kills them with her slipper on the floor. When wishing to rise, she places both palms of her hands on the ground before her, and lifts herself first on four feet (so to speak) and then with a jerk puts herself on her two feet—for this she needs no assistance. After that she goes about the house without difficulty. She did it in my presence yesterday, and saying that she felt chilled, walked out and sat on the stoop to sun herself a while—then came back and resumed her former seat.

I was assured that with support, and occasional rest on a chair taken with her, she walks to her granddaughter's house, distant five hundred yards or more.

Her memory is remarkably fresh on some things and much clouded on others, particularly on her age. She is at times flighty, but with patience, and by asking her questions only upon such matters as she could be conversant with, I found no great difficulty in obtaining intelligible answers. I had to resort to Mrs. White's assistance in asking the questions, because the centenarian lady is quite deaf, though not to the extent of needing to be addressed in an excessively loud tone.

I discontinued my questions as soon as I discovered that she was fatigued, and have not returned to see her because I had to leave the Mission San Gabriel, near which the San Isidro Ranch is, and visit this place.

Spadra,[1] Dec. 11th, 1877.

[signed] Thomas Savage

I, Eulalia Pérez, was born in the Presidio of Loreto in Baja California.

My father's name was Diego Pérez, and he was employed in the Navy Department of said presidio; my mother's name was Antonia Rosalia Cota. Both were pure white.

I do not remember the date of my birth, but I do know that I was fifteen years old when I married Miguel Antonio Guillén, a soldier of the garrison at Loreto Presidio. During the time of my stay at Loreto I had three children—two boys, who died there in infancy, one girl, Petra, who was eleven years old when we moved to San Diego, and another boy, Isidoro, who came with us to this [Alta] California.

I lived eight years in San Diego with my husband, who continued his service in the garrison of the presidio, and I attended women in childbirth.

1. Settlement on former Rancho San Jose, Los Angeles County.

I had relatives in the vicinity of Los Angeles, and even farther north, and asked my husband repeatedly to take me to see them. My husband did not want to come along, and the commandant of the presidio did not allow me to go, either, because there was no other woman who knew midwifery.

In San Diego everyone seemed to like me very much, and in the most important homes they treated me affectionately. Although I had my own house, they arranged for me to be with those families almost all the time, even including my children.

In 1812 I was in San Juan Capistrano attending Mass in church when a big earthquake occurred, and the tower fell down. I dashed through the sacristy, and in the doorway the people knocked me down and stepped over me. I was pregnant[2] and could not move. Soon afterwards I returned to San Diego and almost immediately gave birth to my daughter Maria Antonia who still lives here in San Gabriel.

After being in San Diego eight years, we came to the Mission of San Gabriel, where my husband had been serving in the guard. In 1814, on the first of October, my daughter Maria del Rosario was born, the one who is the wife of Michael White and in whose home I am now living. . . .

When I first came to San Diego the only house in the presidio was that of the commandant and the barracks where the soldiers lived.

There was no church, and Mass was said in a shelter made out of some old walls covered with branches, by the missionary[3] who came from the Mission of San Diego.

The first sturdy house built in San Diego belonged to a certain Sánchez, the father of Don Vicente Sánchez, alcalde of Los Angeles and deputy of the Territorial Council. The house was very small, and every one went to look at it as though it were a palace. That house was built about a year after I arrived in San Diego.

My last trip to San Diego would have been in the year 1818, when my daughter Maria del Rosario was four years old. I seem to remember that I was there when the revolutionaries came to California. I recall that they put a stranger in irons and that afterwards they took them off.

2. If Dona Eulalia were 139 years old when Savage interviewed her in 1877, she would have been born in 1738 and thus 74 years old and pregnant at the time of the earthquake!

3. The words *padre* and *misionero* have been used interchangeably in the dictation. They have been translated as *missionary*.

Some three years later I came back to San Gabriel. The reason for my return was that the missionary at San Gabriel, Father José Sánchez, wrote to Father Fernando at San Diego—who was his cousin or uncle—asking him to speak to the commandant of the presidio at San Diego requesting him to give my son Isidoro Guillén a guard to escort me here with all my family. The commandant agreed.

When we arrived here Father José Sánchez lodged me and my family temporarily in a small house until work could be found for me. There I was with my five daughters—my son Isidoro Guillén was taken into service as a soldier in the mission guard.

At that time Father Sánchez was between sixty and seventy years of age—a white Spaniard, heavy set, of medium stature—a very good, kind, charitable man. He, as well as his companion Father José Maria Zalvidea, treated the Indians very well, and the two were much loved by the Spanish-speaking people and by the neophytes and other Indians.

Father Zalvidea was very tall, a little heavy, white; he was a man of advanced age. I heard it said that they summoned Zalvidea to San Juan Capistrano because there was no missionary priest there. Many years later, when Father Antonio Peyri fled from San Luis Obispo—it was rumored that they were going to kill the priests—I learned that Zalvidea was very sick, and that actually he had been out of his mind ever since they took him away from San Gabriel, for he did not want to abandon the mission. I repeat that the father was afraid, and two Indians came from San Luis Rey to San Juan Capistrano; in a rawhide cart, making him as comfortable as they could, they took him to San Luis, where he died soon after from the grueling hardships he had suffered on the way.

Father Zalvidea was very much attached to his children at the mission, as he called the Indians that he himself had converted to Christianity. He traveled personally, sometimes on horseback and at other times on foot, and crossed mountains until he came to remote Indian settlements, in order to bring them to our religion.

Father Zalvidea introduced many improvements in the Mission of San Gabriel and made it progress a very great deal in every way. Not content with providing abundantly for the neophytes, he planted [fruit] trees in the mountains, far away from the mission, in order that the untamed Indians might have food when they passed by those spots.

When I came to San Gabriel the last time, there were only two women in this part of California who knew how to cook [well]. One was María Luisa Cota, wife of Claudio López, superintendent of the mission; the other was María Ignacia Amador, wife of Francisco Javier

Alvarado. She knew how to cook, sew, read and write and take care of the sick. She was a good healer. She did needlework and took care of the church vestments. She taught a few children to read and write in her home, but did not conduct a formal school.

On special holidays, such as the day of our patron saint, Easter, etc., the two women were called upon to prepare the feast and to make the meat dishes, sweets, etc.

The priests wanted to help me out because I was a widow burdened with a family. They looked for some way to give me work without offending the other women. Fathers Sánchez and Zalvidea conferred and decided that they would have first one woman, then the other and finally me, do the cooking, in order to determine who did it best, with the aim of putting the one who surpassed the others in charge of the Indian cooks so as to teach them how to cook. With that idea in mind, the gentlemen who were to decide on the merits of the three dinners were warned ahead of time. One of these gentlemen was Don Ignacio Tenorio, whom they called the Royal Judge, and who came to live and die in the company of Father Sánchez. He was a very old man, and when he went out, wrapped up in a muffler, he walked very slowly with the aid of a cane. His walk consisted only of going from the missionary's house to the church.

The other judges who also were to give their opinions were Don Ignacio Mancisidor, merchant; Don Pedro Narváez, naval official; Sergeant José Antonio Pico—who later became lieutenant, brother of Governor Pío Pico; Don Domingo Romero, who was my assistant when I was housekeeper at the mission; Claudio López, superintendent at the mission; besides the missionaries. These gentlemen, whenever they were at the mission, were accustomed to eat with the missionaries.

On the days agreed upon for the three dinners, they attended. No one told me anything regarding what it was all about, until one day Father Sánchez called me and said, "Look, Eulalia, tomorrow it is your turn to prepare dinner—because María Ignacia and Luisa have already done so. We shall see what kind of a dinner you will give us tomorrow."

The next day I went to prepare the food. I made several kinds of soup, a variety of meat dishes and whatever else happened to pop into my head that I knew how to prepare. The Indian cook, named Tomás, watched me attentively, as the missionary had told him to do.

At dinner time those mentioned came. When the meal was concluded, Father Sánchez asked for their opinions about it, beginning with the eldest, Don Ignacio Tenorio. This gentleman pondered awhile, saying that for many years he had not eaten the way he had eaten that day—that he doubted that they ate any better at the King's table. The others also praised the dinner highly.

Then the missionary called Tomás and asked him which of the three women he liked best—which one of them knew the most about cooking. He answered that I did.

Because of all this, employment was provided for me at the mission. At first they assigned me two Indians so that I could show them how to cook, the one named Tomás and the other called "The Gentile." I taught them so well that I had the satisfaction of seeing them turn out to be very good cooks, perhaps the best in all this part of the country.

The missionaries were very satisfied; this made them think more highly of me. I spent about a year teaching those two Indians. I did not have to do the work, only direct them, because they already had learned a few of the fundamentals.

After this, the missionaries conferred among themselves and agreed to hand over the mission keys to me. This was in 1821, if I remember correctly. I recall that my daughter María del Rosario was seven years old when she became seriously ill and was attended by Father José Sánchez, who took such excellent care of her that finally we could rejoice at not having lost her. At that time I was already the housekeeper.

The duties of the housekeeper were many. In the first place, every day she handed out the rations for the mess hut. To do this she had to count the unmarried women, bachelors, day-laborers, vaqueros—both those with saddles and those who rode bareback. Besides that, she had to hand out daily rations to the heads of households. In short, she was responsible for the distribution of supplies to the Indian population and to the missionaries' kitchen. She was in charge of the key to the clothing storehouse where materials were given out for dresses for the unmarried and married women and children. Then she also had to take care of cutting and making clothes for the men.

Furthermore, she was in charge of cutting and making the vaqueros' outfits, from head to foot—that is, for the vaqueros who rode in saddles. Those who rode bareback received nothing more than their cotton blanket and loin-cloth, while those who rode in saddles were dressed the same way as the Spanish-speaking inhabitants; that is, they were given shirt, vest, jacket, trousers, hat, cowboy boots, shoes and spurs; and a saddle, bridle and lariat for the horse. Besides, each vaquero was given a big silk or cotton handkerchief, and a sash of Chinese silk or Canton crepe, or whatever there happened to be in the storehouse.

They put under my charge everything having to do with clothing. I cut and fitted, and my five daughters sewed up the pieces. When they could not handle everything, the father was told, and then women from the town of Los Angeles were employed, and the father paid them.

Besides this, I had to attend to the soap-house, which was very large, to the wine-presses. and to the olive-crushers that produced oil, which I worked in myself. Under my direction and responsibility, Domingo Romero took care of changing the liquid.

Luis the soap-maker had charge of the soap-house, but I directed everything.

I handled the distribution of leather, calf-skin, chamois, sheepskin, Morocco leather, fine scarlet cloth, nails, thread, silk, etc.—everything having to do with the making of saddles, shoes and what was needed for the belt- and shoe-making shops.

Every week I delivered supplies for the troops and Spanish-speaking servants. These consisted of beans, corn, garbanzos, lentils, candles, soap and lard. To carry out this distribution, they placed at my disposal an Indian servant named Lucio, who was trusted completely by the missionaries.

When it was necessary, some of my daughters did what I could not find the time to do. Generally, the one who was always at my side was my daughter María del Rosario.

After all my daughters were married—the last one was Rita, about 1832 or 1833—Father Sánchez undertook to persuade me to marry First Lieutenant Juan Mariné, a Spaniard from Catalonia, a widower with family who had served in the artillery. I did not want to get married, but the father told me that Mariné was a very good man—as, in fact, he turned out to be—besides, he had some money, although he never turned his cash-box over to me. I gave in to the father's wishes because I did not have the heart to deny him anything when he had been father and mother to me and to all my family.

I served as housekeeper of the mission for twelve or fourteen years, until about two years after the death of Father José Sánchez, which oc-curred in this same mission.

A short while before Father Sánchez died, he seemed robust and in good health, in spite of his advanced age. When Captain Barroso[4] came and excited the Indians in all the missions to rebel, telling them that

4. Leonardo Díaz Barroso in 1831 was appointed deputy and commissioner of Mis-sion San Diego.

they were no longer neophytes but free men, Indians arrived from San Luis, San Juan and the rest of the missions. They pushed their way into the college, carrying their arms, because it was raining very hard. Outside the mission, guards and patrols made up of the Indians themselves were stationed. They had been taught to shout "Sentinel—on guard!" and "On guard he is!" but they said "Sentinel—open! Open he is!"

On seeing the Indians demoralized, Father Sánchez was very upset. He had to go to Los Angeles to say Mass, because he was accustomed to do so every week or fortnight, I do not remember which. He said to me, "Eulalia, I am going now. You know what the situation is; keep your eyes open and take care of what you can. Do not leave here, neither you nor your daughters." (My daughter María Antonia's husband, named Leonardo Higuera, was in charge of the Rancho de los Cerritos, which belonged to the mission, and María del Rosario's husband, Michael White, was in San Blas.)

The father left for the pueblo, and in front of the guard some Indians surged forward and cut the traces of his coach. He jumped out of the coach, and then the Indians, pushing him rudely, forced him toward his room. He was sad and filled with sorrow because of what the Indians had done and remained in his room for about a week without leaving it. He became ill and never again was his previous self. Blood flowed from his ears, and his head never stopped paining him until he died. He lived perhaps a little more than a month after the affair with the Indians, dying in the month of January, I think it was, of 1833. In that month there was a great flood. The river rose very high and for more than two weeks no one could get from one side to the other. Among our grandchildren was one that they could not bring to the mission for burial for something like two weeks, because of the flood. The same month—a few days after the father's death—Claudio López, who had been superintendent of the mission for something like thirty years, also died.

In the Mission of San Gabriel there was a large number of neophytes. The married ones lived on their rancherías with their small children. There were two divisions for the unmarried ones: one for the women, called the nunnery, and another for the men. They brought girls from the ages of seven, eight or nine years to the nunnery, and they were brought up there. They left to get married. They were under the care of a mother in the nunnery, an Indian. During the time I was at the mission this matron was named Polonia—they called her "Mother Superior." The alcalde was in charge of the unmarried men's division.

Every night both divisions were locked up, they keys were delivered to me, and I handed them over to the missionaries.

A blind Indian named Andresillo stood at the door of the nunnery and called out each girl's name, telling her to come in. If any girl was missing at admission time, they looked for her the following day and brought her to the nunnery. Her mother, if she had one, was brought in and punished for having detained her, and the girl was locked up for having been careless in not coming in punctually.

In the morning the girls were let out. First they went to Father Zalvidea's Mass, for he spoke the Indian language; afterwards they went to the mess hut to have breakfast, which sometimes consisted of corn gruel with chocolate, and on holidays with sweets and bread. On other days, ordinarily they had boiled barley and beans and meat. After eating breakfast each girl began the task that had been assigned to her beforehand—sometimes it was at the looms, or unloading, or sewing, or whatever there was to be done.

When they worked at unloading, at eleven o'clock they had to come up to one or two of the carts that carried refreshments out to the Indians working in the fields. This refreshment was made of water with vinegar and sugar, or sometimes with lemon and sugar. I was the one who made up that refreshment and sent it out, so the Indians would not get sick. That is what the missionaries ordered.

All work stopped at eleven, and at twelve o'clock the Indians came to the mess hut to eat barley and beans with meat and vegetables. At one o'clock they returned to their work, which ended for the day at sunset. Then all came to the mess hut to eat supper, which consisted of gruel with meat, sometimes just pure gruel. Each Indian carried his own bowl, and the mess attendant filled it up with the allotted portion. . . .

The Indians were taught the various jobs for which they showed an aptitude. Others worked in the fields, or took care of the horses, cattle, etc. Still others were carters, oxherds, etc.

At the mission, coarse cloth, scrapes, and blankets were woven, and saddles, bridles, boots, shoes and similar things were made. There was a soap-house, and a big carpenter shop as well as a small one, where those who were just beginning to learn carpentry worked; when they had mastered enough they were transferred to the big shop.

Wine and oil, bricks and adobe bricks were also made. Chocolate was manufactured from cocoa, brought in from the outside; and sweets were made. Many of these sweets, made by my own hands, were sent to Spain by Father Sánchez.

There was a teacher in every department, an instructed Indian who was Christianized. A white man headed the looms, but when the Indians were finally skilled, he withdrew.

My daughters and I made the chocolate, oil, sweets, lemonade and other things ourselves. I made plenty of lemonade—it was even bottled and sent to Spain.

The Indians also were taught to pray. A few of the more intelligent ones were taught to read and write. Father Zalvidea taught the Indians to pray in their Indian tongue; some Indians learned music and played instruments and sang at Mass. The sextons and pages who helped with Mass were Indians of the mission.

The punishments that were meted out were the stocks and confinement. When the misdemeanor was serious, the delinquent was taken to the guard, where they tied him to a pipe or a post and gave him twenty-five or more lashes, depending on his crime. Sometimes they put them in the head-stocks; other times they passed a musket from one leg to the other and fastened it there, and also they tied their hands. That punishment, called "The Law of Bayona," was very painful.

But Fathers Sánchez and Zalvidea were always very considerate with the Indians. I would not want to say what others did because they did not live in the mission. . . .

12

"Beginning to Work," from
A New England Girlhood (1889)

LUCY LARCOM

LUCY LARCOM (1824–1893), born in Beverly, Massachusetts, was one of ten children, eight of them daughters. The death of her father Benjamin, a sea captain and merchant, left the family with his large debt. Larcom's mother, Lois, moved the family to Lowell, Massachusetts, where the girls took jobs in the Lowell Mills and their mother established a boarding house for female mill employees. Larcom had several jobs—as a doffer charged with keeping the bobbins full, then as a spinner and a dresser. While working at the mill, she became active in an "improvement circle" of young mill women. The members of this circle read one another's poetry and prose, and supported each other's publications in various newspapers and magazines, notably the *Lowell Offering* (1840–45). Lowell editor and poet John Greenleaf Whittier recognized Larcom's talent and encouraged her writing. The two maintained a lifelong friendship in which Whittier acted as editor, "agent," and mentor.

In 1846 Larcom moved to the Midwest with two of her sisters and taught school until she entered the Monticello Seminary in Godfrey, Illinois, to study the liberal arts. After graduation in 1854, she accepted a teaching position at Wheaton College in Norton, Massachusetts, where she became a popular professor of English and rhetoric and founder of several societies and publications. With the publication of her poem "Hannah Binding Shoes," she won public acclaim and left Wheaton to devote herself to writing and editing the children's periodical *Our Young Folks* from 1854 to 1862. Her work, including poems, hymns, biographical sketches, a blank-verse novel, and articles, was widely published in popular journals, including the new literary magazine *The Atlantic Monthly*.

Larcom, who never married, was socially active and acquainted with writers Harriet Beecher Stowe and Ralph Waldo Emerson. Her coming-of-age narrative, *A New England Girlhood* (subtitled *Outlined from Memory*), was written in her fifties and published by Houghton Mifflin. This life story chronicles both the difficult conditions in the mills and the congenial sociality of working girls. This autobiography brought her the most recognition upon publication in 1889. In her last years she returned to Beverly. She died in Boston on April 17, 1893.

The chapter included from Larcom's *A New England Girlhood* explores the demands of work and the conflicting meanings of being gendered "girl," suggesting the shifts in identity and class affiliation she experienced on entering the mills. Carol Holly reads Larcom's narrative as a story of women's affiliation that invites the female reader into this dialogical process (223–26). While Larcom's narrative has not yet received the sustained critical attention as autobiography that it deserves, the discussion of "Industrialization" by Susan Albertine (in *The Oxford Companion to Women's Writing in the United States*) provides helpful contexts and a bibliographic overview.

A New England Girlhood
Outlined from Memory
Boston, New York, and Chicago
Houghton, Mifflin and Company
The Riverside Press, Cambridge

VII. Beginning to Work.

A child does not easily comprehend even the plain fact of death. Though I had looked upon my father's still, pale face in his coffin, the impression it left upon me was of sleep; more peaceful and sacred than common slumber, yet only sleep. My dreams of him were for a long time so vivid that I would say to myself, "He was here yesterday; he will be here again to-morrow," with a feeling that amounted to expectation.

We missed him, we children large and small who made up the yet untrained home crew, as a ship misses the man at the helm. His grave, clear perception of what was best for us, his brief words that decided, once for all, the course we were to take, had been far more to us than we knew.

It was hardest of all for my mother, who had been accustomed to depend entirely upon him. Left with her eight children, the eldest a boy of eighteen years, and with no property except the roof that sheltered us and a small strip of land, her situation was full of perplexities which we little ones could not at all understand. To be fed like the ravens and clothed like the grass of the field seemed to me, for one, a perfectly natural thing, and I often wondered why my mother was so fretted and anxious.

I knew that she believed in God, and in the promises of the Bible, and yet she seemed sometimes to forget everything but her troubles and her helplessness. I felt almost like preaching to her, but I was too small a child to do that, I well knew; so I did the next best thing I could think of—I sang hymns as if singing to myself, while I meant them for her. Sitting at the window with my book and my knitting, while she was preparing dinner or supper with a depressed air because she missed the abundant provision to which she had been accustomed, I would go from hymn to hymn, selecting those which I thought would be most comforting to her, out of the many that my memory book contained, and taking care to pronounce the words distinctly.

I was glad to observe that she listened to

> "Come, ye disconsolate,"

and

> "How firm a foundation;"

and that she grew more cheerful; though I did not feel sure that my singing cheered her so much as some happier thought that had come to her out of her own heart. Nobody but my mother, indeed, would have called my chirping singing. But as she did not seem displeased, I went on, a little more confidently, with some hymns that I loved for their starry suggestions,—

"When marshaled on the nightly plain,"

and

"Brightest and best of the sons of the morning,"

and

"Watchman, tell us of the night?"

The most beautiful picture in the Bible to me, certainly the loveliest in the Old Testament had always been that one painted by prophecy, of the time when wild and tame creatures should live together in peace, and children should be their fearless playmates. Even the savage wolf Poverty would be pleasant and neighborly then, no doubt! A Little Child among them, leading them, stood looking wistfully down through the soft sunrise of that approaching day, into the cold and darkness of the world. Oh, it would be so much better than the garden of Eden!

Yes, and it would be a great deal better, I thought, to live in the millennium, than even to die and go to heaven, although so many people around me talked as if that were the most desirable thing of all. But I could never understand why, if God sent us here, we should be in haste to get away, even to go to a pleasanter place.

I was perplexed by a good many matters besides. I had learned to keep most of my thoughts to myself, but I did venture to ask about the Resurrection—how it was that those who had died and gone straight to heaven, and had been singing there for thousands of years, could have any use for the dust to which their bodies had returned. Were they not already as alive as they could be? I found that there were different ideas of the resurrection among "orthodox" people, even then. I was told however, that this was too deep a matter for me, and so I ceased asking questions. But I pondered the matter of death; what did it mean? The Apostle Paul gave me more light on the subject than any of the ministers did. And, as usual, a poem helped me. It was Pope's Ode, beginning with,—

"Vital spark of heavenly flame,"—

which I learned out of a reading-book. To die was to "languish into life." That was the meaning of it! and I loved to repeat to myself the words,—

> Hark! they whisper: angels say,
> "Sister spirit, come away!"—
>
> The world recedes; it disappears!
> Heaven opens on my eyes! my ears
> With sounds seraphic ring.

A hymn that I learned a little later expressed to me the same satisfying thought:—

> For strangers into life we come,
> And dying is but going home.

The Apostle's words, with which the song of "The Dying Christian to his Soul" ends, left the whole cloudy question lit up with sunshine, to my childish thoughts:—

> O grave, where is thy victory?
> O death, where is thy sting?

My father was dead; but that only meant that he had gone to a better home than the one he lived in with us, and by and by we should go home, too.

Meanwhile the millennium was coming, and some people thought it was very near. And what was the millennium? Why, the time when everybody on earth would live just as they do in heaven. Nobody would be selfish, nobody would be unkind; no! not so much as in a single thought. What a delightful world this would be to live in then! Heaven itself could scarcely be much better! Perhaps people would not die at all, but, when the right time came, would slip quietly away into heaven, just as Enoch did.

My father had believed in the near millennium. His very last writing, in his sick- room, was a penciled computation, from the prophets, of the time when it would begin. The first minister who preached in our church, long before I was born, had studied the subject much, and had written books upon this, his favorite theme. The thought of it was continually breaking out, like bloom and sunshine, from the stern doctrines of the period.

One question in this connection puzzled me a good deal. Were people going to be made good in spite of themselves, whether they wanted to or not? And what would be done with the bad ones, if there were any left? I did not like to think of their being killed off, and yet everybody must be good, or it would not be a true millennium.

It certainly would not matter much who was rich, and who was poor, if goodness, and not money, was the thing everybody cared for. Oh, if the millennium would only begin now! I felt as if it were hardly fair to me that I should not be here during those happy thousand years, when I wanted to so much. But I had not lived even my short life in the world without learning something of my own faults and perversities; and when I saw that there was no sign of an approaching millennium in my heart I had to conclude that it might be a great way off, after all. Yet the very thought of it brought warmth and illumination to my dreams by day and by night. It was coming, some time! And the people who were in heaven would be as glad of it as those who remained on earth.

That it was a hard world for my mother and her children to live in at present I could not help seeing. The older members of the family found occupations by which the domestic burdens were lifted a little; but, with only the three youngest to clothe and to keep at school, there was still much more outgo than income, and my mother's discouragement every day increased.

My eldest brother had gone to sea with a relative who was master of a merchant vessel in the South American trade. His inclination led him that way; it seemed to open before him a prospect of profitable business, and my mother looked upon him as her future stay and support.

One day she came in among us children looking strangely excited. I heard her tell some one afterwards that she had just been to hear Father Taylor preach, the sailors' minister, whose coming to our town must have been a rare occurrence. His words had touched her personally, for he had spoken to mothers whose first-born had left them to venture upon strange seas and to seek unknown lands. He had even given to the wanderer he described the name of her own absent son—"Benjamin." As she left the church she met a neighbor who informed her that the brig "Mexican" had arrived at Salem, in trouble. It was the vessel in which my brother had sailed only a short time before, expecting to be absent for months. "Pirates" was the only word we children caught, as she hastened away from the house, not knowing whether her son was alive or not. Fortunately, the news hardly reached the town before my brother himself did. She met him in the street, and brought him home with her, forgetting all her anxieties in her joy at his safety.

The "Mexican" had been attacked on the high seas by the piratical craft "Panda," robbed of twenty thousand dollars in specie, set on fire, and abandoned to her fate, with the crew fastened down in the hold. One small skylight had accidentally been overlooked by the freebooters. The captain discovered it, and making his way through it to the deck, succeeded in putting out the fire, else vessel and sailors would have sunk together, and their fate would never have been known.

Breathlessly we listened whenever my brother would relate the story, which he did not at all enjoy doing, for a cutlass had been swung over his head, and his life threatened by the pirate's boatswain, demanding more money, after all had been taken. A Genoese messmate, Iachimo, shortened to plain "Jack" by the "Mexican's" crew, came to see my brother one day, and at the dinner table he went through the whole adventure in pantomime, which we children watched with wide-eyed terror and amusement. For there was some comedy mixed with what had been so nearly a tragedy, and Jack made us see the very whites of the black cook's eyes, who, favored by his color, had hidden himself all except that dilated whiteness between two great casks in the hold. Jack himself had fallen through a trap-door, was badly hurt, and could not extricate himself.

It was very ludicrous. Jack crept under the table to show us how he and the cook made eyes at each other down there in the darkness, not daring to speak. The pantomime was necessary, for the Genoese had very little English at his command.

When the pirate crew were brought into Salem for trial, my brother had the questionable satisfaction of identifying in the court-room the ruffian of a boatswain who had threatened his life. This boatswain and several others of the crew were executed in Boston. The boy found his brief sailor-experience quite enough for him, and afterward settled down quietly to the trade of a carpenter.

Changes thickened in the air around us. Not the least among them was the burning of "our meeting-house," in which we had all been baptized. One Sunday morning we children were told, when we woke, that we could not go to meeting that day, because the church was a heap of smoking ruins. It seemed to me almost like the end of the world.

During my father's life, a few years before my birth, his thoughts had been turned towards the new manufacturing town growing up on the banks of the Merrimack. He had once taken a journey there, with the possibility in his mind of making the place his home, his limited income furnishing no adequate promise of a maintenance for his large family of daughters. From the beginning, Lowell had a high reputation for good order, morality, piety, and all that was dear to the old-fashioned New Englander's heart.

After his death, my mother's thoughts naturally followed the direction his had taken; and seeing no other opening for herself, she sold her small estate, and moved to Lowell, with the intention of taking a corporation-house for mill-girl boarders. Some of the family objected, for the Old World traditions about factory life were anything but attractive; and they were current in New England until the experiment at Lowell had shown that independent and intelligent workers invariably give their own character to their occupation. My mother had visited Lowell, and she was willing and glad, knowing all about the place, to make it our home.

The change involved a great deal of work. "Boarders" signified a large house, many beds, and an indefinite number of people. Such piles of sewing accumulated before us! A sewing-bee, volunteered by the neighbors, reduced the quantity a little, and our child-fingers had to take their part. But the seams of those sheets did look to me as if they were miles long!

My sister Lida and I had our "stint,"—so much to do every day. It was warm weather, and that made it the more tedious, for we wanted to be running about the fields we were so soon to leave. One day, in sheer desperation, we dragged a sheet up with us into an apple-tree in the yard, and sat and sewed there through the summer afternoon, beguiling the irksomeness of our task by telling stories and guessing riddles.

It was hardest for me to leave the garret and the garden. In the old houses the garret was the children's castle. The rough rafters,—it was always an unfinished room, otherwise not a true garret,—the music of the rain on the roof, the worn sea-chests with their miscellaneous treasures, the blue-roofed cradle that had sheltered ten blue-eyed babies, the tape-looms and reels and spinning-wheels, the herby smells, and the delightful dream corners, these could not be taken with us to the new home. Wonderful people had looked out upon us from under those garret-eaves. Sindbad the Sailor and Baron Munchausen had sometimes strayed in and told us their unbelievable stories; and we had there made acquaintance with the great Caliph Haroun Alraschid.

To go away from the little garden was almost as bad. Its lilacs and peonies were beautiful to me; and in a corner of it was one tiny square of earth that I called my own, where I was at liberty to pull up my pinks and lady's delights, every day, to see whether they had taken root, and where I could give my lazy morning-glory seeds a poke, morning after morning, to help them get up and begin their climb. Oh, I should miss the garden very much indeed!

It did not take long to turn over the new leaf of our home experience. One sunny day three of us children, my youngest sister, my brother John, and I, took with my mother the first stage-coach journey of our lives, across Lynnfield plains and over Andover hills to the banks of the Merrimack. We were set down before an empty house in a yet unfinished brick block, where we watched for the bib wagon that was to bring our household goods.

It came at last; and the novelty of seeing our old furniture settled in new rooms kept us from being homesick. One after another they appeared, bedsteads, chairs, tables, and, to me most welcome of all, the old mahogany secretary with brass-handled drawers, that had always stood in the "front room" at home. With it came the barrel full of books that had filled its shelves, and they took their places as naturally as if they had always lived in this strange town.

There they all stood again side by side on their shelves, the dear, dull, good old volumes that all my life I had tried in vain to take a sincere Sabbath-day interest in,—Scott's Commentaries on the Bible, Hervey's "Meditations," Young's "Night Thoughts," "Edwards on the Affections," and the Writings of Baxter and Doddridge. Besides these, there were bound volumes of the "Repository Tracts," which I had read and re-read; and the delightfully miscellaneous "Evangelicana," containing an account of Gilbert Tennent's wonderful trance; also the "History of the Spanish Inquisition," with some painfully realistic illustrations; a German Dictionary, whose outlandish letters and words I liked to puzzle myself over; and a descriptive History of Hamburg, full of fine steel engravings—which last two or three volumes my father had brought with him from the countries to which he had sailed in his sea-faring days. A complete set of the " Missionary Herald," unbound, filled the upper shelves.

Other familiar articles journeyed with us: the brass-headed shovel and tongs, that it had been my especial task to keep bright; the two card tables (which were as unacquainted as ourselves with ace, face, and trump); the two china mugs, with their eighteenth-century lady and gentleman figures, curiosities brought from over the sea; and reverently laid away by my mother with her choicest relics in the secretary-desk, my father's miniature, painted in Antwerp, a treasure only shown occasionally to us children as a holiday treat; and my mother's easy-chair, I should have felt as if I had lost her, had that been left behind. The earliest unexpressed ambition of my infancy had been to grow up and wear a cap, and sit in an easy-chair knitting, and look comfortable, just as my mother did.

Filled up with these things, the little one-windowed sitting-room easily caught the home feeling and gave it back to us. Inanimate objects do gather into themselves something of the character of those who live among them, through association; and this alone makes heirlooms valuable. They are family treasures, because they are part of the family life, full of memories and inspirations. Bought or sold, they are nothing but old furniture. Nobody can buy the old associations; and nobody who has really felt how everything that has been in a horde makes part of it, can willingly bargain away the old things.

My mother never thought of disposing of her best furniture, whatever her need. It traveled with her in every change of her abiding-place, as long as she lived, so that to us children home seemed to accompany her wherever she went. And, remaining yet in the family, it often brings back to me pleasant reminders of my childhood. No other Bible seems quite so sacred to me as the old Family Bible, out of which my father used to read when we were all gathered around him for worship. To turn its leaves and look at its pictures was one of our few Sabbath-day indulgences; and I cannot touch it now except with feelings of profound reverence.

For the first time in our lives, my little sister and I became pupils in a grammar school for both girls and boys, taught by a man. I was put with her into the sixth class, but was sent the very next day into the first. I did not belong in either, but somewhere between. And I was very uncomfortable in my promotion, for though the reading and spelling and grammar and geography were perfectly easy, I had never studied anything but mental arithmetic, and did not know how to "do a sum." We had to show, when called up to recite, a slateful of sums, "done" and "proved." No explanations were ever asked of us.

The girl who sat next to me saw my distress, and offered to do my sums for me. I accepted her proposal, feeling, however, that I was a miserable cheat. But I was afraid of the master, who was tall and gaunt, and used to stalk across the school-room, right over the desk-tops, to find out if there was any mischief going on. Once, having caught a boy annoying a seat-mate with a pin, he punished the offender by pursuing him around the school-room, sticking a pin into his shoulder whenever he could overtake him. And he had a fearful leather strap, which was sometimes used even upon the shrinking palm of a little girl. If he should find out that I was a pretender and deceiver, as I knew that I was, I could not guess what might happen to me. He never did, however. I was left unmolested in the ignorance which I deserved. But I never liked the girl who did my sums, and I fancied she had a decided contempt for me.

There was a friendly looking boy always sitting at the master's desk; they called him "the monitor." It was his place to assist scholars who were in trouble about their lessons, but I was too bashful to speak to him, or to ask assistance of anybody. I think that nobody learned much under that regime, and the whole school system was soon after entirely reorganized.

Our house was quickly filled with a large feminine family. As a child, the gulf between little girlhood and young womanhood had always looked to me very wide. I supposed we should get across it by some sudden jump, by and by. But among these new companions of all ages, from fifteen to thirty years, we slipped into womanhood without knowing when or how.

Most of my mother's boarders were from New Hampshire and Vermont, and there was a fresh, breezy sociability about them which made them seem almost like a different race of beings from any we children had hitherto known.

We helped a little about the housework, before and after school, making beds, trimming lamps, and washing dishes. The heaviest work was done by a strong Irish girl, my mother always attending to the cooking herself. She was, however, a better caterer than the circumstances required or permitted. She liked to make nice things for the table, and, having been accustomed to an abundant supply, could never learn to economize. At a dollar and a quarter a week for board (the price allowed for mill-girls by the corporations) great care in expenditure was necessary. It was not in my mother's nature closely to calculate costs, and in this way there came to be a continually increasing leak in the family purse. The older members of the family did everything they could, but it was not enough. I heard it said one day, in a distressed tone, "The children will have to leave school and go into the mill."

There were many pros and cons between my mother and sisters before this was positively decided. The mill-agent did not want to take us two little girls, but consented on condition we should be sure to attend school the full number of months prescribed each year. I, the younger one, was then between eleven and twelve years old.

I listened to all that was said about it, very much fearing that I should not be permitted to do the coveted work. For the feeling had already frequently come to me, that I was the one too many in the overcrowded family nest. Once, before we left our old home, I had heard a neighbor condoling with my mother because there were so many of us, and her emphatic reply had been a great relief to my mind:—

"There isn't one more than I want. I could not spare a single one of my children."

But her difficulties were increasing, and I thought it would be a pleasure to feel that I was not a trouble or burden or expense to any-body. So I went to my first day's work in the mill with a light heart. The novelty of it made it seem easy, and it really was not hard, just to change the bobbins on the spinning-frames every three quarters of an hour or so, with half a dozen other little girls who were doing the same thing. When I came back at night, the family began to pity me for my long, tiresome day's work, but I laughed and said,—

"Why, it is nothing but fun. It is just like play."

And for a little while it was only a new amusement; I liked it better than going to school and "making believe" I was learning when I was not. And there was a great deal of play mixed with it. We were not occupied more than half the time. The intervals were spent frolicking around among the spinning-frames, teasing and talking to the older girls, or entertaining ourselves with games and stories in a corner, or exploring, with the overseer's permission, the mysteries of the carding-room, the dressing-room, and the weaving room.

I never cared much for machinery. The buzzing and hissing and whizzing of pulleys and rollers and spindles and flyers around me often grew tiresome. I could not see into their complications, or feel interested in them. But in a room below us we were sometimes al-lowed to peer in through a sort of blind door at the great waterwheel that carried the works of the whole mill. It was so huge that we could only watch a few of its spokes at a time, and part of its dripping ring, moving with a slow, measured strength through the darkness that shut it in. It impressed me with something of the awe which comes to us in thinking of the great Power which keeps the mechanism of the universe in motion. Even now, the remembrance of its large, mysteri-ous movement, in which every little motion of every noisy little wheel was involved, brings back to me a verse from one of my favorite hymns:—

> Our lives through various scenes are drawn,
> And vexed by trifling cares,
> While Thine eternal thought moves on
> Thy undisturbed affairs.

There were compensations for being shut in to daily toil so early. The mill itself had its lessons for us. But it was not, and could not be, the right sort of life for a child, and we were happy in the knowledge that, at the longest, our employment was only to be temporary.

When I took my next three months at the grammar school, everything there was changed, and I too was changed. The teachers were kind, and thorough in their instruction; and my mind seemed to have been ploughed up during that year of work, so that knowledge took root in it easily. It was a great delight to me to study, and at the end of the three months the master told me that I was prepared for the high school.

But alas! I could not go. The little money I could earn—one dollar a week, besides the price of my board—was needed in the family, and I must return to the mill. It was a severe disappointment to me, though I did not say so at home. I did not at all accept the conclusion of a neighbor whom I heard talking about it with my mother. His daughter was going to the high school, and my mother was telling him how sorry she was that I could not.

"Oh," he said, in a soothing tone, "my girl has not got any such head-piece as yours has. Your girl doesn't need to go."

Of course I knew that whatever sort of a "head-piece" I had, I did need and want just that very opportunity to study. I think the resolution was then formed, inwardly, that I would go to school again, some time, whatever happened. I went back to my work, but now without enthusiasm. I had looked through an open door that I was not willing to see shut upon me.

I began to reflect upon life rather seriously for a girl of twelve or thirteen. What was I here for? What could I make of myself? Must I submit to be carried along with the current, and do just what everybody else did? No: I knew I should not do that, for there was a certain Myself who was always starting up with her own original plan or aspiration before me, and who was quite indifferent as to what people generally thought.

Well, I would find out what this Myself was good for, and that she should be!

It was but the presumption of extreme youth. How gladly would I know now, after these long years, just why I was sent into the world, and whether I have in any degree fulfilled the purpose of my being!

In the older times it was seldom said to little girls, as it always has been said to boys, that they ought to have some definite plan, while they were children, what to be and do when they were grown up. There was usually but one path open before them, to become good wives and housekeepers. And the ambition of most girls was to follow their mothers' footsteps in this direction; a natural and laudable ambition.

But girls, as well as boys, must often have been conscious of their own peculiar capabilities,—must have desired to cultivate and make use of their individual powers. When I was growing up, they had already begun to be encouraged to do so. We were often told that it was our duty to develop any talent we might possess, or at least to learn how to do some one thing which the world needed, or which would make it a pleasanter world.

When I thought what I should best like to do, my first dream—almost a baby's dream—about it was that it would be a fine thing to be a schoolteacher, like Aunt Hannah. Afterward, when I heard that there were artists, I wished I could some time be one. A slate and pencil, to draw pictures, was my first request whenever a day's ailment kept me at home from school; and I rather enjoyed being a little ill, for the sake of amusing myself in that way. The wish grew up with me; but there were no good drawing-teachers in those days, and if there had been, the cost of instruction would have been beyond the family means. My sister Emilie, however, who saw my taste and shared it herself, did her best to assist me, furnishing me with pencil and paper and paint-box.

If I could only make a rose bloom on paper, I thought I should be happy! or if I could at last succeed in drawing the outline of winter-stripped boughs as I saw them against the sky, it seemed to me that I should be willing to spend years in trying. I did try a little, and very often. Jack Frost was my most inspiring teacher. His sketches on the bedroom window-pane in cold mornings were my ideal studies of Swiss scenery, crags and peaks and chalets and fir-trees, and graceful tracery of ferns, like those that grew in the woods where we went huckleberry-ing, all blended together by his touch of enchantment. I wondered whether human fingers ever succeeded in imitating that lovely work.

The taste has followed me all my life through, but I could never indulge it except as a recreation. I was not to be an artist, and I am rather glad that I was hindered, for I had even stronger inclinations in other directions; and art, really noble art, requires the entire devotion of a lifetime.

I seldom thought seriously of becoming an author, although it seemed to me that anybody who had written a book would have a right to feel very proud. But I believed that a person must be exceedingly wise, before presuming to attempt it: although now and then I thought I could feel ideas growing in my mind that it might be worth while to put into a book,—if I lived and studied until I was forty or fifty years old.

I wrote my little verses, to be sure, but that was nothing; they just grew. They were the same as breathing or singing. I could not help writing them, and I thought and dreamed a great many that never were put on paper. They seemed to fly into my mind and away again, like birds going with a carol through the air. It seemed strange to me that people should notice them, or should think my writing verses anything peculiar; for I supposed that they were in everybody's mind, just as they were in mine, and that anybody could write them who chose.

One day I heard a relative say to my mother,—

"Keep what she writes till she grows up, and perhaps she will get money for it. I have heard of somebody who earned a thousand dollars by writing poetry."

It sounded so absurd to me. Money for writing verses! One dollar would be as ridiculous as a thousand. I should as soon have thought of being paid for thinking! My mother, fortunately, was sensible enough never to flatter me or let me be flattered about my scribbling. It never was allowed to hinder any work I had to do. I crept away into a corner to write what came into my head, just as I ran away to play; and I looked upon it only as my most agreeable amusement, never thinking of preserving anything which did not of itself stay in my memory. This too was well, for the time did not come when I could afford to look upon verse-writing as an occupation. Through my life, it has only been permitted to me as an aside from other more pressing employments. Whether I should have written better verses had circumstances left me free to do what chose, it is impossible now to know.

All my thoughts about my future sent me back to Aunt Hannah and my first infantile idea of being a teacher. I foresaw that I should be that before I could be or do anything else. It had been impressed upon me that I must make myself useful in the world, and certainly one could be useful who could "keep school" as Aunt Hannah did. I did not see anything else for a girl to do who wanted to use her brains as well as her hands. So the plan of preparing myself to be a teacher gradually and almost unconsciously shaped itself in my mind as the only practicable one. I could earn my living in that way,—an all-important consideration.

I liked the thought of self-support, but I would have chosen some artistic or beautiful work if I could. I had no especial aptitude for teaching, and no absorbing wish to be a teacher, but it seemed to me that I might succeed if I tried. What I did like about it was that one must know something first. I must acquire knowledge before I could impart it, and that was just what I wanted. I could be a student, wherever I was and whatever else I had to be or do, and I would!

I knew I should write; I could not help doing that, for my hand seemed instinctively to move towards pen and paper in moments of leisure. But to write anything worth while, I must have mental cultivation; so, in preparing myself to teach, I could also be preparing myself to write.

This was the plan that indefinitely shaped itself in my mind as I returned to my work in the spinning-room, and which I followed out, not without many breaks and hindrances and neglects, during the next six or seven years, to learn all I could, so that I should be fit to teach or to write, as the way opened. And it turned out that fifteen or twenty of my best years were given to teaching.

13

"Looking Back on Girlhood" (1892)

Sarah Orne Jewett

SARAH ORNE JEWETT (1849–1909) was born on September 3, 1849, in South Berwick, Maine, where she lived for most of her life. The small-town New England settings and themes that figure prominently in Jewett's work have contributed to critical characterization of Jewett as a "local color" fiction writer. Although landscape and place are, indeed, key in Jewett's work, she is now being recognized as not merely a regional writer, but as a major figure in late nineteenth- and early twentieth-century letters, and a subject for feminist and queer critical interrogations.

Jewett was the second of three daughters of Theodore H. Jewett, a doctor, and his wife, Caroline Perry Jewett. While her relatively affluent family was able to provide her with some formal education at Miss Raynes School and Berwick Academy, chronic childhood illnesses prevented her from attending school regularly. Instead, Sarah accompanied her father on his rounds, an experience that she claimed was her formative education. Her best-known novel, *A Country Doctor* (1884), details the life of a female physician and incorporates rural vernacular.

Jewett published her first short story, "Jenny Garrow's Lovers," in 1868, shortly after graduation. With the support of William Dean

Howells, her work subsequently appeared in other magazines, including *The Atlantic Monthly*. In 1877, her first short story collection, *Deephaven*, was published. Jewett's prolific literary output includes *The Country of the Pointed Firs* (1896), a novella widely acclaimed as her finest work.

In addition to her fiction, Jewett corresponded with and sustained friendships with many luminaries of her day, including Henry James, Harriet Beecher Stowe, John Greenleaf Whittier, and Rudyard Kipling. Her most passionate relationship, however, was with Annie Fields, wife of Boston publisher James T. Fields. After his death, the two women lived together, spending part of the year at Annie's Boston residence, part of the year at Sarah's home in Maine, and traveled to Europe and the Caribbean. Sarah's romantic friendship with Annie, fifteen years her senior, may have inspired relationships in her fiction in which older women mentor younger women in affectionate friendships.

Injuries sustained in a carriage accident on her birthday in 1902 cut short Jewett's literary career. Chronic pain made it impossible for her to concentrate on writing for the remainder of her life, although she continued corresponding with and visiting intellectuals and writers, including Willa Cather, whom Jewett met in 1908 and upon whom she was a powerful influence. Cather dedicated her early novel *O, Pioneers!* (1913) to Jewett's memory. Jewett died of a cerebral hemorrhage in 1909.

The selection included here, "Looking Back on Girlhood," written in 1892, first appeared in the small magazine *Youth's Companion*, and was later reprinted in *The Uncollected Short Stories of Sarah Orne Jewett*, edited by Richard Cary (1971). To date we do not know of critical treatments of this essay as autobiography. For discussions of Jewett's fiction, see Sarah Way Sherman (1989), Marilyn Sanders Mobley (1991), and the edited volume by Karen L. Kilcup and Thomas S. Edwards (1999).

"Looking Back on Girlhood"

Prefatory

In giving this brief account of my childhood, or, to speak exactly, of the surroundings which have affected the course of my work as a writer, my first thought flies back to those who taught me to observe, and to know the deep pleasures of simple things, and to be interested in the lives of people about me.

With its high hills and pine forests, and all its ponds and brooks and distant mountain views, there are few such delightful country towns in New England as the one where I was born. Being one of the oldest colonial settlements, it is full of interesting traditions and relics of the early inhabitants, both Indians and Englishmen. Two large rivers join just below the village at the head of tide-water, and these, with the great inflow from the sea, make a magnificent stream, bordered on its seaward course now by high-wooded banks of dark pines and hemlocks, and again by lovely green fields that slope gently to long lines of willows at the water's edge.

There is never-ending pleasure in making one's self familiar with such a region. One may travel at home in a most literal sense, and be always learning history, geography, botany, or biography—whatever one chooses.

I have had a good deal of journeying in my life, and taken great delight in it, but I have never taken greater delight than in my rides and drives and tramps and voyages within the borders of my native town. There is always something fresh, something to be traced or discovered, something particularly to be remembered. One grows rich in memories and associations.

I believe that we should know our native towns much better than most of us do, and never let ourselves be strangers at home. Particularly when one's native place is so really interesting as my own!

Above tide-water the two rivers are barred by successive falls. You hear the noise of them by night in the village like the sound of the sea, and this fine water power so near the coast, beside a great salmon fishery famous among the Indians, brought the first English settlers to the town in 1627. I know some families who still live upon the lands which their ancestors bought from the Indians, and their single deed bears the queer barbaric signatures.

There are many things to remind one of these early settlers beside the old farms upon which they and their descendants have lived for six or seven generations. One is a quaint fashion of speech which survives among the long-established neighborhoods, in words and phrases common in England in the sixteenth and seventeenth centuries.

One curious thing is the pronunciation of the name of the town: Berwick by the elder people has always been called *Barvik,* after the fashion of Danes and Northmen; never *Berrik,* as the word has so long been pronounced in modern England.

The descendants of the first comers to the town have often been distinguished in the affairs of their time. No village of its size in New England could boast, particularly in the early part of the present century, of a larger number of men and women who kept themselves more closely in touch with "the best that has been thought and said in the world."

As I write this, I keep in mind the truth that I have no inheritance from the ancient worth and dignity of Berwick—or what is now North Berwick—in Maine. My own people are comparatively late comers. I was born in a pleasant old colonial house built near 1750, and bought by my grandfather sixty or seventy years ago, when he brought his household up the river to Berwick from Portsmouth.

He was a sea-captain, and had run away to sea in his boyhood and led a most adventurous life, but was quite ready to forsake seafaring in his early manhood, and at last joined a group of acquaintances who were engaged in the flourishing West India trade of that time.

For many years he kept and extended his interests in shipping, building ships and buying large quantities of timber from the northward and eastward, and sending it down the river and so to sea.

This business was still in existence in my early childhood, and the manner of its conduct was primitive enough, the barter system still prevailing by force of necessity. Those who brought the huge sticks of oak and pine timber for masts and plank were rarely paid in money, which was of comparatively little use in remote and sparsely settled districts. When the sleds and long trains of yoked oxen returned from the river wharves to the stores, they took a lighter load in exchange of flour and rice and barrels of molasses, of sugar and salt and cotton cloth and raisins and spices and tea and coffee; in fact, all the household necessities and luxuries that the northern farms could not supply.

They liked to have a little money with which to pay their taxes and their parish dues, if they were so fortunate as to be parishioners, but they needed very little money besides.

So I came in contact with the up-country people as well as with the sailors and shipmasters of the other side of the business. I used to linger about the busy country stores, and listen to the graphic country talk. I heard the greetings of old friends, and their minute details of neighborhood affairs, their delightful jokes and Munchausen-like reports of tracts of timber-pines ever so many feet through at the butt.

When the great teams came in sight at the head of the village street, I ran to meet them over the creaking snow, if possible to mount and ride into town in triumph; but it was not many years before I began to feel sorry at the sight of every huge lopped stem of oak or pine that came trailing along after the slow-stepping, frosted oxen. Such trees are unreplaceable. I only know of one small group now in all this part of the country of those great timber pines.

My young ears were quick to hear the news of a ship's having come into port, and I delighted in the elderly captains, with their sea-tanned faces, who came to report upon their voyages, dining cheerfully and heartily with my grandfather, who listened eagerly to their exciting tales of great storms on the Atlantic, and winds that blew them northabout, and good bargains in Havana, or Barbadoes, or Havre.

I listened as eagerly as any one; this is the charming way in which I was taught something of a fashion of life already on the wane, and of that subsistence upon sea and forest bounties which is now almost a forgotten thing in my part of New England.

Much freight still came and went by the river gundelows and packets long after the railroad had made such changes, and every village along its line lost its old feeling of self-sufficiency.

In my home the greater part of the minor furnishings had come over in the ships from Bristol and Havre. My grandfather seemed to be a citizen of the whole geography. I was always listening to stories of three wars from older people—the siege of Louisburg, the Revolution, in which my father's ancestors had been honest but mistaken Tories, and in which my mother's, the Gilmans of Exeter, had taken a nobler part.

As for the War of 1812, "the last war," as everybody called it, it was a thing of yesterday in the town. One of the famous privateer crews was gathered along our own river shore, and one member of the crew, in his old age, had been my father's patient.

The Berwick people were great patriots, and were naturally proud of the famous Sullivans, who were born in the upper part of the town, and came to be governors and judge and general.

I often heard about Lafayette, who had made an ever-to-be-remembered visit in order to see again some old friends who lived in the town. The name of a famous Colonel Hamilton, the leader in the last century of the West India trade, and the histories of the old Berwick houses of Chadbourn and Lord were delightfully familiar, and one of the traditions of the latter family is more than good enough to be told again.

There was a Berwick lad who went out on one of the privateers that sailed from Portsmouth in the Revolution. The vessel was taken by a British frigate, and the crew put in irons. One day one of the English midshipmen stood near these prisoners as they took their airing on deck, and spoke contemptuously about "the rebels."

Young Lord heard what he said, and turned himself about to say boldly, "If it were not for your rank, sir, I would make you take that back!"

"No matter about my rank," said the gallant middy. "If you can whip me, you are welcome to."

So they had a "capital good fight," standing over a tea-chest, as proud tradition tells, and the Berwick sailor was the better fighter of the two, and won.

The Englishman shook hands, and asked his name and promised not to forget him—which was certainly most handsome behavior.

When they reached an English port all the prisoners but one were sent away under guard to join the other American prisoners of war; but the admiral sent for a young man named Nathan Lord, and told him that his Grace the Duke of Clarence, son of his majesty the King, begged for his pardon, and had left a five-pound note at his disposal.

This was not the first or last Berwick lad who proved himself of good courage in a fight, but there never was another to whip a future King of England, and moreover to be liked the better for it by that fine gentleman.

My grandfather died in my eleventh year, and presently the Civil War began.

From that time the simple village life was at an end. Its provincial character was fading out; shipping was at a disadvantage, and there were no more bronzed sea-captains coming to dine and talk about their voyages, no more bags of filberts or oranges for the children, or great red jars of olives; but in these childish years I had come in contact with many delightful men and women of real individuality and breadth of character, who had fought the battle of life to good advantage, and sometimes against great odds.

In these days I was given to long, childish illnesses, and it must be honestly confessed, to instant drooping if ever I were shut up in school. I had apparently not the slightest desire for learning, but my father was always ready to let me be his companion in long drives about the country.

In my grandfather's business household, my father, unconscious of tonnage and timber measurement, of the markets of the Windward Islands or the Mediterranean ports, had taken to his book, as old people said, and gone to college and begun that devotion to the study of medicine which only ended with his life.

I have tried already to give some idea of my father's character in my story of "The Country Doctor," but all that is inadequate to the gifts and character of the man himself. He gave me my first and best knowledge of books by his own delight and dependence upon them, and ruled my early attempts at writing by the severity and simplicity of his own good taste.

"Don't try to write *about* people and things, tell them just as they are!"

How often my young ears heard these words without comprehending them! But while I was too young and thoughtless to share in an enthusiasm for Sterne or Fielding, and Smollett or Don Quixote, my mother and grandmother were leading me into the pleasant ways of "Pride and Prejudice," and "The Scenes of Clerical Life," and the delightful stories of Mrs. Oliphant.

The old house was well provided with leather-bound books of a deeply serious nature, but in my youthful appetite for knowledge, I could even in the driest find something vital, and in the more entertaining I was completely lost.

My father had inherited from his father an amazing knowledge of human nature, and from his mother's French ancestry, that peculiarly French trait, called *gaieté de cœur*. Through all the heavy responsibilities and anxieties of his busy professional life, this kept him young at heart and cheerful. His visits to his patients were often made perfectly delightful and refreshing to them by his kind heart, and the charm of his personality.

I knew many of the patients whom he used to visit in lonely inland farms, or on the seacoast in York and Wells. I used to follow him about silently, like an undemanding little dog, content to follow at his heels.

I had no consciousness of watching or listening, or indeed of any special interest in the country interiors. In fact, when the time came that my own world of imaginations was more real to me than any other, I was sometimes perplexed at my father's directing my attention to certain points of interest in the character or surroundings of our acquaintances.

I cannot help believing that he recognized, long before I did myself, in what direction the current of purpose in my life was setting. Now, as I write my sketches of country life, I remember again and again the wise things he said, and the sights he made me see. He was only impatient with affectation and insincerity.

I may have inherited something of my father's and grandfather's knowledge of human nature, but my father never lost a chance of trying to teach me to observe. I owe a great deal to his patience with a heedless little girl given far more to dreams than to accuracy, and with perhaps too little natural sympathy for the dreams of others.

The quiet village life, the dull routine of farming or mill life, early became interesting to me. I was taught to find everything that an imaginative child could ask, in the simple scenes close at hand.

I say these things eagerly, because I long to impress upon every boy and girl this truth: that it is not one's surroundings that can help or hinder—it is having a growing purpose in one's life to make the most of whatever is in one's reach.

If you have but a few good books, learn those to the very heart of them. Don't for one moment believe that if you had different surroundings and opportunities you would find the upward path any easier to climb. One condition is like another, if you have not the determination and the power to grow in yourself.

I was still a child when I began to write down the things I was thinking about, but at first I always made rhymes and found prose so difficult that a school composition was a terror to me, and I do not remember ever writing one that was worth anything. But in course of time rhymes themselves became difficult and prose more and more enticing, and I began my work in life, most happy in finding that I was to write of those country characters and rural landscapes to which I myself belonged, and which I had been taught to love with all my heart.

I was between nineteen and twenty when my first sketch was accepted by Mr. Howells for the *Atlantic*. I already counted myself as by no means a new contributor to one or two other magazines—*Young Folks* and *The Riverside*—but I had no literary friends "at court."

I was very shy about speaking of my work at home, and even sent it to the magazine under an assumed name, and then was timid about asking the post-mistress for those mysterious and exciting editorial letters which she announced upon the post-office list as if I were a stranger in the town.

14

"The Club Movement among Colored Women of America" (1900)

Fannie Barrier Williams

FRANCES "FANNIE" BARRIER WILLIAMS (1855–1944) was born in Brockport, New York, in 1855, one of three children of Anthony and Harriet Barrier, free African Americans. There, the family suffered little discrimination, and she lived a childhood she would later describe as idyllic. Although the Barriers were the only African American family at the First Baptist Church, they were active in its affairs and had a vibrant social life in a community relatively free of interracial tensions.

Following her 1870 graduation from Brockport Normal School (now SUNY-Brockport), where she was the first African American to receive a degree, Barrier Williams encountered difficulties. After teaching in Washington D.C.'s public schools in hope of assisting freedmen, she left to explore her own artistic and musical inclinations. Despite racial discrimination at the School of Fine Arts in Washington and the New England Conservatory of Music in Boston, she became an accomplished portraitist and pianist. Her education was cut short in Boston, however, when she was asked to leave the Conservatory after Southern students threatened to quit if she remained. A visit to the South, which exposed her to lynching and Jim Crow laws, forced her to rethink her early notions of racial harmony. Returning to teaching, she met and married S. Laing Williams, a law student at Columbian University (now George Washington University Law School) in 1887. He established a practice in Chicago with Ferdinand Barnett, Ida B. Wells-Barnett's husband, and with help from his wife's friend, Booker T. Washington, later became assistant district attorney in Chicago.

Meanwhile Barrier Williams became an active reformer. She and her husband worked for the Hyde Park Colored Voters Republican Club and the Taft Colored League. She also became director of art and music in the Prudence Crandall Study Club, founded by influential members of the African American community. In 1891 she helped establish the interracial Provident Hospital and its training school, which accepted African American women. Becoming increasingly conscious of gender discrimination, especially toward African American women, she established the National League of Colored Women in 1893, and co-founded the National Association of Colored Women in 1896. She served as the African American representative and chairperson of state schools for dependent children in the Illinois Women's Alliance and spoke in support of women's suffrage. She also wrote for the *Chicago Record-Herald* and the *New York Age*.

In 1893 Barrier Williams worked for the inclusion of African Americans in Chicago's Columbian Exposition. She was granted a position as clerk in the department of publicity and promotions, where she handled "Colored Interests" and worked for African American staff appointments and issues on the agenda. At the Exposition she made a now famous speech, "The Intellectual Progress of the Colored Women of the United States Since the Emancipation Proclamation," praised by Frederick Douglass, and another speech entreating churches to desegregate. In 1894 she was nominated for membership in the prestigious all-white Chicago Women's Club, which caused dissension in the club but did not deter her, although many members eventually withdrew from the organization. Barrier Williams's essay on the club movement, included here, was first published in the essays and polemics collected by Booker T. Washington in *A New Negro for a New Century* (1900), which intended to provide both African American and white readers with "an Accurate and Up-to-Date record of the Upward Struggles of the Negro Race," particularly "The Colored Woman and

Her Part in Race Regeneration." At the National Colored Women's Congress, Barrier Williams and several other renowned African American women, including Ida B. Wells, broke with Booker T. Washington's position of appeasement to the white supremacist South to side with W. E. B. Du Bois's assertion of African American nationalism.

Barrier Williams remained a supporter of Du Bois and helped found the NAACP. When she attended the 1907 National American Women's Suffrage Association convention, she was the only African American chosen to eulogize Susan B. Anthony. After her husband's death in 1921, she stayed in Chicago, where she became the first woman and the first African American to serve on the Chicago Library Board (from 1924 to 1926). Thereafter she returned to live with her sister in Brockport, where she continued her activist work for African American women until her death.

In this selection, Barrier Williams's emphasis on the importance of women's affiliation in club movements and her efforts to integrate the suffragist movement mark her as a new-model African American woman writer in the Reconstruction and post-Reconstruction eras: educated, middle-class, socially prominent, politically both pragmatic and theoretically grounded.

"The Club Movement among Colored Women of America"

Afro-American women of the United States have never had the benefit of a discriminating judgment concerning their worth as women made up of the good and bad of human nature. What they have been made to be and not what they are, seldom enters into the best or worst opinion concerning them.

In studying the status of Afro-American women as revealed in their club organizations, it ought to be borne in mind that such social differentiations as "women's interests, children's interests, and men's interests" that are so finely worked out in the social development of the more favored races are but recent recognitions in the progressive life of the negro race. Such specializing had no economic value in slavery days, and the degrading habit of regarding the negro race as an unclassified people has not yet wholly faded into a memory.

The negro as an "alien" race, as a "problem," as an "industrial factor," as "ex-slaves," as "ignorant" etc., are well known and instantly recognized; but colored women as mothers, as home-makers, as the center and source of the social life of the race have received little or no attention. These women have been left to grope their way unassisted toward a realization of those domestic virtues, moral impulses and standards of family and social life that are the badges of race respectability. They have had no special teachers to instruct them. No conventions of distinguished women of the more favored race have met to consider their peculiar needs. There has been no fixed public opinion to which they could appeal; no protection against the libelous attacks upon their characters, and no chivalry generous enough to guarantee their safety against man's inhumanity to woman. Certain it is that colored women have been the least known and the most ill-favored class of women in this country.

Thirty-five years ago they were unsocialized, unclassed and unrecognized as either maids or matrons. They were simply women whose character and personality excited no interest. If within thirty-five years they have become sufficiently important to be studied apart from the general race problem and have come to be recognized as an integral part of the general womanhood of American civilization, that fact is a gratifying evidence of real progress.

In considering the social advancement of these women, it is important to keep in mind the point from which progress began, and the fact that they have been mainly self-taught in all those precious things that make for social order, purity and character. They have gradually become conscious of the fact that progress includes a great deal more than what is generally meant by the terms culture, education and contact.

The club movement among colored women reaches into the sub-social condition of the entire race. Among white women clubs mean the forward movement of the best women in the interest of the best womanhood. Among colored women the club is the effort of the few competent in behalf of the many incompetent; that is to say that the club is only one of many means for the social uplift of a race. Among white women the club is the onward movement of the already uplifted.

The consciousness of being fully free has not yet come to the great masses of the colored women in this country. The emancipation of the mind and spirit of the race could not be accomplished by legislation. More time, more patience, more suffering and more charity are still needed to complete the work of emancipation.

The training which first enabled colored women to organize and successfully carry on club work was originally obtained in church work. These churches have been and still are the great preparatory schools in which the primary lessons of social order, mutual trustfulness and united effort have been taught. The churches have been sustained, enlarged and beautified principally through the organized efforts of their women members. The meaning of unity of effort for the common good, the development of social sympathies grew into woman's consciousness through the privileges of church work.

Still another school of preparation for colored women has been their secret societies. "The ritual of these secret societies is not without a certain social value." They demand a higher order of intelligence than is required for church membership. Care for the sick, provisions for the decent burial of the indigent dead, the care for orphans and the enlarging sense of sisterhood all contributed to the development of the very conditions of heart that qualify women for the more inclusive work of those social reforms that are the aim of women's clubs. The churches and secret societies have helped to make colored women acquainted with the general social condition of the race and the possibilities of social improvement.

With this training the more intelligent women of the race could not fail to follow the example and be inspired by the larger club movement of the white women. The need of social reconstruction became more and more apparent as they studied the results of women's organizations. Better homes, better schools, better protection for girls of scant home training. Better sanitary conditions, better opportunities for competent young women to gain employment, and the need of being better known to the American people appealed to the conscience of progressive colored women from many communities.

The clubs and leagues organized among colored women have all been more or less in direct response to these appeals. Seriousness of purpose has thus been the main characteristic of all these organizations. While the National Federation of Woman's Clubs has served as a guide and inspiration to colored women, the club movement among them is something deeper than a mere imitation of white women. It is nothing less than the organized anxiety of women who have become intelligent enough to recognize their own low social condition and strong enough to initiate the forces of reform.

The club movement as a race influence among the colored women of the country may be fittingly said to date from July, 1895, when the first national conference of colored women was held in Boston, Mass. Prior to this time there were a number of strong clubs in some of the larger cities of the country, but they were not affiliated and the larger idea of effecting the social regeneration of the race was scarcely conceived of.

Among the earlier clubs the Woman's League of Washington, D.C., organized in 1892, and the Woman's Era Club of Boston, organized in January, 1893, were and are still the most thorough and influential organizations of the kind in the country.

The kind of work carried on by the Washington League since its organization is best indicated by its standing committees, as follows:

Committee on Education.
Committee on Industries.
Committee on Mending and Sewing.
Committee on Free Class Instruction.
Committee on Day Nursery.
Committee on Building Fund.

These various activities include sewing schools, kindergartens, well-conducted night schools, and mother's meetings, all of which have been developed and made a prominent part of the educational and social forces of the colored people of the capital. The league has made itself the recognized champion of every cause in which colored women and children have any special interests in the District of Columbia.

The league is also especially strong in the personnel of its membership, being made up largely of teachers, many of whom are recognized as among the most cultured and influential women of the negro race in this country.

Mrs. Helen Cook, of Washington, was the first president elected by the league, and still holds that position. Mrs. Cook belongs to one of the oldest and best-established colored families in the country. She has had all the advantages of culture, contact, and experience to make her an ideal leader of the leading woman's organization of the colored race.

The Woman's League claims to have originated the idea of a national organization of colored women's clubs. In its annual report for 1895 there occurs the following language:

The idea of national organization has been embodied in the Woman's League of Washington from its formation. It existed fully developed in the minds of the original members even before they united themselves into an association which has national union for its central thought, its inspiring motive, its avowed purpose—its very reason for being.

Having assumed a national character by gaining the affiliations of such clubs as the Kansas City League, the Denver League, and associations in Virginia, South Carolina and Pennsylvania, the Washington League was admitted into the membership of the National Council of Women of the United States.

The league is very tenacious of its name and claim as the originator of the idea of nationalizing the colored women's clubs of America, but its claim has always been challenged with more or less spirit by some of the clubs composing the National Association.

The New Era Club of Boston was organized in the month of February, 1893. The desire of the cultured and public-spirited colored women of that city to do something in the way of promoting a more favorable public opinion in behalf of the negro race was the immediate incentive to this organization. The club began its work of agitation by collecting data and issuing leaflets and tracts containing well-edited matter in reference to Afro-American progress. Its most conspicuous work has been the publication of the Woman's Era, the first newspaper ever published by colored women in this country. This paper gained a wide circulation and did more than any other single agency to nationalize the club idea among the colored women of the country. The New Era Club has sustained its reputation as the most representative organization of colored people in New England. It has taken the initiative in many reforms and helpful movements that have had a wide influence on race development. This club has been especially useful and influential in all local affairs that in any way effect the colored people. Deserving young men and women struggling to obtain an education, and defenseless young women in distress have always been able to find substantial assistance in the New Era Club.

This Boston organization embraces a membership of about one hundred women, many of whom are prominent in the ranks of New England's strongest women.

Mrs. Josephine St. Pierre Ruffin has been the president of the Era Club all the time since its organization. She is an active member in many of the influential women's organizations in Massachusetts. She is a woman of rare force of character, mental alertness and of generous impulses. She has played a leading part in every movement that has tended to the emancipation of colored women from the thraldom of past conditions. Her husband, the late judge Ruffin, held the first position of a judicial character ever held by a colored man in New England.

These two clubs, located respectively in Washington and Boston, were worthy beginnings of the many local efforts that were destined to grow and spread until there should be such a thing in the United States as a national uprising of the colored women of the country pledged to the serious work of a social reconstruction of the negro race.

But these two clubs were not the only examples of the colored woman's capacity for organization. The following clubs were thoroughly organized and actively engaged in the work of reform contemporaneously with the clubs of Boston and Washington:

The Harper Woman's Club of Jefferson City, Mo., was formed in 1890 and had established a training school for instruction in sewing; a temperance department and mothers' meetings were also carried on. The Loyal Union of Brooklyn and New York was organized in December, 1892. It had a membership of seventy-five women and was engaged largely in agitating for better schools and better opportunities for young women seeking honorable employment; the I. B. W. Club of Chicago, Ill., organized in 1893; the Woman's Cub of Omaha, Neb., organized February, 1895; the Belle Phoebe League of Pittsburg, Pa., organized November, 1894; the Woman's League of Denver; the Phyllis Wheatley Club of New Orleans; the Sojourner Club of Providence, R. I., and the Woman's Mutual Improvement Club of Knoxville, Tenn., organized in 1894.

It will thus be seen that from 1890 to 1895 the character of Afro-American womanhood began to assert itself in definite purposes and efforts in club work. Many of these clubs came into being all unconscious of the influences of the larger club movement among white women. The incentive in most cases was quite simple and direct. How to help and protect some defenseless and tempted young woman; how to aid some poor boy to complete a much-coveted education; how to lengthen the short school term in some impoverished school district; how to instruct and interest deficient mothers in the difficulties of child training are some of the motives that led to the formation of the great majority of these clubs. These were the first out-reachings of sympathy and fellowship felt by women whose lives had been narrowed by the petty concerns of the struggle for existence and removed by human cruelty from all the harmonies of freedom, love and aspirations.

Many of these organizations so humble in their beginnings and meager in membership clearly needed behind them the force and favor of some larger sanction to save them from timidity and pettiness of effort. Many of them clearly needed the inspirations, the wider vision and supporting strength that come from a national unity. The club in Mississippi could have a better understanding of its own possibilities by feeling the kinship of the club in New England or Chicago, and the womanhood sympathy of these northern clubs must remain narrow and inefficient if isolated in interest from the self-emancipating struggles of southern clubs.

As already noted some of the more progressive clubs had already conceived the idea of a National organization. The Woman's Era journal of Boston began to agitate the matter in the summer of 1894, and requested the clubs to express themselves through its columns the question of holding a National convention. Colored women everywhere were quick to see the possible benefits to be derived from a National conference of representative women. It was everywhere believed that such a convention, conducted with decorum, and along the lines of serious purpose might help in a decided manner to change public opinion concerning the character and worth of colored women. This agitation had the effect of committing most of the clubs to the proposal for a call in the summer of 1895. While public-spirited Afro-American women everywhere were thus aroused to this larger vision in plans for race amelioration, there occurred an incident of aggravation that swept away all timidity and doubt as to the necessity of a National conference. Some obscure editor in a Missouri town sought to gain notoriety by publishing a libelous article in which the colored women of the country were described as having no sense of virtue and altogether without character. The article in question was in the form of an open letter addressed to Miss Florence Belgarnie of England, who had manifested a kindly interest in behalf of the American negro as a result of Miss Ida B. Wells' agitation. This letter is too foul for reprint, but the effect of its publication stirred the intelligent colored women of America as nothing else had ever done. The letter, in spite of its wanton meanness, was not without some value in showing to what extent the sensitiveness of colored women had grown. Twenty years prior to this time a similar publication would scarcely have been noticed, beyond the small circles of the few who could read, and were public-spirited. In 1895 this open and vulgar attack on the character of a whole race of women was instantly and vehemently resented, in every possible way, by a whole race of women conscious of being slandered. Mass meetings were held in every part of the country to denounce the editor and refute the charges.

The calling of a National convention of colored women was hastened by this coarse assault upon their character. The Woman's Era Club of Boston took the initiative in concentrating the widespread anxiety to do something large and effective, by calling a National conference of representative colored women. The conference was appointed to meet in Berkeley Hall, Boston, for a three days' session, July 29, 30 and 31, 1895.

In pursuance to this call the 29th day of July, 1895, witnessed in Berkeley Hall the first National convention of colored women ever held in America. About one hundred delegates were present from ten States and representatives of about twenty-five different clubs.

The convention afforded a fine exhibition of capable women. There was nothing amateurish, uncertain or timid in the proceedings. Every subject of peculiar interest to colored women was discussed and acted upon as if by women disciplined in thinking out large and serious problems. The following named women were elected as officers of the conference:

Mrs. Josephine St. P. Ruffin, president; vice-presidents, Mrs. Helen Cook, of Washington, and Mrs. Booker T. Washington; secretary, Miss Eliza Carter.

The sanity of these colored women in their first National association was shown in the fact that but little time was spent in complaints and fault-finding about conditions that were inevitable. Almost for the first time in the history of negro gatherings, this Boston conference frankly studied the status of their own race and pointed out their own shortcomings. They set for themselves large and serious tasks in suggestions of plans and work to redeem the unredeemed among them. The convention did credit to itself by sending far and wide a warning note that the race must begin to help itself to live better, strive for a higher standard of social purity, to exercise a more helpful sympathy with the many of the race who are without guides and enlightenment in the ways of social righteousness.

Of course the Missouri editor was roundly scored in resolutions that lacked nothing of the elements of resentment, but the slanderous article against colored women that was the immediate incentive to the calling of the conference, became of the least importance when the women came together and realized the responsibility of larger considerations.

They very soon felt that a National convention of responsible women would be a misplacement of moral force, if it merely exhausted itself in replying to a slanderous publication. The convention, therefore, easily shaped itself toward the consideration of themes and policies more in keeping with its responsibilities to the thousands of women and interests represented.

The chief work of the convention was the formation of National organization. The name adopted was "The National Association of Colored Women." The first officers of the National association were as follows:

The importance of this Boston conference to the club movement among colored women can scarcely be overestimated. The bracing effect of its vigorous proceedings and stirring addresses to the public gave a certain inspiration to the women throughout the whole country. The clubs that already existed became stronger and more positive and aggressive in their helpful work.

The National association has steadily grown in power and influence as an organized body, composed of the best moral and social forces of the negro race. It has held three National conventions since its organization, in 1895: At Washington, D.C., in 1896; Nashville, Tenn., in 1897; and Chicago, in 1899. At the Chicago convention one hundred and fifty delegates were present, representing clubs from thirty States of the Union. The growing importance of the National organization was evidenced by the generous notices and editorial comments in the press of the country. Fraternal greetings were extended to the Chicago convention from many of the prominent white clubs of the city. It is not too much to say that no National convention of colored people held in the country ever made such a deep impression upon the public and told a more thrilling story of the social progress of the race than the Chicago convention. The interest awakened in colored women, and their peculiar interests, was evidenced in many ways. The National association has made it possible for many bright colored women to enjoy the fellowship and helpfulness of many of the best organizations of American women. It has certainly helped to emancipate the white women from the fear and uncertainty of contact or association with women of the darker race. In other words the National Association of Colored Women's Clubs is helping to give respect and character to a race of women who had no place in the classification of progressive womanhood in America. The terms good and bad, bright and dull, plain and beautiful are now as applicable to colored women as to women of other races.

There has been created such a thing as public faith in the sustained virtue and social standards of the women who have spoken and acted so well in these representative organizations. The National body has also been felt in giving a new importance and a larger relationship to the purposes and activities of local clubs throughout the country. Colored women everywhere in this club work began to feel themselves included in a wider and better world than their immediate neighborhood. Women who have always lived and breathed the air of ample freedom and whose range of vision has been world-wide, will scarcely know what it means for women whose lives have been confined and dependent to feel the first consciousness of a relationship to the great social forces that include whole nationalities in the sweep of their influences. To feel that you are something better than a slave, or a descendant of an ex-slave, to feel that you are a unit in the womanhood of a great nation and a great civilization, is the beginning of self-respect and the respect of your race. The National Association of Colored Women's Clubs has certainly meant all this and much more to the women of the ransomed race in the United States.

The National association has also been useful to an important extent in creating what may be called a race public opinion. When the local clubs of the many States became nationalized, it became possible to reach the whole people with questions and interests that concerned the whole race. For example, when the National association interested itself in studying such problems as the Convict Lease System of the Southern States, or the necessity of kindergartens, or the evils of the one-room cabin, it was possible to unite and interest the intelligent forces of the entire race. On these and other questions it has become possible to get the cooperation of the colored people in Mississippi and Minnesota and of New York and Florida. Such co-operation is new and belongs to the new order of things brought about by nationalized efforts.

Through the united voice of the representative colored women of the country the interests of the race are heard by the American women with more effect than they were in other days. There is certainly more power to demand respect and righteous treatment since it has become possible to organize the best forces of all the race for such demands.

The influence of the National association has been especially felt in the rapid increase of women's clubs throughout the country, and especially in the South. There are now about three hundred of such clubs in the United States. There is an average membership of about sixty women to each club. Some have an enrollment of over two hundred women and there are but few with less than twenty-five. Wherever there is a nucleus of intelligent colored women there will be found a woman's club. The following is only a partial list of the clubs composing the National association.

COLORADO.
   Denver, The Woman's League.

CONNECTICUT.
   Norwich, Rose of New England League.

FLORIDA.
   Jacksonville Woman's Christian Industrial and Protective Union.
   The Phyllis Wheatley Chautauqua Circle, Jacksonville.
   The Afro-American Woman's Club, Jacksonville.

GEORGIA.
   Atlanta Woman's Club.
   Harriet Beecher Stowe, Macon.
   Columbus. Douglass Reading Circle.
   Augusta, Woman's's Protective Club.
   Woman's Club of Athens.

INDIANA.
   The Booker T. Washington Club, Logansport.

ILLINOIS.
   Chicago, Ida B. Wells Club.
   Chicago, Phyllis Wheatley Club.
   Chicago, Woman's Civic League.
   Chicago, Woman's Conference. Chicago, Women's Circle.
   Chicago, Progressive Circle of King's Daughters.

KANSAS.
   Sierra Leone Club.
   Woman's Club, Paola.

TENNESSEE.
   Knoxville, Woman's Mutual Improvement Club.
   Memphis, Coterie Migratory Assembly.
   Memphis, Hook's School Association.
   Phyllis Wheatley, Nashville.
   Jackson, Woman's Club.
   Jackson, W. C. T. U.

TEXAS.
Fort Worth Phyllis Wheatley Club.

VIRGINIA.
Woman's League of Roanoke.
Richmond Woman's League.
Cappahoosie Gloucester A. and I. School.
Urbanna Club.
Lynchburg Woman's League.
Lexington Woman's Club.

DISTRICT OF COLUMBIA.
Washington, D.C., Ladies' Auxiliary Committee.
Washington League.
Washington, Lucy Thurman W. C. T. U.
Woman's Protective Union, Washington, D.C.

WEST VIRGINIA.
Wheeling, Woman's Fortnightly Club.

There are of course hundreds of clubs that are not yet members of the
National association, but these outside clubs have all been brought into
being by the influence of the National body, and have received their inspiration and direction from the same source.

A study of the plans and purposes of these clubs reveals an interesting similarity. They show the wants, needs, limitations and aspirations
of the Afro-American are about the same everywhere North, South,
East and West.

If the question be asked: "What do these clubs do; what do they
stand for in their respective communities, and what have they actually
accomplished?" satisfactory answer will be found by studying them a
little at short range.

The first thing to be noted is that these club women are students of
their own social condition, and the clubs themselves are schools in
which are taught and learned, more or less thoroughly, the near lessons
of life and living. All these clubs have a program for study. In some of
the more ambitious clubs literature, music and art are studied more or
less seriously, but in all of them race problems and sociological questions directly related to the condition of the negro race in America are
the principal subjects for study and discussion.

Many of the clubs, in their programs for study, plan to invite from
time to time prominent men and women to address them on questions
of vital interest. In this way club members not only become wide

awake and interested in questions of importance to themselves and their community, but men and women who help to make and shape public opinion have an opportunity to see and know the better side of the colored race.

Race prejudice yields more readily to this interchange of service and helpfulness than to any other force in the relationship of races.

The lessons learned in these women's organizations of the country all have a direct bearing on the social conditions of the negro race. They are such lessons that are not taught in the schools or preached from the pulpits. Home-making has been new business to the great majority of the women whom the women's clubs aim to reach and influence. For this reason the principal object of club studies is to teach that homes are something better and dearer than rooms, furniture, comforts and food. How to make the homes of the race the shrines of all the domestic virtues rather than a mere shelter, is the important thing that colored women are trying to learn and teach through their club organizations.

Take for example one club in Chicago, known as the "Colored Woman's Conference," and it will be found that its aims and efforts are typical of the best purposes of club life among colored women. The special activities and aims of this particular club are the establishment of kindergartens, mothers' meetings, sewing schools for girls, day nurseries, employment bureau; promoting the cause of education by establishing a direct line of interest between the teacher and the home life of every child; friendly visiting and protection to friendless and homeless girls; and a penny savings bank as a practical lesson in frugality and economy. The special thing to be noted in this program is that colored women are not afraid to set for themselves hard and serious tasks and to make whatever sacrifices necessary to realize their high purposes.

A lack of kindergarten teachers more than a lack of money has retarded the work of establishing kindergartens, especially in the South, where they are specially needed. The progressive woman feels that an increased number of kindergartens would have a determining influence in shaping and moulding the character of thousands of colored children whose home lives are scant and meager.

The success of the kindergarten work in St. Louis, Mo., under the direction of Mrs. Haydee Campbell and her able assistant, Miss Helene Abbott, is a happy justification of the wisdom and anxiety of the colored club woman to extend these schools wherever it is possible to do so.

The mothers' meetings established in connection with almost every club have probably had a more direct and beneficial influence on everyday problems of motherhood and home-making than any other activity. Meetings of this sort have been the chief feature of the women's clubs organized by the Tuskegee teachers among the women of the hard plantation life, within reach of the Tuskegee Institute. Thousands of these women in the rural life of the South continue to live under the shadow of bondaged conditions. There has come to them scarcely a ray of light as to a better way of how to live for themselves and their offspring.

It is to the credit of the high usefulness of the colored club woman that she has taken the initiative in doing something to reach and help a class of women who have lived isolated from all the regenerating and uplifting influences of freedom and education. It is the first touch of sympathy that has connected the progressive colored woman with her neglected and unprogressive sister.

In this connection especial word ought to be said in behalf of these clubs as agencies of rescue and protection to the many unprotected and defenseless colored girls to be found in every large city. No race of young women in this country have so little done for them as the young colored woman. She is unknown, she is not believed in, and in respect to favors that direct and uplift, she is an alien, and unheeded. They have been literally shut out from the love, favor and protection that chivalry and a common pride have built up around the personality and character of the young women of almost every other race. The colored women's clubs have lead heart enough and intelligence enough to recognize their opportunity and duty toward their own young women, and in numerous instances have been the very salvation of unfortunate colored girls.

An interesting example of the usefulness of these clubs in this rescue work was recently shown by the success of the Colored Woman's Conference, above mentioned, in saving a girl, friendless, and a victim of unfortunate circumstances, from the stain of the penitentiary by pledging to take her in charge and to save her to herself and society by placing her under good and redeeming influences.

These women's clubs have never failed to champion the cause of every worthy applicant for advice and assistance. They have made the cause of the neglected young colored woman one of commanding interest, and are interesting in her behalf every possible means of education, and are endeavoring to create for her a kindlier feeling and a better degree of respect, and to improve her standing among young women generally. The clubs have entered upon this department of their work with great heartiness and have enlisted in behalf of young women new influences of helpfulness and encouragement. Colored girls with poor homes and no homes are many. Thousands of them are the poor, weak and misguided daughters of ill-starred mothers. To reach out for and save them from a bitter fate; to lift them into a higher sphere of hopefulness and opportunity is a task altogether worthy of the best efforts of club women.

What has been said of the earnestness and practical aim of colored women's clubs in behalf of kindergartens for the children and salvation for the girls may also be said of the practical way in which they have established and sustained sewing schools, mending schools and friendly visitations in behalf of neighborhood respectability and decency, and of their various committees that visit reformatory institutions and jails in search of opportunities to be useful. Numerous and interesting instances might be given to show to what extent these women are realizing their desire to be useful in the social regeneration of their race.

This chapter on the club movement among colored women would be incomplete without some notice of the leaders of the movement. Nothing that these club women have done or aimed to do is more interesting than themselves. What a variety of accomplishments, talents, successes and ambitions have been brought into view and notice by these hitherto obscure women of a ransomed race! Educated? Yes, besides the thousands educated in the common schools, hundreds of them have been trained in the best colleges and universities in the country, and some of them have spent several years in the noted schools of Europe.

The women thus trained and educated are busily pursuing every kind of avocation not prohibited by American prejudices. As educators, fully twenty thousand of them are at work in the schools, colleges and universities of the country, and some of them teach everything required to be taught from the kindergarten to the university. Among these educators and leaders of Afro-American womanhood are to be found linguists, mathematicians, musicians, artists, authors, newspaper writers, lecturers and reform agitators, with varying degrees of excellence and success. There are women in the professions of law, medicine, dentistry, preaching, trained nursing, managers of successful business enterprises, and women of small independent fortunes made and saved within the past twenty-five years.

There are women plain, beautiful, charming, bright conversationalists, fluent, resourceful in ideas, forceful in execution, and women of all sorts of temperament and idiosyncracies and force and delicacy of character.

All this of course is simply amazing to people trained in the habit of rating colored women too low and knowing only the menial type. To such people she is a revelation.

The woman thus portrayed is the real new woman in American life. This woman, as if by magic, has succeeded in lifting herself as completely from the stain and meanness of slavery as if a century had elapsed since the day of emancipation. This new woman, with the club behind her and the club service in her heart and mind, has come to the front in an opportune time. She is needed to change the old idea of things implanted in the minds of the white race and there sustained and hardened into a national habit by the debasing influence of slavery estimates. This woman is needed as an educator of public opinion. She is a happy refutation of the idle insinuations and common skepticism as to the womanly worth and promise of the whole race of women. She has come to enrich American life with finer sympathies, and to enlarge the boundary of fraternity and the democracy of love among American women. She has come to join her talents, her virtues, her intelligence, her sacrifices and her love in the work of redeeming the unredeemed from stagnation, from cheapness and from narrowness.

Quite as important as all this she has come to bring new hope and fresh assurances to the hapless young women of her own race. Life is not a failure. All avenues are not closed. Womanly worth of whatever race or complexion is appreciated. Love, sympathy, opportunity and helpfulness are within the reach of those who can deserve them. The world is still yearning for pure hearts, willing hands, and bright minds. This and much more is the message brought by this new woman to the hearts of thousands discouraged and hopeless young colored women.

It is a real message of courage, a real inspiration that has touched more sides of the Afro-American race than any other message or thing since the dawn of freedom.

This is not exaggeration or fancy. Demonstration of it can be seen, heard and felt in the widespread renewal of hope and effort among the present generation of young Afro-American women.

These young women, thus aroused to courage, to hope and self-assertion toward better things, can find inspiring examples of success and achievements in the women of their own race. They have begun to feel something of the exaltation of race pride and race ideals. They have been brought face to face with standards of living that are high and en-nobling, and have been made conscious of the severe penalties of social misdoings.

Around them has been created a sentiment of care, pride, protection and chivalry that is every day deepening and widening the distinctions between right and wrong in woman's relationship to man, child and society. The glow of optimism has coursed so easily through this chapter concerning the work done and attempted by colored women that the importance of it all may seem somewhat exaggerated.

It, perhaps, should be confessed that in spite of the actual good already realized, the club movement is more of a prophecy than a thing accomplished. Colored women organized have succeeded in touching the heart of the race, and for the first time the thrill of unity has been felt. They have set in motion moral forces that are beginning to socialize interests that have been kept apart by ignorance and the spirit of dependence.

They have begun to make the virtues as well as the wants of the colored women known to the American people. They are striving to put a new social value on themselves. Yet their work has just begun. It takes more than five or ten years to effect the social uplift of a whole race of people.

The club movement is well purposed. There is in it a strong faith, an enthusiasm born of love and sympathy, and an ever-increasing intelligence in the ways and means of affecting noble results. It is not a fad. It is not an imitation. It is not a passing sentiment. It is not an expedient, or an experiment. It is rather the force of a new intelligence against the old ignorance. The struggle of an enlightened conscience against the whole brood of social miseries born out of the stress and pain of a hated past.

Fannie Barrier Williams.

15

Sketches from
The Atlantic Monthly

ZITKALA-ŠA

ZITKALA-ŠA (née Gertrude Simmons Bonnin; 1876–1938) was
born at the Yankton Sioux Agency on what is now the Pine Ridge
Reservation in South Dakota. Her white father left before she was
born, and her mother, Ellen Tate Iyohinwin (Reaches for the Wind)
Simmons, raised her within the Yankton Sioux community. In 1884
visiting missionaries recruited her for White's Manual Institute, a
Quaker boarding school for Native Americans in Wabash, Indiana,
and she enrolled despite her mother's misgivings. Her six years at
the Institute, when she began learning English, are portrayed in her
"Sketches" as a bitter struggle. She then completed two years of study
at Earlham College from 1895 to 1897, winning awards for oratory, but
increasing pressures to assimilate intensified her conflicted feelings
about indigenous culture. After graduating, she studied violin briefly
at the Boston Conservatory before accepting a teaching position at
Carlisle Indian Industrial School (CIIS) in Pennsylvania.

During her time at CIIS, she took the pen name Zitkala-Ša ("Red
Bird" in Lakota) for the "Sketches" of her life she published in *The
Atlantic Monthly* in 1900, as well as the "Old Indian Legends" she
published in *Harper's Magazine*. Her autobiographical narratives
portrayed the treatment of Indian students as inhumane exploitation
in the name of Christian conversion and assimilation. As Zitkala-Ša,

she entered literary, political, and social circles on the East Coast, where she spoke on behalf of indigenous peoples. Her criticism of the use of Christianity as an instrument of political domination and her celebration of indigenous ways of knowing are powerfully expressed in her 1902 essay, "Why I Am a Pagan."

Zitkala-Ša was also dedicated to music throughout her life. In 1900 she traveled to Paris as a violin soloist representing CIIS at the Paris Exposition. In 1913 she collaborated with classical composer William Hanson on the opera *Sundance,* which dramatized stories and issues of Plains Indians. The opera was revived and voted Opera of the Year in 1937 by the New York Light Opera Guild.

She married Raymond Talesfase Bonnin, also a Sioux Indian and an employee of the Bureau of Indian Affairs, who supported her activism. Living on a reservation in Utah with him in 1911, she joined the Society for the American Indian (SAI), became its secretary in 1916, and was the editor of its publication, the *American Indian Magazine,* for two years from 1918 to 1919. After the collapse of the SAI in 1920, she began to work with the General Federation of Women's Clubs to found an Indian Welfare Committee. In 1921 she reclaimed her name Zitkala-Ša to publish *American Indian Stories* as a book. She also remained a staunch activist, traveling and lecturing on Indian rights, frequently dressed in Sioux robes. In 1924 she was employed by the Indian Rights Association to research and co-author a piece on the treatment of Oklahoma Indian peoples. The commission report, *Oklahoma's Poor Rich Indians: An Orgy of Graft and Exploitation of the Five Civilized Tribes—Legalized Robbery,* was an indictment that led to the establishment of the Merriam Commission and its report to Congress in 1928. Dedicated to preserving oral Indian cultures and stories, she founded the National Council of American Indians in 1926 to inform Indian peoples of pertinent local and national issues and served as its president until her death. She is buried in Arlington National Cemetery, beneath a headstone that reads: "Gertrude Simmons Bonnin—'Zitkala-Ša' of the Sioux Indians—1876–1938."

Feminist interest in the life narratives of women of color fueled a reawakening of interest in the work and life of Zitkala-Ša. Dexter Fisher called attention to her importance, as did Kathleen M. Sands and Gretchen M. Bataille. Sidonie Smith's essay explores her narrative's importance for changing concepts of American identity and nationhood in the early twentieth century. The extensive notes to the collection of Zitkala-Ša's writing by P. Jane Hafen focus on her significance as both a writer and artist and an influential public figure.

"Impressions of an Indian Childhood" (1900)

I. My Mother.

A wigwam of weather-stained canvas stood at the base of some irregularly ascending hills. A footpath wound its way gently down the sloping land till it reached the broad river bottom; creeping through the long swamp grasses that bent over it on either side, it came out on the edge of the Missouri.

Here, morning, noon, and evening, my mother came to draw water from the muddy stream for our household use. Always, when my mother started for the river, I stopped my play to run along with her. She was only of medium height. Often she was sad and silent, at which times her full arched lips were compressed into hard and bitter lines, and shadows fell under her black eyes. Then I clung to her hand and begged to know what made the tears fall.

"Hush; my little daughter must never talk about my tears;" and smiling through them, she patted my head and said, "Now let me see how fast you can run to-day." Whereupon I tore away at my highest possible speed, with my long black hair blowing in the breeze.

I was a wild little girl of seven. Loosely clad in a slip of brown buckskin, and light-footed with a pair of soft moccasins on my feet, I was as free as the wind that blew my-hair, and no less spirited than a bounding deer. These were my mother's pride,—my wild freedom and overflowing spirits. She taught me no fear save that of intruding myself upon others.

Having gone many paces ahead I stopped, panting for breath, and laughing with glee as my mother watched my every movement. I was not wholly conscious of myself, but was more keenly alive to the fire within. It was as if I were the activity, and my hands and feet were only experiments for my spirit to work upon.

Returning from the river, I tugged beside my mother, with my hand upon the bucket I believed I was carrying. One time, on such a return, I remember a bit of conversation we had. My grown-up cousin, Warca-Ziwin (Sunflower), who was then seventeen, always went to the river alone for water for her mother. Their wigwam was not far from ours.; and I saw her daily going to and from the river. I admired my cousin greatly. So I said: "Mother, when I am tall as my cousin Warca-Ziwin, you shall not have to come for water. I will do it for you."

With a strange tremor in her voice which I could no understand, she answered, "If the paleface does not take away from us the river we drink."

"Mother, who is this bad paleface?" I asked.

"My little daughter, he is a sham,—a sickly sham! The bronzed Dakota is the only real man."

I looked up into my mother's face while she spoke; and seeing her bite her lips, I knew she was unhappy. This aroused revenge in my small soul. Stamping my foot on the earth, I cried aloud, "I hate the paleface that makes my mother cry!"

Setting the pail of water on the ground, my mother stooped, and stretching her left hand out on the level with my eyes, she placed her other arm about me; she pointed to the hill where my uncle and my only sister lay buried.

"There is what the paleface has done! Since then your father too has been buried in a hill near the rising sun. We were once very happy. But the paleface has stolen our lands and driven us hither. Having defrauded us of our land, the paleface forced us away.

"Well, it happened on the day we moved camp that your sister and uncle were both very sick. Many others were ailing, but there seemed to be no help. We traveled many days and nights; not in the grand happy way that we moved camp when I was a little girl, but we were driven, my child, driven like a herd of buffalo. With every step, your sister, who was not as large as you are now, shrieked with the painful jar until she was hoarse with crying. She grew more and more feverish. Her little hands and cheeks were burning hot. Her little lips were parched and dry, but she would not drink the water I gave her. Then I discovered that her throat was swollen and red. My poor child, how I cried with her because the Great Spirit had forgotten us!

"At last, when we reached this western country, on the first weary night your sister died. And soon your uncle died also, leaving a widow and an orphan daughter, your cousin Warca-Ziwin. Both your sister and uncle might have been happy with us today, had it not been for the heartless paleface."

My mother was silent the rest of the way to our wigwam. Though I saw no tears in her eyes, I knew that was because I was with her. She seldom wept before me.

II. The Legends.

During the summer days, my mother built her fire in the shadow of our wigwam.

In the early morning our simple breakfast was spread upon the grass west of our tepee. At the farthest point of the shade my mother sat beside her fire, toasting a savory piece of dried meat. Near her, I sat upon my feet, eating my dried meat with unleavened bread, and drinking strong black coffee.

The morning meal was our quiet hour, when we two were entirely alone. At noon, several who chanced to be passing by stopped to rest, and to share our luncheon with us, for they were sure of our hospitality.

My uncle, whose death my mother ever lamented, was one of our nation's bravest warriors. His name was on the lips of old men when talking of the proud feats of valor; and it was mentioned by younger men, too, in connection with deeds of gallantry. Old women praised him for his kindness toward them; young women held him up as an ideal to their sweethearts. Every one loved him, and my mother worshiped his memory. Thus it happened that even strangers were sure of welcome in our lodge, if they but asked a favor in my uncle's name.

Though I heard many strange experiences related by these wayfarers, I loved best the evening meal, for that was the time old legends were told. I was always glad when the sun hung low in the west, for then my mother sent me to invite the neighboring old men and women to eat supper with us. Running all the way to the wigwams, I halted shyly at the entrances. Sometimes I stood long moments without saying a word. It was not any fear that made me so dumb when out upon such a happy errand; nor was it that I wished to withhold the invitation, for it was all I could do to observe this very proper silence. But it was a sensing of the atmosphere, to assure myself that I should not hinder other plans. My mother used to say to me, as I was almost bounding away for the old people: "Wait a moment before you invite any one. If other plans are being discussed, do not interfere, but go elsewhere."

The old folks knew the meaning of my pauses; and often they coaxed my confidence by, asking, "What do you seek, little granddaughter."

"My mother says you are to come to our tepee this evening," I instantly exploded, and breathed the freer afterwards.

"Yes, yes, gladly, gladly I shall come!" each replied. Rising at once and carrying their blankets across one shoulder, they flocked leisurely from their various wigwams toward our dwelling.

My mission done, I ran back, skipping and jumping with delight. All out of breath, I told my mother almost the exact words of the answers to my invitation. Frequently she asked, "What were they doing when you entered their tepee?" This taught me to remember all I saw at a single glance. Often I told my mother my impressions without being questioned.

While in the neighboring wigwams sometimes an old Indian woman asked me, "What is your mother doing?" Unless my mother had cautioned me not to tell, I generally answered her questions without reserve.

At the arrival of our guests I sat close to my mother, and did not leave her side without first asking her consent. I ate my supper in quiet, listening patiently to the talk of the old people, wishing all the time that they would begin the stories I loved best. At last, when I could not wait any longer, I whispered in my mother's ear, "Ask them to tell an Iktomi story, mother."

Soothing my impatience, my mother said aloud, "My little daughter is anxious to hear your legends." By this time all were through eating, and the evening was fast deepening into twilight.

As each in turn began to tell a legend, I pillowed my head in my mother's lap; and lying flat upon my back, I watched the stars as they peeped down upon me, one by one. The increasing interest of the tale aroused me, and I sat up eagerly listening for every word. The old women made funny remarks, and laughed so heartily that I could not help joining them.

The distant howling of a pack of wolves or the hooting of an owl in the river bottom frightened me, and I nestled into my mother's lap. She added some dry sticks to the open fire, and the bright flames leaped up into the faces of the old folks as they sat around in a great circle.

One such an evening, I remember the glare of the fire shone on a tattooed star upon the brow of the old warrior who was telling a story. I watched him curiously as he made his unconscious gestures. The blue star upon his bronzed forehead was a puzzle to me. Looking about, I saw two parallel lines on the chin of one of the old women. The rest had none. I examined my mother's face, but found no sign there.

After the warrior's story was finished, I asked the old woman the meaning of the blue lines on her chin, looking all the while out of the corners of my eyes at the warrior with the star on his forehead. I was a little afraid that he would rebuke me for my boldness.

Here the old woman began: "Why, my grandchild, they are signs, secret signs I dare not tell you. I shall, however, tell you a wonderful story about a woman who had a cross tattooed upon each of her cheeks."

It was a long story of a woman whose magic power lay hidden behind the marks upon her face. I fell asleep before the story was completed.

Ever after that night I felt suspicious of tattooed people. Wherever I saw one I glanced furtively at the mark and round about it, wondering what terrible magic power was covered there.

It was rarely that such a fearful story as this one was told by the camp fire. Its impression was so acute that the picture still remains vividly clear and pronounced.

III. The Beadwork.

Soon after breakfast, mother sometimes began her beadwork. On a bright clear day, she pulled out the wooden pegs that pinned the skirt of our wigwam to the ground, and rolled the canvas part way up on its frame of slender poles. Then the cool morning breezes swept freely through our dwelling, now and then wafting the perfume of sweet grasses from newly burnt prairie.

Untying the long tasseled strings that bound a small brown buckskin bag, my mother spread upon a mat beside her bunches of colored beads, just as an artist arranges the paints upon his palette. On a lapboard she smoothed out a double sheet of soft white buckskin and drawing from a beaded case that hung on the left of her wide belt a long, narrow blade, she trimmed the buckskin into shape. Often she worked upon small moccasins for her small daughter. Then I became intensely interested in her designing. With a proud, beaming face, I watched her work. In imagination, I saw myself walking in a new pair of snugly fitting moccasins. I felt the envious eyes of my playmates upon the pretty red beads decorating my feet.

Close beside my mother I sat on a rug, with a scrap of buckskin in one hand and an awl in the other. This was the beginning of my practical observation lessons in the art of beadwork. From a skein of finely twisted threads of silvery sinews my mother pulled out a single one. With an awl she pierced the buckskin, and skillfully threaded it with the white sinew. Picking up the tiny beads one by one, she strung them with the point of her thread, always twisting it carefully after every stitch.

It took many trials before I learned how to knot my sinew thread on the point of my finger, as I saw her do. Then the next difficulty was in keeping my thread stiffly twisted, so that I could easily string my beads upon it. My mother required of me original designs for my lessons in beading. At first I frequently ensnared many a sunny hour into working a long design. Soon I learned from self-inflicted punishment to refrain from drawing complex patterns, for I had to finish whatever I began.

After some experience I usually drew easy and simple crosses and squares. These were some of the set forms. My original designs were not always symmetrical nor sufficiently characteristic, two faults with which my mother had little patience. The quietness of her oversight made me feel strongly responsible and dependent upon my own judgment. She treated me as a dignified little individual as long as I was on my good behavior; and how humiliated I was when some boldness of mine drew forth a rebuke from her!

In the choice of colors she left me to my own taste. I was pleased with an outline of yellow upon a background of dark blue, or a combination of red and myrtle-green. There was another of red with a bluish gray that was more conventionally used. When I became a little familiar with designing and the various pleasing combinations of color, a harder lesson was given me. It was the sewing on, instead of beads, some tinted porcupine quills, moistened and flattened between the nails of the thumb and forefinger. My mother cut off the prickly ends and burned them at once in the centre fire. These sharp points were poisonous, and worked into the flesh wherever they lodged. For this reason, my mother said, I should not do much alone in quills until I was as tall as my cousin Warca-Ziwin.

Always after these confining lessons I was wild with surplus spirits, and found joyous relief in running loose in the open again. Many a summer afternoon, a party of four or five of my playmates roamed over the hills with me. We each carried a light sharpened rod about four feet long, with which we pried up certain sweet roots. When we had eaten all the choice roots we chanced upon, we shouldered our rods and strayed off into patches of a stalky plant under whose yellow blossoms we found little crystal drops of gum. Drop by drop we gathered this nature's rock candy, until each of us could boast of a lump the size of a small bird's egg. Soon satiated with its woody flavor, we tossed away our gum, to return again to the sweet roots.

I remember well how we used to exchange our necklaces, beaded belts, and sometimes even our moccasins. We pretended to offer them as gifts to one another. We delighted in impersonating our own mothers. We talked of things we had heard them say in their conversations. We imitated their various manners, even to the inflection of their voices. In the lap of the prairie we seated ourselves upon our feet; and leaning our painted cheeks in the palms of our hands, we rested our elbows on our knees, and bent forward as old women were most accustomed to do.

While one was telling of some heroic deed recently done by a near relative, the rest of us listened attentively, and exclaimed in undertones, "Han! han!" (yes! Yes!) whenever the speaker paused for breath, or sometimes for our sympathy. As the discourse became more thrilling, according to our ideas, we raised our voices in these interjections. In these impersonations our parents were led to say only those things that were in common favor.

No matter how exciting a tale we might be rehearsing, the mere shifting of a cloud shadow in the landscape nearby was sufficient to change our impulses; and soon we were all chasing the great shadows that played among the hills. We shouted and whooped in the chase; laughing and calling to one another, we were like little sportive nymphs on that Dakota sea of rolling green.

On one occasion, I forgot the cloud shadow in a strange notion to catch up with my own shadow. Standing straight and still, I began to glide after it, putting out one foot cautiously. When, with the greatest care, I set my foot in advance of myself, my shadow crept onward too. Then again I tried it; this time with the other foot. Still again my shadow escaped me. I began to run; and away flew my shadow, always just a step beyond me. Faster and faster I ran, setting my teeth and clenching my fists, determined to overtake my own fleet shadow. But ever swifter it glided before me, while I was growing breathless and hot. Slackening my speed, I was greatly vexed that my shadow should check its pace also. Daring it to the utmost, as I thought, I sat down upon a rock imbedded in the hillside.

So! my shadow had the impudence to sit down beside me!

Now my comrades caught up with me, and began to ask why I was running away so fast.

"Oh, I was chasing my shadow! Didn't you ever do that?" I inquired, surprised that they should not understand.

They planted their moccasined feet firmly upon my shadow to stay it, and I arose. Again my shadow slipped away, and moved as often as I did. Then we gave up trying to catch my shadow.

Before this peculiar experience I have no distinct memory of having recognized any vital bond between myself and my own shadow. I never gave it an afterthought.

Returning our borrowed belts and trinkets, we rambled homeward. That evening, as on other evenings, I went to sleep over my legends.

IV. The Coffee-Making.

One summer afternoon, my mother left me alone in our wigwam, while she went across the way to my aunt's dwelling.

I did not much like to stay alone in our tepee, for I feared a tall, broad-shouldered crazy man, some forty years old, who walked loose among the hills. Wiyaka-Napbina (Wearer of a Feather Necklace) was harmless, and whenever he came into a wigwam he was driven there by extreme hunger. He went nude except for the half of a red blanket he girdled around his waist. In one tawny arm he used to carry a heavy bunch of wild sunflowers that he gathered in his aimless ramblings. His black hair was matted by the winds, and scorched into a dry red by the constant summer sun. As he took great strides, placing one brown bare foot directly in front of the other, he swung his long lean arm to and fro.

Frequently he paused in his walk and gazed far, backward, shading his eyes with his hand. He was under the belief that an evil spirit was haunting his steps. This was what my mother told me once, when I sneered at such a silly big man. I was brave when my mother was nearby, and Wiyaka-Napbina walking farther and farther away.

"Pity the man, my child. I knew him when he was a brave and handsome youth." He was overtaken by a malicious spirit among the hills, one day, when he went hither and thither after his ponies. Since then he cannot stay away from the hills," she said.

I felt so sorry for the man in his misfortune that I prayed to the Great Spirit to restore him. But though I pitied him at a distance, I was still afraid of him when he appeared near our wigwam.

Thus, when my mother left me by myself that afternoon, I sat in a fearful mood within our tepee. I recalled all I had ever heard about Wiyaka-Napbina; and I tried to assure myself that though he might pass nearby, he would not come to our wigwam because there was no little girl around our grounds.

Just then, from without a hand lifted the canvas covering of the entrance; the shadow of a man fell within the wigwam; and a large roughly moccasined foot was planted inside.

For a moment I did not dare to breathe or stir, for I thought that could be no other than Wiyaka-Napbina. The next instant I sighed aloud in relief. It was an old grandfather who had often told me Iktomi legends.

"Where is your mother, my little grandchild?" were his first words.

"My mother is soon coming back from my aunt's tepee," I replied.

"Then I shall wait awhile for her return," he said, crossing his feet and seating himself upon a mat.

At once I began to play the part of a generous hostess. I turned to my mother's coffeepot.

Lifting the lid, I found nothing but coffee grounds in the bottom. I set the pot on a heap of cold ashes in the centre, and filled it half full of warm Missouri River water. During this performance I felt conscious of being watched. Then breaking off a small piece of our unleavened bread, I placed it in a bowl. Turning soon to the coffeepot, which would never have boiled on a dead fire had I waited forever, I poured out a cup of worse than muddy warm water. Carrying the bowl in one hand and cup in the other, I handed the light luncheon to the old warrior. I offered them to him with the air of bestowing generous hospitality.

"How! how!" he said, and placed the dishes on the ground in front of his crossed feet. He nibbled at the bread and sipped from the cup. I sat back against a pole watching him. I was proud to have succeeded so well in serving refreshments to a guest all by myself. Before the old warrior had finished eating, my mother entered. Immediately she wondered where I had found coffee, for she knew I had never made any, and that she had left the coffeepot empty. Answering the question in my mother's eyes, the warrior remarked, "My granddaughter made coffee on a heap of dead ashes, and served me the moment I came."

They both laughed, and mother said, "Wait a little longer, and I shall build a fire." She meant to make some real coffee. But neither she nor the warrior, whom the law of our custom had compelled to partake of my insipid hospitality, said anything to embarrass me. They treated my best judgment, poor as it was, with the utmost respect. It was not till long years afterward that I learned how ridiculous a thing I had done.

V. The Dead Man's Plum Bush.

One autumn afternoon, many people came streaming toward the dwelling of our near neighbor. With painted faces, and wearing broad white bosoms of elk's teeth, they hurried down the narrow footpath to Haraka Wambdi's wigwam. Young mothers held their children by the hand, and half pulled them along in their haste. They overtook and passed by the bent old grandmothers who were trudging along with crooked canes toward the centre of excitement. Most of the young braves galloped hither on their ponies. Toothless warriors, like the old women, came more slowly, though mounted on lively ponies. They sat proudly erect on their horses. They wore their eagle plumes, and waved their various trophies of former wars.

In front of the wigwam a great fire was built, and several large black kettles of venison were suspended over it. The crowd were seated about it on the grass in a great circle. Behind them some of the braves stood leaning against the necks of their ponies, their tall figures draped in loose robes which were well drawn over their eyes.

Young girls, with their faces glowing like bright red autumn leaves, their glossy braids falling over each ear, sat coquettishly beside their chaperons. It was a custom for young Indian women to invite some older relative to escort them to the public feasts. Though it was not an iron law, it was generally observed.

Haraka Wambdi was a strong young brave, who had just returned from his first battle, a warrior. His near relatives, to celebrate his new rank, were spreading a feast to which the whole of the Indian village was invited.

Holding my pretty striped blanket in readiness to throw over my shoulders, I grew more and more restless as I watched the gay throng assembling. My mother was busily broiling a wild duck that my aunt had that morning brought over.

"Mother, mother, why do you stop to cook small meal when we are invited to a feast?" I asked, with a snarl in my voice.

"My child, learn to wait. On our way to the celebration we are going to stop at Chanyu's wigwam. His aged mother-in-law is lying very ill and I think he would like a taste of this small game."

Having once seen the suffering on the thin, pinched features of this dying woman, I felt a momentary shame that I had not remembered her before.

On our way, I ran ahead of my mother, and was reaching out my hand to pick some purple plums that grew on a small bush, when I was checked by a low "Sh!" from my mother.

"Why, mother, I want to taste the plum!" I exclaimed, as I dropped my hand to my aid in disappointment.

"Never pluck a single plum from this bush, my child, for its roots are wrapped around an Indian's skeleton. A brave is buried here. While he lived, he was so fond of playing the game of striped plum seeds that, at his death, his set of plum seeds were buried in his hands. From them sprang up this little bush."

Eyeing the forbidden fruit, I trod lightly on the sacred ground, and dared to speak only in whispers, until we had gone many paces from it. After that time, I halted in my ramblings whenever I came in sight of the plum bush. I grew sober with awe, and was alert to hear a long-drawn-out whistle rise from the roots of it. Though I had never heard with my own ears this strange whistle of departed spirits, yet I had listened so frequently to hear the old folks describe it that I knew I should recognize it at once.

The lasting impression of that day, as I recall it now, is what my mother told me about the dead man's plum bush.

VI. The Ground Squirrel.

In the busy autumn days, my cousin Warca-Ziwin's mother cam to our wigwam to help my mother preserve foods for our winter use. I was very fond of my aunt, because she was not so quiet as my mother. Though she was older, she was more jovial and less reserved. She was slender and remarkably erect. While my mother's hair was heavy and black, my aunt had unusually thin locks.

Ever since I knew her, she wore a string of large blue beads around her neck,—beads that were precious because my uncle had given them to her when she was a younger woman. She had a peculiar swing in her gait, caused by a long stride rarely natural to so slight a figure. It was during my aunt's visit with us that my mother forgot her accustomed quietness, often laughing heartily at some of my aunt's witty remarks.

I loved my aunt threefold: for her hearty laughter, for the cheerfulness she caused my mother, and most of all for the times she dried my tears and held me in her lap, when my mother had reproved me.

Early in the cool mornings, just as the yellow rim of the sun rose above the hills, we were up and eating our breakfast. We awoke so early that we saw the sacred hour when a misty smoke hung over a pit surrounded by an impassable sinking mire. This strange smoke appeared every morning, both winter and summer; but most visibly in midwinter it rose immediately above the marshy spot. By the time the full face of the sun appeared above the eastern horizon, the smoke vanished. Even very old men, who had known this country the longest, said that the smoke from this pit had never failed a single day to rise heavenward.

As I frolicked about our dwelling, I used to stop suddenly, and with a fearful awe watch the smoking of the unknown fires. While the vapor was visible, I was afraid to go very far from our wigwam unless I went with my mother.

From a field in the fertile river bottom my mother and aunt gathered an abundant supply of corn. Near our tepee, they spread a large canvas upon the grass, and dried their sweet corn in it. I was left to watch the corn, that nothing should disturb it. I played around it with dolls made of ears of corn. I braided their soft fine silk for hair, and gave them blankets as various as the scraps I found in my mother's workbag.

There was a little stranger with a black-and-yellow-striped coat that used to come to the drying corn. It was a little ground squirrel, who was so fearless of me that he came to one corner of the canvas and carried away as much of the sweet corn as he could hold. I wanted very much to catch him, and rub his pretty fur back, but my mother said he would be so frightened if I caught him that he would bite my fingers. So I was as content as he to keep the corn between us. Every morning he came for more corn. Some evenings I have seen him creeping about our grounds; and when I gave a sudden whoop of recognition, he ran quickly out of sight.

When mother had dried all the corn she wished, then she sliced great pumpkins into thin rings; and these she doubled and linked together into long chains. She hung them on a pole that stretched between two forked posts. The wind and sun soon thoroughly dried the chains of pumpkin. Then she packed them away in a case of thick and stiff buckskin.

In the sun and wind she also dried many wild fruits,—cherries, berries, and plums. But chiefest among my early recollections of autumn is that one of the corn drying and the ground squirrel.

I have few memories of winter days, at this period of my life, though many of the summer. There is one only which I can recall.

Some missionaries gave me a little bag of marbles. They were all sizes and colors. Among them were some of colored glass. Walking with my mother to the river, on a late winter day, we found great chunks of ice piled all along the bank. The ice on the river was floating in huge pieces. As I stood beside one large block, I noticed for the first time the colors of the rainbow in the crystal ice. Immediately I thought of my glass marbles at home. With my bare fingers I tried to pick out some of the colors, for they seemed so near the surface. But my fingers began to sting with the intense cold, and I had to bite them hard to keep from crying.

From that day on, for many a moon, I believed that glass marbles had river ice inside of them.

VII. The Big Red Apples.

The first turning away from the easy, natural flow of my life occurred in an early spring. It was in my eighth year; in the month of March, I afterward learned. At this age I knew but one language, and that was my mother's native tongue.

From some of my playmates I heard that two paleface missionaries were in our village. They were from that class of white men who wore big hats and carried large hearts, they said. Running direct to my mother, I began to question her why these two strangers were among us. She told me, after I had teased much, that they had come to take away Indian boys and girls to the East. My mother did not seem to want me to talk about them. But in a day or two, I gleaned many wonderful stories from my playmates concerning the strangers.

"Mother, my friend Judéwin is going home with the missionaries. She is going to a more beautiful country than ours; the palefaces told her so!" I said wistfully, wishing in my heart that I too might go.

Mother sat in chair, and I was hanging on her knee. Within the last two seasons my big brother Dawée had returned from a three years' education in the East, and his coming back influenced my mother to take a farther step from her native way of living. First it was a change from the buffalo skin to the white man's canvas that covered our wigwam. Now she had given up her wigwam of slender poles, to live, a foreigner, in a home of clumsy logs.

"Yes, my child, several others besides Judéwin are going away with the palefaces. Your brother said the missionaries had inquired about his little sister," she said, watching my face very closely.

My heart thumped so hard against my breast, I wondered if she could hear it.

"Did he tell them to take me, mother?" I asked, fearing lest Dawée had forbidden the palefaces to see me, and that my hope of going to the Wonderland would be entirely blighted.

With a sad, slow smile, she answered "There! I knew you were wishing to go, because Judéwin has filled your ears with the white men's lies. Don't believe a word they say! Their words are sweet, but, my child, their deeds are bitter. You will cry for me, but they will not even soothe you. Stay with me, my little one! Your brother Dawée says that going East, away from your mother, is too hard an experience for his baby sister."

Thus my mother discouraged my curiosity about the lands beyond our eastern horizon; for it was not yet an ambition for Letters that was stirring me. But on the following day the missionaries did come to our very house. I spied them coming up the footpath leading to our cottage. A third man was with them, but he was not my brother Dawée. It was another, a young interpreter, a paleface who had a smattering of the Indian language. I was ready to run out to meet them, but I did not dare to displease my mother. With great glee, I jumped up and down on our ground floor. I begged my mother to open the door, that they would be sure to come to us. Alas! They came, they saw, and they conquered!

Judéwin had told me of the great tree where grew red, red apples; and how we could reach out our hands and pick all the red apples we could eat. I had never seen apple trees. I had never tasted more than a dozen red apples in my life; and when I heard of the orchards of the East, I was eager to roam among them. The missionaries smiled into my eyes, and patted my head. I wondered how mother could say such hard words against them.

"Mother, ask them if little girls may have all the red apples they want, when they go East," I whispered aloud, in my excitement.

The interpreter heard me, and answered: "Yes, little girl, the nice red apples are for those who pick them; and you will have a ride on the iron horse if you go with these good people."

I had never seen a train, and he knew it.

"Mother, I'm going East! I like big red apples, and I want to ride on the iron horse! Mother, say yes!" I pleaded.

My mother said nothing. The missionaries waited in silence; and my eyes began to blur with tears, though I struggled to choke them back. The corners of my mouth twitched, and my mother saw me.

"I am not ready to give you any word," she said to them. "Tomorrow I shall send you my answer by my son."

With this they left us. Alone with my mother, I yielded to my tears, and cried aloud, shaking my head so as not to hear what she was saying to me. This was the first time I had ever been so unwilling to give up my own desire that I refused to hearken to my mother's voice.

There was a solemn silence in our home that night. Before I went to bed I begged the Great Spirit to make my mother willing I should go with the missionaries.

The next morning came, and my mother called me to her side. "My daughter, do you still persist in wishing to leave your mother?" she asked.

"Oh, mother, it is not that I wish to leave you, but I want to see the wonderful Eastern land," I answered.

My dear old aunt came to our house that morning, and I heard her say, "Let her try it."

I hoped that, as usual, my aunt was pleading on my side. My brother Dawée came for mother's decision. I dropped my play, and crept close to my aunt.

"Yes, Dawée, my daughter, though she does not understand what it all means, is anxious to go. She will need an education when she is grown, for then there will be fewer real Dakotas, and many more pale-faces. This tearing her away, so young, from her mother is necessary, if I would have her an educated woman. The palefaces, who owe us large debt for stolen lands, have begun to pay a tardy justice in offering some education to our children. But I know my daughter must suffer keenly in this experiment. For her sake, I dread to tell you my reply to the missionaries. Go, tell them that they may take my little daughter, and that the Great Spirit shall not fail to reward them according to their hearts."

Wrapped in my heavy blanket, I walked with my mother to the carriage that was soon to take us to the iron horse. I was happy. I met my playmates, who were also wearing their best thick blankets. We showed one another our new beaded moccasins, and the width of the belts that girdled our new dresses. Soon we were being drawn rapidly away by the white man's horses. When I saw the lonely figure of my mother vanish in the distance, a sense of regret settled heavily upon me. I felt suddenly weak, as if I might fall limp to the ground. I was in the hands of strangers whom my mother did not fully trust. I no longer felt free to be myself, or to voice my own feelings. The tears trickled down my cheeks, and I buried my face in the folds of my blanket. Now the first step, parting me from my mother, was taken, and all my be-lated tears availed nothing.

Having driven thirty miles to the ferryboat, we crossed the Missouri in the evening. Then riding again a few miles eastward, we stopped before a massive brick building. I looked at it in amazement, and with a vague misgiving, for in our village I had never seen so large a house. Trembling with fear and distrust of the palefaces, my teeth chattering from the chilly ride, I crept noiselessly in my soft moccasins along the narrow hall, keeping very close to the bare wall. I was as frightened and bewildered as the captured young of a wild creature.

Zitkala-Ša

"The School Days of an Indian Girl" (1900)

I. The Land of Red Apples.

There were eight in our party of bronzed children who were going East with the missionaries. Among us were three young braves, two tall girls, and we three little ones, Judéwin, Thowin, and I.

We had been very impatient to start on our journey to the Red Apple Country, which, we were told, lay a little beyond the great circular horizon of the Western prairie. Under a sky of rosy apples we dreamt of roaming as freely and happily as we had chased the cloud shadows on the Dakota plains. We had anticipated much pleasure from a ride on the iron horse, but the throngs of staring palefaces disturbed and troubled us.

On the train, fair women, with tottering babies on each arm, stopped their haste and scrutinized the children of absent mothers. Large men, with heavy bundles in their hands, halted near by, and riveted their glassy blue eyes upon us.

I sank deep into the corner of my seat, for I resented being watched. Directly in front of me, children who were no larger than I hung themselves upon the backs of their seats, with their bold white faces toward me. Sometimes they took their forefingers out of their mouths and pointed at my moccasined feet. Their mothers, instead of reproving such rude curiosity, looked closely at me, and attracted their children's further notice to my blanket. This embarrassed me, and kept me constantly on the verge of tears.

I sat perfectly still, with my eyes downcast, daring only now and then to shoot long glances around me. Chancing to turn to the window at my side, I was quite breathless upon seeing one familiar object. It was the telegraph pole which strode by at short paces. Very near my mother's dwelling, along the edge of a road thickly bordered with wild sunflowers, some poles like these had been planted by white men. Often I had stopped, on my way down the road, to hold my ear against the pole, and, hearing its low moaning, I used to wonder what the paleface had done to hurt it. Now I sat watching for each pole that glided by to be the last one.

In this way I had forgotten my uncomfortable surroundings, when I heard one of my comrades call out my name. I saw the missionary standing very near, tossing candies and gums into our midst. This amused us all, and we tried to see who could catch the most of the sweet-meats. The missionary's generous distribution of candies was impressed upon my memory by a disastrous result which followed. I had caught more than my share of candies and gums, and soon after our arrival at the school I had a chance to disgrace myself, which, I am ashamed to say, I did.

Though we rode several days inside of the iron horse, I do not recall a single thing about our luncheons.

It was night when we reached the school grounds. The lights from the windows of the large buildings fell upon some of the icicled trees that stood beneath them. We were led toward an open door, where the brightness of the lights within flooded out over the heads of the excited palefaces who blocked the way. My body trembled more from fear than from the snow I trod upon.

Entering the house, I stood close against the wall. The strong glaring light in the large whitewashed room dazzled my eyes. The noisy hurrying of hard shoes upon a bare wooden floor increased the whirring in my ears. My only safety seemed to be in keeping next to the wall. As I was wondering in which direction to escape from all this confusion, two warm hands grasped me firmly, and in the same moment I was tossed high in midair. A rosy-cheeked paleface woman caught me in her arms. I was both frightened and insulted by such trifling. I stared into her eyes, wishing her to let me stand on my own feet, but she jumped me up and down with increasing enthusiasm. My mother had never made a plaything of her wee daughter. Remembering this I began to cry aloud.

They misunderstood the cause of my tears, and placed me at a white table loaded with food. There our party were united again. As I did not hush my crying, one of the older ones whispered to me, "Wait until you are alone in the night."

It was very little I could swallow besides my sobs, that evening.

"Oh, I want my mother and my brother Dawée! I want to go to my aunt!" I pleaded; but the ears of the palefaces could not hear me.

From the table we were taken along an upward incline of wooden boxes, which I learned afterward to call a stairway. At the top was a quiet ball, dimly lighted. Many narrow beds were in one straight line down the entire length of the wall. In them lay sleeping brown faces, which peeped just out of the coverings. I was tucked into bed with one of the tall girls, because she talked to me in my mother tongue and seemed to soothe me.

I had arrived in the wonderful land of rosy skies, but I was not happy, as I had thought I should be. My long travel and the bewildering sights had exhausted me. I fell asleep, heaving deep, tired sobs. My tears were left to dry themselves in streaks, because neither my aunt nor my mother was near to wipe them away.

II. The Cutting of my Long Hair.

The first day in the land of apples was a bitter-cold one; for the snow still covered the ground, and the trees were bare. A large bell rang for breakfast, its loud metallic voice crashing through the belfry overhead and into our sensitive ears. The annoying clatter of shoes on bare floors gave us no peace. The constant clash of harsh noises, with an undercurrent of many voices murmuring an unknown tongue, made a bedlam within which I was securely tied. And though my spirit tore itself in struggling for its lost freedom, all was useless.

A paleface woman, with white hair, came up after us. We were placed in a line of girls who were marching into the dining room. These were Indian girls, in stiff shoes and closely clinging dresses. The small girls wore sleeved aprons and shingled hair. As I walked noiselessly in my soft moccasins, I felt like sinking to the floor, for my blanket had been stripped from my shoulders. I looked hard at the Indian girls, who seemed not to care that they were even more immodestly dressed than I, in their tightly fitting clothes. While we marched in, the boys entered at an opposite door. I watched for the three young braves who came in our party. I spied them in the rear ranks, looking as uncomfortable as I felt.

A small bell was tapped, and each of the pupils drew a chair from under the table. Supposing this act meant they were to be seated, I pulled out mine and at once slipped into it from one side. But when I turned my head, I saw that I was the only one seated, and all the rest at our table remained standing. Just as I began to rise, looking shyly around to see how chairs were to be used, a second bell was sounded. All were seated at last, and I had to crawl back into my chair again. I heard a man's voice at one end of the hall, and I looked around to see him. But all the others hung their heads over their plates. As I glanced at the long chain of tables, I caught the eyes of a paleface woman upon me. Immediately I dropped my eyes, wondering why I was so keenly watched by the strange woman. The man ceased his mutterings, and then a third bell was tapped. Every one picked up his knife and fork and began eating. I began crying instead, for by this time I was afraid to venture anything more.

But this eating by formula was not the hardest trial in that first day. Late in the morning, my friend Judéwin gave me a terrible warning. Judéwin knew a few words of English; and she had overheard the paleface woman talk about cutting our long, heavy hair. Our mothers had taught us that only unskilled warriors who were captured had their hair shingled by the enemy. Among our people, short hair was worn by mourners, and shingled hair by cowards!

We discussed our fate some moments, and when Judéwin said, "We have to submit, because they are strong," I rebelled.

"No, I will not submit! I will struggle first!" I answered.

I watched my chance and when no one noticed I disappeared. I crept up the stairs as quietly as I could in my squeaking shoes,—my moccasins had been exchanged for shoes. Along the hall I passed, without knowing whither I was going. Turning aside to an open door, I found a large room with three white beds in it. The windows were covered with dark green curtains, which made the room very dim. Thankful that no one was there, I directed my steps toward the corner farthest from the door. On my hands and knees I crawled under the bed, and cuddled myself in the dark corner.

From my hiding place I peered out shuddering with fear whenever I heard footsteps nearby. Though in the hall loud voices were calling my name and I knew that even Judéwin was searching for me, I did not open my mouth to answer. Then the steps were quickened and the voices became excited. The sounds came nearer and nearer. Women and girls entered the room. I held my breath, and watched them often closet doors and peep behind large trunks. Some one threw up the curtains, and the room was filled with sudden light. What caused them to stoop and look under the bed I do not know. I remember being dragged out, though I resisted by kicking and scratching wildly. In spite of myself, I was carried downstairs and tied fast in a chair.

I cried aloud, shaking my head all the while until I felt the cold blades of the scissors against my neck, and heard them gnaw off one of my thick braids. Then I lost my spirit. Since the day I was taken from my mother I had suffered extreme indignities. People had stared at me. I had been tossed about in the air like a wooden puppet. And now my long hair was shingled like a coward's! In my anguish I moaned for my mother, but no one came to comfort me. Not a soul reasoned quietly with me, as my own mother used to do; for now I was only one of many little animals driven by a herder.

III. The Snow Episode.

A short time after our arrival we three Dakotas were playing in the snowdrifts. We were all still deaf to the English language, excepting Judéwin, who always heard such puzzling things. One morning we learned through her ears that we were forbidden to fall lengthwise in the snow, as we had been doing, to see our own impressions. However, before many hours we had forgotten the order, and were having great sport in the snow, when a shrill voice called us. Looking up, we saw an imperative hand beckoning us into the house. We shook the snow off ourselves, and started toward the woman as slowly as we dared.

Judéwin said: "Now the paleface is angry with us. She is going to punish us for falling into the snow. If she looks straight into your eyes and talks loudly, you must wait until she stops. Then, after a tiny pause, say, 'No.'" The rest of the way we practiced upon the little word "no."

As it happened, Thowin was summoned to judgment first. The door shut behind her with a click.

Judéwin and I stood silently listening at the keyhole. The paleface woman talked in very severe tones. Her words fell from her lips like crackling embers, and her inflection ran up like the small end of a switch. I understood her voice better than the things she was saying. I was certain we had made her very impatient with us. Judéwin heard enough of the words to realize all too late that she had taught us the wrong reply.

"Oh, poor Thowin!" she gasped, as she put both hands over her ears. Just then I heard Thowin's tremulous answer, "No."

With an angry exclamation, the woman gave her a hard spanking. Then she stopped to say something. Judéwin said it was this: "Are you going to obey my word the next time?"

Thowin answered again with the only word at her command, "No."

This time the woman meant her blows to smart, for the poor frightened girl shrieked at the top of her voice. In the midst of the whipping the blows ceased abruptly, and the woman asked another question: "Are you going to fall in the snow again?"

Thowin gave her bad password another trial. We heard her say feebly, "No! No!"

With this the woman hid away her half-worn slipper, and led the child out, stroking her black shorn head. Perhaps it occurred to her that brute force is not the solution for such a problem. She did nothing to Judéwin nor to me. She only returned to us our unhappy comrade, and left us alone in the room.

During the first two or three seasons misunderstandings as ridiculous as this one of the snow episode frequently took place, bringing unjustifiable frights and punishments into our little lives.

Within a year I was able to express myself somewhat in broken English. As soon as I comprehended a part of what was said and done, a mischievous spirit of revenge possessed me. One day I was called in from my play for some misconduct. I had disregarded a rule which seemed to me very needlessly binding. I was sent into the kitchen to mash the turnips for dinner. It was noon, and steaming dishes were hastily carried into the dining room. I hated turnips, and their odor which came from the brown jar was offensive to me. With fire in my heart, I took the wooden tool that the paleface woman held out to me. I stood upon a step, and, grasping the handle with both hands, I bent in hot rage over the turnips. I worked my vengeance upon them. All were so busily occupied that no one noticed me. I saw that the turnips were in a pulp, and that further beating could not improve them; but the order was, "Mash these turnips," and mash them I would! I renewed my energy; and as I sent the masher into the bottom of the jar, I felt a satisfying sensation that the weight of my body had gone into it.

Just here a paleface woman came up to my table. As she looked into the jar, she shoved my hands roughly aside. I stood fearless and angry. She placed her red hands upon the rim of the jar. Then she gave one lift and a stride away from the table. But lo! the pulpy contents fell through the crumbled bottom to the floor! She spared me no scolding phrases that I had earned. I did not heed them. I felt triumphant in my revenge, though deep within me I was a wee bit sorry to have broken the jar.

As I sat eating my dinner, and saw that no turnips were served, I whooped in my heart for having once asserted the rebellion within me.

IV. The Devil.

Among the legends the old warriors used to tell me were many stories of evil spirits. But I was taught to fear them no more than those who stalked about in material guise. I never knew there was an insolent chieftain among the bad spirits, who dared to array his forces against the Great Spirit, until I heard this white man's legend from a paleface woman.

Out of a large book she showed me a picture of the white man's devil. I looked in horror upon the strong claws that grew out of his fur-covered fingers. His feet were like his hands. Trailing at his heels was a scaly tail tipped with a serpent's open jaws. His face was a patchwork: he had bearded cheeks, like some I had seen palefaces wear; his nose was an eagle's bill, and his sharp-pointed ears were pricked up like those of a sly fox. Above them a pair of cow's horns curved upward. I trembled with awe, and my heart throbbed in my throat, as I looked at the king of evil spirits. Then I heard the paleface woman say that this terrible creature roamed loose in the world, and that little girls who disobeyed school regulations were to be tortured by him.

That night I dreamt about this evil divinity. Once again I seemed to be in my mother's cottage. An Indian woman had come to visit my mother. On opposite sides of the kitchen stove, which stood in the centre of the small house, my mother and her guest were seated in straight-backed chairs. I played with a train of empty spools hitched together on a string. It was night, and the wick burned feebly. Suddenly I heard some one turn our door-knob from without.

My mother and the woman hushed their talk, and both looked toward the door. It opened gradually. I waited behind the stove. The hinges squeaked as the door was slowly, very slowly pushed inward.

Then in rushed the devil! He was tall! He looked exactly like the picture I had seen of him in the white man's papers. He did not speak to my mother, because he did not know the Indian language, but his glittering yellow eyes were fastened upon me. He took long strides around the stove, passing behind the woman's chair. I threw down my spools, and ran to my mother. He did not fear her, but followed closely after me. Then I ran round and round the stove, crying aloud for help. But my mother and the woman seemed not to know my danger. They sat still, looking quietly upon the devil's chase after me. At last I grew dizzy. My head revolved as on a hidden pivot. My knees became numb, and doubled under my weight like a pair of knife blades without a spring. Beside my mother's chair I fell in a heap. Just as the devil stooped over me with outstretched claws my mother awoke from her quiet indifference, and lifted me on her lap. Whereupon the devil vanished, and I was awake.

On the following morning I took my revenge upon the devil. Stealing into the room where a wall of shelves was filled with books, I drew forth The Stories of the Bible. With a broken slate pencil I carried in my apron pocket, I began by scratching out his wicked eyes. A few moments later, when I was ready to leave the room, there was a ragged hole in the page where the picture of the devil had once been.

V. Iron Routine.

A loud-clamoring bell awakened us at half past six in the cold winter mornings. From happy dreams of Western rolling lands and unlassoed freedom we tumbled out upon chilly bare floors back again into a paleface day. We had short time to jump into our shoes and clothes, and wet our eyes with icy water, before a small hand bell was vigorously rung for roll call.

There were too many drowsy children and too numerous orders for the day to waste a moment in any apology to nature for giving her children such a shock in the early morning. We rushed downstairs, bounding over two high steps at a time, to land in the assembly room.

A paleface woman, with a yellow-covered roll book open on her arm and gnawed pencil in her hand, appeared at the door. Her small, tired face was coldly lighted with a pair of large gray eyes.

She stood still in a halo of authority, while over the rim of her spectacles her eyes pried nervously about the room. Having glanced at her long list of names and called out the first one, she tossed up her chin and peered through the crystals of her spectacles to make sure of the answer "Here."

Relentlessly her pencil black-marked our daily records if we were not present to respond to our names, and no chum of ours had done it successfully for us. No matter if a dull headache or the painful cough of slow consumption had delayed the absentee, there was only time enough to mark the tardiness. It was next to impossible to leave the iron routine after the civilizing machine had once begun its day's buzzing; and as it was inbred in me to suffer in silence rather than to appeal to the ears of one whose open eyes could not see my pain, I have many times trudged in the day's harness heavy-footed, like a dumb sick brute.

Once I lost a dear classmate. I remember well how she used to mope along at my side, until one morning she could not raise her head from her pillow. At her deathbed I stood weeping, as the paleface woman sat near her moistening the dry lips. Among the folds of the bedclothes I saw the open pages of the white man's Bible. The dying Indian girl talked disconnectedly of Jesus the Christ and the paleface who was cooling her swollen hands and feet.

I grew bitter, and censured the woman for cruel neglect of our physical ills. I despised the pencils that moved automatically, and the one teaspoon which dealt out, from a large bottle, healing to a row of variously ailing Indian children. I blamed the hard-working, well-meaning, ignorant woman who was inculcating in our hearts her superstitious ideas. Though I was sullen in all my little troubles, as soon as I felt better I was ready again to smile upon the cruel woman. Within a week I was again actively testing the chains which tightly bound my individuality like a mummy for burial.

The melancholy of those black days has left so long a shadow that it darkens the path of years that have since gone by. These sad memories rise above those of smoothly grinding school days. Perhaps my Indian nature is the moaning wind which stirs them now for their present record. But, however tempestuous this is within me, it comes out as the low voice of a curiously colored seashell, which is only for those ears that are bent with compassion to hear it.

VI. Four Strange Summers.

After my first three years of school, I roamed again in the Western country through four strange summers.

During this time I seemed to hang in the heart of chaos, beyond the touch or voice of human aid. My brother, being almost ten years my senior, did not quite understand any feelings. My mother had never gone inside of a schoolhouse, and so she was not capable of comforting her daughter who could read and write. Even nature seemed to have no place for me. I was neither a wee girl nor a tall one; neither a wild Indian nor a tame one. This deplorable situation was the effect of my brief course in the East, and the unsatisfactory "teenth" in a girl's years.

It was under these trying conditions that, one bright afternoon, as I sat restless and unhappy in my mother's cabin, I caught the sound of the spirited step of my brother's pony on the road which passed by our dwelling. Soon I heard the wheels of a light buckboard, and Dawée's familiar "Ho!" to his pony. He alighted upon the bare ground in front of our house. Tying his pony to one of the projecting corner logs of the low-roofed cottage, he stepped upon the wooden doorstep.

I met him there with a hurried greeting, and, as I passed by, he looked a quiet "What?" into my eyes.

When he began talking with my mother, I slipped the rope from the pony's bridle. Seizing the reins and bracing my feet against the dashboard, I wheeled around in an instant. The pony was ever ready to try his speed. Looking backward, I saw Dawée waving his hand to me. I turned with the curve in the road and disappeared. I followed the winding road which crawled upward between the bases of little hillocks. Deep water-worn ditches ran parallel on either side. A strong wind blew against my cheeks and fluttered my sleeves. The pony reached the top of the highest hill, and began an even race on the level lands. There was nothing moving within that great circular horizon of the Dakota prairies save the tall grasses, over which the wind blew and rolled off in long, shadowy waves.

Within this vast wigwam of blue and green I rode reckless and insignificant. It satisfied my small consciousness to see the white foam fly from the pony's mouth.

Suddenly, out of the earth a coyote came forth at a swinging trot that was taking the cunning thief toward the hills and the village beyond. Upon the moment's impulse I gave him a long chase and a wholesome fright. As I turned away to go back to the village, the wolf sank down upon his haunches for rest, for it was a hot summer day; and as I drove slowly homeward, I saw his sharp nose still pointed at me, until I vanished below the margin of the hilltops.

In a little while I came in sight of my mother's house. Dawée stood in the yard, laughing at an old warrior who was pointing his forefinger, and again waving his whole hand, toward the hills. With his blanket drawn over one shoulder, he talked and motioned excitedly. Dawée turned the old man by the shoulder and pointed me out to him.

"Oh han!" (Oh yes) the warrior muttered, and went his way. He had climbed the top of his favorite barren hill to survey the surrounding prairies, when he spied my chase after the coyote. His keen eyes recognized the pony and driver. At once uneasy for my safety, he had come running to my mother's cabin to give her warning. I did not appreciate his kindly interest, for there was an unrest gnawing at my heart.

As soon as he went away, I asked Dawée about something else.

"No, my baby sister, I cannot take you with me to the party tonight," he replied. Though I was not far from fifteen, and I felt that before long I should enjoy all the privileges of my tall cousin, Dawée persisted in calling me his baby sister.

That moonlight night, I cried in my mother's presence when I heard the jolly young people pass by our cottage. They were no more young braves in blankets and eagle plumes, nor Indian maids with prettily-painted cheeks. They had gone three years to school in the East, and had become civilized. The young men wore the white man's coat and trousers, with bright neckties. The girls wore tight muslin dresses, with ribbons at neck and waist. At these gatherings they talked English. I could speak English almost as well as my brother, but I was not properly dressed to be taken along. I had no hat, no ribbons, and no closefitting gown. Since my return from school I had thrown away my shoes, and wore again the soft moccasins.

While Dawée was busily preparing to go I controlled my tears. But when I heard him bounding away on his pony, I buried my face in my arms and cried hot tears.

My mother was troubled by my unhappiness. Coming to my side, she offered me the only printed matter we had in our home. It was an Indian Bible, given her some years ago by a missionary. She tried to console me. "Here, my child, are the white man's papers. Read a little from them," she said most piously.

I took it from her hand, for her sake; but my enraged spirit felt more like burning the book, which afforded me no help, and was a perfect delusion to my mother. I did not read it, but laid it unopened on the floor, where I sat on my feet. The dim yellow light of the braided muslin burning in a small vessel of oil flickered and sizzled in the awful silent storm which followed my rejection of the Bible.

Now my wrath against the fates consumed my tears before they reached my eyes. I sat stony, with a bowed head. My mother threw a shawl over her head and shoulders, and stepped out into the night.

After an uncertain solitude, I was suddenly aroused by a loud cry piercing the night. It was my mother's voice wailing among the barren hills which held the bones of buried warriors. She called aloud for her brothers' spirits to support her in her helpless misery. My fingers grew icy cold, as I realized that my unrestrained tears had betrayed my suffering to her, and she was grieving for me.

Before she returned, though I knew she was on her way, for she had ceased her weeping, I extinguished the light, and leaned my head on the window sill.

Many schemes of running away from my surroundings hovered about in my mind. A few more moons of such a turmoil drove me away to the Eastern school. I rode on the white man's iron steed, thinking it would bring me back to my mother in a few winters, when I should be grown tall, and there would be congenial friends awaiting me.

VII. Incurring my Mother's Displeasure.

In the second journey to the East I had not come without some precautions. I had a secret interview with one of our best medicine men, and when I left his I wigwam I carried securely in my sleeve a tiny bunch of magic roots. This possession assured me of friends wherever I should go. So absolutely did I believe in its charms that I wore it through all the school routine for more than a year. Then, before I lost my faith in the dead roots, I lost the little buckskin bag containing all my good luck.

At the close of this second term of three years I was the proud owner of my first diploma. The following autumn I ventured upon a college career against my mother's will.

I had written for her approval, but in her reply I found no encouragement. She called my notice to her neighbors' children, who had completed their education in three years. They had returned to their homes, and were then talking English with the frontier settlers. Her few words hinted that I had better give up my slow attempt to learn the white man's ways, and be content to roam over the prairies and find my living upon wild roots. I silenced her by deliberate disobedience.

Thus, homeless and heavy-hearted, I began anew my life among strangers.

As I hid myself in my little room in the college dormitory, away from the scornful and yet curious eyes of the students, I pined for sympathy. Often I wept in secret, wishing I had gone West, to be nourished by my mother's love, instead of remaining among a cold race whose hearts were frozen hard with prejudice.

During the fall and winter seasons I scarcely had a real friend, though by that time several of my classmates were courteous to me at a safe distance.

My mother had not yet forgiven my rudeness to her, and I had no moment for letter-writing. By daylight and lamplight, I spun with reeds and thistles, until my hands were tired from their weaving, the magic design which promised me the white man's respect.

At length, in the spring term, I entered an oratorical contest among the various classes. As the day of competition approached, it did not seem possible that the event was so near at hand, but it came. In the chapel the classes assembled together, with their invited guests. The high platform was carpeted, and gayly festooned with college colors. A bright white light illumined the room, and outlined clearly the great polished beams that arched the domed ceiling. The assembled crowds filled the air with pulsating murmurs. When the hour for speaking arrived all were hushed. But on the wall the old clock which pointed out the trying moment ticked calmly on.

One after another I saw and heard the orators. Still, I could not realize that they longed for the favorable decision of the judges as much as I did. Each contestant received a loud burst of applause, and some were cheered heartily. Too soon my turn came, and I paused a moment behind the curtains for a deep breath. After my concluding words, I heard the same applause that the others had called out.

Upon my retreating steps, I was astounded to receive from my fellow students a large bouquet of roses tied with flowing ribbons. With the lovely flowers I fled from the stage. This friendly token was a rebuke to me for the hard feelings I had borne them.

Later, the decision of the judges awarded me the first place. Then there was a mad uproar in the hall, here my classmates sang and shouted my name at the top of their lungs; and the disappointed students howled and brayed in fearfully dissonant tin trumpets. In this excitement, happy students rushed forward to offer their congratulations. And I could not conceal a smile when they wished to escort me in a procession to the students' parlor, where all were going to calm themselves. Thanking them for the kind spirit which prompted them to make such a proposition, I walked alone with the night to my own little room.

A few weeks afterward, I appeared as the college representative in another contest. This time the competition was among orators from different colleges in our state. It was held at the state capital, in one of the largest opera houses.

Here again was a strong prejudice against my people. In the evening, as the great audience filled the house, the student bodies began warring among themselves. Fortunately, I was spared witnessing any of the noisy wrangling before the contest began. The slurs against the Indian that stained the lips of our opponents were already burning like a dry fever within my breast.

But after the orations were delivered a deeper burn awaited me. There, before that vast ocean of eyes, some college rowdies threw out a large white flag, with a drawing of a most forlorn Indian girl on it. Under this they had printed in bold black letters words that ridiculed the college which was represented by a "squaw." Such worse than barbarian rudeness embittered me. While we waited for the verdict of the judges, I gleamed fiercely upon the throngs of palefaces. My teeth were hard set, as I saw the white flag still floating insolently in the air.

Then anxiously we watched the man carry toward the stage the envelope containing the final decision.

There were two prizes given, that night, and one of them was mine!

The evil spirit laughed within me when the white flag dropped out of sight, and the hands which furled it hung limp in defeat.

Leaving the crowd as quickly as possible, I was soon in my room. The rest of the night I sat in an armchair and gazed into the crackling fire. I laughed no more in triumph when thus alone. The little taste of victory did not satisfy a hunger in my heart. In my mind I saw my mother far away on the Western plains, and she was holding a charge against me.

Zitkala-Ša

"An Indian Teacher among Indians" (1900)

I. My First Day.

Though an illness left me unable to continue my college course, my pride kept me from returning to my mother. Had she known of my worn condition, she would have said the white man's papers were not worth the freedom and health I had lost by them. Such a rebuke from my mother would have been unbearable, and as I felt then it would be far too true to be comfortable.

Since the winter when I had my first dreams about red apples I had been traveling slowly toward the morning horizon. There had been no doubt about the direction in which I wished to go to spend my energies in a work for the Indian race. Thus I had written my mother briefly, saying my plan for the year was to teach in an Eastern Indian school. Sending this message to her in the West I started at once eastward.

Thus I found myself, tired and hot, in a black veiling of car smoke, as I stood wearily on a street corner of an old, fashioned town, waiting for a car. In a few moments more I should be on the school grounds, where a new work was ready for my inexperienced hands.

Upon entering the school campus, I was surprised at the thickly clustered buildings which made it a quaint little village, much more interesting than the town itself. The large trees among the houses gave the place a cool, refreshing shade, and the grass a deeper green. Within this large court of grass and trees stood a low green pump. The queer box-like case had a revolving handle on its side, which clanked and creaked constantly.

I made myself known, and was shown to my room,—a small, carpeted room, with ghastly walls and ceiling. The two windows, both on the same side, were curtained with heavy muslin yellowed with age. A clean white bed was in one corner of the room, and opposite it was a square pine table covered with a black woolen blanket.

Without removing my hat from my head, I seated myself in one of the two stiff-backed chairs that were placed beside the table. For several heart throbs I sat still, looking from ceiling to floor, from wall to wall, trying hard to imagine years of contentment there. Even while I was wondering if my exhausted strength would sustain me through this undertaking, I heard a heavy tread stop at my door. Opening it, I met the imposing figure of a stately gray-haired man. With a light straw hat in one hand, and the right hand extended for greeting, he smiled kindly upon me. For some reason I was awed by his wondrous height and his strong square shoulders, which I felt were a finger's length above my head.

I was always slight, and my serious illness in the early spring had made me look rather frail and languid. His quick eye measured my height and breadth. Then he looked into my face. I imagined that a visible shadow flitted across his countenance as he let my hand fall. I knew he was no other than my employer.

"Ah ha! so you are the little Indian girl who created the excitement among the college orators!" he said, more to himself than to me. I thought I heard a subtle note of disappointment in his voice. Looking in from where he stood, with one sweeping glance, he asked if I lacked anything for my room.

After he turned to go, I listened to his step until it grew faint and was lost in the distance. I was aware that my car-smoked appearance had not concealed the lines of pain on my face.

For a short moment my spirit laughed at my ill fortune, and I entertained the idea of exerting myself to make an improvement. But as I tossed my hat off a leaden weakness came over me, and I felt as if years of weariness lay like water-soaked logs upon me. I threw myself upon the bed, and, closing my eyes, forgot my good intention.

II. A Trip Westward.

One sultry month I sat at a desk heaped up with work. Now, as I recall it, I wonder how I could have dared to disregard nature's warning with such recklessness. Fortunately, my inheritance of a marvelous endurance enabled me to bend without breaking.

Though I had gone to and fro, from my room to the office, in an unhappy silence, I was watched by those around me. On an early morning I was summoned to the superintendent's office. For a half hour I listened to his words and when I returned to my room I remembered one sentence above the rest. It was this: "I am going to turn you loose to pasture!" He was sending me West to gather Indian pupils for the school, and this was his way of expressing it.

I needed nourishment, but the mid-summer's travel across the continent to search the hot prairies for overconfident parents who would intrust their children to strangers was a lean pasturage. However, I dwelt on the hope of seeing my mother. I tried to reason that a change was a rest. Within a couple of days I started toward my mother's home.

The intense heat and the sticky car smoke that followed my homeward trail did not noticeably restore my vitality. Hour after hour I gazed upon the country which was receding rapidly from me. I noticed the gradual expansion of the horizon as we emerged out of the forest into the plains. The great high buildings, whose towers overlooked the dense woodlands, and whose gigantic cluster formed large cities, diminished together with the groves, until only little log cabins lay snugly in the bosom of the vast prairie. The cloud shadows which drifted about on the waving yellow of long-dried grasses thrilled me like the meeting of old friends.

At a small station, consisting of a single frame house with a rickety board walk around it, I alighted from the iron horse, just thirty miles from my mother and my brother Dawée. A strong hot wind seemed determined to blow my hat off, and return me to olden days when I roamed bareheaded over the hills. After the puffing engine of my train was gone, I stood on the platform in deep solitude. In the distance I saw the gently rolling land leap up into bare hills. At their bases a broad gray road was winding itself round about them until it came by the station. Among these hills, I rode in a light conveyance, with is trusty driver, whose unkempt flaxen hair hung shaggy about his ears and his leather neck of reddish tan. From accident or decay he had lost one of his long front teeth.

Though I call him a paleface, his cheeks were of a brick red. His moist blue eyes, blurred and bloodshot, twitched involuntarily. For a long time he had driven through grass and snow from this solitary station to the Indian village. His weather-stained clothes fitted badly his warped shoulders. He was stooped, and his protruding chin, with its tuft of dry flax, nodded as monotonously as did the head of his faithful beast.

All the morning I looked about me, recognizing old familiar sky lines of rugged bluffs and-round-topped hills. By the roadside I caught glimpses of various plants whose sweet roots were delicacies among my people. When I saw the first cone-shaped wigwam, I could not help uttering an exclamation which caused my driver a sudden jump out of his drowsy nodding.

At noon, as we drove through the eastern edge of the reservation, I grew very impatient and restless. Constantly I wondered what my mother would say upon seeing her little daughter grown tall. I had not written her the day of my arrival, thinking I would surprise her. Crossing a ravine thicketed with low shrubs and plum bushes, we approached a large yellow acre of wild sunflowers. Just beyond this nature's garden we drew near to my mother's cottage. Close by the log cabin stood a little canvas-covered wigwam. The driver stopped in front of the open door, and in a long moment my mother appeared at the threshold.

I had expected her to run out to greet me, but she stood still, all the while staring at the weather-beaten man at my side. At length, when her loftiness became unbearable, I called to her, "Mother, why do you stop?"

This seemed to break the evil moment, and she hastened out to hold my head against her cheek.

"My daughter, what madness possessed you to bring home such a fellow?" she asked, pointing at the driver, who was fumbling in his pockets for change while he held the bill I gave him between his jagged teeth.

"Bring him! Why, no, mother, he has brought me! He is a driver!" I exclaimed.

Upon this revelation, my mother threw her arms about me and apologized for her mistaken inference. We laughed away the momentary hurt. Then she built a brisk fire on the ground in the tepee, and hung a blackened coffeepot on one of the prongs of a forked pole which leaned over the flames. Placing a pan on a heap of red embers, she baked some unleavened bread. This light luncheon she brought into the cabin, and arranged on a table covered with a checkered oilcloth.

My, mother had never gone to school, and though she meant always to give up her own customs for such of the white man's ways as pleased her, she made only compromises. Her two windows, directly opposite each other, she curtained with a pink-flowered print. The naked logs were unstained, and rudely carved with the axe so as to fit into one another. The sod roof was trying to boast of tiny sunflowers, the seeds of which had probably been planted by the constant wind. As I leaned my head against the logs, I discovered the peculiar odor that I could not forget. The rains had soaked the earth and roof so that the smell of damp clay was but the natural breath of such a dwelling.

"Mother, why is not your house cemented? Do you have no interest in a more comfortable shelter?" I asked, when the apparent inconveniences of her home seemed to suggest indifference on her part.

"You forget, my child, that I am now old, and I do not work with beads any more. Your brother Dawée, too, has lost his position, and we are left without means to buy even a morsel of food," she replied.

Dawée was a government clerk in our reservation when I last heard from him. I was surprised upon hearing what my mother said concerning his lack of employment. Seeing the puzzled expression on my face, she continued: "Dawée! Oh, has he not told you that the Great Father at Washington sent a white son to take your brothers pen from him? Since then Dawée has not been able to make use of the education the Eastern school has given him."

I found no words with which to answer satisfactorily. I found no reason with which to cool my inflamed feelings.

Dawée was a whole day's journey off on the prairie, and my mother did not expect him until the next day. We were silent.

When, at length, I raised my head to hear more clearly the moaning of the wind in the corner logs, I noticed the daylight streaming into the dingy room through several places where the logs fitted unevenly. Turning to my mother, I urged her to tell me more about Dawée's trouble, but she only said: "Well, my daughter, this village has been these many winters a refuge for white robbers. The Indian cannot complain to the Great Father in Washington without suffering outrage for it here. Dawée tried to secure justice for our tribe in a small matter, and to-day you see the folly of it."

Again, though she stopped to hear what I might say, I was silent.

"My child, there is only one source of justice, and I have been praying steadfastly to the Great Spirit to avenge our wrongs," she said, seeing I did not move my lips.

My shattered energy was unable to hold longer any faith, and I cried out desperately: "Mother, don't pray again! The Great Spirit does not care if we live or die! Let us not look for good or justice: then we shall not be disappointed!"

"Sh! my child, do not talk so madly. There is Taku Iyotan Wasaka,[1] to which I pray," she answered, as she stroked my head again as she used to do when I was a smaller child.

III. My Mother's Curse Upon White Settlers.

One black night mother and I sat alone in the dim starlight, in front of our wigwam. We were facing the river, as we talked about the shrinking limits of the village. She told me about the poverty stricken white settlers, who lived in caves dug in the long ravines of the high hills across the river.

A whole tribe of broad-footed white beggars had rushed hither to make claims on those wild lands. Even as she was telling this I spied a small glimmering light in the bluffs.

"That is a white man's lodge where you see the burning fire," she said. Then, a short distance from it, only a little lower than the first, was another light. As I became accustomed to the night, I saw more and more twinkling lights, here and there, scattered all along the wide black margin of the river.

Still looking toward the distant firelight, my mother continued: "My daughter, beware of the paleface. It was the cruel paleface who caused the death of your sister and your uncle, my brave brother. It is this same paleface who offers in one palm, the holy papers, and with the other gives a holy baptism of firewater. He is the hypocrite who reads with one eye, 'Thou shalt not kill,' and with the other gloats upon the

---

1. An absolute Power.

sufferings of the Indian race." Then suddenly discovering a new fire in the bluffs, she exclaimed, "Well, well, my daughter, there is the light of another white rascal!"

She sprang to her feet, and, standing firm beside her wigwam, she sent a curse upon those who sat around the hated white man's light. Raising her right arm forcibly into line with her eye, she threw her whole might into her doubled fist as she shot it vehemently at the strangers. Long she held her outstretched fingers toward the settler's lodge, as if an invisible power passed from them to the evil at which she aimed.

IV. Retrospection.

Leaving my mother, I returned to the school in the East. As months passed over me, I slowly comprehended that the large army of white teachers in Indian schools had a larger missionary creed than I had suspected.

It was one which included self-preservation quite as much as Indian education. When I saw an opium-eater holding a position as teacher of Indians, I did not understand what good was expected, until a Christian in power replied that this pumpkin-colored creature had a feeble mother to support. An inebriate paleface sat stupid in a doctor's chair, while Indian patients carried their ailments to untimely graves, because his fair wife was dependent upon him for her daily food.

I find it hard to count that white man a teacher who tortured an ambitious Indian youth by frequently reminding the brave changeling that he was nothing but a "government pauper."

Though I burned with indignation upon discovering on every side instances no less shameful than those I have mentioned, there was no present help. Even the few rare ones who have worked nobly for my race were powerless to choose workmen like themselves. To be sure, a man was sent from the Great Father to inspect Indian schools, but what he saw was usually the students' sample work made for exhibition. I was nettled by this sly cunning of the workmen who hoodwinked the Indian's pale Father at Washington.

My illness, which prevented the conclusion of my college course, together with my mother's stories of the encroaching frontier settlers, left me in no mood to strain my eyes in searching for latent good in my white co-workers.

At this stage of my own evolution, I was ready to curse men of small capacity for being the dwarfs their God had made them. In the process of my education I had lost all consciousness of the nature world about me. Thus, when a hidden rage took me to the small white-walled prison which I then called my room, I unknowingly turned away from my one salvation.

Alone in my room, I sat like the petrified Indian woman of whom my mother used to tell me. I wished my heart's burdens would turn me to unfeeling stone. But alive, in my tomb, I was destitute!

For the white man's papers I had given up my faith in the Great Spirit. For these same papers I had forgotten the beating in trees and brooks. On account of my mother's simple view of life, and my lack of any, I gave her up, also. I made no friends among the race of people I loathed. Like a slender tree, I had been uprooted from my mother, nature, and God. I was shorn of my branches, which had waved in sympathy and love for home and friends. The natural coat of bark which had protected my oversensitive nature was scraped off to the very quick.

Now a cold bare pole I seemed to be, planted in a strange earth. Still, I seemed to hope a day would come when my mute aching head, reared upward to the sky, would flash a zigzag lightning across the heavens. With this dream of vent for a long-pent consciousness, I walked again amid the crowds.

At last, one weary day in the schoolroom, a new idea presented itself to me. It was a new way of solving the problem of my inner self. I liked it. Thus I resigned my position as teacher; and now I am in an Eastern city, following the long course of study I have set for myself. Now, as I look back upon the recent past, I see it from a distance, as a whole. I remember how, from morning till evening, many specimens of civilized peoples visited the Indian school. The city folks with canes and eyeglasses, the countrymen with sunburnt cheeks and clumsy feet, forgot their relative social ranks in an ignorant curiosity. Both sorts of these Christian palefaces were alike astounded at seeing the children of savage warriors so docile and industrious.

As answers to their shallow inquiries they received the students' sample work to look upon. Examining the neatly figured pages, and gazing upon the Indian girls and boys bending over their books, the white visitors walked out of the schoolhouse well satisfied: they were educating the children of the red man! They were paying a liberal fee to the government employees, in whose able hands lay the small forest of Indian timber.

In this fashion many have passed idly through the Indian schools during the last decade, afterward to boast of their charity to the North American Indian. But few there are who have paused to question whether real life or long-lasting death lies beneath this semblance of civilization.

"Why I am a Pagan" (1902)

When the spirit swells my breast I love to roam leisurely among the green hills; or sometimes, sitting on the brink of the murmuring Missouri, I marvel at the great blue overhead. With half closed eyes I watch the huge cloud shadows in their noiseless play upon the high bluffs opposite me, while into my ear ripple the sweet, soft cadences of the river's song. Folded hands lie in my lap, for the time forgot. My heart and I lie small upon the earth like a grain of throbbing sand. Drifting clouds and tinkling waters, together with the warmth of a genial summer day, bespeak with eloquence the loving Mystery round about us. During the idle while I sat upon the sunny river brink, I grew somewhat, though my response be not so clearly manifest as in the green grass fringing the edge of the high bluff back of me.

At length retracing the uncertain footpath scaling the precipitous embankment, I seek the level lands where grow the wild prairie flowers. And they, the lovely little folk, soothe my soul with their perfumed breath.

Their quaint round faces of varied hue convince the heart which leaps with glad surprise that they, too, are living symbols of omnipotent thought. With a child's eager eye I drink in the myriad star shapes wrought in luxuriant color upon the green. Beautiful is the spiritual essence they embody.

I leave them nodding in the breeze, but take along with me their impress upon my heart. I pause to rest me upon a rock embedded on the side of a foothill facing the low river bottom. Here the Stone-Boy, of whom the American aborigine tells, frolics about, shooting his baby arrows and shouting aloud with glee at the tiny shafts of lightning that flash from the flying arrow-beaks. What an ideal warrior he became, baffling the siege of the pests of all the land till he triumphed over their united attack. And here he lay,—Inyan our great-great-grandfather, older than the hill he rested on, older than the race of men who love to tell of his wonderful career.

Interwoven with the thread of this Indian legend of the rock, I fain would trace a subtle knowledge of the native folk which enabled them to recognize a kinship to any and all parts of this vast universe. By the leading of an ancient trail I move toward the Indian village.

With the strong, happy sense that both great and small are so surely enfolded in His magnitude that, without a miss, each has his allotted individual ground of opportunities, I am buoyant with good nature.

Yellow Breast, swaying upon the slender stem of a wild sunflower, warbles a sweet assurance of this as I pass by. Breaking off the clear crystal song, he turns his wee head from side to side eyeing me wisely as slowly I plod with moccasined feet. Then again he yields himself to his song of joy. Flit, flit hither and yon, he fills the summer sky with his swift, sweet melody. And truly does it seem his vigorous freedom lies more in his little spirit than in his wing.

With these thoughts I reach the log cabin whither I am strongly drawn by the tie of a child to an aged mother. Out bounds my four-footed friend to meet me, frisking about my path with unmistakable delight. Chan is a black shaggy dog, "a thorough bred little mongrel" of whom I am very fond. Chan seems to understand many words in Sioux, and will go to her mat even when I whisper the word, though generally I think she is guided by the tone of the voice. Often she tries to imitate the sliding inflection and long drawn out voice to the amusement of our guests, but her articulation is quite beyond my ear. In both my hands I hold her shaggy head and gaze into her large brown eyes. At once the dilated pupils contract into tiny black dots, as if the roguish spirit within would evade my questioning.

Finally resuming the chair at my desk I feel in keen sympathy with my fellow creatures, for I seem to see clearly again that all are akin.

The racial lines, which once were bitterly real, now serve nothing more than marking out a living mosaic of human beings. And even here men of the same color are like the ivory keys of one instrument where each resembles all the rest, yet varies from them in pitch and quality of voice. And those creatures who are for a time mere echoes of all other's note are not unlike the fable of the thin sick man whose distorted shadow, dressed like a real creature, came to the old master to make him follow as a shadow. Thus with a compassion for all echoes in human guise, I greet the solemn-faced "native preacher" whom I find awaiting me. I listen with respect for God's creature, though he mouth most strangely the jangling phrases of a bigoted creed.

As our tribe is one large family, where every person is related to all the others, he addressed me :—

"Cousin, I came from the morning church service to talk with you."

"Yes?" I said interrogatively, as he paused for some word from me.

Shifting uneasily about in the straight-backed chair he sat upon, he began: "Every holy day (Sunday) I look about our little God's house, and not seeing you there, I am disappointed. This is why I come to-day. Cousin, as I watch you from afar, I see no unbecoming behavior and hear only good reports of you, which all the more burns me with the wish that you were a church member. Cousin, I was taught long years ago by kind missionaries to read the holy book. These godly men taught me also the folly of our old beliefs.

"There is one God who gives reward or punishment to the race of dead men. In the upper region the Christian dead are gathered in unceasing song and prayer. In the deep pit below, the sinful ones dance in torturing flames.

"Think upon these things, my cousin, and choose now to avoid the after-doom of hell fire!" Then followed a long silence in which he clasped tighter and unclasped again his interlocked fingers.

Like instantaneous lightning flashes came pictures of my own mother's making, for she, too, is now a follower of the new superstition.

"Knocking out the chinking of our log cabin, some evil hand thrust in a burning taper of braided dry grass, but failed of his intent for the fire died out and the half burned brand fell inward to the floor. Directly above it, on a shelf, lay the holy book. This is what we found after our return from a several days' visit. Surely some great power is hid in the sacred book!"

Brushing away from my eyes many like pictures, I offered midday meal to the converted Indian sitting wordless and with downcast face. No sooner had he risen from the table with "Cousin, I have relished it," than the church bell rang.

Thither he hurried forth with his afternoon sermon. I watched him as he hastened along, his eyes bent fast upon the dusty road till he disappeared at the end of a quarter of a mile.

The little incident recalled to mind the copy of a missionary paper brought to my notice a few days ago, in which a "Christian" pugilist commented upon a recent article of mine, grossly perverting the spirit of my pen. Still I would not forget that the pale-faced missionary and the hoodooed aborigine are both God's creatures, though small indeed their own conceptions of Infinite Love. A wee child toddling in a wonder world, I prefer to their dogma my excursions into the natural gardens where the voice of the Great Spirit is heard in the twittering of birds, the rippling of mighty waters and the sweet breathing of flowers. If this is Paganism, then at present, at least, I am a Pagan.

Zitkala-Ša

16

"Nurslings of the Sky," from *The Land of Little Rain* (1903)

Mary Hunter Austin

MARY HUNTER AUSTIN (1868–1934), born on September 9, 1868, in Carlinville, Illinois, was one of nine children (of whom four survived) of a lawyer, George, and a teacher, Susanna. Her childhood interests in nature and literature were stimulated when, after graduating from Blackburn College in 1888, she and her widowed mother moved to California. After touring San Francisco and Los Angeles, they settled in the San Joaquin Valley. Overland travel inspired Austin's early essay, "One Hundred Miles on Horseback."

In 1892 Austin married Wallace Stafford Austin and moved to Lone Pine, California, in the shadow of Mount Whitney, which inspired further writing. Her husband, however, was critical of her writing and her politics; she in turn resented domestic duties, which she felt constrained her creative energies. They had one daughter, Ruth, who was finally institutionalized for severe mental disability.

While in California, Austin traveled to Carmel, where she met such writers as Jack London, Ambrose Bierce, and Mark Twain. She began publishing in literary magazines, including *The Atlantic Monthly* and *Munsey's*. In 1903 she published her first book, *The Land of Little Rain*, a narrative sympathetically observing the landscape and wildlife around the Mojave Desert. The following excerpt, a chapter near the end of *The Land of Little Rain*, captures Austin's keen environmental sensibility, her gift for metaphor, and her attention to the evocative power of landscape. Austin traveled frequently throughout California and to New York City, separating from her husband in 1914 and stepping up her work in support of the women's suffrage movement and the Women's Political Union. In 1924 she moved to Santa Fe, New Mexico, and built a home that she called *Casa Querida*. In Santa Fe Austin became active in indigenous rights movements and published *The Land of Journey's Ending*. Her New Mexico literary circle included D. H. Lawrence, Georgia O'Keeffe, and Mabel Dodge Luhan.

Her political activism is reflected in several of her novels, including such feminist novels as *A Woman of Genius* (1912) and *No. 26 Jayne Street* (1920). Austin was also a prodigious writer of poetry, plays, short stories, and essays, although she was plagued by physical and emotional ailments—what now might be called eating disorders, along with several breakdowns, breast cancer, and heart attacks. In 1932 Austin assembled a series of autobiographical sketches linking herself to nature, published as *Earth Horizon,* that innovatively tell her story through a combination of the third-person character "Mary" and the first-person reflexive "I." She died in 1934.

Critics have noted Austin's prescient attention to autobiographical reflexivity and her situating of subjectivity in an interplay with richly detailed regions of the Southwest. Melody Graulich's essays, as well as many other essays on Austin, offer suggestive analyses of a writer whose importance for life narrative is yet to be fully recognized.

Boston and New York
Houghton, Mifflin and Company
The Riverside Press, Cambridge
1903.

Nurslings of the Sky

Choose a hill country for storms. There all the business of the weather is carried on above your horizon and loses its terror in familiarity. When you come to think about it, the disastrous storms are on the levels, sea or sand or plains. There you get only a hint of what is about to happen, the fume of the gods rising from their meeting place under the rim of the world; and when it breaks upon you there is no stay nor shelter. The terrible mewings and mouthings of a Kansas wind have the added terror of viewlessness. You are lapped in them like uprooted grass; suspect them of a personal grudge. But the storms of hill countries have other business. They scoop watercourses, manure, the pines, twist them to a finer fibre, fit the firs to be masts and spars, and, if you keep reasonably out of the track of their affairs, do you no harm.

They have habits to be learned, appointed paths, seasons, and warnings, and they leave you in no doubt about their performances. One who builds his house on a water scar or the rubble of a steep slope must take chances. So they did in Overtown who built in the wash of Argus water, and at Kearsarge at the foot of a steep, treeless swale. After twenty years Argus water rose the wash against the frail houses, and the piled snows of Kearsarge slid down at a thunder peal over the cabins and the camp, but you could conceive that it was the fault of neither the water nor the snow.

The first effect of cloud study is a sense of presence and intention in storm processes. Weather does not happen. It is the visible manifestation of the Spirit moving itself in the void. It gathers itself together under the heavens; rains, snows, yearns mightily in wind, smiles; and the Weather Bureau, situated advantageously for that very business, taps the record on his instruments and going out on the streets denies his God, not having gathered the sense of what he has seen. Hardly anybody takes account of the fact that John Muir who knows more of mountain storms than any other, is a devout man.

Of the high Sierras choose the neighborhood of the splintered peaks about the Kern and King's river divide for storm study, or the short, wide-mouthed cañons opening eastward on high valleys. Days when the hollows are steeped in a warm, winey flood the clouds come walking on the floor of heaven, flat and pearly gray beneath, rounded and pearly white above. They gather flock-wise, moving on the level currents that roll about the peaks, lock hands and settle with the cooler air, drawing a veil about those places where they do their work. If their meeting or parting takes place at sunrise or sunset, as it often does, one gets the splendor of the apocalypse. There will be cloud pillars miles high, snow-capped, glorified, and preserving an orderly perspective before the unbarred door of the sun, or perhaps mere ghosts of clouds that dance to some pied piper of an unfelt wind. But be it day or night, once they have settled to their work, one sees from the valley only the blank wall of their tents stretched along the ranges. To get the real effect of a mountain storm you must be inside.

One who goes often into a hill country learns not to say: What if it should rain? It always does rain somewhere among the peaks: the unusual thing is that one should escape it. You might suppose that if you took any account of plant contrivances to save their pollen powder against showers. Note how many there are deep-throated and bell-flowered like the pentstemons, how many have nodding pedicels as the columbine, how many grow in copse shelters and grow there only. There is keen delight in the quick showers of summer cañons, with the added comfort, born of experience, of knowing that no harm comes of a wetting at high altitudes. The day is warm; a white cloud spies over the cañon wall, slips up behind the ridge to cross it by some windy pass, obscures your sun. Next you hear the rain drum on the broad-leaved hellebore, and beat down the mimulus beside the brook. You shelter on the lee of some strong pine with shut-winged butterflies and merry, fiddling creatures of the wood. Runnels of rain water from the glacier-slips swirl through the pine needles into rivulets; the streams froth and rise in their banks. The sky is white with cloud; the sky is gray with rain; the sky is clear. The summer showers leave no wake.

Such as these follow each other day by day for weeks in August weather. Sometimes they chill suddenly into wet snow that packs about the lake gardens clear to the blossom frills, and melts away harmlessly. Sometimes one has the good fortune from a heather-grown headland to watch a rain-cloud forming in mid-air. Out over meadow or lake region begins a little darkling of the sky,—no cloud, no wind, just a smokiness such as spirits materialize from in witch stories.

It rays out and draws to it some floating films from secret cañons. Rain begins, "slow dropping veil of thinnest lawn;" a wind comes up and drives the formless thing across a meadow, or a dull lake pitted by the glancing drops, dissolving as it drives. Such rains relieve like tears.

The same season brings the rains that have work to do, ploughing storms that alter the face of things. These come with thunder and the play of live fire along the rocks. They come with great winds that try the pines for their work upon the seas and strike out the unfit. They shake down avalanches of splinters from sky-line pinnacles and raise up sudden floods like battle fronts in the cañons against towns, trees, and boulders. They would be kind if they could, but have more important matters. Such storms, called cloud-bursts by the country folk, are not rain, rather the spillings of Thor's cup, jarred by the Thunderer. After such a one the water that comes up in the village hydrants miles away is white with forced bubbles from the wind-tormented streams.

All that storms do to the face of the earth you may read in the geographies, but not what they do to our contemporaries. I remember one night of thunderous rain made unendurably mournful by the houseless cry of a cougar whose lair, and perhaps his family, had been buried under a slide of broken boulders on the slope of Kearsarge. We had heard the heavy denotation of the slide about the hour of the alpenglow, a pale rosy interval in a darkling air, and judged he must have come from hunting to the ruined cliff and paced the night out before it, crying a very human woe. I remember, too, in that same season of storms, a lake made milky white for days, and crowded out of its bed by clay washed into it by a fury of rain, with the trout floating in it belly up, stunned by the shock of the sudden flood. But there were trout enough for what was left of the lake next year and the beginning of a meadow about its upper rim. What taxed me most in the wreck of one of my favorite cañons by cloudburst was to see a bobcat mother mouthing her drowned kittens in the ruined lair built in the wash, far above the limit of accustomed waters, but not far enough for the unexpected. After a time you get the point of view of gods about these things to save you from being too pitiful.

The great snows that come at the beginning of winter, before there is yet any snow except the perpetual high banks, are best worth while to watch. These come often before the late bloomers are gone and while the migratory birds are still in the piney woods. Down in the valley you see little but the flocking of blackbirds in the streets, or the low flight of mallards over the tulares, and the gathering of clouds behind Williamson. First there is a waiting stillness in the wood; the pine trees creak although there is no wind, the sky glowers, the firs rock by the water borders. The noise of the creek rises insistently and falls off a full note like a child abashed by sudden silence in the room. This changing of the stream-tone following tardily the changes of the sun on melting snows is most meaningful of wood notes. After it runs a little trumpeter wind to cry the wild creatures to their holes. Sometimes the warning hangs in the air for days with increasing stillness. Only Clark's crow and the strident jays make light of it; only they can afford to. The cattle get down to the foothills and ground inhabiting creatures make fast their doors. It grows chill, blind clouds fumble in the cañons; there will be a roll of thunder, perhaps, or a flurry of rain, but mostly the snow is born in the air with quietness and the sense of strong white pinions softly stirred. It increases, is wet and clogging, and makes a white night of midday.

There is seldom any wind with first snows, more often rain, but later, when there is already a smooth foot or two over all the slopes, the drifts begin. The late snows are fine and dry, mere ice granules at the wind's will. Keen mornings after a storm they are blown out in wreaths and banners from the high ridges sifting into the cañons.

Once in a year or so we have a "big snow." The cloud tents are widened out to shut in the valley and an outlying range or two and are drawn tight against the sun. Such a storm begins warm, with a dry white mist that fills and fills between the ridges, and the air is thick with formless groaning. Now for days you get no hint of the neighboring ranges until the snows begin to lighten and some shouldering peak lifts through a rent. Mornings after the heavy snows are steely blue, two-edged with cold, divinely fresh and still, and these are times to go up to the pine borders. There you may find floundering in the unstable drifts "tainted wethers" of the wild sheep, faint from age and hunger; easy prey. Even the deer make slow going in the thick fresh snow, and once we found a wolverine going blind and feebly in the white glare.

No tree takes the snow stress with such ease as the silver fir. The star-whorled, fan-spread branches droop under the soft wreaths — droop and press flatly to the trunk; presently the point of overloading is reached, there is a soft sough and muffled dropping, the boughs recover, and the weighting goes on until the drifts have reached the midmost whorls and covered up the branches. When the snows are particularly wet and heavy they spread over the young firs in green-ribbed tents wherein harbor winter loving birds.

All storms of desert hills, except wind storms, are impotent. East and east of the Sierras they rise in nearly parallel ranges, desertward, and no rain breaks over them, except from some far-strayed cloud or roving wind from the California Gulf, and these only in winter. In summer the sky travails with thunderings and the flare of sheet lightnings to win a few blistering big drops, and once in a lifetime the chance of a torrent. But you have not known what force resides in the mindless things until you have known a desert wind. One expects it at the turn of the two seasons, wet and dry, with electrified tense nerves. Along the edge of the mesa where it drops off to the valley, dust devils begin to rise white and steady, fanning out at the top like the genii out of the Fisherman's bottle. One supposes the Indians might have learned the use of smoke signals from these dust pillars as they learn most things direct from the tutelage of the earth. The air begins to move fluently, blowing hot and cold between the ranges. Far south rises a murk of sand against the sky; it grows, the wind shakes itself, and has a smell of earth. The cloud

of small dust takes on the color of gold and shuts out the neighborhood, the push of the wind is unsparing. Only man of all folk is foolish
enough to stir abroad in it. But being in a house is really much worse;
no relief from the dust, and a great fear of the creaking timbers. There is
no looking ahead in such a wind, and the bite of the small sharp sand
on exposed skin is keener than any insect sting. One might sleep, for the
lapping of the wind wears one to the point of exhaustion very soon, but
there is dread, in open sand stretches sometimes justified, of being over
blown by the drift. It is hot, dry, fretful work, but by going along the
ground with the wind behind, one may come upon strange things in its
tumultuous privacy. I like these truces of wind and heat that the desert
makes, otherwise I do not know how I should come by so many acquaintances with furtive folk. I like to see hawks sitting daunted in
shallow holes, not daring to spread a feather, and doves in a row by the
prickle bushes, and shut-eyed cattle, turned tail to the wind in a patient
doze. I like the smother of sand among the dunes, and finding small
coiled snakes in open places, but I never like to come in a wind upon
the silly sheep. The wind robs them of what wit they had, and they
seem never to have learned the self-induced hypnotic stupor with
which most wild things endure weather stress. I have never heard that
the desert winds brought harm to any other than the wandering shep-
herds and their flocks. Once below Pastaria Little Pete showed me
bones sticking out of the sand where a flock of two hundred had been
smothered in a bygone wind. In many places the four-foot posts of a
cattle fence had been buried by the wind-blown dunes.

It is enough occupation, when no storm is brewing, to watch the
cloud currents and the chambers of the sky. From Kearsarge, say, you
look over Inyo and find pink soft cloud masses asleep on the level
desert air; south of you hurries a white troop late to some gathering of
their kind at the back of Oppapago; nosing the foot of Waban, a woolly
mist creeps south. In the clean, smooth paths of the middle sky and
highest up in air, drift, unshepherded, small flocks ranging contrarily.
You will find the proper names of these things in the reports of the
Weather Bureau—cirrus, cumulus, and the like—and charts that will
teach by study when to sow and take up crops. It is astonishing the
trouble men will be at to find out when to plant potatoes, and glaze
over the eternal meaning of the skies. You have to beat out for yourself
many mornings on the windly headlands the sense of the fact that you
get the same rainbow in the cloud drift over Waban and the spray of
your garden hose. And not necessarily then do you live up to it.

17

"Mary MacLane Meets the Vampire on the Isle of Treacherous Delights" (1910)

MARY MACLANE

MARY (ELIZABETH) MACLANE (1881–1929) was born on May 1, 1881, in Winnipeg, Canada, to Scotch-Canadian parents. When she was four, the family, including a sister and two brothers, moved to Western Minnesota, about which she wrote a short memoir, "The Kid Primitive." After her father died in 1889, MacLane's mother married longtime friend Henry Klenze and moved to Butte, Montana. As a teenager MacLane wrote a narrative of her coming-of-age in dated entries addressed to "The Devil," whom she called on to rescue her from what she called the barren wasteland of Butte. *The Story of Mary MacLane*, published in 1902 when she was nineteen, became an immediate, controversial bestseller, selling almost 100,000 copies within the first month. It was translated into several languages and influenced American modernist writers such as Ernest Hemingway.

MacLane moved to bohemian Greenwich Village in New York City and for a few years enjoyed literary celebrity and wealth. She made book tours during which she read flamboyantly from her narrative. Her frank, brazen, and proud depictions of and musings on sexuality, friendship, and herself invited censorship and parody as well as praise. Her literary celebrity was unlike any America had seen before.

The New York World ran headlines such as "Mary Will Skip New York, Miss MacLane to Ignore Us on Her Trip East," and featured a forum in which readers wrote in response to the question "What do you think of Mary MacLane?" In 1905 MacLane led a Fourth of July parade, lying languorously on a float outfitted with a divan and silk canopy.

MacLane's second book failed to attract a fickle public. Unable to secure royalties owed her by her publisher, she was forced to return to Butte in 1908. Making a living by writing short essays for the *Butte Evening News,* she was condemned by most of Butte's citizens as the "wild woman." The essay included here from the March 27, 1910, *Evening News* frames her restless migration between the "barren" West of the Rocky Mountains and the treacherous seductions of Manhattan. In 1918 MacLane moved to Chicago where she wrote and starred in a film (now lost) entitled *Men Who Have Made Love to Me.* Her second autobiographical narrative, *I, Mary MacLane* (1917), reflecting on her career but without the passionate invective of her first memoir, was unsuccessful. In 1929 she died in a Chicago hotel room fire.

MacLane's work remained out of print from 1917 to 1993. Interest in her and her writing revived in the 1970s and 1980s with the awakening attention to Western women writers. Lillian Faderman has read MacLane as a proto-lesbian writer, focusing attention on her infatuation with a teacher and her allusions to liaisons in Greenwich Village. Elisabeth Pruitt collected MacLane's first book, along with several of her articles and an interview, in her 1993 *Tender Darkness: A Mary MacLane Anthology.* Julia Watson has recently published an essay on the sense of place in MacLane's work, and Cathryn Halverson discusses MacLane's life and work in *Maverick Autobiographies* (2004).

"Mary MacLane Meets the Vampire on the Isle of Treacherous Delights"

It is close upon the witching hour of midnight. I, of womankind and something-and-twenty years, sit alone in my little blue and white room, fallow and eke somewhat forlorn. I am surrounded by the silence of West Park street, than which the vast stillnesses of the everlasting hills to the southwest are not more profound. It sets somberly upon me for I, who imagined myself built for silences, solitudes, sunsets, still gray dawns—I am longing for little old New York.

New York—oh, New York—the mere thought of it fills me with a subtle restlessness, a half-insane emotion of far desire. Its name calls up a throng of turbulent memories, of mingled mournfulness and the utter reckless joy of living such as nothing but a dweller in New York can know.

All—all that is in the soul, the body, the mind, the heart of a human being, New York, the vampire, *the cruel and much-loved,* drags out. It demands the last fluttering gasp of breath, the last drop of blood, the last thrill of the worn nerves. While there's left one glimmer of light in one's mind, or one conscious nerve in one's body, the lips of the vampire are pressed close upon one's human lips, passionate, insatiate, mad until all is over and one lies abandoned, cold and dead.

There's nothing, nothing, nothing that New York gathers in and holds as it does youth. The mind and the body in the fullness of their youth arc the food of the vampire. It devours, but, oh, it gives in exchange—life!

All the life, the youth; all the brain, such as it is, and all the restless heart; all the wild, nameless vitalities that make me human, every treasured thing I have to give, I waft at this moment, over frozen river and snow-clad hill—a thousand leagues—to New York, the exquisite vampire, merciless, bewitching.

I know New York as I know Butte-Montana, for exactly what it is. I have no roseate illusions about it. It has lodged me not as a transient bird of passage, but as one of the four million who call it home. I well know that it is no place to go to gather lilies. Its paving stones are the paving stones of hell. But on them walk people who are more wonderful than lilies. And the lesson it teaches is the adamant truth itself.

I first went to New York in the summer of 1902, at the age of 19, when I was a crude but successful child, guarded and looked-after and chaperoned to the point of atrophy. New York seemed to me then a vast, tiresome Babel, with a mingled atmosphere of skyscrapers and of alcoholic beverages, which latter continually were being offered me and which I did not like. I last went to New York at the age of five-and-twenty, when I was cast into it as into a seething whirlpool, "broke," at the time, heavyhearted, and alone. My little body, like Juliet's, was already aweary of this great world. But what it and the heart in it had to suffer before they caught the meaning and the pace of the seething whirlpool only the silent gods know. I may one day write it or I may keep it, a black memory, locked fast within me. But this much let me say for myself, that I bore misfortune in solitude and with cold disdain for its slings and arrows, and New York, though it has got everything else out of me that I could give it, wrung not one salt tear from my tired eyes. It gives me infinite satisfaction to be able to say it now and before I left New York, but a little time ago—yet, I remembered even that crucial time as a precious and informing experience. Also before I left I could gauge New York—I could grasp it, as I now grasp Butte, in the hollow of my hand. Nothing in it could faze or frighten me. The skyscrapers had become something attractive and beloved, and the quick fire of the alcoholic things, absinthe, vermouth, chartreuse, had run a thousand times, a negative passion, in my veins. In short, on the altar of the exquisite vampire I had offered up, madly and gladly, what was left of the first half of my youth. I am conscious as I sit here, in the chaste silence of West Park street, in my blue and white room, of but just entering on the second half of my youth—which is a fuller half than the first, if less radiant; light-hearted and care-freer, if less innocent—and by those tokens I fain would haste with it to where the North and East rivers wash the glittering shores of the Isle of Treacherous Delights—to lay it upon the same broad altar, already piled high with a million like gifts.

There is nothing at all in New York that is not fascinating to those who love it. For them there is poetry in every seething subway station, in every low-down Italian, with his banana cart on the Third and Fourth avenue corners, in the Siegel and Macy and Wanamaker department stores, as well as in the wonderful shops on the avenue, in the vaudeville theaters, and even in the piano-organs that awaken the echoes and the dwellers in the apartment buildings on the side streets. To them the look of New York is beautiful. No turreted castle overlooking a desolate sea could show more picturesque than the Flatiron building at sunset, with the dying lights on its battlements, and the Twenty-third street mob, like scurrying insects, at its base. And close to it is another thing of beauty which to me typifies the spirit of all New York—the great bronze Diana of St Gaudens, which rests a-tiptoe on the Madison Square tower. She suggests youth in its gay and triumphant freedom.

But, however, it's not for those chaste delights alone I'm longing in the midst of West Park street's remote gloom. One can not live on even Flatiron buildings, and Diana, though she's inspiring, is not satisfying to the emotions she rouses. Besides, she's bronze.

But the quality that is so distinctively New Yorkish, and which Butte-Montana conspicuously lacks (having in its place the deadly thrall we all wot of), is the quality of deep and intimate humanness. It is that and not the glitter which makes people, after a half-year of living in it, fall so abandonedly in love with New York; it is that which makes New York people think there's no other town in the world. They may tell you it's the glitter of the gay white way, or the cafes, or the theaters, or the Fifth avenue parade, or what not, but those are only the delectable setting. It's the subtle freemasonry among the millions, the silent recognition and understanding of each other's humanness and the half suggestion of intimacy that one feels toward all or any of the persons one meets and passes on Broadway—it's that that's all the glitter and enchantment of it. And, too, it's that together with the glitter of the white way that is the most alluring and treacherous and annihilating of all the attributes of the vampire. In truth, it is that quality that is the vampire. For it's intimacy with human beings and all that it betokens—the exchanging of bits of one's personality for bits of another's, the idiosyncrasies of friendship, the nerve-racking experience of being in love, the hypnotic effects of one personality upon another, the utter throwing to the winds of all one's reserves of body and soul before the compelling magnetisms of some, and the lesser intoxication of knowing one's domination of others—it is all these things that devour flesh and blood and nerve. They eat their way from the outer wall that guards the crude human being to the inmost keep of the citadel. One's loves and friendships have effects on one's slim young body and one's wayward mind that are more malignant than cocaine and more subtle than absinthe. But it's all so exquisitely and poetically and seductively worth while. Not one affair of the heart—and even friendships with me seem to be affairs of the heart—that New York has given me, though they left me, times, battered, stung, wounded, a bundle of frazzled nerves—not one would I exchange for any non-human treasure that life could bring. If there's one tenet that I cling to with sincerity and faith, it's that which enjoins absolute freedom of action, to follow not the precepts but the impulses, to grasp one's heart's desires, to emulate the surging voice of all New York in its wild cry "More Life, More Life!"—to turn everything outward, to let slip all one's emotions, all one's glittering passion, all one's dormant lights-o'-love.

That's what you do in New York. And it's that that makes the deadly thrall of Butte seem deadlier and the stillness of West Park street more deep. No solitary cell at Sing Sing could rival my little blue and white room at this moment for aloofness, for there's no such thing as human intimacy in this young, young town.

I did not know that when I lived in Butte before I had myself no intimate friendships, but I knew that I was entirely abnormal, anyway. But since I've been gone from it I realize that the people in Butte are all abnormal in that they form no real intimacies. The are as shy as wild sea-fowl with each other, and absolutely dead-locked in iron-hound personal isolation. They have what they call friendships, and there are little clubs of women who foregather, and people take drinks together and that—but with it all they are not, they seemingly can't be, intimate with each other. They think they exchange bits of their personalities, when they are really exchanging only talk. They exchange kisses and hand-clasps and even lingering caresses, but all in the deadly thrall way. I idly wonder as I sit here whether there would be anything intimate about even the doing of a murder in Butte. "But no," I think to myself, "there would be more of passion, let loose, in New York in a mere brushing together of finger-tips, or in gazing into eyes across a little table, than in anything that's done in Butte. It's the way you do them in New York."

Butte's way is without doubt the wiser of the two, but what's that to do with it? Butte's way makes for more strength in that since one turns nothing outward, one's resources are husbanded, but what's the use? What do we do with our strength after we husband it? There's no development where there's no intimacy. One barely begins to live only after one has rubbed hard against at least two live people, with nerves in their finger-ends and lights in their eyes.

I have in Butte two deadly, thrall friendships—or are they a love and a friendship, I don't myself quite know—upon which I've been bold enough, since I've been back, to try out the methods in favor on and hard-by the white way. It's fascinating to watch their effects, which are to one-third perplex, one-third frighten, and one-third allure. I get nothing of the kind myself in return, since the wild sea-bird shyness is fast upon them and I have all the advancing to do, but, withal, I have at least the pleasure of making two people writhe at the unusualness, in Butte, of friendship in the nude.

But pungent though it is, it is not a wholly satisfying pursuit and the half-lenient gods, after all, do not limit me to those two. There are one or two people in Butte who have themselves lived on the Isle of Treacherous Delights. I find they know the game as it's played there, and they go to it with a recognizing, if shy, eagerness. But—this is Butte-Montana, where the on-lookers make scarlet mountains of drab mole hills—and when all's said I believe I, M. MacLane, am the one citizen Butte will ever have who is absolutely undisturbed and undeterred by the whispering tongues. Contempt is the word which correctly pictures my attitude toward them. And contempt is the correct attitude to maintain. Why should they judge me? Why should any one judge any one else? Which brings me back to little old New York, where no one judges any one else. How much better to be living than slowly drying up inwardly. How much better to be in New York, where people are really let live. How I long at this witching hour of midnight, with the staid quietness of West Park street oppressing me, and at the threshold of my second half of youth, to feel once more the lips of the vampire very close against mine.

On the corner of Fifth avenue and Twenty-sixth street, close to where the bronze Diana stands, poised against the blue, is the Cafe Martin, where the Dry Martini is more palely golden than anywhere else on the Isle, where the people are more attractive and all the delights more bewitchingly treacherous. It has been the scene of more new and well nigh insane adventures for me—and a million other feminine youths— than probably any cafe could be outside London. It is swagger, extremely French (for America), and cordial in its welcome to unescorted women before the bell tolls six in the evening. The place is so pallidly, prettily decorated, the music is so thin and sensuous, the women such high wrought things. It is consequently crowded with them from lunch-time until then. There are also men to be sure—at about four in the afternoon, when one type of the masculine absinthe-drinker of New York assembles to steep its sodden soul in anise. But the restaurant which looks on the Avenue is mostly filled with women, such a picturesque crowd, with a freedom of mood upon them which is remarkable even in New York. They are nearly all young women—(but New York women are still in the throes of youth at five-and-forty)—there are artists, writers, chorus-girls, vaudeville people, *habitues* of Bohemia, *dilettantes* of all sorts—all the loose young feminine fish in New York. It is the one cafe on the Isle wherein the crowd is not specialized—where that most fascinating, most complex, most unexplainable of human beings, the New York young woman, may be seen in the mixed aggregate. In that the Martin is unlike the Knickerbocker, up at Forty-second street, the center of the Rialto and the haunt of the moneyed but unaristocratic theatrical people, or the Cafe des Beaux Arts, frequented chiefly by the high-browed followers of the arts, or Rector's, beloved of the refined *demimondaines,* or Churchill's, loved of the unrefined ones, or Sherry's, the feeding-place of the swagger, or the Waldorf, where the ungrammatical and heavily upholstered inhabitants of Pittsburgh feel at home, or Maria's, the resort of the not-too-successful *literateurs*, or Jack's, where the hippodrome ballet nightly grazes. Any or all of those types are to be seen at Martin's, whereas they would be unlikely to find themselves at any two of the others.

What a picture of youth it is in the Martin, at four in the afternoon!—a picture of tired, tired youth, women like crushed lilies or half-wilted jonquils. They are all in the clinch of the vampire. The mark of the vampire is upon their delicately-rouged and faintly-drooping lips, in the glint of their all-knowing eyes, upon their insolent brows and in the movements of their slender hands. Their hearts and bodies are weary from the ceaseless glitter of the world and from their endless pursuit of Pleasure—a Pleasure like an *ignis fatuus* that is always a little way beyond, that never, never waits. I have seen it myself around corners, behind doors, at the top of flights of stairs—always beyond, never in my hands or by my side. I have sat, times, in the Martin, with some delectable companion, twirling the stem of my absinthe glass with my thumb and finger and with my chin on my hand, and looked about at the gay-hearted company and wondered if they knew they had never caught up with the *ignis fatuus* Pleasure, and never would—and if they did that the flavor of the Grape would become wormwood on their lips, and the daylight shadowed, and the music stilled.

But no, assuredly they never think of it all. The generality of the amblers down the primrose path are happily not given to introspection. That is a seething curse peculiar to those to whom the birth-stars are not kind, with whom it plays perennial mischief. And if one is both lured by the primrose path and, too, given to introspection—so much the more grievous the curse—so much the more.

For as one sits here, in the aforesaid silence, it comes over one like a cold, distracting breath, and the look of all of life makes one but shudder. One's longing for the Isle of Delights falls away like a mantle—that mad utter folly, that dedication of all things to life at its last and utmost tension, that picture of the flower-faces, of tired youth, in the Cafe Martin—float across one's mind with a suggestion of blackness like death itself.

One wants no human intimacy either in the marts of New York or the little by-ways of Butte. One sees one's portion in an aloofness and isolation far beyond what even Butte can give. For the having fed at the flesh-pots in the Isle of the Delights one pays a heavy, heavy reckoning—and to introspection that does it all. It once made the Delights more seductive, and it now makes the heavy reckoning so much the more heavy—so much the more, and—

"The Flower that once has bloomed forever dies."

New York or Butte-Montana, is it worth while—or isn't it? I ask me, with my hands pressed upon my eyes.

18

"The Promised Land," from *The Promised Land* (1912)

MARY ANTIN

MARY ANTIN (1881–1949) was born in the small Russian town of Polotzk in 1881. Her father, a trader constrained by the social and economic circumstances of Czarist rule, immigrated to the United States in 1891, and the rest of the family immigrated three years later with borrowed money. After several failed business attempts, the Antins settled in Boston's South End, where they lived meagerly on their combined earnings.

While her father, mother, and oldest sister worked, Antin was allowed to attend public school in Chelsea, a predominately Jewish suburb. She was a remarkable student, and with much support from her teachers and prominent figures in the Jewish community, in 1899, while still a student, she published her first book of juvenilia — a collection of letters she had written to an uncle that she translated from Yiddish to English.

Shortly afterward Antin met geologist Amadeus William Grabau, who was ten years her senior and hailed from a staunchly Lutheran family. Antin's own educational goal of attending Radcliffe College was thwarted by their marriage, the birth of their daughter, and their 1901 move to New York, where Grabau was offered a position at Columbia University. In New York Antin mingled with intellectuals, including Josephine Lazarus, whose sister, Emma, had written the poem "The New Colossus" inscribed on the Statue of Liberty. Josephine became Antin's mentor and introduced her to Emersonian transcendentalism. The Lazarus sisters' arguments regarding the importance of transcendentalism for thinking about the citizenship of diverse American immigrants, especially women, inspired Antin's beliefs and writing.

Josephine, who had encouraged Antin to write an autobiography, died in 1910, motivating Antin to begin her project. First published as a set of articles in *The Atlantic Monthly*, and finally collected as *The Promised Land* in 1912, Antin's idealistic assimilationist autobiography, in its quest to realize the American Dream, met with critical success and became a bestseller, reprinted thirty-three times. Subsequently, she became a popular speaker on patriotic American themes. In 1914 she published another book, a defense of immigration entitled *They Who Knock at the Gates,* and actively campaigned to loosen restrictions on immigration. During and after World War I, however, widespread xenophobia and anti-German sentiment made life difficult for Antin and her husband, who ultimately left Columbia University and moved to China, where he died in 1946. These events left Antin devastated. Save for a few articles in magazines such as *The Atlantic Monthly* and *Common Ground,* she did not publish again. These articles, however, suggest that Antin, despite the xenophobia of World War I and the anti-Semitism of World War II, maintained her idealistic belief in the relationship of spiritualism to social justice and equality until her death after a lengthy illness in 1949.

Antin's life narrative is now read more critically in the wake of the New American studies, but its delineation of immigrant Russian-Jewish life remains important for conceptualizing urban American life in the early twentieth century. Antin's address to the reader as "my American friend," however, may suggest the anxieties and ambivalence about becoming an American in her immigrant narrative (see Sidonie Smith, "Cheesecake"). The excerpt here comes midway through *The Promised Land* and narrates the transitional moment when the old world of Russian Polotzk has been left behind and the new world of urban Boston calls for a new kind of identity.

Boston and New York
Houghton Mifflin Company
The Riverside Press, Cambridge
1912

To the Memory of
Josephine Lazarus
Who lives in the fulfillment
of her prophecies

Chapter IX. The Promised Land

Having made such good time across the ocean, I ought to be able to proceed no less rapidly on *terra firma*, where, after all, I am more at home.
And yet here is where I falter. Not that I hesitated, even for the space of
a breath, in my first steps in America. There was no time to hesitate. The
most ignorant immigrant, on landing, proceeds to give and receive
greetings, to eat, sleep, and rise, after the manner of his own country;
wherein he is corrected, admonished, and laughed at, whether by interested friends or the most indifferent strangers; and his American experience is thus begun. The process is spontaneous on all sides, like the
education of the child by the family circle. But while the most stupid
nursery maid is able to contribute her part toward the result, we do not
expect an analysis of the process to be furnished by any member of the
family, least of all by the engaging infant. The philosophical maiden
aunt alone, or some other witness equally psychological and aloof, is
able to trace the myriad efforts by which the little Johnnie or Nellie ac-
quires a secure hold on the disjointed parts of the huge plaything, life.

Now I was not exactly an infant when I was set down, on a May day
some fifteen years ago, in this pleasant nursery of America. I had long
since acquired the use of my faculties, and had collected some bits of experience, practical and emotional, and had even learned to give an account of them. Still, I had very little perspective, and my observations
and comparisons were superficial. I was too much carried away to ana-
lyze the forces that were moving me. My Polotzk I knew well before I
began to judge it and experiment with it. America was bewilderingly
strange, unimaginably complex, delightfully unexplored. I rushed im-
petuously out of the cage of my provincialism and looked eagerly about
the brilliant universe. My question was, What have we here?—not,

What does this mean? That query came much later. When I now become retrospectively introspective, I fall into the predicament of the centipede in the rhyme, who got along very smoothly until he was asked which leg came after which, whereupon he became so rattled that he could n't take a step. I know I have come on a thousand feet, on wings, winds, and American machines,—I have leaped and run and climbed and crawled,—but to tell which step came after which I find a puzzling matter. Plenty of maiden aunts were present during my second infancy, in the guise of immigrant officials, school-teachers, settlement workers, and sundry other unprejudiced and critical observers. Their statistics I might properly borrow to fill the gaps in my recollections, but I am prevented by my sense of harmony. The individual, we know, is a creature unknown to the statistician, whereas I undertook to give the personal view of everything. So I am bound to unravel, as well as I can, the tangle of events, outer and inner, which made up the first breathless years of my American life.

During his three years of probation, my father had made a number of false starts in business. His history for that period is the history of thousands who come to America, like him, with pockets empty, hands untrained to the use of tools, minds cramped by centuries of repression in their native land. Dozens of these men pass under your eyes every day, my American friend, too absorbed in their honest affairs to notice the looks of suspicion which you cast at them, the repugnance with which you shrink from their touch. You see them shuffle from door to door with a basket of spools and buttons, or bending over the sizzling irons in a basement tailor shop, or rummaging in your ash can, or moving a pushcart from curb to curb, at the command of the burly policeman. "The Jew peddler!" you say, and dismiss him from your premises and from your thoughts, never dreaming that the sordid drama of his days may have a moral that concerns you. What if the creature with the untidy beard carries in his bosom his citizenship papers? What if the cross-legged tailor is supporting a boy in college who is one day going to mend your state constitution for you? What if the ragpicker's daughters are hastening over the ocean to teach your children in the public schools? Think, every time you pass the greasy alien on the street, that he was born thousands of years before the oldest native American; and he may have something to communicate to you, when you two shall have learned a common language. Remember that his very physiognomy is a cipher the key to which it behooves you to search for most diligently.

By the time we joined my father, he had surveyed many avenues of approach toward the coveted citadel of fortune. One of these, heretofore untried, he now proposed to essay, armed with new courage, and cheered on by the presence of his family. In partnership with an energetic little man who had an English chapter in his history, he prepared to set up a refreshment booth on Crescent Beach. But while he was completing arrangements at the beach we remained in town, where we enjoyed the educational advantages of a thickly populated neighborhood; namely, Wall Street, in the West End of Boston.

Anybody who knows Boston knows that the West and North Ends are the wrong ends of that city. They form the tenement district, or, in the newer phrase, the slums of Boston. Anybody who is acquainted with the slums of any American metropolis knows that that is the quarter where poor immigrants foregather, to live, for the most part, as unkempt, half-washed, toiling, unaspiring foreigners; pitiful in the eyes of social missionaries, the despair of boards of health, the hope of ward politicians, the touchstone of American democracy. The well-versed metropolitan knows the slums as a sort of house of detention for poor aliens, where they live on probation till they can show a certificate of good citizenship.

He may know all this and yet not guess how Wall Street, in the West End, appears in the eyes of a little immigrant from Polotzk. What would the sophisticated sight-seer say about Union Place, off Wall Street, where my new home waited for me? He would say that it is no place at all, but a short box of an alley. Two rows of three-story tenements are its sides, a stingy strip of sky is its lid, a littered pavement is the floor, and a narrow mouth its exit.

But I saw a very different picture on my introduction to Union Place. I saw two imposing rows of brick buildings, loftier than any dwelling I had ever lived in. Brick was even on the ground for me to tread on, instead of common earth or boards. Many friendly windows stood open, filled with uncovered heads of women and children. I thought the people were interested in us, which was very neighborly. I looked up to the topmost row of windows, and my eyes were filled with the May blue of an American sky!

In our days of affluence in Russia we had been accustomed to upholstered parlors, embroidered linen, silver spoons and candlesticks, goblets of gold, kitchen shelves shining with copper and brass. We had featherbeds heaped halfway to the ceiling; we had clothes presses dusky with velvet and silk and fine woollen. The three small rooms into which my father now ushered us, up one flight of stairs, contained only the necessary beds, with lean mattresses; a few wooden chairs; a table or two; a mysterious iron structure, which later turned out to be a stove; a couple of unornamental kerosene lamps; and a scanty array of cooking-utensils and crockery. And yet we were all impressed with our new home and its furniture. It was not only because we had just passed through our seven lean years, cooking in earthen vessels, eating black bread on holidays and wearing cotton; it was chiefly because these wooden chairs and tin pans were American chairs and pans that they shone glorious in our eyes. And if there was anything lacking for comfort or decoration we expected it to be presently supplied—at least, we children did. Perhaps my mother alone, of us newcomers, appreciated the shabbiness of the little apartment, and realized that for her there was as yet no laying down of the burden of poverty.

Our initiation into American ways began with the first step on the new soil. My father found occasion to instruct or correct us even on the way from the pier to Wall Street, which journey we made crowded together in a rickety cab. He told us not to lean out of the windows, not to point, and explained the word "greenhorn." We did not want to be "greenhorns," and gave the strictest attention to my father's instructions. I do not know when my parents found opportunity to review together the history of Polotzk in the three years past, for we children had no patience with the subject; my mother's narrative was constantly interrupted by irrelevant questions, interjections, and explanations.

The first meal was an object lesson of much variety. My father produced several kinds of food, ready to eat, without any cooking, from little tin cans that had printing all over them. He attempted to introduce us to a queer, slippery kind of fruit, which he called "banana," but had to give it up for the time being. After the meal, he had better luck with a curious piece of furniture on runners, which he called "rocking-chair." There were five of us newcomers, and we found five different ways of getting into the American machine of perpetual motion, and as many ways of getting out of it. One born and bred to the use of a rocking-chair cannot imagine how ludicrous people can make themselves when attempting to use it for the first time. We laughed immoderately over our various experiments with the novelty, which was a wholesome way of letting off steam after the unusual excitement of the day.

In our flat we did not think of such a thing as storing the coal in the bathtub. There was no bathtub. So in the evening of the first day my father conducted us to the public baths. As we moved along in a little procession, I was delighted with the illumination of the streets. So many lamps, and they burned until morning, my father said, and so people did not need to carry lanterns. In America, then, everything was free, as we had heard in Russia. Light was free; the streets were as bright as a synagogue on a holy day. Music was free; we had been serenaded, to our gaping delight, by a brass band of many pieces, soon after our installation on Union Place.

Education was free. That subject my father had written about repeatedly, as comprising his chief hope for us children, the essence of American opportunity, the treasure that no thief could touch, not even misfortune or poverty. It was the one thing that he was able to promise us when he sent for us; surer, safer than bread or shelter. On our second day I was thrilled with the realization of what this freedom of education meant. A little girl from across the alley came and offered to conduct us to school. My father was out, but we five between us had a few words of English by this time. We knew the word school. We understood. This child, who had never seen us till yesterday, who could not pronounce our names, who was not much better dressed than we, was able to offer us the freedom of the schools of Boston! No application made, no questions asked, no examinations, rulings, exclusions; no machinations, no fees. The doors stood open for every one of us. The smallest child could show us the way.

This incident impressed me more than anything I had heard in advance of the freedom of education in America. It was a concrete proof— almost the thing itself. One had to experience it to understand it.

It was a great disappointment to be told by my father that we were not to enter upon our school career at once. It was too near the end of the term, he said, and we were going to move to Crescent Beach in a week or so. We had to wait until the opening of the schools in September. What a loss of precious time—from May till September!

Not that the time was lost. Even the interval on Union Place was crowded with lessons and experiences. We had to visit the stores and be dressed from head to foot in American clothing; we had to learn the mysteries of the iron stove, the washboard, and the speaking-tube; we had to learn to trade with the fruit peddler through the window, and not to be afraid of the policeman; and, above all, we had to learn English.

The kind people who assisted us in these important matters form a group by themselves in the gallery of my friends. If I had never seen them from those early days till now, I should still have remembered them with gratitude. When I enumerate the long list of my American teachers, I must begin with those who came to us on Wall Street and taught us our first steps. To my mother, in her perplexity over the cook-stove, the woman who showed her how to make the fire was an angel of deliverance. A fairy godmother to us children was she who led us to a wonderful country called "uptown," where, in a dazzlingly beautiful palace called a "department store," we exchanged our hateful home-made European costumes, which pointed us out as "greenhorns" to the children on the street, for real American machine-made garments, and issued forth glorified in each other's eyes.

With our despised immigrant clothing we shed also our impossible Hebrew names. A committee of our friends, several years ahead of us in American experience, put their heads together and concocted Ameri-can names for us all. Those of our real names that had no pleasing American equivalents they ruthlessly discarded, content if they retained the initials. My mother, possessing a name that was not easily translat-able, was punished with the undignified nickname of Annie. Fetchke, Joseph, and Deborah issued as Frieda, Joseph, and Dora, respectively. As for poor me, I was simply cheated. The name they gave me was hardly new. My Hebrew name being Maryashe in full, Mashke for short, Russianized into Marya (Mar-ya), my friends said that it would hold good in English as Mary; which was very disappointing, as I longed to possess a strange-sounding American name like the others.

I am forgetting the consolation I had, in this matter of names, from the use of my surname, which I have had no occasion to mention until now. I found on my arrival that my father was "Mr. Antin" on the slightest provocation, and not, as in Polotzk, on state occasions alone. And so I was "Mary Antin," and I felt very important to answer to such a dignified title. It was just like America that even plain people should wear their surnames on week days.

As a family we were so diligent under instruction, so adaptable, and so clever in hiding our deficiencies, that when we made the journey to Crescent Beach, in the wake of our small wagon-load of household goods, my father had very little occasion to admonish us on the way, and I am sure he was not ashamed of us. So much we had achieved toward our Americanization during the two weeks since our landing.

Crescent Beach is a name that is printed in very small type on the maps of the environs of Boston, but a life-size strip of sand curves from Winthrop to Lynn; and that is historic ground in the annals of my fam-ily. The place is now a popular resort for holiday crowds, and is famous under the name of Revere Beach. When the reunited Antins made their stand there, however, there were no boulevards, no stately bath-houses, no hotels, no gaudy amusement places, no illuminations, no showmen, no tawdry rabble. There was only the bright clean sweep of sand, the summer sea, and the summer sky. At high tide the whole Atlantic rushed in, tossing the seaweeds in his mane; at low tide he rushed out, growling and gnashing his granite teeth. Between tides a baby might play on the beach, digging with pebbles and shells, till it lay asleep on the sand. The whole sun shone by day, troops of stars by night, and the great moon in its season.

Into this grand cycle of the seaside day I came to live and learn and play. A few people came with me, as I have already intimated; but the main thing was that *I* came to live on the edge of the sea—I, who had spent my life inland, believing that the great waters of the world were spread out before me in the Dvina. My idea of the human world had grown enormously during the long journey; my idea of the earth had expanded with every day at sea; my idea of the world outside the earth now budded and swelled during my prolonged experience of the wide and unobstructed heavens.

Not that I got any inkling of the conception of a multiple world. I had had no lessons in cosmogony, and I had no spontaneous revelation of the true position of the earth in the universe. For me, as for my fathers, the sun set and rose, and I did not feel the earth rushing through space. But I lay stretched out in the sun, my eyes level with the sea, till I seemed to be absorbed bodily by the very materials of the world around me; till I could not feel my hand as separate from the warm sand in which it was buried. Or I crouched on the beach at full moon, wondering, wondering, between the two splendors of the sky and the sea. Or I ran out to meet the incoming storm, my face full in the wind, my being a-tingle with an awesome delight to the tips of my fog-matted locks flying behind; and stood clinging to some stake or upturned boat, shaken by the roar and rumble of the waves. So clinging, I pretended that I was in danger, and was deliciously frightened; I held on with both hands, and shook my head, exulting in the tumult around me, equally ready to laugh or sob. Or else I sat, on the stillest days, with my back to the sea, not looking at all, but just listening to the rustle of the waves on the sand; not thinking at all, but just breathing with the sea.

Thus courting the influence of sea and sky and variable weather, I was bound to have dreams, hints, imaginings. It was no more than this, perhaps: that the world as I knew it was not large enough to contain all that I saw and felt; that the thoughts that flashed through my mind, not half understood, unrelated to my utterable thoughts, concerned something for which had as yet no name. Every imaginative growing child has these flashes of intuition, especially one that becomes intimate with some one aspect of nature. With me it was the growing time, that idle summer by the sea, and I grew all the faster because I had been so cramped before. My mind, too, had so recently been worked upon by the impressive experience of a change of country that I was more than commonly alive to impressions, which are the seeds of ideas.

Let no one suppose that I spent my time entirely, or even chiefly, in inspired solitude. By far the best part of my day was spent in play—frank, hearty, boisterous play, such as comes natural to American children. In Polotzk, I had already begun to be considered too old for play, excepting set games or organized frolics. Here I found myself included with children who still played, and I willingly returned to childhood. There were plenty of playfellows. My father's energetic little partner had a little wife and a large family. He kept them in the little cottage next to ours; and that the shanty survived the tumultuous presence of that brood is a wonder to me to-day. The young Wilners included an assortment of boys, girls, and twins, of every possible variety of age, size, disposition, and sex. They swarmed in and out of the cottage all day long, wearing the door-sill hollow and trampling the ground to powder. They swung out of windows like monkeys, slid up the roof like flies, and shot out of trees like fowls. Even a small person like me couldn't go anywhere without being run over by a Wilner; and I could never tell which Wilner it was because none of them ever stood still long enough to be identified; and also because I suspected that they were in the habit of interchanging conspicuous articles of clothing, which was very confusing.

You would suppose that the little mother must have been utterly lost, bewildered, trodden down in this horde of urchins; but you are mistaken. Mrs. Wilner was a positively majestic little person. She ruled her brood with the utmost coolness and strictness. She had even the biggest boy under her thumb, frequently under her palm. If they enjoyed the wildest freedom outdoors, indoors the young Wilners lived by the clock. And so at five o'clock in the evening, on seven days in the week, my father's partner's children could be seen in two long rows around the supper table. You could tell them apart on this occasion, because they all had their faces washed. And this is the time to count them: there are twelve little Wilners at table.

I managed to retain my identity in this multitude somehow, and while I was very much impressed with their numbers, I even dared to pick and choose my friends among the Wilners. One or two of the smaller boys I liked best of all, for a game of hide-and-seek or a frolic on the beach. We played in the water like ducks, never taking the trouble to get dry. One day I waded out with one of the boys, to see which of us dared go farthest. The tide was extremely low, and we had not wet our knees when we began to look back to see if familiar objects were still in sight. I thought we had been wading for hours, and still the water was so shallow and quiet. My companion was marching straight ahead, so I did the same. Suddenly a swell lifted us almost off our feet, and we clutched at each other simultaneously. There was a lesser swell, and little waves began to run, and a sigh went up from the sea. The tide was turning—perhaps a storm was on the way—and we were miles, dreadful miles from dry land.

Boy and girl turned without a word, four determined bare legs ploughing through the water, four scared eyes straining toward the land. Through an eternity of toil and fear they kept dumbly on, death at their heels, pride still in their hearts. At last they reached high-water mark—six hours before full tide.

Each has seen the other afraid, and each rejoices in the knowledge. But only the boy is sure of his tongue.

"You was scared, war n't you?" he taunts.

The girl understands so much, and is able to reply:—

"You can schwimmen, I not."

"Betcher life I can schwimmen," the other mocks.

And the girl walks off, angry and hurt.

"An' I can walk on my hands," the tormentor calls after her. "Say, you greenhorn, why don'tcher look?"

The girl keeps straight on, vowing that she would never walk with that rude boy again, neither by land nor sea, not even though the waters should part at his bidding.

I am forgetting the more serious business which had brought us to Crescent Beach. While we children disported ourselves like mermaids and mermen in the surf, our respective fathers dispensed cold lemonade, hot peanuts, and pink popcorn, and piled up our respective fortunes, nickel by nickel, penny by penny. I was very proud of my connection with the public life of the beach. I admired greatly our shining soda fountain, the rows of sparkling glasses, the pyramids of oranges, the sausage chains, the neat white counter, and the bright array of tin spoons. It seemed to me that none of the other refreshment stands on the beach—there were a few—were half so attractive as ours. I thought my father looked very well in a long white apron and shirt sleeves. He dished out ice cream with enthusiasm, so I supposed he was getting rich. It never occurred to me to compare his present occupation with the position for which he had been originally destined; or if I thought about it, I was just as well content, for by this time I had by heart my father's saying, "America is not Polotzk." All occupations were respectable, all men were equal, in America.

If I admired the soda fountain and the sausage chains, I almost worshipped the partner, Mr. Wilner. I was content to stand for an hour at a time watching him make potato chips. In his cook's cap and apron, with a ladle in his hand and a smile on his face, he moved about with the greatest agility, whisking his raw materials out of nowhere, dipping into his bubbling kettle with a flourish, and bringing forth the finished product with a caper. Such potato chips were not to be had anywhere else on Crescent Beach. Thin as tissue paper, crisp as dry snow, and salt as the sea—such thirst-producing, lemonade-selling, nickel-bringing potato chips only Mr. Wilner could make. On holidays, when dozens of family parties came out by every train from town, he could hardly keep up with the demand for his potato chips. And with a waiting crowd around him our partner was at his best. He was as voluble as he was skilful, and as witty as he was voluble; at least so I guessed from the laughter that frequently drowned his voice. I could not understand his jokes, but if I could get near enough to watch his lips and his smile and his merry eyes, I was happy. That any one could talk so fast, and in English, was marvel enough, but that this prodigy should belong to *our* establishment was a fact to thrill me. I had never seen anything like Mr. Wilner, except a wedding jester; but then he spoke common Yiddish. So proud was I of the talent and good taste displayed at our stand that if my father beckoned to me in the crowd and sent me on an errand, I hoped the people noticed that I, too, was connected with the establishment.

And all this splendor and glory and distinction came to a sudden end. There was some trouble about a license—some fee or fine—there was a storm in the night that damaged the soda fountain and other fixtures—there was talk and consultation between the houses of Antin and Wilner—and the promising partnership was dissolved. No more would the merry partner gather the crowd on the beach; no more would the twelve young Wilners gambol like mermen and mermaids in the surf. And the less numerous tribe of Antin must also say farewell to the jolly seaside life; for men in such humble business as my father's carry their families, along with their other earthly goods, wherever they go, after the manner of the gypsies. We had driven a feeble stake into the sand. The jealous Atlantic, in conspiracy with the Sunday law, had torn it out. We must seek our luck elsewhere.

In Polotzk we had supposed that "America" was practically synonymous with "Boston." When we landed in Boston, the horizon was pushed back, and we annexed Crescent Beach. And now, espying other lands of promise, we took possession of the province of Chelsea, in the name of our necessity.

In Chelsea, as in Boston, we made our stand in the wrong end of the town. Arlington Street was inhabited by poor Jews, poor Negroes, and a sprinkling of poor Irish. The side streets leading from it were occupied by more poor Jews and Negroes. It was a proper locality for a man without capital to do business. My father rented a tenement with a store in the basement. He put in a few barrels of flour and of sugar, a few boxes of crackers, a few gallons of kerosene, an assortment of soap of the "save the coupon" brands; in the cellar, a few barrels of potatoes, and a pyramid of kindling-wood; in the showcase, an alluring display of penny candy. He put out his sign, with a gilt-lettered warning of "Strictly Cash," and proceeded to give credit indiscriminately. That was the regular way to do business on Arlington Street. My father, in his three years' apprenticeship, had learned the tricks of many trades. He knew when and how to "bluff." The legend of "Strictly Cash" was a protection against notoriously irresponsible customers; while none of the "good" customers, who had a record for paying regularly on Saturday, hesitated to enter the store with empty purses.

If my father knew the tricks of the trade, my mother could be counted on to throw all her talent and tact into the business. Of course she had no English yet, but as she could perform the acts of weighing, measuring, and mental computation of fractions mechanically, she was able to give her whole attention to the dark mysteries of the language, as intercourse with her customers gave her opportunity. In this she made such rapid progress, that she soon lost all sense of disadvantage, and conducted herself behind the counter very much as if she were back in her old store in Polotzk. It was far more cosey than Polotzk—at least, so it seemed to me; for behind the store was the kitchen, where, in the interval of slack trade, she did her cooking and washing. Arlington Street customers were used to waiting while storekeeper salted the soup or rescued a loaf from the oven.

Once more Fortune favored my family with a thin little smile, and my father, in reply to a friendly inquiry would say, "One makes a living," with a shrug of the shoulders that added "but nothing to boast of." It was characteristic of my attitude toward bread-and-butter matters that this contented me, and I felt free to devote myself to the conquest of my new world. Looking back to those critical first years, I see myself always behaving like a child let loose in a garden to play and dig and chase the butterflies. Occasionally, indeed, I was stung by the wasp of family trouble; but I knew a healing ointment—my faith in America. My father had come to America to make a living. America, which was free and fair and kind, must presently yield him what he sought. I had come to America to see a new world, and I followed my own ends with the utmost assiduity; only, as I ran out to explore, I would look back to see if my house were in order behind me—if my family still kept its head above water.

In after years, when I passed as an American among Americans, if I was suddenly made aware of the past that lay forgotten,—if a letter from Russia, or a paragraph in the newspaper, or a conversation overheard in the street-car, suddenly reminded me of what I might have been,—I thought it miracle enough that I, Mashke, the granddaughter of Raphael the Russian, born to a humble destiny, should be at home in an American metropolis, be free to fashion my own life, and should dream my dreams in English phrases. But in the beginning my admiration was spent on more concrete embodiments of the splendors of America; such as fine houses, gay shops, electric engines and apparatus, public buildings, illuminations, and parades. My early letters to my Russian friends were filled with boastful descriptions of these glories of my new country. No native citizen of Chelsea took such pride and delight in its institutions as I did. It required no fife and drum corps, no Fourth of July procession, to set me tingling with patriotism. Even the common agents and instruments of municipal life, such as the letter carrier and the fire engine, I regarded with a measure of respect. I know what I thought of people who said that Chelsea was a very small, dull, unaspiring town, with no discernible excuse for a separate name or existence.

The apex of my civic pride and personal contentment was reached on the bright September morning when I entered the public school. That day I must always remember, even if I live to be so old that I cannot tell my name. To most people their first day at school is a memorable occasion. In my case the importance of the day was a hundred times magnified, on account of the years I had waited, the road I had come, and the conscious ambitions I entertained.

I am wearily aware that I am speaking in extreme figures, in superlatives. I wish I knew some other way to render the mental life of the immigrant child of reasoning age. I may have been ever so much an exception in acuteness of observation, powers of comparison, and abnormal self-consciousness; none the less were my thoughts and conduct typical of the attitude of the intelligent immigrant child toward American institutions. And what the child thinks and feels is a reflection of the hopes, desires, and purposes of the parents who brought him overseas, no matter how precocious and independent the child may be. Your immigrant inspectors will tell you what poverty the foreigner brings in his baggage, what want in his pockets. Let the overgrown boy of twelve, reverently drawing his letters in the baby class, testify to the noble dreams and high ideals that may be hidden beneath the greasy caftan of the immigrant. Speaking for the Jews, at least, I know I am safe in inviting such an investigation.

Who were my companions on my first day at school? Whose hand was in mine, as I stood, overcome with awe, by the teacher's desk, and whispered my name as my father prompted? Was it Frieda's steady, capable hand? Was it her loyal heart that throbbed, beat for beat with mine, as it had done through all our childish adventures? Frieda's heart did throb that day, but not with my emotions. My heart pulsed with joy and pride and ambition; in her heart longing fought with abnegation. For I was led to the schoolroom, with its sunshine and its singing and the teacher's cheery smile; while she was led to the workshop, with its foul air, care-lined faces, and the foreman's stern command. Our going to school was the fulfillment of my father's best promises to us, and Frieda's share in it was to fashion and fit the calico frocks in which the baby sister and I made our first appearance in a public schoolroom.

I remember to this day the gray pattern of the calico, so affectionately did I regard it as it hung upon the wall—my consecration robe awaiting the beatific day. And Frieda, I am sure, remembers it, too, so longingly did she regard it as the crisp, starchy breadths of it slid between her fingers. But whatever were her longings, she said nothing of them; she bent over the sewing-machine humming an Old-World melody. In every straight, smooth seam, perhaps, she tucked away some lingering impulse of childhood; but she matched the scrolls and flowers with the utmost care. If a sudden shock of rebellion made her straighten up for an instant, the next instant she was bending to adjust a ruffle to the best advantage. And when the momentous day arrived, and the little sister and I stood up to be arrayed, it was Frieda herself who patted and smoothed my stiff new calico; who made me turn round and round, to see that I was perfect; who stooped to pull out a disfiguring basting-thread.

If there was anything in her heart besides sisterly love and pride and good-will, as we parted that morning, it was a sense of loss and a woman's acquiescence in her fate; for we had been close friends, and now our ways would lie apart. Longing she felt, but no envy. She did not grudge me what she was denied. Until that morning we had been children together, but now, at the fiat of her destiny, she became a woman, with all a woman's cares; whilst I, so little younger than she, was bidden to dance at the May festival of untroubled childhood.

I wish, for my comfort, that I could say that I had some notion of the difference in our lots, some sense of the injustice to her, of the indulgence to me. I wish I could even say that I gave serious thought to the matter. There had always been a distinction between us rather out of proportion to the difference in our years. Her good health and domestic instincts had made it natural for her to become my mother's right hand, in the years preceding the emigration, when there were no more servants or dependents. Then there was the family tradition that Mary was the quicker, the brighter of the two, and that hers could be no common lot. Frieda was relied upon for help, and her sister for glory. And when I failed as a milliner's apprentice, while Frieda made excellent progress at the dressmaker's, our fates, indeed, were sealed. It was understood, even before we reached Boston, that she would go to work and I to school. In view of the family prejudices, it was the inevitable course. No injustice was intended. My father sent us hand in hand to school, before he had ever thought of America. If, in America, he had been able to support his family unaided, it would have been the culmination of his best hopes to see all his children at school, with equal advantages at home. But when he had done his best, and was still unable to provide even bread and shelter for us all, he was compelled to make us children self-supporting as fast as it was practicable. There was no choosing possible; Frieda was the oldest, the strongest, the best prepared, and the only one who was of legal age to be put to work.

My father has nothing to answer for. He divided the world between his children in accordance with the laws of the country and the compulsion of his circumstances. I have no need of defending him. It is myself that I would like to defend, and I cannot. I remember that I accepted the arrangements made for my sister and me without much reflection, and everything that was planned for my advantage I took as a matter of course. I was no heartless monster, but a decidedly self-centred child. If my sister had seemed unhappy it would have troubled me; but I am ashamed to recall that I did not consider how little it was that contented her. I was so preoccupied with my own happiness that I did not half perceive the splendid devotion of her attitude towards me, the sweetness of her joy in my good luck. She not only stood by approvingly when I was helped to everything; she cheerfully waited on me herself. And I took everything from her hand as if it were my due.

The two of us stood a moment in the doorway of the tenement house on Arlington Street, that wonderful September morning when I first went to school. It was I that ran away, on winged feet of joy and expectation; it was she whose feet were bound in the treadmill of daily toil. And I was so blind that I did not see that the glory lay on her, and not on me.

Father himself conducted us to school. He would not have delegated that mission to the President of the United States. He had awaited the day with impatience equal to mine, and the visions he saw as he hurried us over the sun-flecked pavements transcended all my dreams. Almost his first act on landing on American soil, three years before, had been his application for naturalization. He had taken the remaining steps in the process with eager promptness, and at the earliest moment allowed by the law, he became a citizen of the United States. It is true that he had left home in search of bread for his hungry family, but he went blessing the necessity that drove him to America. The boasted freedom of the New World meant to him far more than the right to reside, travel, and work wherever he pleased; it meant the freedom to speak his thoughts, to throw off the shackles of superstition, to test his own fate, unhindered by political or religious tyranny. He was only a young man when he landed—thirty-two; and most of his life he had been held in leading-strings. He was hungry for his untasted manhood.

Three years passed in sordid struggle and disappointment. He was not prepared to make a living even in America, where the day laborer eats wheat instead of rye. Apparently the American flag could not protect him against the pursuing Nemesis of his limitations; he must expiate the sins of his fathers who slept across the seas. He had been endowed at birth with a poor constitution, a nervous, restless temperament, and an abundance of hindering prejudices. In his boyhood his body was starved, that his mind might be stuffed with useless learning. In his youth this dearly gotten learning was sold, and the price was the bread and salt which he had not been trained to earn for himself. Under the wedding canopy he was bound for life to a girl whose features were still strange to him; and he was bidden to multiply himself, that sacred learning might be perpetuated in his sons, to the glory of the God of his fathers. All this while he had been led about as a creature without a will, a chattel, an instrument. In his maturity he awoke, and found himself poor in health, poor in purse, poor in useful knowledge, and hampered on all sides. At the first nod of opportunity he broke away from his prison, and strove to atone for his wasted youth by a life of useful labor; while at the same time he sought to lighten the gloom of his narrow scholarship by freely partaking of modern ideas. But his utmost endeavor still left him far from his goal. In business, nothing prospered with him. Some fault of hand or mind or temperament led him to failure where other men found success. Wherever the blame for his disabilities be placed, he reaped their bitter fruit. "Give me bread!" he cried to America. "What will you do to earn it?" the challenge came back. And he found that he was master of no art, of no trade; that even his precious learning was of no avail, because he had only the most antiquated methods of communicating it.

So in his primary quest he had failed. There was left him the compensation of intellectual freedom. That he sought to realize in every possible way. He had very little opportunity to prosecute his education, which, in truth, had never been begun. His struggle for a bare living left him no time to take advantage of the public evening school; but he lost nothing of what was to be learned through reading, through attendance at public meetings, through exercising the rights of citizenship. Even here he was hindered by a natural inability to acquire the English language. In time, indeed, he learned to read, to follow a conversation or lecture; but he never learned to write correctly, and his pronunciation remains extremely foreign to this day.

If education, culture, the higher life were shining things to be worshipped from afar, he had still a means left whereby he could draw one step nearer to them. He could send his children to school, to learn all those things that he knew by fame to be desirable. The common school, at least, perhaps high school; for one or two, perhaps even college! His children should be students, should fill his house with books and intellectual company; and thus he would walk by proxy in the Elysian Fields of liberal learning. As for the children themselves, he knew no surer way to their advancement and happiness.

So it was with a heart full of longing and hope that my father led us to school on that first day. He took long strides in his eagerness, the rest of us running and hopping to keep up.

At last the four of us stood around the teacher's desk; and my father, in his impossible English, gave us over in her charge, with some broken word of his hopes for us that his swelling heart could no longer contain.

I venture to say that Miss Nixon was struck by something uncommon in the group we made, something outside of Semitic features and the abashed manner of the alien. My little sister was as pretty as a doll, with her clear pink-and-white face, short golden curls, and eyes like blue violets when you caught them looking up. My brother might have been a girl, too, with his cherubic contours of face, rich red color, glossy black hair, and fine eyebrows. Whatever secret fears were in his heart, remembering his former teachers, who had taught with the rod, he stood up straight and uncringing before the American teacher, his cap respectfully doffed. Next to him stood a starved-looking girl with eyes ready to pop out, and short dark curls that would not have made much of a wig for a Jewish bride.

All three children carried themselves rather better than the common run of "green" pupils that were brought to Miss Nixon. But the figure that challenged attention to the group was the tall, straight father, with his earnest face and fine forehead, nervous hands eloquent in gesture, and a voice full of feeling. This foreigner, who brought his children to school as if it were an act of consecration, who regarded the teacher of the primer class with reverence, who spoke of visions, like a man inspired, in a common schoolroom, was not like other aliens, who brought their children in dull obedience to the law; was not like the native fathers, who brought their unmanageable boys, glad to be relieved of their care. I think Miss Nixon guessed what my father's best English could not convey. I think she divined that by the simple act of delivering our school certificates to her he took possession of America.

19

Lives in *The Independent* and the Question of Race

ANONYMOUS

THERE IS NO INFORMATION on the lives of anonymous contributors to *The Independent*. Published from 1848 to the early decades of the twentieth century, *The Independent* was "devoted to the consideration of politics, social and economic tendencies, history, literature, and the arts," and has been an important source for American literary scholars and historians. It regularly included short narratives by everyday people reflecting on political and social issues. We include three such narratives, written in 1904 and 1912, that focus on the persistence of racism in the Reconstruction era as observed by two Southern African American women and a Northern white woman.

The narrative of a "Southern Colored Woman" details the teller's experience as the daughter of freed, independent parents who owned a home and did everything possible to prevent her from contact with Southern white men and their inevitable slurs. Writing as a self-sufficient, educated wife and mother of three, she chronicles the humiliations she has encountered and decries the outcast state of African Americans by *de facto* segregationist practices.

The narrative of a "Northern Woman" from the western United States who has lived in the South points to the persistence of white supremacy in attitudes ascribed to "colored" servants that are equally—or even more—characteristic of white domestics. Heralding the rise of a southern literature, she nonetheless descries its biases.

Another narrative, originally published with these two as "Experiences of the Race Problem" by a "Southern White Woman," not included here, rehearses the racist stereotypes of former slaves and the defense of white supremacy that persisted, using examples both vivid and vicious.

The narrative of the "Negro Nurse," by contrast, attests to the persistence of slavery conditions during Reconstruction and her own poverty and lack of leisure in the "Mammy" syndrome. Citing conditions that perpetuate the moral debasement of former slaves, she states, "I live a treadmill life."

"The Race Problem—An Autobiography" (1904)
A SOUTHERN COLORED WOMAN

[The present article and the two following ones on the negro problem which we print this week are respectively by a Southern colored woman, a Southern white woman, and a Northern white woman now a resident of the South. We know of no women in the whole South better qualified to write on this painful topic from their various standpoints. The articles are especially timely owing to last week's race war in Ohio, and are remarkable for their extraordinary frankness. For reasons that will be evident to the reader and that concern their social if not personal safety, the names of the writers are withheld.—EDITOR.]

My father was slave in name only, his father and master being the same. He lived on a large plantation and knew many useful things. The blacksmith shop was the place he liked best, and he was allowed to go there and make little tools as a child. He became an expert blacksmith before he was grown. Before the war closed he had married and was the father of one child. When his father wanted him to remain on the plantation after the war, he refused because the wages offered were too small. The old man would not even promise an increase later; so my father left in a wagon he had made with his own hands, drawn by a horse he had bought from a passing horse drover with his own money.

He had in his wagon his wife and baby, some blacksmith tools he had made from time to time, bedding, their clothing, some food, and twenty dollars in his pocket. As he drove by the house he got out of the wagon to bid his father good-by. The old man came down the steps and, pointing in the direction of the gate, said: "Joseph, when you get on the outside of that gate—stay." Turning to my mother, he said: "When you get hungry and need clothes for yourself and the baby as you are sure to do, come to me," and he pitched a bag of silver in her lap, which my father immediately took and placed at his father's feet on the steps and said. "I am going to feed and clothe them and I can do it on a bare rock." My father drove twenty-five miles to the largest town in the State, where he succeeded in renting a small house.

The next day he went out to buy something to eat. On his way home a lady offered him fifty cents for a string of fish for which he had only paid twenty cents. That gave him an idea. Why not buy fish every day and sell them? He had thought to get work at his trade, but here was money to be made and quickly. So from buying a few strings of fish he soon saved enough to buy a wagon load of fish.

My mother was very helpless, never having done anything in her life except needlework. She was unfitted for the hard work, and most of this my father did. He taught my mother to cook, and he would wash and iron himself at night.

Many discouraging things happened to them—often sales were slow and fish would spoil; many would not buy of him because he was colored; another baby was born and died, and my father came very near losing his life for whipping a white man who insulted my mother. He got out of the affair finally, but had to take on a heavy debt, besides giving up all of his hard earned savings.

My father said after the war his ambition was first to educate himself and family, then to own a white house with green blinds, as much like his father's as possible, and to support his family by his own efforts; never to allow his wife and daughters to be thrown in contact with Southern white men in their homes. He succeeded.

The American Missionary Association had opened schools by this time, and my father went to night school and sent his wife and child to school in the day.

By hard work and strict economy two years after he left his father's plantation he gave two hundred dollars for a large plot of ground on a high hill on the outskirts of the town.

Three years later I was born in my father's own home, in his coveted white house with green blinds—his father's house in miniature. Here my father kept a small store, was burned out once and had other trials, but finally he had a large grocery store and feed store attached.

I have never lived in a rented house except for one year since I've been grown. I have never gone to a public school in my life, my parents preferring the teaching of the patient "New England schoolmarm" to the Southern "poor white," who thought it little better than a disgrace to teach colored children—so much of a disgrace that she taught her pupils not to speak to her on the streets. My mother and her children never performed any labor outside of my father's and their own homes.

To-day I have the same feeling my parents had. There is no sacrifice I would not make, no hardship I would not undergo rather than allow my daughters to go in service where they would be thrown constantly in contact with Southern white men, for they consider the colored girl their special prey.

It is commonly said that no girl or woman receives a certain kind of insult unless she invites it. That does not apply to a colored girl and woman in the South. The color of her face alone is sufficient invitation to the Southern white man—these same men who profess horror that a white gentleman can entertain a colored one at his table. Out of sight of their own women they are willing and anxious to entertain colored women in various ways. Few colored girls reach the age of sixteen without receiving advances from them—maybe from a young "upstart," and often from a man old enough to be their father, a white haired veteran of sin. Yes, and men high in position, whose wives and daughters are leaders of society. I have had a clerk in a store hold my hand as I gave him the money for some purchase and utter some vile request; a shoe man to take liberties, a man in a crowd to place his hands on my person, others to follow me to my very door, a school director to assure me a position if I did his bidding.

It is true these particular men never insulted me but once; but there are others. I might write more along this line and worse things—how a white man of high standing will systematically set out to entrap a colored girl—but my identification would be assured in some quarters. My husband was also educated in an American Missionary Association school (God bless the name!), and after graduating took a course in medicine in another school. He has practiced medicine now for over ten years. By most frugal living and strict economy he saved enough to buy for a home a house of four rooms, which has since been increased to eight. Since our marriage we have bought and paid for two other places, which we rent. My husband's collections average one hundred dollars a month. We have an iron-bound rule that we must save at least fifty dollars a month. Some months we lay by more, but never less. We do not find this very hard to do with the rent from our places, and as I do all of my work except the washing and ironing.

We have three children, two old enough for school. I try to be a good and useful neighbor and friend to those who will allow me. I would be content and happy if I, an American citizen, could say as Axel Jarlson (the Swedish emigrant, whose story appeared in *The Independent* of January 8th, 1903) says, "There are no aristocrats to push him down and say that he is not worthy because his father was poor." There are "aristocrats" to push me and mine down and say we are not worthy because we are colored. The Chinaman, Lee Chew, ends his article in The Independent of February 19th, 1903, by saying, "Under the circumstances how can I call this my home, and how can any one blame me if I take my money and go back to my village in China?"

Happy Chinaman! Fortunate Lee Chew! You can go back to your village and enjoy your money. This is my village, my home, yet am I an outcast. See what an outcast! Not long since I visited a Southern city where the "Jim Crow" car law is enforced. I did not know of this law, and on boarding an electric car took the most convenient seat. The conductor yelled, "What do you mean? Niggers don't sit with white folks down here. You must have come from 'way up yonder. I'm not Roosevelt. We don't sit with niggers, much less eat with them."

I was astonished and said, "I am a stranger and did not know of your law." His answer was: "Well, no back talk now; that's what I'm here for—to tell niggers their places when they don't know them."

Every white man, woman and child was in a titter of laughter by this time at what they considered the conductor's wit.

These Southern men and women, who pride themselves on their fine sense of feeling, had no feeling for my embarrassment and unmerited insult, and when I asked the conductor to stop the car that I might get off, one woman said in a loud voice, "These niggers get more impudent every day; she doesn't want to sit where she belongs."

No one of them thought that I was embarrassed, wounded and outraged by the loud, brutal talk of the conductor and the sneering, contemptuous expressions on their own faces. They considered me "impudent" when I only wanted to be alone that I might conquer my emotion. I was nervous and blinded by tears of mortification which will account for my second insult on this same day.

I walked downtown to attend to some business and had to take an elevator in an office building. I stood waiting for the elevator, and when the others, all of whom were white, got in I made a move to go in also, and the boy shut the cage door in my face. I thought the elevator was too crowded and waited; the same thing happened the second time. I would have walked up, but I was going to the fifth story, and my long walk downtown had tired me. The third time the elevator came down the boy pointed to a sign and said, " I guess you can't read; but niggers don't ride in this elevator; we're white folks here, we are. Go to the back and you'll find an elevator for freight and niggers."

The occupants of the elevator also enjoyed themselves at my expense. This second insult in one day seemed more than I could bear. I could transact no business in my frame of mind, so I slowly took the long walk back to the suburbs of the city, where I was stopping.

My feelings were doubly crushed and in my heart, I fear, I rebelled not only against man but God. I have been humiliated and insulted often, but I never get used to it: it is new each time, and it stings and hurts more and more

The very first humiliation I received I remember very distinctly to this day. It was when I was very young. A little girl playmate said to me: "I like to come over to your house to play, we have such good times, and your ma has such good preserves; but don't you tell my ma I eat over here. My ma says you all are nice, clean folks and she'd rather live by you than the white people we moved away from; for you don't borrow things. I know she would whip me if I ate with you, tho, because you are colored, you know."

I was very angry and forgot she was my guest, but told her to go home and bring my ma's sugar home her ma borrowed, and the rice they were always wanting a cup of.

After she had gone home I threw myself upon the ground and cried, for I liked the little girl, and until then I did not know that being "colored" made a difference. I am not sure I knew anything about "colored." I was very young and I know now I had been shielded from all unpleasantness.

My mother found me in tears and I asked her why was I colored, and couldn't little girls eat with me and let their mothers know it.

My mother got the whole story from me, but she couldn't satisfy me with her explanation—or, rather, lack of explanation. The little girl came often to play with me after that and we were little friends again, but we never had any more play dinners. I could not reconcile the fact that she and her people could borrow and eat our rice in their own house and not sit at my table and eat my mother's good, sweet preserves.

The second shock I received was horrible to me at the time. I had not gotten used to real horrible things then. The history of Christian men selling helpless men and women's children to far distant States was unknown to me; a number of men burning another chained to a post an impossibility, the whipping of a grown woman by a strong man unthought of. I was only a child, but I remember to this day what a shock I received. A young colored woman of a lovely disposition and character had just died. She was a teacher in the Sunday school I attended—a self-sacrificing, noble young woman who had been loved by many. Her coffin, room, hall, and even the porch of her house were filled with flowers sent by her friends. There were lovely designs sent by the more prosperous and simple bouquets made by untrained, childish hands. I was on my way with my own last offering of love, when I was met by quite a number of white boys and girls. A girl of about fifteen years said to me, "More flowers for that dead nigger? I never saw such a to-do made over a dead nigger before. Why, there must be thousands of roses alone in that house. I've been standing out here for hours and there has been a continual stream of niggers carrying flowers, and beautiful ones, too, and what makes me madder than anything else, those Yankee teachers carried flowers, too!" I, a little girl, with my heart full of sadness for the death of my friend, could make no answer to these big, heartless boys and girls, who threw stones after me as I ran from them.

When I reached home I could not talk for emotion. My mother was astonished when I found voice to tell her I was not crying because of the death of Miss W., but because I could not do something, anything, to avenge the insult to her dead body. I remember the strongest feeling I had was one of revenge. I wanted even to kill that particular girl or do something to hurt her. I was unhappy for days. I was told that they were heartless, but that I was even worse, and that Miss W. would be the first to condemn me could she speak.

That one encounter made a deep impression on my childish heart; it has been with me throughout the years. I have known real horrors since, but none left a greater impression on me.

My mother used to tell me if I were a good little girl everybody would love me, and if I always used nice manners it would make others show the same to me.

I believed that literally until I entered school, when the many encounters I had with white boys and girls going to and from school made me seriously doubt that goodness and manners were needed in this world. The white children I knew grew meaner as they grew older—more capable of saying things that cut and wound.

I was often told by white children whose parents rented houses: "You think you are white because your folks own their own home; but you ain't, you're a nigger just the same, and my pa says if he had his rights he would own niggers like you, and your home, too."

A child's feelings are easily wounded, and day after day I carried a sad heart. To-day I carry a sad heart on account of my children. What is to become of them? The Southern whites dislike more and more the educated colored man. They hate the intelligent colored man who is accumulating something. The respectable, intelligent colored people are "carefully unknown"; their good traits and virtues are never mentioned. On the other hand, the ignorant and vicious are carefully known and all of their traits cried aloud.

In the natural order of things our children will be better educated than we, they will have our accumulations and their own. With the added dislike and hatred of the white man, I shudder to think of the outcome.

In this part of the country, where the Golden Rule is obsolete, the commandment, "Love thy neighbor as thyself" is forgotten; anything is possible.

I dread to see my children grow. I know not their fate. Where the white girl has one temptation, mine will have many. Where the white boy has every opportunity and protection, mine will have few opportunities and no protection. It does not matter how good or wise my children may be, they are colored. When I have said that, all is said. Everything is forgiven in the South but color.

"Observations of the Southern Race Feeling" (1904)
A NORTHERN WOMAN

I am a native of the Northwest. My father was a college boy at the time of the Civil War, and, coming West a year or two after his graduation, he fell a victim first to fever and then to a disease whose most pronounced symptom was loss of memory—of his "college widow," and somewhat later he married the girl to whom the attack of this malady was solely due. The only ex-soldier in my immediate family was the young man who, after the establishment of peace, married my mother's oldest sister. This is probably one reason why my childhood was not enveloped in an especially polemical atmosphere, but even had my father and uncles all been "boys in blue," I fancy that I should have grown up with not very different feelings in regard to the South and the war. The people of the Northwest, with a new country to subdue and develop, and in the stress and zest of such a life and its promise for the future, had neither time nor desire to fill the minds of their children with thoughts of a war which was ended before they were born. Of course, I liked to hear stories of the war (altho my grandfather had an assortment of "wolf stories" which thrilled me far more), and I took it for granted that the South must have been wrong, while my political sympathies— politics and theology being subjects of profound concern with me at one period of my extreme youth—were naturally colored by my nativity in a State strongly Republican. But the point which I wish to emphasize as a preface to what I am about to say is that the war stories were only *stories* to me, and that, like the other young Westerners of any generation, I grew up more nearly free from sectional prejudice than perhaps would have been possible had I been reared in any of the longer settled States. I do not claim any peculiar virtue for myself or my fellow Westerners in this. We have had too many interests and ambitions of other sorts to allow us to care greatly for what we have considered practically dead issues, and I for one hardly knew that there *was* a negro question until I went South to live.

There is the most widespread misapprehension in the South upon two points—the sentiment of Northerners toward the Southern people, and the modifications which that sentiment undergoes after a visit to the South. I have spoken of conditions which have tended to lessen prejudice in the Northwest; I believe that I am not mistaken in saying that in Eastern and Western States alike there has been another agency at work whose effect has been to create interest in and sympathy with the Southern white people, rather than to prolong hostility. That agency has been the rise of Southern literature.

From the talk of my elders I am led to believe that in ante-bellum days the good people of the North, tho they outwardly reprobated, secretly were fascinated by the splendid lavishness of the "old plantation days" as a thing belonging to a beautiful (altho depraved) world apart from their "plain living and high thinking." And when, in these latter days, the novel and the short story of Southern life began to appear, they were welcomed so enthusiastically that from the first appearance of Cable's works up to the present hour no one school of American literature has been so much the fashion as the Southern school.

Southerners have small idea of the degree of romantic interest with which they are regarded by those of the North, especially of the fiction-reading classes. But I am not so sure that better acquaintance with the real South would increase Northern tolerance for its ideals and mode of life. At least that has not been my experience. No one could have gone to a new country with more amiable intentions or more filled with rose-colored expectations as to place and people than was I when I set out for the Southern city where I have lived for some years past. If I had gone there to teach negroes, or under conditions which would have brought me into contact with the worst side of the white population, there would be good reason to accuse me of having formed my opinions under the influence of pique at personal slights and snubs (which I should certainly have received had I served in the former capacity), or from acquaintance with the lower classes; but my acquaintances belong to what admittedly represents the best of blood and culture in the South, and it is the people who invite me to dinner who have furnished the most of the material for whatever sentiments I now entertain upon the negro and other questions concerning which North and South are at variance.

One of the first shocks which I received, and which has been repeated so often that I suppose it ought by this time to have ceased to be a shock, was in respect to something to which reference is made in one of the preceding articles. If its author has never discussed the race question before colored auditors or made the inferiority of the negro the topic of conversation at her table before colored servants she has cause for just pride. If my own experiences furnish any ground for conclusions, there is neither man nor woman like her in the whole length and breadth of the South. I have long ceased to be surprised at this talk, which seems peculiarly inspired by a dining-room atmosphere, but to this day I have an impulse to "duck" my head to avoid the dishes which I feel must inevitably fly at some of the white conversationalists. That they never do fly seemed to me at first a proof that self-control at least could be set down to the credit of the colored race, but I am assured by "those who know the negro best" that it is a proof of his profound inferiority that he "has not spirit enough" to resent insults which a white man would avenge with promptness and finality.

The first time, too, that I heard a lady of supposed Christianity and culture defend the thesis that negro mothers could not possibly love their children as white mothers do, because of their lack of all the finer and nobler sentiments which enter into real love, I did not take her views as representing overmuch intelligent reflection, because the same woman, among other things, had said to me at her own table that "any one could see that Northern young women, educated in co-educational schools, were not as modest and had not such ladylike manners as our Southern girls." But I discovered that no very different theory was held by people whose judgment in other matters I respected, and whose standard of "ladylike manners" did not differ so essentially as hers from my primitive Western one.

Generally speaking, my associations in the South have been of a sort to impress me more with the white man's attitude toward the negro than with any other side of the question, but I cannot believe that for this reason my view is a wholly one-sided one, or founded upon that ignorance of the real conditions which is the Southerner's stock-in-trade of argument against his Northern critic. For I consider the state of white sentiment in the South to be the supremely important factor in the problem. Even if all that has been said of universal negro ignorance, thriftlessness and beastly immorality were true, the destiny of the theoretically free black man is still so largely in the white man's hand that the danger—and that it is becoming a serious one I cannot doubt—lies much less in the brutal instincts of the negro than in the white man's blind adherence to a policy which must surely aggravate those instincts.

The whole Southern creed is contained in two words: *White supremacy.* They admit that the maintenance of this does not square in all details with "the ethical theories of Northern sentimentalists." To our Northerner (who has heard herself accused by Southerners of anything rather than too much sentiment) it seems to square even less with the practical and the possible. If I may be allowed a somewhat startling comparison, the Southerner's position on the negro is about the same as his attitude toward woman; he will treat the former with kindness, as he will the latter with adulation, "in his place." That "place" in either case, stripped of the accidental externals which make the one seem menial and the other exalted, means dependence and helpfulness. Southerners like to tell you that all negro depravity has developed since emancipation. The "old mammy" is the object not only of much show of sentiment but of real affection; in the recent Confederate reunion the crowd went wild over the gray-haired negro who walked by his "old

master's" side as he had done all through the war; and yet, if we may
believe stories told by Southerners themselves, horrible uprisings of the
half-savage plantation hands were by no means an unknown thing in
slavery times. But, however successful the old slaveholders may have
been in producing irreproachable negro character, their children of
today, now over-indulgent and now over-cruel, make no effort to train
their colored hirelings to be self-respecting wage-earners or to develop
in them a sense of honor and independence—and then they tell you
how negroes steal! "Well, I can't find a bit of my monogram note-
paper," said a friend to me last winter. "I suppose Daisy (the nurse) has
used it all up. Dear no! I never say anything to her about it—she always
uses our note-paper and stamps. I wouldn't be so mean as not to let the
poor thing have paper to write to her beaux."

It may be "Yankee stinginess," but I confess that it never had occurred to me to supply stamps and fine note-paper for my chambermaid. Perhaps no better example than this of the difference between
Northern and Southern treatment of the negro could be cited. If a servant appropriated my postage stamps she would hear from me, but
I do not grudge her and her race what I consider the more valuable
tribute of saying that personally I have not found them the universal
thieves that they are represented. I have lived principally in boarding-
houses, where my room has been open all day, not only to the house
servants but to the horde of washerwomen, nurses and other uncata-
loged negroes who swarm about a large Southern house, and twice
only during my entire residence in the South have I had anything stolen
from me. In one case the culprit was never discovered, but in the other
and more serious one all the missing articles were found in the trunk of
a white maid of German parentage. As with dishonesty, so with immorality. I have yet to discover among Southern whites the slightest effort
to correct this evil. I have heard refined ladies discuss in their parlors as
something deliciously amusing the amours of their cooks and house-
girls. It seems a pity that they take so much more solemn a view of these
affairs when they recite them for publication. And their lack of experience with white servants makes them ascribe solely to colored women
what, unfortunately, is not unknown among white ones of the same
class. One of my friends, disgusted with negro servants, thought to
usher in a household millennium by the employment of two white girls
of pleasing appearance. Within a few months she had discharged them
both because of their undoubted and shameless immorality, and a talk
with the mother of one of them revealed a state of things in their social

circle which made it a cause for thankfulness that in estimating the purity of Anglo-Saxon womanhood people do not reason, as they do with our colored sisters, from the bottom up. Of course, this "You're another" sort of argument does not really prove anything, and yet, whatever justification there may be for "Jim Crow" street cars, I fail to perceive any for providing separate moral standards as well as separate seats for the two races. Whenever anything like the "Booker Washington incident" touches off the powder in the "social equality" cannon there is a discharge of virtuous eloquence from the editorial page of every Southern paper, calling upon the people of the South to "highly resolve" to save their noble race from degeneration through the scandal of miscegenation. For the life of me I cannot see why the breaking of bread with a colored gentleman should logically result in an epidemic of marriage between white girls and black men; in fact, the intermarriage of the races to any appreciable extent seems to me the last thing likely to happen; but if it is true that the only negroes of any promise are those of mixed blood, why object to elevating the colored race by doing legally what has been going on illegitimately for generations? Does it make the sin so much less offensive to Southern ideals of virtue that hitherto one-half of the parties to the crime have been gentlemen endowed with "superlative virtues that surpass mere morality?"

The truth is, the Southerner, no less than the Northerner, has a collection of negro theories, and upon all occasions he brings them out draped in the same lurid rhetoric, and arranges them as a screen behind which to conceal his relentless purpose to deny the negro every right and every pleasure which resemble those of the white man.

Let me give a few examples of how he denies them. During the bicycle craze our cook, a neat and modest appearing mulatto of perhaps thirty-five, asked one evening to borrow my bicycle pump, adding that she had left hers at home and dared not go to the bicycle shop nearby because of the insulting speeches of the white men who frequented it. A few years ago a class in a colored school happened to select and display the same colors as a class in a white institution in the same city. The result was a small riot growing out of the prompt avenging of their outraged dignity by the young white *gentlemen*, and the most embarrassing feature in the disciplining of the latter was found in the fact that nearly all were supported in their resolve to maintain their "honor" by their parents, all "leading citizens."

These petty tyrannies are in a way more indicative of the real Southern spirit toward the colored people than some of the affairs which get into the papers, because they show how strong is the tendency to perse-cute the negro for acts inoffensive and naturally attendant upon the "pursuit of happiness." And murder is committed by the rougher white element with as little excuse as insult is offered by the better classes.

One Christmas night a well dressed colored man, sober and peace-able, was shot down in front of our house by three white men, who es-caped without the slightest attempt at pursuit, and the murder was scarcely noticed in the next morning's papers. Fancy what would have happened had the colors of the actors in this little Christmas drama been reversed.

Last February an unknown negro engaged a room in a cheap lodging-house in the "downtown" district of New Orleans. The Mardi-Gras season brought in an influx of visitors to this as to the hotels of the fashionable sort, and at a late hour one night the negro was aroused with some lack of ceremony and ordered to share his quarters with sev-eral newly arrived guests. Of course, it was not commendable on his part that after more or less discussion he began to emphasize his refusal of a room-mate with pistol shots, but even better men have been known to be cross when rudely awakened from pleasant dreams. He suc-ceeded in dispersing his unbidden callers, and barricaded his door, whereupon the excluded ones summoned a goodly squad from the po-lice force to "get him out." To make a long story short, they did get him out, burned and riddled with bullets. The significant feature of all newspaper comment upon this incident was that, altho absolutely nothing was known of the negro's previous history, it was generally as-sumed that he must have been a criminal hiding from justice or he would not have been afraid to let other men into his room. It may have been so—the negro when brought out was much too dead to deny it—but would that assumption have been taken concerning a white gentle-man who fancied a room to himself at the St. Charles Hotel, or, in fact, is Southern history entirely lacking in precedents to indicate that he might have adopted the same indiscreet method of defending his privacy?

When, last spring, a peculiarly revolting murder was committed in Shreveport, La., the enraged populace promptly set out, as usual, to "find the nigger." In a few hours they found one, a man with blood stains on his overalls, and who took to the woods when accosted. While the high-minded citizens were even yet exulting in the proud work of having avenged—with the customary rites—the dead woman, evi-dence was discovered which proved beyond doubt that the murderer, if a negro at all, was not this particular one, who was acquitted of having shed any other recent blood than that of some cattle on a neighboring plantation. Louisiana papers in commenting upon this incident admitted that some regrettable precipitation had marked the occasion, but generally inclined to the view that not much harm had been done, because if the man had not committed this crime, he probably had some other one on his conscience—otherwise he would not have tried to run away! Of course, in view of the methods usually pursued by white mobs, it is entirely reasonable to suppose that a truly virtuous negro, strong in his conscious innocence, would just have stood still and let himself be lynched.

It would be unjust to assert that the better Southern newspapers, like the better people, do not deprecate lynchings, yet they frequently print communications, and quotations from the news sheets of the rougher districts, containing sentiments which they would not dare place upon their editorial pages. And they find a comfort which would be funny, if there could be an amusing side to a national disgrace, in the occurrence of similar acts of violence along the Northern borders of our traditional dividing line. I have no more wish to excuse these outrages in the North than I have to argue against the legal punishment of negro crime. But I have this to say in regard to the popular Southern argument based upon "innate race antipathy": that the perpetual assertion that Northern prejudice against the negro is as strong as that of the South is not true, and that the increasing antagonism of each new generation of white children does not strike me as being "inborn." The apparent indications of the former, of which Southerners make so much, are confined to the ignorant, who have been misled to believe that the black man injures them as wage-earners, and to a certain class of the educated, whose kindly feelings toward the South and honest desire to be "broadminded" lead them to express a sympathy and tolerance which a better acquaintance with the facts would hardly fail to modify. As to the latter, when every "reduced gentlewoman" who keeps a private school in the South makes it her business to instil into the minds of her little pupils the concentrated bitterness forty years of poverty and sad reminiscence, it seems slightly inaccurate to charge the result wholly to the Creator. Even were this race prejudice innate, that would scarcely prove its right to go unrestrained. Picture the demoralization of our theology if such treatment were applied to Original Sin!

In regard to the educated negro, perhaps the only people really qualified to speak of his actual character are the white men and women who have devoted themselves to his education, and have spent years enough in the work justly to estimate the results. I myself have known negroes in the main as servants, and among them there have not been many college graduates. But I have seen enough of the work of one colored university to feel persuaded that where, as there, it is conducted upon sound principles, the result is more than a surface polish. It should be borne in mind that the negro "universities" are of very various degrees of excellence, and also that it is hard to get fair judgment for the educated negro. The moment the Southern housekeeper knows that she has a "college graduate" (who may, after all, have had barely a high school course) in her kitchen, she is promptly upon the alert for "airs," and she glories in and magnifies every little slip which would pass unnoticed in an unlettered maid. An acquaintance discharged a house-girl whom she found glancing through a copy of Emerson's Essays while dusting.

"I wasn't going to have that kind of nigger around—and she knew more about Emerson than I did, too!"

There seems, too, something of inconsistency in the reasoning which, having proclaimed Booker Washington and Bishop Turner "two of the noblest men whom the South has ever produced," declares that the educated negro is an "artificial product" whose "character and disposition education does not change but intensifies."

As I have already said, to my mind it is the prejudice of the white man more than the worthlessness and depravity of the black which has given us a negro question. So long as a part of our population persistently shuts its eyes to what education has done for the negro, and stubbornly refuses to let him live peaceably the life toward which that education naturally inclines him, so long a problem which I believe might, if allowed to do so, work itself out naturally to the good of both races, will not fail to present the difficulties which always beset a solution based upon that worst kind of shortsightedness—injustice.

"More Slavery at the South" (1912)
A NEGRO NURSE

[The following thrilling story was obtained by a representative of *The Independent* specially commissioned to gather the facts. The reporting is, of course, our representative's, but the facts are those given by the nurse.—EDITOR.]

I am a negro woman, and I was born and reared in the South. I am now past forty years of age and am the mother of three children. My husband died nearly fifteen years ago, after we had been married about five years. For more than thirty years—or since I was ten years old—I have been a servant in one capacity or another in white families in a thriving Southern city, which has at present a population of more than 50,000. In my early years I was at first what might be called a "house-girl," or, better, a "house-boy." I used to answer the doorbell, sweep the yard, go on errands and do odd jobs. Later on I became a chambermaid and performed the usual duties of such a servant in a home. Still later I was graduated into a cook, in which position I served at different times for nearly eight years in all. During the last ten years I have been a nurse. I have worked for only four different families during all these thirty years. But, belonging to the servant class, which is the majority class among my race at the South, and associating only with servants, I have been able to become intimately acquainted not only with the lives of hundreds of household servants, but also with the lives of their employers. I can, therefore, speak with authority on the so-called servant question; and what I say is said out of an experience which covers many years.

To begin with, then, I should say that more than two-thirds of the negroes of the town where I live are menial servants of one kind or another and besides that more than two-thirds of the negro women here, whether married or single, are compelled to work for a living—as nurses, cooks, washerwomen, chambermaids, seamstresses, hucksters, janitresses, and the like. I will say, also, that the condition of this vast host of poor colored people is just as bad as, if not worse than, it was during the days of slavery. Tho today we are enjoying nominal freedom, we are literally slaves. And, not to generalize, I will give you a sketch of the work I have to do and I'm only one of many.

I frequently work from fourteen to sixteen hours a day. I am compelled by my contract, which is oral only, to sleep in the house. I am allowed to go home to my own children, the oldest of whom is a girl of 18 years, only once in two weeks, every other Sunday afternoon—even then I'm not permitted to stay all night. I not only have to nurse a little white child, now eleven months old, but I have to act as playmate or "handy-andy," not to say governess, to three other children in the home, the oldest of whom is only nine years of age. I wash and dress the baby two or three times each day; I give it its meals, mainly from a bottle; I have to put it to bed each night; and, in addition, I have to get up and attend to its every call between midnight and morning. If the baby falls to sleep during the day as it has been trained to do every day about eleven o'clock, I am not permitted to rest. It's "Mammy, do this," or "Mammy, do that," or "Mammy, do the other," from my mistress, all the time. So it is not strange to see "Mammy" watering the lawn in front with the garden hose, sweeping the sidewalk, mopping the porch and halls, dusting around the house, helping the cook, or darning stockings. Not only so, but I have to put the other three children to bed each night as well as the baby, and I have to wash them and dress them each morning. I don't know what it is to go to church; I don't know what it is to go to a lecture or entertainment or anything of the kind: I live a treadmill life and I see my own children only when they happen to see me on the streets when I am out with the children, or when my children come to the "yard" to see me, which isn't often, because my white folks don't like to see their servants' children hanging around their premises. You might as well say that I'm on duty all the time—from sunrise to sunrise, every day in the week. I am the slave, body and soul, of this family. And what do I get for this work—this lifetime bondage? The pitiful sum of ten dollars a month! And what am I expected to do with these ten dollars? With this money I'm expected to pay my house rent, which is four dollars per month, for a little house of two rooms, just big enough to turn round in; and I'm expected, also, to feed and clothe myself and three children. For two years my oldest child, it is true, has helped a little toward our support by taking in a little washing at home. She does the washing and ironing of two white families, with a total of five persons; one of these families pays her $1.00 per week, and the other 75 cents per week, and my daughter has to furnish her own soap and starch and wool. For six months my youngest child, a girl about thirteen years old, has been nursing, and she receives $1.50 per week but has no night work. When I think of the low rate of wages we poor colored people receive, and when I hear so much said about our unreliability, our untrustworthiness, and even our vices, I recall the story of the private soldier in a certain army who, once upon a time, being upbraided by the commanding officer because the heels of his shoes were not polished, is said to have replied: "Captain, do you expect all the virtues for $13 per month?"

Of course, nothing is being done to increase our wages, and the way things are going at present it would seem that nothing could be done to cause an increase of wages. We have no labor unions or organizations of any kind that could demand for us a uniform scale of wages for cooks, washerwomen, nurses, and the like; and, for another thing, if some negroes did here and there refuse to work for seven and eight and ten dollars a month, there would be hundreds of other negroes right on the spot ready to take their places and do the same work, or more, for the low wages that had been refused. So that, the truth is, we have to work for little or nothing or become vagrants! And that, of course, in this State would mean that we would be arrested, tried, and de-spatched to the "State Farm," where we would surely have to work for nothing or be beaten with many stripes!

Nor does this low rate of pay tend to make us efficient servants. The most that can be said of us negro household servants in the South—and I speak as one of them—is that we are to the extent of our ability willing and faithful slaves. We do not cook according to scientific principles be-cause we do not know anything about scientific principles. Most of our cooking is done by guesswork or by memory. We cook well when our "hand" is in, as we say, and when anything about the dinner goes wrong, we simply say, "I lost my hand today!" We don't know anything about scientific food for babies, nor anything about what science says must be done for infants at certain periods of their growth or when cer-tain symptoms of disease appear; but somehow we "raise" more of the children than we kill, and, for the most part, they are lusty chaps—all of them. But the point is, we do not go to cooking-schools nor to nurse-training schools, and so it cannot be expected that we should make as efficient servants without such training as we should make were such training provided. And yet with our cooking and nursing, such as it is, the white folks seem to be satisfied—perfectly satisfied. I sometimes wonder if this satisfaction is the outgrowth of the knowledge that more highly trained servants would be able to demand better pay!

Perhaps some might say, if the poor pay is the only thing about which we have to complain, then the slavery in which we daily toil and struggle is not so bad after all. But the poor pay isn't all—not by any means! I remember very well the first and last place from which I was dismissed. I lost my place because I refused to let the madam's husband kiss me. He must have been accustomed to undue familiarity with his servants, or else he took it as a matter of course, because without any lovemaking at all, soon after I was installed as cook, he walked up to me, threw his arms around me, and was in the act of kissing me, when I demanded to know what he meant, and shoved him away. I was young then, and newly married, and didn't know then what has been a burden to my mind and heart ever since that a colored woman's virtue in this part of the country has no protection. I at once went home, and told my husband about it. When my husband went to the man who had insulted me, the man cursed him, and slapped him, and—had him arrested! The police judge fined my husband $25. I was present at the hearing, and testified on oath to the insult offered me. The white man, of course, denied the charge. The old judge looked up and said: "This court will never take the word of a nigger against the word of a white man." Many and many a time since I have heard similar stories repeated again and again by my friends. I believe nearly all white men take, and expect to take, undue liberties with their colored female servants—not only the fathers, but in many cases the sons also. Those servants who rebel against such familiarity must either leave or expect a mighty hard time, if they stay. By comparison, those who tamely submit to these improper relations live in clover. They always have a little "spending change," wear better clothes, and are able to get off from work at least once a week—and sometimes oftener. This moral debasement is not at all times unknown to the white women in these homes. I know of more than one colored woman who was openly importuned by white women to become the mistresses of their white husbands on the ground that they, the white wives, were afraid that, if their husbands did not associate with colored women, they would certainly do so with outside white women, and the white wives, for reasons which ought to be perfectly obvious, preferred to have their husbands do wrong with colored women in order to keep their husbands *straight*! And again, I know at least fifty places in my small town where white men are positively raising two families—a white family in the "Big House" in front, and a colored family in a "Little House" in the backyard. In most cases, to be sure, the colored women involved are the cooks or chambermaids or seamstresses, but it cannot be true that their real connection with the white men of the families is unknown to the white women of the families. The results of this concubinage can be seen in all of our colored churches and in all of our colored public schools in the South, for in most of our churches and schools the majority of the young men and women and boys and girls are light-skinned mulattoes. The real, Simon-pure, blue-gum, thick-lip, coal-black negro is passing away—certainly in the cities; and the fathers of the new generation of negroes are white men, while their mothers are unmarried colored women.

Another thing—it's a small indignity, it may be, but an indignity just the same. No white person, not even the little children just learning to talk, no white person at the South ever thinks of addressing any negro man or woman as *Mr.*, or *Mrs.*, or *Miss*. The women are called, "Cook," or "Nurse," or "Mammy," or "Mary Jane," or "Lou," or "Dilcey," as the case might be, and the men are called "Bob," or "Boy," or "Old Man," or "Uncle Bill," or "Pate." In many cases our white employers refer to us and in our presence, too, as their "niggers." No matter what they call us—no matter what they teach their children to call us—we must tamely submit, and answer when we are called; we must enter no protest; if we did object, we should be driven out without the least ceremony, and, in applying for work at other places, we should find it very hard to procure another situation. In almost every case, when our intending employers would be looking up our record, the information would be given by telephone or otherwise that we were "impudent," "saucy," "dishonest," and "generally unreliable." In our town we have no such thing as an employment agency or intelligence bureau, and, therefore, when we want work, we have to get out on the street and go from place to place, always with hat in hand, hunting for it.

Another thing. Sometimes I have gone on the street cars or the railroad trains with the white children, and, so long as I was in charge of the children, I could sit anywhere I desired, front or back. If a white man happened to ask some other white man, "What is that nigger doing in here?" and was told, "Oh, she's the nurse of those white children in front of her!" immediately there was the hush of peace. Everything was all right, so long as I was in the white man's part of the street car or in the white man's coach as a servant—a slave—but as soon as I did not present myself as a menial, and the relationship of master and servant was abolished by my not having the white children with me, I would be forthwith assigned to the "nigger" seats or the "colored people's coach." Then, too, any day in my city, and I understand that it is so in every town in the South, you can see some "great big black burly" negro coachman or carriage driver huddled up beside some aristocratic Southern white woman, and nothing is said about it, nothing is done about it, nobody resents the familiar contact. But let that same colored man take off his brass buttons and his high hat, and put on the plain livery of an average American citizen, and drive one block down any thoroughfare in any town in the South with that same white woman, as her equal or companion or friend, and he'd be shot on the spot!

You hear a good deal nowadays about the "service pan." The "service pan" is the general term applied to "left-over" food, which in many a Southern home is freely placed at the disposal of the cook, or, whether so placed or not, it is usually disposed of by the cook. In my town, I know, and I guess in many other towns also, every night when the cook starts for her home she takes with her a pan or a plate of cold victuals. The same thing is true on Sunday afternoons after dinner—and most cooks have nearly every Sunday afternoon off. Well, I'll be frank with you, if it were not for the service pan, I don't know what the majority of our Southern colored families would do. The service pan is the main-stay in many a home. Good cooks in the South receive on an average $8 per month. Porters, butlers, coachmen, janitors, "office boys" and the like receive on an average $16 per month. Few and far between are the colored men in the South who receive $1 or more per day. Some mechanics do; as, for example, carpenters, brick masons, wheelwrights, blacksmiths, and the like. The vast majority of negroes in my town are serving in menial capacities in homes, stores and offices. Now taking it for granted, for the sake of illustration, that the husband receives, $16 per month and the wife $8. That would be $24 between the two. The chances are that they will have anywhere from five to thirteen children between them. Now, how far will $24 go toward housing and feeding and clothing ten or twelve persons for thirty days? And, I tell you, with all of us poor people the service pan is a great institution; it is a great help to us, as we wag along the weary way of life. And then most of the white folks expect their cooks to avail themselves of these perquisities; they allow it; they expect it. I do not deny that the cooks find opportu-nity to hide away at times, along with the cold "grub," a little sugar, a little flour, a little meal, or a little piece of soap; but I indignantly deny that we are thieves. We don't steal; we just "take" things—they are a part of the oral contract, exprest or implied. We understand it, and most of the white folks understand it. Others may denounce the service pan, and say that it is used only to support idle negroes, but many a time, when I was a cook, and had the responsibility of rearing my three chil-dren upon my lone shoulders, many a time I have had occasion to bless the Lord for the service pan!

I have already told you that my youngest girl was a nurse. With scores of other colored girls who are nurses, she can be seen almost any afternoon when the weather is fair, rolling the baby carriage or lolling about on some one of the chief boulevards of our town. The very first week that she started out on her work she was insulted by a white man, and many times since has been improperly approached by other white men. It is a favorite practice of young white sports about town—and they are not always young, either—to stop some colored nurse, inquire the name of the "sweet little baby," talk baby talk to the child, fondle it, kiss it, make love to it. etc., etc., and in nine of ten cases every such white man will wind up by making love to the colored nurse and seeking an appointment with her.

I confess that I believe it to be true that many of our colored girls are as eager as the white men are to encourage and maintain these improper relations; but where the girl is not willing, she has only herself to depend upon for protection. If their fathers, brothers or husbands seek to redress their wrongs, under our peculiar conditions, the guiltless negroes will be severely punished, if not killed, and the white blackleg will go scot-free!

Ah, we poor colored women wage-earners in the South are fighting a terrible battle, and because of our weakness, our ignorance, our poverty, and our temptations we deserve the sympathies of mankind. Perhaps a million of us are introduced daily to the privacy of a million chambers thruout the South, and hold in our arms a million white children, thousands of whom, as infants are suckled at our breasts—during my lifetime I myself have served as "wet nurse" to more than a dozen white children. On the one hand, we are assailed by white men, and, on the other hand, we are assailed by black men, who should be our natural protectors; and, whether in the cook kitchen, at the washtub, over the sewing machine, behind the baby carriage, or at the ironing board, we are but little more than pack horses, beasts of burden, slaves! In the distant future, it may be, centuries and centuries hence, a monument of brass or stone will be erected to the Old Black Mammies of the South, but what we need is present help, present sympathy, better wages, better hours, more protection, and a chance to breathe for once while alive as free women. If none others will help us it would seem that the Southern white women themselves might do so in their own defense, because we are rearing their children—we feed them, we bathe them, we teach them to speak the English language, and in numberless instances we sleep with them—and it is inevitable that the lives of their children will in some measure be pure or impure according as they are affected by contact with their colored nurses.

Georgia.

20

"How I Made My First Big Flight Abroad: My Flight Across the English Channel" (1912)

Harriet Quimby

HARRIET QUIMBY (1875?–1912), in a narrative alleging she was the daughter of wealthy parents who provided her with a first-class education, claimed she was born in Arroyo Grande, California, in 1884. It is believed, however, that she was born on May 11, 1875, in Kinderhook Township, Michigan, and raised on a farm. In 1900 the family moved to San Francisco, where Quimby dreamt of becoming an actress and began, in 1902, to write for the *Dramatic Review*. After working as one of the first female newspaper reporters at *The San Francisco Call*, she moved to New York where she worked for *Leslie's Illustrated Weekly* as a writer and photojournalist from 1903 to 1912. Her award-winning photographs and clever articles made her a chief contributor to the periodical and a key figure in the New York literary scene, and she was promoted to an editorial position.

Thrilled by John Moisant's performance at the 1910 Belmont Park Aviation Meet, Quimby asked this daredevil aviator to give her flying lessons. She and Moisant's sister Matilde took lessons at his school of aviation on Long Island, scheduling them at dawn in order not to interfere with Quimby's work at *Leslie's*. Although Matilde began her lessons earlier, Quimby, after four months and thirty-three lessons, earned her pilot's license fifteen days before Matilde, making her the first licensed woman pilot in America. Subsequently America's first two women fliers joined the Moisant International Aviators and performed in Mexico City, shocking the amazed spectators. Quimby determined that she would become the first woman to fly the English Channel, but she kept her plan to herself to prevent others from attempting it first.

Quimby's initial worries that flying might jeopardize her career were allayed when her employer sponsored her proposed flight and provided a letter of introduction to French airplane designer Louis Blériot, who supplied a 50-horsepower monoplane. Quimby was undaunted by the fact that she had never flown a Blériot before and by the widespread belief that a woman could not accomplish such a feat. Quimby's advisor, pilot Gustav Hamel, offered to make the flight disguised as her. On the morning of April 16, 1912, Quimby, in her notorious violet flying suit and matching jewelry, took off from Dover. An hour and nine minutes later, she landed twenty-five miles short of the proposed destination, making her historic landing on a beach in the isolated town of Hardelot, France. Public response to her flight ranged from wild enthusiasm to condescension and indifference.

Quimby continued to travel on the lucrative air-show exhibition circuit. On July 1, 1912, she flew the Blériot in a publicity stunt at the Harvard-Boston Aviation Meet. She and her passenger, air show manager William Willard, took off for a flight around the Boston lighthouse, but the plane lurched and began to nose dive, and they were thrown to their deaths in the shallow water. Strangely enough, the plane then landed itself, coming out of the nosedive and gliding to a stop without much damage.

While Quimby left behind prolific accounts of American life in the early twentieth century and played a major role in aviation and women's history, only scant facts are known about her personal life. She never married or had children, but lived with and supported her mother and drove her own car. The article included here (from *Fly Magazine,* June 1912) indicates, however, that Quimby's flight experiences contributed to remaking her view of herself as a future-oriented subject, as Sidonie Smith suggests (2001).

(The first woman to fly the English Channel)

"How I Made My First Big Flight Abroad: My Flight Across the English Channel"

While flying in Mexico, at President Madero's inauguration, last December, an ambition to be the first woman aviator to cross the English Channel alone entered my mind. The more I thought of it, the less formidable the feat seemed to be. Without mentioning the matter to a soul, for fear that some one across the sea might anticipate my idea, I waited until my return to New York. There I secured a letter of introduction to Louis Bleriot and prepared to present it to him at his factory in Paris.

On the seventh of March I sailed on the Hamburg-American liner *Amerika,* went to London and disclosed my project to the wide-awake editor of the London *Mirror.* He was delighted with the idea and immediately offered me a handsome inducement if I would make the trip as the *Mirror*'s representative. The next thing necessary was to get a monoplane. I went to Paris, saw Mr. Bleriot and placed an order with him for a seventy-horse-power passenger machine, regarding which I had had some correspondence with the firm. At the same time I readily arranged with Mr. Bleriot for the loan of a fifty-horse-power monoplane of the type I had been accustomed to use in the United States.

Mr. Bleriot has a hangar at Hardelot, where he has a seaside home. It seemed prudent to try out the new machine first in some quiet way. So it was shipped Hardelot. I followed soon after. The control of the new machine was a trifle different from that which I had been using in the United States, hence my desire to have a trial flight.

I was eager to test the new machine and rose early the following morning, to find the wind blowing a gale. Patiently we waited all day long for it to diminish. Usually it dies out in the evening, but it kept constantly increasing, until it whistled around the corners of the house at a velocity of forty miles. The next morning, at five, once more I prepared to go out into the chilly air to make a trial. Still the wind blew a gale, and it continued to blow throughout the day.

The persistent gale at Hardelot would not permit me to carry out my plan to try out the machine. Time was flying—even if I was not. I had promised the Mirror editor to be at Dover promptly. So I arranged to have the Bleriot monoplane shipped across to Dover at once and wired the Mirror to have its photographers and reporters meet me at the Hotel Lord Warden, at Dover. It was vitally important that nothing should be known of my contemplated journey, so the machine was shipped very secretly to the aerodome on Dover heights, about three miles back from the channel, a fine, smooth ground from which to make a good start. The famous Dover Castle stands on the cliffs, overlooking the channel. It points the way clearly to Calais.

I saw at once that I had only to rise in my machine, fix my eyes upon the castle, fly over it and speed directly across to the French coast. It seemed so easy that it looked like a cross-country flight. I am glad I thought so and felt so, otherwise I might have had more hesitation about flying in the fog with an untried compass, in a new and untried machine, knowing that the treacherous North Sea stood ready to receive me if I drifted only five miles too far out of my course. This was the fate of D. Leslie Allen, the English aviator, who started the same day as I did, in a monoplane similar to mine, on a fight over the Irish Channel from London to Dublin. He started, but he never came back. It is a mystery of the Irish Channel.

Sunday, April 14th, was a perfect day for flying across the channel. There was no wind. The sun was bright and warm. The air was so clear that by straining our eyes a little we could see the French coast dimly outlined across the channel. Everybody said, "Start now. It is your chance. We may have high winds tomorrow and they may last two weeks. That has been the experience of every one who has come here to make the channel flight." I have made it a rule not to fly on Sunday, so we all agreed to try it early Monday morning if the weather would permit.

Our movements, of course, attracted attention. Fortunately, Gustave Hamel, the famous English aviator, was with us, as he had volunteered to try out my new machine and get the engine in tune. He did this on Sunday, while a number of persons gathered around the aerodrome fences to see what was going on. Somehow, the rumor had gone out that a woman was to attempt to cross the channel alone in an aeroplane. A few reporters visited the aerodrome with watchful eyes, but as nothing happened they retired one after the other, until we had the field to ourselves.

After all our patient waiting and hoping against hope that the wind would go down toward evening, there was no abatement in its strength. We went back to our hotel at seven P.M., tired, chilled and disgusted. The wide-awake *Mirror* reporters who had taken a tug out into the choppy sea in midchannel and another group who were waiting back of Calais to witness my landing were even more disappointed than we. My greatest disappointment was that I had had no chance to try out the new machine.

"All things come to him who waits." At three-thirty Tuesday morning we were called, had our hot tea, got into our automobiles and at four o'clock were on the flying grounds. There was no wind. Scarcely a breath of air was stirring. The monoplane was hurried out of the hangar. We knew that we must hasten, for it was almost certain that the wind would rise again within an hour. Mr. Hamel, whose courtesy and consideration I shall always remember, jumped into the machine and was off for a short "try-out" of the engine and to report atmospheric conditions. He found everything satisfactory and hurried back, making one of the beautiful and easy landings for which he is famous.

It was my turn at last. Everybody was expectant. I was eager to get into my seat and be off. My heart was not in my mouth. I felt impatient to realize the project on which I was determined, despite the protest of my best friends. For the first time I was to fly a Bleriot monoplane. For the first time I was to fly by compass. For the first time I was to make a journey across the water. For the first time I was to fly on the other side of the Atlantic. My anxiety was to get off quickly.

The sky seemed clear, but patches of cloud and masses of fog here and there obscured the shore. The French coast was wholly invisible, by reason of moving masses of mist. The wind had not come up yet. The smooth grounds of the aerodrome gave fine a chance for a perfect start. I heeded Mr. Hamel's warning about the coldness of the channel flight and had prepared accordingly. Under my flying suit of wool-back satin I wore two pairs of silk combinations, over it a long woolen coat, over this an American raincoat, and around and across my shoulders a long, wide stole of sealskin. Even this did not satisfy my solicitous friends. At the last minute they handed up a large hot-water bag, which Mr. Hamel insisted on tying to my waist like an enormous locket.

I soon found that I was not too warm. The channel passage was chilly enough, especially when I shot through the damp banks of mist that speedily enveloped me. I did not suffer, for the excitement stimulated my warmth; but I noticed, when I landed, that the hot-water bag was as cold as ice. It surely saved me something.

It was five-thirty A. M. when my machine got off the ground. The preliminaries were brief. Hearty handshakes were quickly given, the motor began to make its twelve hundred revolutions a minute, and I put up my hand to give the signal of release. Then I was off. The noise of the motor drowned the shouts and cheers of friends below. In a moment I was in the air, climbing steadily in a long circle. I was up fifteen hundred feet within thirty seconds. From this high point of vantage my eyes lit at once on Dover Castle. It was half hidden in a fog bank. I felt that trouble was coming, but I made directly for the flagstaff of the castle, as I had promised the waiting *Mirror* photographers and the moving-picture men I should do.

In an instant I was beyond the cliffs and over the channel. Far beneath me I saw the *Mirror*'s tug, with its stream of black smoke. It was trying to keep ahead of me, but I passed it in a jiffy. Then the thickening fog obscured my view. Calais was out of sight. I could not see ahead of me at all nor could I see the water below. There was only one thing for me to do and that was to keep my eyes fixed on the compass.

My hands were covered with long, Scotch woolen gloves, which gave me good protection from the cold and fog; but the machine was wet and my face was so covered with dampness that I had to push my goggles up on my forehead. I could not see through them. I was traveling at over a mile a minute. The distance straight across from Dover to Calais is only twenty- two miles, and I knew that land must be in sight if I could only get below the fog and see it. So I dropped from an altitude of about two thousand feet until I was half that height. The sunlight struck upon my face and my eyes lit upon the white and sandy shores of France. I felt happy, but I could not find Calais. Being unfamiliar with the coast line, I could not locate myself. I determined to reconnoiter and come down to a height of about five hundred feet and traverse the shore.

Meanwhile, the wind had risen and the currents were coming in billowy gusts. I flew a short distance inland to locate myself or find a good place on which to alight. It was all tilled land below me, and rather than tear up the farmers' fields I decided to drop down on the hard and sandy beach. I did so at once, making an easy landing. Then I jumped from my machine and was alone upon the shore. But it was only for a few moments. A crowd of fishermen—men, women and children each carrying a pail of sand worms—came rushing from all directions toward me. They were chattering in French, of which I comprehended sufficient to discover that they knew I had crossed the channel. These humble fisherfolk knew what had happened. They were congratulating themselves that the first woman to cross in an aeroplane had landed on their fishing beach.

An incident that pleased me more than anything else was the hospitality of one of the fisherwomen. She insisted upon serving me with a very welcome cup of hot tea, accompanied by bread and cheese. The tea was served in a cup fully six times as large as an ordinary teacup and was so old and quaint that I could not conceal my admiration of it. The goodhearted woman insisted upon giving it to me, and no cup that I have ever won or ever shall win as an aero trophy will be prized more than this.

It was not long before all of Hardelot was racing to the beach.

The newspaper representatives, as soon as they arrived from Calais, produced a bottle of champagne from a place of careful concealment and insisted that I permit them to drink my health while seated in the machine. Of course I did so—anything to oblige these faithful recorders of the events of the day.

I had no change of garments, but the *Mirror* men had taken my long seal coat on the tug across the channel, the day before, while they were waiting my arrival, and it covered my flying suit effectively. Then I got into an automobile and motored to Calais, about thirty miles distant, in time to catch a fast train that took me into Paris at seven P. M., a very tired but a very happy woman.

21

Autobiographical Essays

Sᴜɪ Sɪɴ Fᴀʀ

SUI SIN FAR (1865–1914), a writer and activist, was born Edith
Maude Eaton in Macclesfield, England, in 1865. Her father, Edward
Eaton, was a British merchant and her mother was a Chinese
immigrant named Lotus Blossom. They lived unconventionally as
an interracial couple in an English borough twenty miles south of
Manchester that relied on the silk trade. Close to her mother, Sui Sin
Far grew up a witness to the bitter prejudice her mother endured
during the British colonization of parts of China and came to
recognize the societal consequences of ethnic difference in a racist
world. When she was seven, her family migrated from England,
living in New York for a while, and then settling in Québec. In
North America her biracial identity provoked verbal and physical
abuse. Although the Eatons had belonged to the merchant class in
England, in North America they were seen as an impoverished
working-class family. As the oldest child, Sui Sin Far had to quit
school when she was ten to care for her brothers and sisters and to
earn additional money for the family.

During the late 1880s and 1890s, Sui Sin Far began writing,
working as a short fiction writer, a stenographer, and a journalist
with the Montréal newspaper, *The Star*. She gained acclaim writing
in the United States under the name Sui Sin Far, which means
"Narcissus," linking her to a significant flower in Chinese culture.

Her only published book of stories, *Mrs. Spring Fragrance,* appeared in a small print run (2,500) in 1912, shortly before her death, and was the first book-length collection by a Chinese North American writer.

Sui Sin Far lived most of her life in Boston, Seattle, and San Francisco, traveling extensively, and never married. Throughout 1897 she resided in Jamaica. She died of heart failure on April 7, 1914, at age 49, after suffering bouts of rheumatoid arthritis, malaria, and rheumatic fever throughout her life.

Sui Sin Far is acclaimed as the first writer to sympathetically portray immigrant Chinese life in North America and is the first Chinese-North American to write her own narratives in English. Her sister Winifred Lillie Eaton, who wrote as Onoto Watanna, was a best-selling romance writer. A 1995 biography of Sui Sin Far by Annette White-Parks has brought her accomplishments to wider attention. Critical investigations by Amy Ling, Xio-Huang-Yin, and Elizabeth Ammons, among others, indicate the foundational significance of Sui Sin Far for an Asian American literary tradition. The two selections we include (the first from *The Independent,* the second from the *Boston Globe*), her only autobiographical sketches, oscillate interestingly between the writerly reflections and political testimony of a biracial subject bearing witness to her painful yet productive experience of marginalization.

"Leaves from the Mental Portfolio of an Eurasian" (1909)

When I look back over the years I see myself, a little child of scarcely four years of age, walking in front of my nurse, in a green English lane, and listening to her tell another of her kind that my mother is Chinese. "Oh, Lord!" exclaims the informed. She turns me around and scans me curiously from head to foot. Then the two women whisper together. Tho the word "Chinese" conveys very little meaning to my mind, I feel that they are talking about my father and mother and my heart swells with indignation. When we reach home I rush to my mother and try to tell her what I have heard. I am a young child. I fail to make myself intelligible. My mother does not understand, and when the nurse declares to her, "Little Miss Sui is a story-teller," my mother slaps me.

Many a long year has past over my head since that day—the day on which I first learned that I was something different and apart from other children, but tho my mother has forgotten it, I have not.

I see myself again, a few years older. I am playing with another child in a garden. A girl passes by outside the gate. "Mamie," she cries to my companion. "I wouldn't speak to Sui if I were you. Her mamma is Chinese."

"I don't care," answers the little one beside me. And then to me, "Even if your mamma is Chinese, I like you better than I like Annie."

"But I don't like you," I answer, turning my back on her. It is my first conscious lie.

I am at a children's party, given by the wife of an Indian officer whose children were schoolfellows of mine. I am only six years of age, but have attended a private school for over a year, and have already learned that China is a heathen country, being civilized by England. However, for the time being, I am a merry romping child. There are quite a number of grown people present. One, a white haired old man, has his attention called to me by the hostess. He adjusts his eyeglasses and surveys me critically. "Ah, indeed!" he exclaims, "Who would have thought it at first glance. Yet now I see the difference between her and other children. What a peculiar coloring! Her mother's eyes and hair and her father's features, I presume. Very interesting little creature!"

I had been called from my play for the purpose of inspection. I do not return to it. For the rest of the evening I hide myself behind a hall door and refuse to show myself until it is time to go home.

My parents have come to America. We are in Hudson City, N. Y., and we are very poor. I am out with my brother, who is ten months older than myself. We pass a Chinese store, the door of which is open. "Look!" says Charlie, "Those men in there are Chinese!" Eagerly I gaze into the long low room. With the exception of my mother, who is English bred with English ways and manner of dress, I have never seen a Chinese person. The two men within the store are uncouth specimens of their race, drest in working blouses and pantaloons with queues hanging down their backs. I recoil with a sense of shock.

"Oh, Charlie," I cry, "Are we like that?"

"Well, we're Chinese, and they're Chinese, too, so we must be!" returns my seven-year-old brother.

"Of course you are," puts in a boy who has followed us down the street, and who lives near us and has seen my mother: "Chinky, Chinky, Chinaman, yellow-face, pig-tail, rat-eater." A number of other boys and several little girls join in with him.

"Better than you," shouts my brother, facing the crowd. He is younger and smaller than any there, and I am even more insignificant than he; but my spirit revives.

"I'd rather be Chinese than anything else in the world," I scream.

They pull my hair, they tear my clothes, they scratch my face, and all but lame my brother; but the white blood in our veins fights valiantly for the Chinese half of us. When it is all, over, exhausted and bedraggled, we crawl home, and report to our mother that we have "won the battle."

"Are you sure?" asks my mother doubtfully.

"Of course. They ran from us. They were frightened," returns my brother.

My mother smiles with satisfaction.

"Do you hear?" she asks my father.

"Umm," he observes, raising his eyes from his paper for an instant. My childish instinct, however, tells me that he is more interested than he appears to be.

It is tea time, but I cannot eat. Unobserved I crawl away. I do not sleep that night. I am too excited and I ache all over. Our opponents had been so very much stronger and bigger than we. Toward morning, however, I fall into a doze from which I awake myself, shouting:

> Sound the battle cry;
> See the foe is nigh.

My mother believes in sending us to Sunday school. She has been brought up in a Presbyterian college.

The scene of my life shifts to Eastern Canada. The sleigh which has carried us from the station stops in front of a little French Canadian hotel. Immediately we are surrounded by a number of villagers, who stare curiously at my mother as my father assists her to alight from the sleigh. Their curiosity, however, is tempered with kindness, as they watch, one after another, the little black heads of my brothers and sisters and myself emerge out of the buffalo robe, which is part of the sleigh's outfit. There are six of us, four girls and two boys; the eldest, my brother, being only seven years of age. My father and mother are still in their twenties. "Les pauvres enfants," the inhabitants murmur, as they help to carry us into the hotel. Then in lower tones: "Chinoise, Chinoise."

For some time after our arrival, whenever we children are sent for a walk, our footsteps are dogged by a number of young French and English Canadians, who amuse themselves with speculations as to whether, we being Chinese, are susceptible to pinches and hair pulling, while older persons pause and gaze upon us, very much in the same way that I have seen people gaze upon strange animals in a menagerie. Now and then we are stopt and plied with questions as to what we eat and drink, how we go to sleep, if my mother understands what my father says to her, if we sit on chairs or squat on floors, etc., etc., etc.

There are many pitched battles, of course, and we seldom leave the house without being armed for conflict. My mother takes a great interest in our battles, and usually cheers us on, tho I doubt whether she understands the depth of the troubled waters thru which her little children wade. As to my father, peace is his motto, and he deems it wisest to be blind and deaf to many things.

School days are short, but memorable. I am in the same class with my brother, my sister next to me in the class below. The little girl whose desk my sister shares shrinks close against the wall as my sister takes her place. In a little while she raises her hand.

"Please, teacher!"

"Yes, Annie."

"May I change my seat?"

"No, you may not!"

The little girl sobs. "Why should she have to sit beside a ———"

Happily my sister does not seem to hear, and before long the two little girls become great friends. I have many such experiences.

My brother is remarkably bright; my sister next to me has a wonderful head for figures, and when only eight years of age helps my father with his night work accounts. My parents compare her with me. She is of sturdier build than I, and, as my father says, "Always has her wits about her." He thinks her more like my mother, who is very bright and interested in every little detail of practical life. My father tells me that I will never make half the woman that my mother is or that my sister will be. I am not as strong as my sisters, which makes me feel somewhat ashamed, for I am the eldest little girl, and more is expected of me. I have no organic disease, but the strength of my feelings seems to take from me the strength of my body. I am prostrated at times with attacks of nervous sickness. The doctor says that my heart is unusually large; but in the light of the present I know that the cross of the Eurasian bore too heavily upon my childish shoulders. I usually hide my weakness from the family until I cannot stand. I do not understand myself, and I have an idea that the others will despise me for not being as strong as them. Therefore, I like to wander away alone, either by the river or in the bush. The green fields and flowing water have a charm for me. At the age of seven, as it is today, a bird on the wing is my emblem of happiness.

I have come from a race on my mother's side which is said to be the most stolid and insensible to feeling of all races, yet I look back over the years and see myself so keenly alive to every shade of sorrow and suffering that it is almost a pain to live.

If there is any trouble in the house in the way of a difference between my father and mother, or if any child is punished, how I suffer! And when harmony is restored, heaven seems to be around me. I can be sad, but I can also be glad. My mother's screams of agony when a baby is born almost drive me wild, and long after her pangs have subsided I feel them in my own body. Sometimes it is a week before I can get to sleep after such an experience.

A debt owing by my father fills me with shame. I feel like a criminal when I pass the creditor's door. I am only ten years old. And all the while the question of nationality perplexes my little brain. Why are we what we are? I and my brothers and sisters. Why did God make us to be hooted and stared at? Papa is English, mamma is Chinese. Why couldn't we have been either one thing or the other? Why is my mother's race despised? I look into the faces of my father and mother. Is she not every bit as dear and good as he? Why? Why? She sings us the songs she learned at her English school. She tells us tales of China. Tho a child when she left her native land she remembers it well, and I am never tired of listening to the story of how she was stolen from her home. She tells us over and over again of her meeting with my father in Shanghai and the romance of their marriage. Why? Why?

I do not confide in my father and mother. They would not understand. How could they? He is English, she is Chinese. I am different to both of them—a stranger, tho their own child. "What are we?" I ask my brother. "It doesn't matter, sissy," he responds. But it does. I love poetry, particularly heroic pieces. I also love fairy tales. Stories of everyday life do not appeal to me. I dream dreams of being great and noble; my sisters and brothers also. I glory in the idea of dying at the stake and a great genie arising from the flames and declaring to those who have scorned us: "Behold, how great and glorious and noble are the Chinese people!"

My sisters are apprenticed to a dressmaker; my brother is entered in an office. I tramp around and sell my father's pictures, also some lace which I make myself. My nationality, if I had only known it at that time, helps to make sales. The ladies who are my customers call me "The Little Chinese Lace Girl." But it is a dangerous life for a very young girl. I come near to "mysteriously disappearing" many a time. The greatest temptation was in the thought of getting far away from where I was known, to where no mocking cries of "Chinese!" "Chinese!" could reach.

Whenever I have the opportunity I steal away to the library and read every book I can find on China and the Chinese. I learn that China is the oldest civilized nation on the face of the earth and a few other things. At eighteen years of age what troubles me is not that I am what I am, but that others are ignorant of my superiority. I am small, but my feelings are big—and great is my vanity.

My sisters attend dancing classes, for which they pay their own fees. In spite of covert smiles and sneers, they are glad to meet and mingle with other young folk. They are not sensitive in the sense that I am. And yet they understand. One of them tells me that she overhead a young man say to another that he would rather marry a pig than a girl with Chinese blood in her veins.

In course of time I too learn shorthand and take a position in an office. Like my sister, I teach myself, but, unlike my sister, I have neither the perseverance nor the ability to perfect myself. Besides, to a temperament like mine, it is torture to spend the hours in transcribing other people's thoughts. Therefore, altho I can always earn a moderately good salary, I do not distinguish myself in the business world as does she.

When I have been working for some years I open an office of my own. The local papers patronize me and give me a number of assignments, including most of the local Chinese reporting. I meet many Chinese persons, and when they get into trouble am often called upon to fight their battles in the papers. This I enjoy. My heart leaps for joy when I read one day an article signed by a New York Chinese in which he declares "The Chinese in America owe an everlasting debt of gratitude to Sui Sin Far for the bold stand she has taken in their defense."

The Chinaman who wrote the article seeks me out and calls upon me. He is a clever and witty man, a graduate of one of the American colleges and as well a Chinese scholar. I learn that he has an American wife and several children. I am very much interested in these children, and when I meet them my heart throbs in sympathetic tune with the tales they relate of their experiences as Eurasians. "Why did papa and mamma born us?" asks one. Why?

I also meet other Chinese men who compare favorably with the white men of my acquaintance in mind and heart qualities. Some of them are quite handsome. They have not as finely cut noses and as well developed chins as the white men, but they have smoother skins and their expression is more serene; their hands are better shaped and their voices softer.

Some little Chinese women whom I interview are very anxious to know whether I would marry a Chinaman. I do not answer No. They clap their hands delightedly, and assure me that the Chinese are much the finest and best of all men. They are, however, a little doubtful as to whether one could be persuaded to care for me, full-blooded Chinese people having a prejudice against the half white.

Fundamentally, I muse, all people are the same. My mother's race is as prejudiced as my father's. Only when the whole world becomes as one family will human beings be able to see clearly and hear distinctly. I believe that some day a great part of the world will be Eurasian. I cheer myself with the thought that I am but a pioneer. A pioneer should glory in suffering.

"You were walking with a Chinaman yesterday," accuses an acquaintance.

"Yes, what of it?"

"You ought not to. It isn't right."

"Not right to walk with one of my own mother's people? Oh, indeed!"

I cannot reconcile his notion of righteousness with my own.

I am living in a little town away off on the north shore of a big lake. Next to me at the dinner table is the man for whom I work as a stenographer. There are also a couple of business men, a young girl and her mother.

Some one makes a remark about the cars full of Chinamen that past that morning. A transcontinental railway runs thru the town.

My employer shakes his rugged head. "Somehow or other," says he, "I cannot reconcile myself to the thought that the Chinese are humans like ourselves. They may have immortal souls, but their faces seem to be so utterly devoid of expression that I cannot help but doubt."

"Souls," echoes the town clerk. "Their bodies are enough for me. A Chinaman is, in my eyes, more repulsive than a nigger."

"They always give me such a creepy feeling," puts in the young girl with a laugh.

"I wouldn't have one in my house," declares my landlady.

"Now, the Japanese are different altogether. There is something bright and likeable about those men," continues Mr. K.

A miserable, cowardly feeling keeps me silent. I am in a Middle West town. If I declare what I am, every person in the place will hear about it the next day. The population is in the main made up of working folks with strong prejudices against my mother's countrymen. The prospect before me is not an enviable one—if I speak. I have no longer an ambition to die at the stake for the sake of demonstrating the greatness and nobleness of the Chinese people.

Mr K. turns to me with a kindly smile.

"What makes Miss Far so quiet?" he asks.

"I don't suppose she finds the 'washee washee men' particularly interesting subjects of conversation," volunteers the young manager of the local bank.

With a great effort I raise my eyes from my plate. "Mr. K.," I say, addressing my employer, "the Chinese people may have no souls, no expression on their faces, be altogether beyond the pale of civilization, but whatever they are, I want you to understand that I am—I am a Chinese."

There is silence in the room for a few minutes. Then Mr. K. pushes back his plate and standing up beside me, says:

"I should not have spoken as I did. I knew nothing whatever about the Chinese. It was pure prejudice. Forgive me!"

I admire Mr. K.'s moral courage in apologizing to me; he is a conscientious Christian man, but I do not remain much longer in the little town.

I am under a tropic sky, meeting frequently and conversing with persons who are almost as high up in the world as birth, education and money can set them. The environment is peculiar, for I am also surrounded by a race of people, the reputed descendants of Ham, the son of Noah, whose offspring, it was prophesied, should be the servants of the sons of Shem and Japheth. As I am a descendant, according to the Bible, of both Shem and Japheth, I have a perfect right to set my heel upon the Ham people; but tho I see others around me following out the Bible suggestion, it is not in my nature to be arrogant to any but those who seek to impress me with their superiority, which the poor black maid who has been assigned to me by the hotel certainly does not. My employer's wife takes me to task for this. "It is unnecessary," she says, "to thank a black person for a service."

The novelty of life in the West Indian island is not without its charm. The surroundings, people, manner of living, are so entirely different from what I have been accustomed to up North that I feel as if I were "born again." Mixing with people of fashion, and yet not of them, I am not of sufficient importance to create comment or curiosity. I am busy nearly all day and often well into the night. It is not monotonous work, but it is certainly strenuous. The planters and business men of the island take me as a matter of course and treat me with kindly courtesy. Occasionally an Englishman will warn me against the "brown boys" of the island, little dreaming that I too am of the "brown people" of the earth.

When it begins to be whispered about the place that I am not all white, some of the "sporty" people seek my acquaintance. I am small and look much younger than my years. When, however, they discover that I am a very serious and sober-minded spinster indeed, they retire quite gracefully, leaving me a few amusing reflections.

One evening a card is brought to my room. It bears the name of some naval officer. I go down to my visitor, thinking he is probably some one who, having been told that I am a reporter for the local paper, has brought me an item of news. I find him lounging in an easy chair on the veranda of the hotel—a big, blond, handsome fellow, several years younger than I.

"You are Lieutenant ——?" I inquire.

He bows and laughs a little. The laugh doesn't suit him somehow—and it doesn't suit me, either.

"If you have anything to tell me, please tell it quickly, because I'm very busy."

"Oh, you don't really mean that," he answers, with another silly and offensive laugh. "There's always plenty of time for good times. That's what I am here for. I saw you at the races the other day and twice at King's House. My ship will be here for —— weeks."

"Do you wish that noted?" I ask.

"Oh, no! Why—I came just because I had an idea that you might like to know me. I would like to know you. You look such a nice little body. Say, wouldn't you like to go out for a sail this lovely night? I will tell you all about the sweet little Chinese girls I met when we were at Hong Kong. They're not so shy!"

I leave Eastern Canada for the Far West, so reduced by another attack of rheumatic fever that I only weigh eighty-four pounds. I travel on an advertising contract. It is presumed by the railway company that in some way or other I will give them full value for their transportation across the continent. I have been ordered beyond the Rockies by the doctor, who declares that I will never regain my strength in the East. Nevertheless, I am but two days in San Francisco when I start out in search of work. It is the first time that I have sought work as a stranger in a strange town. Both of the other positions away from home were secured for me by home influence. I am quite surprised to find that there is no demand for my services in San Francisco and that no one is particularly interested in me. The best I can do is to accept an offer from a railway agency to typewrite their correspondence for $5 a month. I stipulate, however, that I shall have the privilege of taking in outside work and that my hours shall be light. I am hopeful that the sale of a story or newspaper article may add to my income, and I console myself with the reflection that, considering that I still limp and bear traces of sickness, I am fortunate to secure any work at all.

The proprietor of one of the San Francisco papers, to whom I have a letter of introduction, suggests that I obtain some subscriptions from the people of Chinatown, that district of the city having never been canvassed. This suggestion I carry out with enthusiasm, tho I find that the Chinese merchants and people generally are inclined to regard me with suspicion. They have been imposed upon so many times by unscrupulous white people. Another drawback—save for a few phrases, I am unacquainted with my mother tongue. How, then, can I expect these people to accept me as their own countrywoman? The Americanized Chinamen actually laugh in my face when I tell them that I am of their race. However, they are not all "doubting Thomases." Some little women discover that I have Chinese hair, color of eyes and complexion, also that I love rice and tea. This settles the matter for them—and for their husbands.

My Chinese instincts develop. I am no longer the little girl who shrunk against my brother at the first sight of a Chinaman. Many and many a time, when alone in a strange place, has the appearance of even an humble laundryman given me a sense of protection and made me feel quite at home. This fact of itself proves to me that prejudice can be eradicated by association.

I meet a half Chinese, half white girl. Her face is plastered with a thick white coat of paint and her eyelids and eyebrows are blackened so that the shape of her eyes and the whole expression of her face is changed. She was born in the East, and at the age of eighteen came West in answer to an advertisement. Living for many years among the working class, she had heard little but abuse of the Chinese. It is not difficult, in a land like California, for a half Chinese, half white girl to pass as one of Spanish or Mexican origin. This the poor child does, tho she lives in nervous dread of being "discovered." She becomes engaged to a young man, but fears to tell him what she is, and only does so when compelled by a fearless American girl friend. This girl, who knows her origin, realizing that the truth sooner or later must be told, and better soon than late, advises the Eurasian to confide in the young man, assuring her that he loves her well enough not to allow her nationality to stand, a bar sinister, between them. But the Eurasian prefers to keep her secret, and only reveals it to the man who is to be her husband when driven to bay by the American girl, who declares that if the halfbreed will not tell the truth she will. When the young man hears that the girl he is engaged to has Chinese blood in her veins, he exclaims: "Oh, what will my folks say?" But that is all. Love is stronger than prejudice with him, and neither he nor she deems it necessary to inform his "folks."

The Americans, having for many years manifested a much higher regard for the Japanese than for the Chinese, several half Chinese young men and women, thinking to advance themselves, both in a social and business sense, pass as Japanese. They continue to be known as Eurasians; but a Japanese Eurasian does not appear in the same light as a Chinese Eurasian. The unfortunate Chinese Eurasians! Are not those who compel them to thus cringe more to be blamed than they?

People, however, are not all alike. I meet white men, and women, too, who are proud to mate with those who have Chinese blood in their veins, and think it a great honor to be distinguished by the friendship of such. There are also Eurasians and Eurasians. I know of one who allowed herself to become engaged to a white man after refusing him nine times. She had discouraged him in every way possible, had warned him that she was half Chinese; that her people were poor, that every week or month she sent home a certain amount of her earnings, and that the man she married would have to do as much, if not more; also, most uncompromising truth of all, that she did not love him and never would. But the resolute and undaunted lover swore that it was a matter of indifference to him whether she was a Chinese or a Hottentot, that it would be his pleasure and privilege to allow her relations double what it was in her power to bestow, and as to not loving him—that did not matter at all. He loved her. So, because the young woman had a married mother and married sisters, who were always picking at her and gossiping over her independent manner of living, she finally consented to marry him, recording the agreement in her diary thus:

"I have promised to become the wife of —— —— on —— ——, 189_, because the world is so cruel and sneering to a single woman— and for no other reason."

Everything went smoothly until one day. The young man was driving a pair of beautiful horses and she was seated by his side, trying very hard to imagine herself in love with him, when a Chinese vegetable gardener's cart came rumbling along. The Chinaman was a jolly-looking individual in blue cotton blouse and pantaloons, his rakish looking hat being kept in place by a long queue which was pulled upward from his neck and wound around it. The young woman was suddenly possest with the spirit of mischief. "Look!" she cried, indicating the Chinaman, "there's my brother. Why don't you salute him?"

The man's face fell a little. He sank into a pensive mood. The wicked one by his side read him like an open book.

"When we are married," said she, "I intend to give a Chinese party every month."

No answer.

"As there are very few aristocratic Chinese in this city, I shall fill up with the laundreymen and vegetable farmers. I don't believe in being exclusive in democratic America, do you"?

He hadn't a grain of humor in his composition, but a sickly smile contorted his features as he replied:

"You shall do just as you please, my darling. But—but—consider a moment. Wouldn't it be just a little pleasanter for us if, after we are married, we allowed it to be presumed that you were—er—Japanese? So many of my friends have inquired of me if that is not your nationality. They would be so charmed to meet a little Japanese lady."

"Hadn't you better oblige them by finding one?"

"Why—er—what do you mean ?"

"Nothing much in particular. Only I am getting a little tired of this," taking off his ring.

"You don't mean what you say! Oh, put it back, dearest! You know I would not hurt your feelings for the world!"

"You haven't. I'm more than pleased. But I do mean what I say."

That evening the "ungrateful" Chinese Eurasian diaried, among other things, the following:

"Joy, oh, joy! I'm free once more. Never again shall I be untrue to my own heart. Never again will I allow any one to 'hound' or 'sneer' me into matrimony."

I secure transportation to many California points. I meet some literary people, chief among whom is the editor of the magazine who took my first Chinese stories. He and his wife give me a warm welcome to their ranch. They are broadminded people, whose interest in me is sincere and intelligent, not affected and vulgar. I also meet some funny people who advise me to "trade" upon my nationality. They tell me that if I wish to succeed in literature in America I should dress in Chinese costume, carry a fan in my hand, wear a pair of scarlet beaded slippers, live in New York, and come of high birth. Instead of making myself familiar with the Chinese-Americans around me, I should discourse on my spirit acquaintance with Chinese ancestors and quote in between the "Good mornings" and How d'ye dos" of editors,

Confucius, Confucius, how great is Confucius, the laundrymen and vegetable farmers. Before Confucius, there never was Confucius. After Confucius, there never came Confucius, etc., etc., etc.,

or something like that, both illuminating and obscuring, don't you know. They forget, or perhaps they are not aware that the old Chinese sage taught "The way of sincerity is the way of heaven."

My experiences as an Eurasian never cease; but people are not now as prejudiced as they have been. In the West, too, my friends are more advanced in all lines of thought than those whom I know in Eastern Canada—more genuine, more sincere, with less of the form of religion, but more of its spirit.

So I roam backward and forward across the continent. When I am East, my heart is West. When I am West, my heart is East. Before long I hope to be in China. As my life began in my father's country it may end in my mother's.

After all I have no nationality and am not anxious to claim any. Individuality is more than nationality. "You are you and I am I," says Confucius. I give my right hand to the Occidentals and my left to the Orientals, hoping that between them they will not utterly destroy the insignificant "connecting link." And that's all.

Seattle, Wash

"Sui Sin Far, the Half Chinese Writer, Tells of Her Career" (1912)

The Interesting Author's Book, *The Dream of a Lifetime,* Which Will Appear This Spring, Tells of Her Vocations.

As the Globe thinks that my experience in life has been unusual, and that a personal sketch will be interesting to its readers, I will try my best to furnish one. Certainly my life has been quite unlike that of any literary worker of whom I have read. I have never met any to know—save editors.

I have resided in Boston now for about two years.

I came here with the intention of publishing a book and planting a few Eurasian thoughts in Western literature. My collection of Chinese-American stories will be brought out very soon, under the title of "Mrs. Spring Fragrance." I have also written another book which will appear next year, if Providence is kind.

In the beginning I opened my eyes in a country place in the County of Chesire, England. My ancestors on my grandfather's side had been known to the county for some generations back. My ancestors on my grandmother's side were unknown to local history. She was a pretty Irish lass from Dublin when she first won my grandfather's affections.

My father, who was educated in England and studied art in France, was established in business by his father at the age of 22, at the Port of Shanghai, China. There he met my mother, a Chinese young girl, who had been educated in England, and who was in training for a missionary. They were married by the British Consul, and the year following their marriage returned to England.

As I swing the door of my mental gallery I find radiant pictures in the opening, and through all the scenes of that period there walks one figure—the figure of my brother, Edward, a noble little fellow, whose heart and intelligence during the brief years of early childhood led and directed mine. I mention this brother because I have recently lost him through an accident, and his death has affected me more than I can say.

At the age of 4 years I started to go to school. I can remember being very much interested in English history. I remember also that my mother was a fascinating story teller and that I was greatly enamored of a French version of "Little Bo-Peep," which my father tried to teach me.

Arrival in America

When I was 6 years old my father brought us to America. Besides my first brother, who was only 10 months older than myself, I had now three sisters and another brother. We settled in Montreal, Can., and hard times befell, upon which I shall not dwell.

I attended school again and must have been about 8 years old when I conceived the ambition to write a book about the half Chinese. This ambition arose from my sensitiveness to the remarks, criticisms and observations on the half Chinese which continually assailed my ears, also from an impulse, born with me, to describe, to impart to others all that I felt, all that I saw, all that I was. I was not sensitive without reason. Some Eurasians may affect that no slur is cast upon them because of their nationality; but I dislike cant and desire to be sincere. Wealth, of course, ameliorates certain conditions. We children, however, had no wealth.

I think as well my mind was stimulated by the readings of my teacher, who sought to impress upon her scholars that the true fathers and mothers of the world were those who battled through great trials and hardships to leave to future generations noble and inspiring truths.

I left school at the age of 10, but shortly thereafter attracted the attention of a lovely old lady, Mrs. William Darling of Hochelaga, who induced my mother to send me to her for a few hours each day. This old lady taught me music and French. I remember her telling her husband that I had a marvelous memory and quoting "Our finest hope is finest memory," which greatly encouraged me, as compared with my brother and sister, who had both splendid heads for figures, I ranked very low intellectually. It was Mrs. Darling who first, aside from my mother, interested me in my mother's people, and impressed upon me that I should be proud that I had sprung from such a race. She also inspired me with the belief that the spirit is more than the body, a belief which helped me through many hours of childish despondency, for my sisters were all much heavier and more muscular than I.

When my parents found that family circumstances made it necessary to withdraw me from Mrs. Darling, my old friend's mind seemed to become wrought with me, and she tried to persuade them to permit her to send me to a boarding school. My father, however, was an Englishman, and the idea of having any of his children brought up on charity, hurt his pride.

I, now in my 11th year, entered into two lives, one devoted entirely to family concerns; the other, a withdrawn life of thought and musing.

This withdrawn life of thought probably took the place of ordinary education with me. I had six keys to it; one, a great capacity for feeling, another, the key of imagination; third, the key of physical pain; fourth, the key of sympathy; fifth, the sense of being differentiated from the ordinary by the fact that I was an Eurasian; sixth, the impulse to create.

Little Lace Girl

The impulse to create was so strong within me that failing all other open avenues of development (I wrote a good deal of secret doggerel verse around this period), I began making Irish crochet lace patterns, which I sold to a clique of ladies to whom I was known as "The Little Lace Girl." I remember that when a Dominion exhibition was held in Montreal a lace pattern which I sent to the art department won first prize—a great surprise to all my people as I was the only little girl competing. My mother was very proud of my work. I remember that when the church asked her to donate something she got me to crochet her a set of my mats as a gift.

At the age of 14 I succumbed to a sickness which affected both head and heart and retarded development both mentally and physically. Which is the chief reason, no doubt, why and ambition conceived in childhood is achieved only as I near the close of half a century. But for all this retardation and the fact that I suffered from recurrent attacks of the terrible fever, I never lost spirit and always maintained my position as the advisory head of the household. We had a large family of children and my father was an artist.

The wiseacres tell us that if we are good we will be big, healthy and contented. I must have been dreadfully wicked. The only thing big about me were my feelings; the only thing healthy, my color; the only content I experienced was when I peeped into the future and saw all the family grown and settled down and myself, far away from all noise and confusion with nothing to do but write a book.

To earn my living I now began to sell my father's pictures. I enjoyed this, and no doubt, it was beneficial, as it took me out into the open air and brought me into contact with a number of interesting persons. To be sure, there was a certain sense of degradation and humiliation in approaching a haughty and contemptuous customer, and also periods of melancholy, when disappointed in a sale I had hoped to effect or payment for a picture was not made when promised. But the hours of hope and elation were worth all the dark ones. I remember starting out one

morning with two pictures in my hand and coming home in the evening with $20. How happy was everybody!

This avocation I followed for some years. Besides affording me opportunities to study human nature, it also enabled me to gratify my
love for landscape beauty—a love which was and is almost a passion.

My 18th birthday saw me in the composing room of the Montreal
Star, where for some months I picked and set type. While there I taught
myself shorthand.

Became Stenographer

At last I took a position in a lawyer's office. I do not think a person of
artistic temperament is fitted for mechanical work and it is impossible
for such to make a success of it. Stenography, in particular, is torturing
to one whose mind must create its own images. Unfortunately, I was
stultified by the work I had undertaken. But it had its advantages in this
respect, that it brought me into judgment and mental ability. I know
that I always took an interest in my employers and their interests, and
therefore, if I did not merit, at least received their commendation.

I recall that the senior member of the firm, now Judge Archibald of
Montreal, occasionally chatted with me about books and writers, read
my little stories and verse as they appeared, and usually commented
upon them with amused interest. I used to tell him that I was ambitious
to write a book. I remember him saying that it would be necessary for
me to acquire some experience of life and some knowledge of character
before I began the work and I assuring him seriously that I intended to
form all my characters upon the model of myself. "They will be very
funny people then," he answered with a wise smile.

While in this office I wrote some humorous articles which were accepted by Peck's Sun, Texas Siftings, and Detroit Free Press. I am not
consciously a humorous person; but now and then unconsciously I
write things, which seem to strike editors as funny.

One day a clergyman suggested to my mother that she should call
upon a young Chinese woman who had recently arrived from China as
the bride of one of the local Chinese merchants. With the exception of
my mother there was but one other Chinese woman in the city besides
the bride. My mother complied with the clergyman's wishes and I accompanied her.

From that time I began to go among my mother's people, and it did
me a world of good to discover how akin I was to them.

Passing by a few years I found myself in Jamaica, W.I., working as a reporter at a local paper. It was interesting work until the novelty wore off, when it became absolute drudgery. However, it was a step forward in development. I had reached my 27th year.

Sir Henry Blake was the Governor of the island while I was there, and I found the Legislative Council reporting both instructive and amusing. How noble and high principled seemed each honorable member while on the floor! How small and mean while compelled to writhe under the scorn and denunciation of some opposing brother! I used to look down form the press gallery upon the heads of the honorable members and think a great many things which I refrained from putting into my report.

I got very weary and homesick tramping the hot dusty streets of Kingston; and contracted malarial fever, the only cure for which, in my case, was a trip up North.

I remained in Montreal about a year, during which period I worked, first, as a stenographer for Mr. Hugh Graham (now Sir Hugh) of the Star, and then in the same capacity for Mr. G.T. Bell of the Grand Trunk Railway. Both of these positions I was compelled to resign because of attacks of inflammatory rheumatism.

At last my physicians declared that I would never gain strength in Montreal, and one afternoon in June what was left of me—84 pounds—set its face westward. I went to San Francisco where I had a sister, a bright girl, who was working as a spotter in one of the photograph galleries. I fell in love with the City of the Golden Gate, and wish I had space in which to write more of the place in which all the old ache in my bones fell away from them, never to return again.

As soon as I could I found myself in a railway agency, the agent of which promised me $5 a month and as well an opportunity to secure outside work. But despite this agency's fascinating situation at the corner of a shopping highway I made slight progress financially, and had it not been for my nature and my office window I might have experienced a season of melancholy. As it was, I looked out of my window, watched a continuously flowing stream of humanity, listened to the passing bands, inhaled the perfume of the curbstone flower sellers' wares, and was very much interested.

To eke out a living, I started to canvas Chinatown for subscribers for the San Francisco Bulletin. During my pilgrimages thereto I met a Chinese whom I had known in Montreal. He inquired if I were still writing Chinese stories. Mr. Charles Lummis made the same inquiry. Latent ambition aroused itself. I recommended writing Chinese stories. Youth's Companion accepted one.

But I suffered many disappointments and rejections and the urgent need for money pressing upon me, I bethought me of Seattle. Perhaps there Fortune would smile a little kinder. This suggestion had come some months before from Lyman E. Knapp, ex-Governor of Alaska, who had dropped into my office one day to get some deeds typewritten. Observing that I understood legal work, he advised me to try "the old Siwash town," where, he added, he was sure I would do better than in San Francisco.

To Seattle I sailed, and the blithe greenness of the shores of Puget Sound seemed to give me the blithest of welcomes. I was in my 29th year, and my sole fortune was $8. Before 5 o'clock of the first day here I had arranged for desk room in a lawyer's office and secured promise of patronage from several attorneys, a loan and mortgage company and a lumber and shingle merchant. I remember that evening I wrote my mother a letter, telling her that I had struck gold, silver, oil, copper, and everything else that luck could strike, in proof of which I grandiloquently shoved into her envelope a part of my remaining wealth.

As always, on account of my inaccuracy as a stenographer and my inability to typewrite continuously, my earning capacity was small; but I managed to hold up my head, and worked intermittently and happily at my Chinese stories.

Chinese Mission Teacher

Occasionally, I taught in a Chinese mission school, as I do here in Boston, but learned far more from my scholars than ever I could impart to them.

I also formed friendships with women who braced and enlightened me, women to whom the things of the mind and the heart appealed, women who were individuals, not merely the daughters of their parents, the wives of their husbands; women who taught me that nationality was no bar to friendship with those whose friendship was worth while.

Ever and again, during the 14 years in which I lived in Seattle, whenever I had a little money put by, some inward impulse would compel me to use it for a passage home. The same impulse would drive me to work my way across the Continent, writing advertisements for the different lines. Once when I saved up $85 toward a rest in which to write the book of my dreams news from home caused me to banish ambition for a while longer; and I sent my little savings to pay a passage out West for one of my younger sisters. The sister remained with me for seven months, during which time I got her to learn shorthand and typewriting, so that upon her return to Montreal she would be enabled to earn her living. Thus did the ties of relationship belate me; but at the same time strengthen.

A year later, a shock of sudden grief so unfitted me for mechanical work that I determined to emancipate myself from the torture of writing other people's thoughts and words with a heart full of my own and throwing up my position, worked my way down South as far as the city of Los Angeles. Arrived there, I gave way to my ruling passion—the passion to write all the emotions of my heart away. But it was hard work—artistic expression, if I may so call it. I had been so long accustomed to dictation that when I sat down to compose, although my mind teemed with ideas tumultuously clamoring for release, I hesitated as if I were waiting for a voice behind me to express them. I had to free myself from that spell. My writings might be imperfect, but they had got to bear the impress of thoughts begotten in my own mind and clothed in my own words.

I struggled for many months. The Century Magazine took a story from me; but I remained discontented with my work. I was not discontented with life, however. If there was nothing but bread to eat and water to drink, absorbed in my work I was immune to material things—for a while. You have to come back to them in the end.

Located in Boston

As I have already said, two years ago I came East with the intention of publishing a book of Chinese-American stories. While I was in Montreal my father obtained for me a letter of introduction from a Chinese merchant of that city to his brother in Boston, Mr. Lew Han Son. I became acquainted with some Americans of the name of Austin who lived in Dorchester and who have been my good friends ever since. I am also acquainted with a lady in Charlestown, Mrs. Henderson, who is a sister of one of my Western friends. Save, however, some visiting among Chinese friends, I do not mingle much in any kind of society. I am not rich and I have my work to do.

I have contributed to many of the leading magazines.

During the past year I have been engaged in writing my first book, and completed it a couple of months ago. In this undertaking, I was encouraged by the managing editor of the Independent. Truth to tell, if I had not received some such encouragement I could not have carried the work to a successful completion as I am one of those persons who have very little staying power.

To accomplish this work, or to enable me to have the leisure in which to accomplish it, I was obliged to obtain some financial assistance, for one cannot live upon air and water alone, even if one is half-Chinese. Two of my lawyer friends in Montreal kindly contributed toward this end. I hope soon to be in a position to repay them.

My people in Montreal, my mother in particular, my Chinese friends in Boston and also American friends are looking forward to the advent of "Mrs. Spring Fragrance" with, I believe, some enthusiasm. I am myself quite excited over the prospect. Would not any one be who had worked as hard as I have—and waited as long as I have—for a book!

22

Selections from *Madeleine: An Autobiography* (1919)

"MADELEINE"

THERE IS NO RELIABLE INFORMATION regarding
the identity of the anonymous author of *Madeleine: An Autobiography*,
although Marcia Carlisle, in her introduction to the 1986 reissue of it,
suggests that the text was not a hoax and that its author was indeed
a prostitute for decades, beginning in the 1890s. Complaints were
filed against *Madeleine* almost immediately following its October
1919 publication. Soon the narrative got caught up in a celebrated
censorship case at an historical moment when the national climate
pitted supporters of strict censorship, xenophobic nationalism, and a
hard line toward the "Red Scare" against those active in progressive
movements for social reform.

Carlisle insists that it was not "descriptions of sexual transactions"
that resulted in the censorship of *Madeleine*, "for there are few"; rather
"it was the author's failure to be humbled by her experiences and
her critical attitude towards Christian reformers that offended" (v).
Madeleine's trial occurred under the rubrics of the Comstock Laws
that prevented the distribution of "obscene literature" (laws intended
largely to prevent the distribution of literature on contraception by
groups such as Margaret Sanger's Planned Parenthood). Conservative
forces calling for censorship of the book included John Sumner, a

lawyer working for the Society for the Prevention of Vice, who believed that if documents about the conditions of prostitution were unavailable, vice would be eliminated. Progressive supporters of the book included Ben B. Lindsey (who wrote the 1919 introduction to *Madeleine*, which asserted that its author was doing a public service by exposing her experience of prostitution to the public), a progressive lawyer and judge who believed that if educational materials were readily available, the causes of prostitution—to his mind, economic— could be remedied on the national and institutional level. C. T. Brainard, the president of Harper and Brothers (*Madeleine*'s publisher), presented a third view, claiming that *Madeleine* was published without his direct knowledge and therefore the charge of obscenity brought against him was untenable. Carlisle suggests that because Brainard did not claim that *Madeleine* was a hoax and complete fiction, its author was likely what she claimed to be. Ultimately, the charges against *Madeleine* were upheld, Brainard was fined a relatively minor penalty, and *Madeleine* was withdrawn from publication until its 1986 reissue.

"Madeleine"'s lengthy autobiography is interesting on several counts. Its narrator details a childhood of poverty and factory work, which she escapes by making her way as an adventurous young woman. Discouraged by the low wages and abuse of domestic work, she is easily drawn into the more lucrative life of the prostitute. Her railroad travels take her from Massachusetts as far west as Montana and north to Calgary, Alberta, where she finally "arrives" as the owner of a profitable brothel. Her experiences contrast such American settings as the metropolis with Western boomtowns and raw mining camps. No Moll Flanders, she is engaged in a moral struggle that pits her addiction to gambling against her desire to sustain a relationship with one man, but she denounces marriage as a form of "white slavery" for middle-class women. Her own tentative and mobile subjectivity shifts with the various social worlds she encounters, but her confessional narrative refuses any easy resolution. This excerpt, which is midway through *Madeleine*, chronicles her life in the mining boomtown of Butte, Montana, and marks a turning point as she links her own experience to the international traffic in sex slavery.

With an Introduction by
Judge Ben B. Lindsey

Harper & Brothers Publishers
New York and London
1919

Madeleine: An Autobiography

Chapter V

Somewhere west of Minneapolis I began to feel a lightening of the burden of grief that I had carried for so many months. Some part of my great love of the out-of-doors came into play as the train rushed through western Minnesota and eastern Dakota; for the young wheat had just begun to thrust its head above the earth, making the prairies one vast, tender, soft cloth of green.

Hour after hour I sat looking out of the car window; but when the fields of growing wheat were left behind us and we had entered into the desolate Bad Lands I pulled down the blind. Their barren desolation brought too vividly to mind the waste desolation of my own heart.

The plains were behind us, and as the train labored upward into the mountains I lay in my berth watching the stars, which did not seem very far away. Somewhere in that vast starlit silence were the children that my heart cried aloud for, and as we ascended the mountain I felt very near to them, but it was a kindly, loving nearness that brought consolation and peace—altogether unlike the haunting presence which was always near me in Chicago.

The beliefs of my childhood were very close to me in those quiet hours. The mountains held a message for me that was as unlike the message of the prairies as they were dissimilar in outline. To me the prairies spoke of the awakening, and the joy of life, the will to dare to do, to live to the utmost. But the mountains were the ramparts of God.

From the sacred Mount of Sinai He had given unto Moses the law for His people. When He would deliver to mankind the sermon which was to ring down through all the ages until man should walk no more on earth, the Great Preacher had gone up into the mountain, thereby placing forever His seal upon the temple of His Father.

A great peace filled my turbulent heart, dispelling the sorrow and bitter pain which for months had darkened my life. To-morrow the aching pain in my arms would be easier to endure, because a train which was bearing me to a city where God was not had passed through the silent places where He dwelt with His little ones.

Chapter VI

In the cab which took me to the hotel where Paul lived I speculated about his probable reception of me. Would he understand and forgive that blow from a grief-crazed mother?

When I registered at the Butte Hotel I tried to ask for him, but my voice failed me. I had been guilty of presumption; he had not asked me to come. Suppose he should refuse to see me? Perhaps he no longer cared for me. No word had come from him since I had driven him from me.

In my room I walked back and forth until I could summon the courage to ring the bell and inquire for him. When the boy came up I asked him to find out when Mr. Martin would be in.

He returned in a few minutes to say that Mr. Martin was out of town and would not return for several weeks.

"Will not return for several weeks." I kept repeating the words after the boy had gone. Here was I, alone in this hole in the top of the world, and Paul would not return for several weeks. The shock of the disappointment was so great that I could not breathe. I walked over to the window and threw it up, but the sulphur-laden air which blew into the room caused me to close it again.

As I stood looking through the window at the hurrying throng in the street I wondered if I had not lost a day somewhere. I had thought it as Sunday, but surely I was mistaken, for men who wore the garb of labor hurried through the streets, carrying dinner-pails in their hands, and Chinamen with laundry baskets on their heads mingled with the crowd of alert-looking business men, debonair gamblers, pasty-faced pimps, overdressed shop-girls, and painted, gaudily garbed harlots.

From a near-by saloon there came the familiar sound of rag-time being pounded out on a wheezy piano, and high above the noise of the street arose the voice of the prompter in the corner dance-hall, "Take your pardner and promenade to the bar."

"The greatest mining-camp on earth," I remembered hearing a well-dressed man in the Pullman asserting about Butte to a party of women from the East. I was not sure what constituted a mining-camp, aside from taking ore out of the ground, but I half expected to see a band of savage Indians ride into that motley throng. I was thoroughly awakened from my self-absorption. I put on my hat and went down into the street to get a nearer view of "the greatest mining-camp on earth."

Although the day *was* Sunday, the big dry-goods stores were the only business houses which were closed. Clothing-stores, groceries, saloons, small dry-goods shops, cigar-stands, dance-halls, and variety shows, elbowing one another and wide open for business, gave a shock to my sense of the fitness of things. I myself did not keep holy the Sabbath day, but my puritanical instincts revolted at the idea of outraging the feelings of those who did.

The strident chords of piano and violin which came from the saloons and dance-halls rivaled the din from the streets. Again rose the stentorian voices of the prompters with their incessant cries of, "Two more couples for the next quadrille," together with the cacophony which came through the swinging-doors of the pool-room: "They're off at Hawthorne! Wildfire in the lead!" "Rubicon against the field!" "It's a hundred-to-one shot you can't win. You're crazy with the heat!" "They're off at Oakland!" "Come on, you Rubicon!" And over all the discordant clamor there hung that awful, thick cloud of sulphur-laden smoke from the smelters, which made one gasp for breath and feel that the city itself with its rampant vice was an outpouring from the slag-pots of hell.

I turned into a side-street to get away from the noise, thankful to find a quiet spot in this horrible place where the sounds of vice did not penetrate, when from a window over my head I heard a loud, clear voice announcing, "She is seventeen, gentlemen, and a black one." I rushed back into the main street, with the belief firm in my mind that they were selling colored women at public auction in that up-stairs room.

When I returned to the hotel I almost walked over a man in the lobby, for my eyes and ears were filled with the sights and sounds of the street. I turned to apologize, and found myself confronting a man I had met some weeks before in Chicago. He had made very little impression on me at the time, but now a stray tomcat from Chicago would have been welcome, and I greeted him as effusively as if he were a long-lost friend.

"What in the world are you doing in Butte?" he inquired. "But pardon me, are you here with some one?"

"I came out to see the wild and woolly West, and I am alone."

"Good!" he answered. "I have to go to Missoula to-morrow, but I can show you the elephant to-night."

"I think I have seen him this afternoon," I said. And we sat down while I told him of my sightseeing tour, personally conducted by myself.

He laughed as I told him of the auction of negro women, and explained that "seventeen and a black one" was a number on a roulette-wheel which had won. I had thought my experiences very thrilling, but the man assured me that I had not seen anything at all; and then, after a dinner in the Butte café, he took me out to see the night life of the town.

We did not tarry long in either of the two first-class houses. They were interesting only because I had not expected to see girls so well dressed nor houses so elaborately furnished in this out-of-the-way place. But the variety shows and the dance-halls were a source of wonder, and the "cribs" a source of horror to me.

I had never seen the seamy side of the underworld in all the five years that I had belonged to it. I had never had any desire to see it, but in Butte it was underfoot at every step and there was no avoiding it even if we had not gone out for the express purpose of sizing it up.

Despite my shuddering horror, the sight fascinated even while it repelled me. It gripped me by the throat and forced me to examine it, even though I was sickened and faint at the horror of it. It filled me with many sad forebodings. I drew my skirts back from contact with the poor creatures who represented this seamy side of prostitution; I could not help it. I wanted to take them by the hand and tell them that I was one of them, but I could not touch them. I could barely touch my lips to the glasses of beer which they served.

In one place where the woman was at least forty my heart was so filled with pity that I urged the man to buy and buy, and when he would no longer order drinks I bought them myself, though I was not in the habit of spending money for booze. But this poor old creature, offering her body for sale, wrung my very heart-strings, and I was determined she should have at least one profitable night. But if my life had depended on it, I could not have fraternized with her, and when we left her place she came to the door and poured forth a stream of filth because I was a "stuck-up parlor-house tart." I did not blame her.

Chapter VII

A few doors farther down the street I heard some one calling my name; I turned, and was surprised to see a woman beckoning me from the doorway of a crib which we had just passed. As we came closer to her I recognized her as a girl who had formerly lived at Allen's.

She caught her breath with a sobbing intake as she shook hands with me, and I was so embarrassed I did not know what to say to her; for girls of the higher class, who have fallen into reduced circumstances, feel their position as keenly as do women in other walks of life; the social gulf between the first-class courtezan and those who have become the dregs of prostitution is as great as the gulf between the sheltered woman in her home and the streetwalker.

When I had last seen this girl, two years before, she had been a star boarder at Allen's and one of the most beautiful women in Chicago. Her face was now so lined with the marks of dissipation and care that she looked ten years older than she had then.

When we had exchanged greetings I introduced my escort, who ordered drinks, and we girls sat down to compare notes, for this sad girl was hungry to talk with some one who had known her in her prosperous days. She begged me not to speak of her when I wrote to old acquaintances in Chicago, and I gave the desired promise.

I was curious to know how she, who had always been so successful, had come to this pass, and she answered my unspoken question by saying:

"It's the same old story, Madeleine. I got stuck on a gambler, who kept me for a while. I am keeping him now. In fact, that is the story of every crib woman. Those who never knew anything different are here because their first lover assigned them the task of supporting him, and the first-class women are here because they have fallen in love with some man whom they have to support if they want to hold him. No girl can meet the expenses in a big parlor-house and keep a man at the same time, even if the landladies would stand for a *macque* in the house, which they won't."

She then explained that she had gone out to Denver after leaving Allen's, and that there she had fallen in with a gambler with a "big roll" who had taken her out of the business and lavished money on her for several months. The previous year they had come out to Butte for the big race meeting, where he had lost all his money. She had pawned her furs and her jewels and given him the money in the hopes of making the "big killing" which every race-track follower looks forward to.

When she had nothing left to pawn she had gone into one of the two first-class houses in Butte. At this point she had interrupted her story to ask me if I intended to "board" in Butte.

"No," I answered, "I came out West to get away from myself; I do not expect to go into a house here."

"Don't try it, Madeleine. It's a tough game in this town. The girls in the big houses are all hundreds of dollars in debt, with no chance to get out. Board is not high, because they pay twenty-five dollars a week straight. All the rest they make is theirs, which would be fine if they cleared anything over their board. But they don't, and the cost of clothes, and laundry, and cleaners' bills, and toilet articles—in fact, everything we use—is double the price it would be in Chicago. The girls are required to dress very elaborately, and when they get in debt they either have to stay or lose everything they have, because the land-ladies in the East will not lend a railway ticket or pay a bill for a girl who has been out here any length of time. They seem to think that the girls in the West, especially in Montana, become tough after they have been here for a short time."

"I do not see why business is not good, if there are only two big houses. I never saw so many people on the streets and in the places of amusement; and at the hotel I saw so many well-dressed, prosperous-looking men that I concluded that any girl who was in business in Butte would have a gold-mine of her own."

"Forget it," said Norma, with an air of disgust.

"If you stay in Butte awhile you will discover that Montana liberality runs to buying booze and playing the races and 'stacking them up' on the high card; never to giving women a good price for their services."

"I don't understand that. In Chicago the men who spend the most money for drinks are those who pay a girl more than the price of the house."

"Well, you will find the contrary in Butte. I have known men to spend a hundred dollars for wine, and then want to stay all night with a girl for nothing. In Butte a girl can be wined and dined and enter-tained to her heart's content, if that kind of thing appeals to her, but she can't earn a living to save her life, nor call her soul her own, for the landladies own them. That's the reason why the first-class women go to the devil so fast when they get stuck in Butte. Take my advice and keep a little cozy corner in your pocketbook for the price of a ticket back to Chicago."

"I don't want to hurt your feelings, Norma, but I do not see how you can stand it. Think of going to bed with one of these unwashed beasts who are tramping up and down these alleys; think of sitting with your face in a window and having them pass along leering and peering, as if you were a part of a live-stock exhibition; and then think of receiving a dollar for entertaining the beasts."

"It isn't the dollar for our personal services that counts; it is the drink-money. We charge a dollar a bottle for beer, just as the big houses do. The saloon that serves us takes twenty-five cents and we keep the remainder. We sometimes make a touch when a man is drunk and we think we can get away with it."

My escort, who had been listening with an expression of disgust on his face, now arose and cut short the conversation. We bade the girl good night, but after we had walked half a block I asked him to turn back with me; I wanted to ask Norma to have breakfast with me the following morning.

When we reached her window she was eagerly talking to a dirty, big laborer who was so drunk that he rolled from side to side, although he tried to steady himself against the window-casement.

Norma appeared embarrassed at having us see her companion, and the creature reached forth his dirty hands to grasp at me, but my escort prevented him. I gave the invitation, which was accepted, and I asked Norma to name the place, since I did not know the town. She made the appointment for two o'clock at the Chaquamegon and we hastened away, leaving her to "rope in" the drunk if she could.

We walked on in silence, for I was too heartsick for words, and my companion did not interrupt my thoughts until we turned into the main street and passed a decent-looking restaurant.

"Let's go in here and have something to eat before we go to bed," he proposed.

At the table he looked so long and earnestly at me that I grew nervous under his gaze. "Why do you stare at me so?" I asked.

"Because I am trying to understand you, but you are too much for me. You remember the night I took you 'hopping' in Chicago a few weeks ago?"

"Yes," I answered, "but what of it, and why do you say I am too much for you?"

"It struck me that night that you were a haughty dame and a darn poor mixer. Or, as one of the other girls in the party said, you were not a good fellow. Yet here you pick up a low crib woman who by her own voluntary confession is a thief, and you invite her to break bread with you. I am wondering why you did it."

"I am sure I don't know," I answered, "but it all seemed so horrible and so hopeless to me, to think of a girl like Norma living in this way. She is only twenty-six and this is the beginning of the end for her. I can't express what I feel about it; my emotions and my thoughts are too chaotic; but this horrible town, and these awful streets of vice, with the women displayed like so much merchandise in the windows, while the endless procession of leering men of all races—whites, negroes, half-breed Indians, and Chinese—pass them in review, fills me with terror. Think of Norma having physical contact with that great, unwashed brute she was talking with when we came back to her. There are no depths of poverty nor stress of circumstances which could make me a thief, but I am not so sure that I would not become a murderess if I were forced to consort with such creatures. I thought I knew all the horrors of prostitution, but I have learned to-night that I know very little about them. I have learned that there is a sheltered class, and that I belong to it, yet I would have laughed yesterday had any one spoken of 'sheltered prostitutes.'"

"But you can't do anything for this girl. Why do you harrow your own soul by association with her? The best thing for you to do is to break your engagement and forget her."

"Never! I know I can't help her, but I must stretch forth my hand; if not to draw her back, at any rate to let her know that somebody cares. It may be a premonition of what is coming to me that makes me want to be kind. I cannot say. It is something I have never felt before."

"Madeleine, it is a premonitory birth-pang of the social consciousness."

"What is the social consciousness?" I asked. "I never heard of it."

"It is summed up in the question you are now asking yourself. 'Am I my sister's keeper?'"

Chapter VIII

The iniquities of Butte lay as heavily on my heart as if I alone had been responsible for them. Here was no kid-gloved vice with a silken veil across its face; but vice naked, raw, and rampant. The noxious fumes from the smelter became as pure ozone when compared with the vitiated moral atmosphere.

Day after day I lingered, fascinated yet frightened, in this upper chamber of hell, my soul racked and agonized by conflicting and contending emotions.

From the hotel clerk I learned that Paul Martin had gone to a remote part of the state on business connected with placer-mines in which he was interested, and that he would not return for several weeks. I wrote to him announcing my presence in Butte and telling him that I had come to Montana for the purpose of begging his forgiveness.

In great trepidation I awaited his answer, which came in the form of a telegram. "There is nothing to forgive," it read. "Come to me at once. Am anxiously waiting for you."

I made inquiries about the place, and learned that it was to be reached by a stage journey of seventy miles from the nearest railroad point, from which station the telegram had been sent.

I was wild with delight at the prospect of seeing Paul again. The thought of being alone with him filled my heart with a glow of joy. The mental picture which I drew of the tiny hamlet in the mountains appealed to my imagination as an ideal setting for our reconciliation. I was still at the age of romance and looked eagerly forward to the proposed journey by stage, not daunted by the stories of its discomforts.

The malodorous, ugly town held me in its grip. I wandered through its hideous streets, and in and out of the dance-halls and variety shows, buying drinks which I did not consume, but because it was the thing to do. Since there was nothing in my manner nor appearance which proclaimed me a member of the profession, I was an object of much curiosity to the habitués and of audible speculation on the part of the inmates.

I spoke only in answer to those who addressed me, but these were few, for my manner did not invite approach.

Returning to the hotel, I made futile efforts to reproduce in drawing some of the scenes which had held me spellbound, and equally futile attempts to put my impressions into words. My impotency to grasp and my inability to portray this living melodrama which was being enacted before my eyes caused me many bitter tears.

Why had nature given me the power to feel these things in every fiber of my being and then denied me the ability to express myself? I paced the floor in an agony which wrung great drops of sweat from my body, my hands clenching and literally tearing at whatever came within their grasp, as if in this senseless manner I could rend the invisible and intangible bonds which held my mind enthralled.

And because I, an untrained girl of twenty-two, could not produce a masterpiece I destroyed my work which mocked my puny efforts at self-expression and thereafter gave up the attempt. "A mustard seed which refused to grow because it could not become a stately oak."

In the early morning of a gloomy day I drove through the dirty streets on my way to the train which was to bear me out of the city which had gone mad of its own lust. Two days later I was in the heart of God's great out-of-doors with the man I loved, and Butte with its raw and rampant vice had become to me as the memory of a bad dream.

Chapter IX

The little mining-town in which I was to spend several weeks was one of the first settlements in Montana, and in the early 'nineties it still preserved its primitive appearance. Except for the dredges on the creek, which had replaced the old-time rockers and gold-pans, everything about the camp still spoke eloquently of the early days when gold had first been discovered.

The straggling main street of the village which stretched out along the creek was lined on either side with great log buildings. Stores, residences, saloons, and the two rival hotels were all of logs. Many of these buildings were whitewashed, and one enterprising hotelkeeper had erected a brick addition to his log structure. This building presented a most incongruous appearance and formed a blot upon the landscape.

The one other street—which was in reality a road—led up through a cañon which bore the euphonious name of Hangman's Gulch.

When questioned about the name, the old-timers told me many thrilling stories of the events which led up to giving this beautiful cañon such a gruesome name. While their stories were widely at variance as to detail, they were agreed upon the fact that a former sheriff of that section had played the dual role of guardian of the place and leader of the road-agents who preyed upon the gold-seekers.

When the Vigilantes had secured undeniable proof of this double-dealing they relentlessly hunted down the man and his gang. Those members of it who were not killed in fights with the Vigilantes were captured and hanged in this gulch, the gibbet being a log beam which projected from the cabin occupied by one of the band.

Cattle-stealing had also been one of the early industries, and neither cattle-stealing nor highway robbery had entirely fallen into desuetude. As Butte was Montana's chief hotbed of vice, so this section was still the most lawless part of the state.

One desperado, who belonged to a family of "bad men," and women hardly less desperate, had been tried for nearly every crime on the calendar, including arson, murder, and incest. But, because of the fear of reprisals by his lawless family, few could be found to give evidence against him, and no jury could or would convict him. A few years later, when he tried his hand at counterfeiting, the United States performed the duty which the state dared not, and he was sent to prison for a long term of years.

As the name of Hangman's Gulch commemorated a phase of the history of the village and the state, so the name of Road-agents' Rock bore evidence of the early activities of this class of criminals. And the private conveyances which now carried out the gold-dust still went through to the railroad under the guard of armed men who gave Road-agents' Rock a wide berth.

The romance of the West held me in its grip, and to me this isolated hamlet in the mountains presented the most fascinating phase of Western life.

I stayed in the same hotel where Paul was living, but I seldom saw him before supper-time, for his days were busy days, and he was up and gone long before I responded to the call of the last bell for breakfast. Every night I resolved to join him at breakfast, but I was not accustomed to undisturbed slumbers nor to early rising. Now, when I went to bed, I wanted to kneel down and thank God that there was no lecherous man present to awaken me at his will, and the health-giving air of the mountains made me sleep like a little child.

I was an object of much curiosity to the natives, both as to my social status and my occupation. They were not long in discovering that I was Paul Martin's girl, and they soon concluded that I must be an Eastern school-teacher, for no one else could possibly be so eager for information nor ask so many questions. I rode horseback over all the trails in the country, dismounting to explore every abandoned mining-shaft or prospect-hole into which I could descend, risking life and limb upon the rotting timbers, and coming back with the inevitable questions upon my lips.

On a bleak, bare hill back of Hangman's Gulch I discovered an old burying-ground, which had long since fallen into disuse. I tore away the weeds which had overgrown the head-boards and found on every one which was as yet decipherable the statement that the deceased had been massacred by the Indians in the early 'sixties. Again I came back to the village with my everlasting "Why?"

Why had they buried those persons on the top of that bleak hill? Why had they not buried them in the valley? But even the old-timers who had survived the massacre could not answer my question.

But the place of all places that I had the most curiosity about was the creek from which the dredges brought up the treasure, and that was forbidden ground.

I spent two months in this place in the mountains, and they were among the happiest months of my life, although my heart and my arms still longed for the child who was gone. Olga had been right when she had referred to Paul as an "understanding" man. When I tried to explain my actions in Chicago and to beg his forgiveness, he only smiled at the idea that there was anything to forgive, and we never discussed the matter again, though we often talked of my little boy. Paul had much of the paternal instinct, and he understood many things of which we never spoke. It was this instinct that made him shield me and shelter me in the bitter years that afterward came to me. There were many times when he ceased to be my lover, but never did he cease to be a father when a father was what I most needed. We hear much of the maternal instinct which causes a woman to look upon the man she loves as her child as well as her lover, but I have known men in whom this instinct of parenthood was equally strong, and Paul was one of them.

We spent the long summer evenings together, talking over every conceivable subject but the one uppermost in my mind, that of our future together.

I spoke to Paul of my long-cherished dream of studying art, but he was filled with the idea of sending me to college. This idea did not appeal to me for several reasons. My hand was never at ease except when I was striving to portray the life that I saw around me. I had never received any training and my drawings were crude, but this was the one thing within myself that gave me the greatest pleasure.

Then, again, nothing could ever induce me to confess to Paul that I had not even been through grammar-school, for this deficiency in my education seemed to me a shameful thing. Through self-study I had acquired a wide knowledge of good literature and general history, but I could not have given the definition of many of the subjects required to enter high-school, to say nothing of trying to break into college.

On one thing I was determined: Paul should never know of my wretched childhood. And because of this determination eventually I built for myself a wall which kept me apart from him through many years; for when once he had conceived the idea of educating me he reverted to it again and again, until he thought that nothing but sheer perversity on my part prevented my going to college.

It was not strange that Paul failed to understand, for he had no way of knowing that to my mind poverty and ignorance were the cardinal sins, and that these accompaniments of my unhappy childhood were to be concealed at the cost of my future happiness, if indeed that were the price of secrecy.

However, I was now so happy with him that I was ready to dismiss the future. I snatched every moment of happiness until I could have cried aloud for joy. But in my supreme moment there came to me a haunting thought that would not be dismissed, try as I would to banish it. When I tried to formulate my thoughts and express to Paul the thing that troubled me I could not make him understand, because I myself did not understand the meaning of many things that are now clear to me.

The wonderful out-of-door life that I was living brought to me such a sense of the Infinite that there were moments when I felt that I stood in the presence of God. Oftentimes after a dash across the uplands I would dismount from my horse and stand looking at the panorama spread out "where the hand of God had hung it"; and then I would kneel down and press my face to the grass, the rocks, and the sage-brush.

But when these brief moments of bliss had passed they were followed by a reaction of sadness, for I stood in that Presence convicted not only of my own sins, but of the sins of all the sinners that I had ever known. And several times I found myself asking aloud, "Am I my brother's keeper?"

In some way the awful conditions which prevailed in Butte had awakened in me a sense of personal responsibility. I had always been deeply conscious of my own transgressions, but only as they tended to destroy me. I was not a "good mixer" and I had always held aloof from most of the women of my class, conscious of the sense of superiority. But since I had seen the dance-hall girls and the crib women of Butte I was filled with a great desire to take them all in my arms, to soothe them and comfort them and heal them.

Poor little fool that I was, I could not even heal myself.

About this time I received a letter telling me the story of one of the girls that I had known in Chicago. She had been, apparently, so corrupt that no thought of her redemption had ever entered the minds of those who knew her. Two years before she had startled us all by announcing that she was going to quit the business. We gave her a month as the longest possible time in which she could remain decent, but now at the end of two years she was still making good.

Of all the girls that I had ever known, she was the last one whom I should have expected to reform. But there was no doubt about it. When I read the story of her redintegration I began to realize something of the wonderful recuperative powers of the human soul.

Then I began to see, as through a glass darkly, that every fallen woman who is restored to decency means more than an individual redeemed. It means the healing of a contagious ulcer on the social body.

I expressed this thought to Paul, but he had the lie of the ages at his tongue's end, "Prostitution is a necessary evil." To be sure, he did not want me to be one of the burnt-offerings, but another man's sweetheart could serve without in the least disturbing his peace of mind.

Chapter X

At the end of two months, when Paul went back to Butte, he took me with him. I had talked of returning to Chicago, but he wanted me to remain with him for another month. He still purposed to send me to college; and I still purposed to circumvent him, without giving the true reason.

I hoped and prayed that he would renew the proposal that he had made to me in Kansas City, but he said nothing which could lead me to believe that he still thought of it. I came to the conclusion that however much he cared for me he had no intention of again asking me to marry him.

I was to remain in a hotel in Butte, though not the one in which Paul was living, for we wanted to avoid scandal. I did not see him every day, as I had in the mountains, for in the city he had his own circle into which he could not take me. There was no longer the wonderful out-of-doors, for the sulphurous atmosphere of Butte precluded the enjoyment of open-air exercises. Time hung heavily on my hands, so that when I met an old acquaintance from Chicago I made the excuse to myself that Paul had neglected me for his society friends and that I was free to accept this man's invitation to dinner.

As we sat at dinner in the café of the leading hotel my companion began a long-drawn-out story of a poker game in which he had sat the night before in this hotel.

This big game was in progress nightly and "the ceiling was the limit." The man asked me if I would like to witness the game. Women are barred from the card-room, but, as he remarked, "Everything goes in Butte, if you know the ropes." He could take me in if I cared to go.

I had no interest whatever in a poker game, but one thing was much like another in Butte. I had let myself "in for it" by going out with this man, and I thought it would be easier to shake him if he became interested in the game; accordingly, I accompanied him to the card-room.

After a brief parley at the door we were admitted to the room, and my escort began to explain the intricacies of "stud" poker.

Fifteen minutes after we had entered the room he had removed his coat, bought a stack of chips, and become oblivious to my presence. Since I was accustomed to being made much of by the men who were my friends, I was not flattered at being ignored for a poker game.

I was wondering if I could not slip out unobserved, when one of the players who was the greatest winner handed me a stack of chips, saying as he did so, "Try your luck, kid."

Instantly an onlooker offered to coach me, and I took the seat of a player who had "gone broke" a few minutes before.

The players had been drinking whisky, but some one ordered a bottle of champagne in my honor and the game went on. I did not know one card from another, so far as their value in the game went. When I got a five-spot in the hole, and on the next turn of the card drew a trey, the man who had constituted himself my tutor in the game told me to throw them in the discard, and I obeyed.

My stack of chips were worth twenty dollars, but they meant nothing to me, since they had cost me nothing. A few minutes later, when I had a nine-spot in the hole, my tutor told me to "stay," and I pushed in a bunch of chips, unconsciously raising the ante. This struck the other players as good sportsmanship on my part, and they all "stayed" with me.

On the next turn of the cards I drew a king. The dealer said, "You are high with the king; it's your bet first," and I bet the remainder of my chips. The other players called me, and the game went on.

On the next turn I drew another nine, but could not bet again, since I was "all in." One man had two jacks in sight, and was making side bets with another player. On the fourth turn this man drew an ace and "bet his head off." His opponent dropped out, and when the dealer turned over the last card I drew the third nine. I had almost forgotten my escort's existence, when he recalled himself to my attention by telling me that I had won a "fat pot" and it was up to me to buy a bottle of wine.

I bought the wine, and then because I was winner the game assumed great interest for me. When I arose from the table at four o'clock in the morning I was two hundred and twenty-five dollars ahead of the game.

This was partly due to "fool's luck" and partly to the generosity of the other players, who could have broken me if they liked.

When I returned to my room I found Paul, white with jealousy and rage, pacing up and down the room. When I came in he walked up to me and, placing his hands on my shoulders, said in an even voice, though his eyes snapped like steel, "Madeleine, where in the world have you been, and is there anything you want to tell me?"

I knew what he meant, but that was not the thing that I had to tell. I related the experiences of the night, and instantly his face softened as he realized the truth of my story. However, he at once began to lecture me on the evils of gambling. "This vice is worse than whisky, Madeleine; promise me that you will never play again."

I was ready to give the promise, for I did not think that I had been caught in the toils, and Paul kissed me and went out.

Since "everything went" in Butte, he could visit my room whenever he liked, or stay as long as he liked, and I was sorry that he had not chosen to remain. But I did not waste much time in thinking about it, for daylight was breaking as I tumbled into bed.

A few days later, disregarding my promise to Paul, I went "down the line" and won a hundred dollars at roulette, and with this winning I placed upon myself shackles which held my soul in bondage for many years. I played poker, roulette, faro, the races, or anything else on which money could be staked. There were times when I would have sold Paul for a stack of red chips.

I had escaped the usual vices of my class, liquor and drugs, only to fall a victim to as great an evil.

Chapter XI

When Paul discovered that I had broken my word to him he was furious and he gave me a curtain-lecture that left my ears tingling. I had violated my word to him and he found it very hard to overlook. A little later he relented of his harshness, though I richly deserved all that he had said.

I renewed my promise never to gamble again, and once more matters ran smoothly between us. But a week later I heard of a system to "beat the wheel," and I went into one of the open gambling-houses and lost every dollar I had. Paul had kept me abundantly supplied with money, and on that day he had given me fifty dollars. When I left the gambling-house I did not have the price of my dinner.

It was the first time that I had ever been completely broke since I had been in the "business," and I could hardly realize that I did not have a penny in the world. I dared not confess to Paul that I had again broken my word to him.

I could easily have made more money if I had chosen to take the easiest way, but with the picture of Paul in the background the thought of doing so was abhorrent to me. At any rate, I would not deceive him in that way. I pawned a valuable ring, and tried to keep my peccadillo a secret from him.

I attempted to appear unconcerned, but I did not succeed in deceiving Paul. He knew that something was troubling me, and then he missed my solitaire, for he had a great admiration for my hands and a fashion of caressing them.

This time he sat very silent after I had confessed the truth. Then he kissed me very gently and went out without saying anything. In an hour he called me up to say that he was sending me some money by messenger and that I had better redeem my ring.

He stayed away for three days, and I was in an agony fearing that I had lost him. Then I received a note from him saying that he would not again ask me not to gamble, since he did not believe in putting a premium on lying. But he hoped that I would feel free to tell him the truth and to come to him when I needed money instead of going to a pawnshop.

I soon returned to the roulette-wheel, though why I played was as great a mystery to me as it was to the onlookers.

It must have been for the sake of the game, for, in the words of one of the interested bystanders who watched me break the bank and then lose hundreds of dollars against a twenty-dollar bill that the dealer took from his pocket: "You were not playing to win. You were only trying to see if you would keep your own money or give it to the dealer."

Then, because I would not ask Paul to keep on paying my gambling debts, and because I would not remain with him and make money in the easiest way, I left him and went East again.

For the next three or four years I wandered over the face of the earth, always finding that the place I was in was the one place where I did not want to be.

I saw them all, the "lost sisterhood" of the nations. I met them in Europe and in the Orient; in Canada and in Mexico. And I met more American women than those of any other nation, for they were in every city and every land that I visited.

I met the public prostitute, the clandestine prostitute, and the occasional prostitute. I met the trusting girl who had been betrayed, and the unfaithful wife. I met the college woman, and the illiterate child of the slums. I met the deserted wife and the wife of the profligate; the girl from the sheltered home and the girl who had been allowed to run wild; the girl who had sold her honor for bread, and the girl who had sold it for luxury and fine clothes. I met the girl who should have been a nun, and those others who were "predestined by ancient conditions" for the life of a harlot.

But the one girl I never met in all these years and in all the cities and the countries that I visited was the pure girl who had been trapped and violated and sold into slavery, and held a prisoner unable to effect her escape—the so-called "white slave."

Because I had more intelligence than the average harlot I was enabled to go into many places that they could not enter, and to make money in many ways not open to them. But whenever I found myself up against a blank wall I came back to Paul or he came to my rescue.

At length I went to live with him, and after this I gambled no more. For one year I had much happiness, mingled with much sorrow and bitterness; for we belonged to different spheres of life, and we had but the one point of contact, our love for each other. And that was not great enough to cover the multitude of disparities between us.

Bibliography

Albertine, Susan. "Industrialization." In *The Oxford Companion to Women's Writing in the United States,* edited by Cathy N. Davidson, Linda Wagner-Martin, and Elizabeth Ammons, 421–23. New York: Oxford University Press, 1995.

Ammons, Elizabeth. *Conflicting Stories: American Women Writers at the Turn into the Twentieth Century.* New York: Oxford University Press, 1991.

Andrews, William L. *To Tell a Free Story: The First Century of Afro-American Autobiography, 1760–1865.* Urbana: University of Illinois Press, 1986.

Andrews, William L., et al., eds. *Sisters of the Spirit: Three Black Women's Autobiographies of the Nineteenth Century.* Bloomington: Indiana University Press, 1986.

Anonymous. [Negro Nurse] "More Slavery at the South." *The Independent* 72 (January 25, 1912): 196–200.

———. [Northern Woman] "Observations of the Southern Race Feeling" *The Independent* 56 (March 17, 1904): 594–99.

———. [Southern Colored Woman] "The Race Problem—An Autobiography." *The Independent* 56 (March 17, 1904): 586–89.

———. [Southern White Woman] "Experiences of the Race Problem." *The Independent* 56 (March 17, 1904): 590–94.

Antin, Mary. *The Promised Land.* Boston: Houghton Mifflin, 1912.

Austin, Mary Hunter. *Earth Horizon: Autobiography.* Boston: Houghton Mifflin, 1932.

———. *The Land of Little Rain.* Boston: Houghton Mifflin, 1903.

Baepler, Paul, ed. *White Slaves, African Masters: An Anthology of American Barbary Captivity Narratives.* Chicago: University of Chicago Press, 1999.

Bataille, Gretchen M., and Kathleen M. Sands. *American Indian Women Telling Their Lives.* Lincoln: University of Nebraska Press, 1984.

Bauer, Dale M., and Philip Gould. *The Cambridge Companion to Nineteenth-Century American Women's Writing.* Cambridge and New York: Cambridge University Press, 2001.

Bergland, Betty. "Postmodernism and the Autobiographical Subject: Reconstructing the 'Other.'" In *Autobiography and Postmodernism,* edited by Kathleen Ashley, Leigh Gilmore, and Gerald Peters, 130–66. Amherst: University of Massachusetts Press, 1994.

Bloom, Lynn Z. "I Write for Myself and Strangers": Private Diaries as Public Documents. In *Inscribing the Daily: Critical Essays on Women's Diaries,* edited by Suzanne L. Bunkers and Cynthia A. Huff, 23–37. Amherst: University of Massachusetts Press, 1996.

Boardman, Kathleen and Gioia Woods, eds. *Western Subjects: Autobiographical Writing in the North American West.* Salt Lake City: University of Utah Press, 2004.

Boyle, Eleanor, ed. *The Terrific Kemble: A Victorian Self-Portrait from the Writings of Fanny Kemble.* London: H. Hamilton, 1978.

Brumble, H. David. *American Indian Autobiography.* Berkeley: University of California Press, 1988.

Buell, Lawrence. "Autobiography in the American Renaissance." In *American Autobiography: Retrospect and Prospect,* edited by Paul John Eakin, 47–69. Madison: University of Wisconsin Press, 1991.

Bunkers, Suzanne L., ed. *Diaries of Girls and Women : A Midwestern American Sampler.* Madison: University of Wisconsin Press, 2001.

Bunkers, Suzanne L., and Cynthia Anne Huff, eds. *Inscribing the Daily: Critical Essays on Women's Diaries.* Amherst: University of Massachusetts Press, 1996.

Bush, Laura L. *Faithful Transgressions in the American West: Six Twentieth-Century Mormon Women's Autobiographical Acts.* Logan: Utah State University Press, 2004.

Buss, Helen M. *Mapping Our Selves: Canadian Women's Autobiography.* Montréal: McGill-Queen's University Press, 1993.

———. *Repossessing the World: Reading Memoirs by Contemporary Women.* Waterloo, Ontario: Wilfrid Laurier University Press, 2002.

Buss, Helen M., and Marlene Kadar, eds. *Working in Women's Archives: Researching Women's Private Literature and Archival Documents.* Waterloo, Ontario: Wilfrid Laurier University Press, 2001.

Butler, Rose. *An Authentic Statement of the Case and Conduct of Rose Butler, who was tried, convicted, and executed for the crime of arson.* New York: Broderick and Ritter, 1819.

Carlisle, Marcia. "Introduction." In *Madeleine: An Autobiography,* by "Madeleine," v–xxviii. New York: Persea Books, 1986

Cary, Richard. "Introduction." In *The Uncollected Short Stories of Sarah Orne Jewett,* edited by Richard Cary, iii–xviii. Waterville, ME: Colby College Press, 1971.

Casper, Scott E. *Constructing American Lives: Biography and Culture in Nineteenth-Century America.* Chapel Hill: University of North Carolina Press, 1999.

Cogan, Frances. *All-American Girl: The Ideal of Real Womanhood in Mid-Nineteenth-Century America.* Athens: University of Georgia Press, 1989.

Culley, Margo, ed. *American Women's Autobiography: Fea(s)ts of Memory.* Madison: University of Wisconsin Press, 1992.

Culley, Margo. *A Day at a Time : The Diary Literature of American Women from 1764 to the Present.* New York: Feminist Press at the City University of New York, 1985.

Davidson, Cathy N., and Jessamyn Hatcher. "Introduction." In *No More Separate Spheres!: A Next Wave American Studies Reader,* edited by Cathy N. Davidson and Jessamyn Hatcher, 7–26. Durham, N.C.: Duke University Press, 2002.

Davidson, Cathy N., Linda Wagner-Martin, and Elizabeth Ammons, eds. *The Oxford Companion to Women's Writing in the United States.* New York: Oxford University Press, 1995.

Derounian-Stodola, Kathryn Zabelle. "Captivity and the Literary Imagination." In *The Cambridge Companion to Nineteenth-Century American Women's Writing,* edited by Dale M. Bauer and Philip Gould, 105–121. Cambridge and New York: Cambridge University Press, 2001.

———, ed. *Women's Indian Captivity Narratives.* New York: Penguin Books, 1998.

Dobkin, Marjorie Housepian, ed. *The Making of a Feminist: Early Journals and Letters of M. Carey Thomas.* Kent, Ohio: Kent State University Press, 1979.

Douglass-Chin, Richard J. *Preacher Woman Sings the Blues: The Autobiographies of Nineteenth-Century African American Evangelists.* Columbia: University of Missouri Press, 2001.

Eakin, Paul John, ed. *American Autobiography: Retrospect and Prospect.* Madison: University of Wisconsin Press, 1991.

Encyclopedia of Life Writing, edited by Margaretta Jolly. London and Chicago: Fitzroy Dearborn, 2001.

Fabian, Ann. *The Unvarnished Truth: Personal Narratives in Nineteenth-Century America.* Berkeley: University of California Press, 2000.

Faderman, Lillian. *Surpassing the Love of Men: Romantic Friendship and Love between Women from the Renaissance to the Present.* New York: Morrow, 1981.

Far, Sui Sin. "Leaves from the Mental Portfolio of an Eurasian." *The Independent* (January 21, 1909): 125–32.

———. Sui Sin Far, the Half Chinese Writer, Tells of Her Career." *Boston Globe,* May 5, 1912, morning edition, 31.126.

Fisher, Dexter. *The Third Woman: Minority Women Writers of the United States.* Boston: Houghton Mifflin, 1980.

Fuller, Margaret, et al. *Memoirs of Margaret Fuller Ossoli.* Boston: Phillips, Sampson and Co., 1852.

———. *The Portable Margaret Fuller,* edited by Mary Kelley. New York: Penguin Books, 1994.

Furnas, J. C. *Fanny Kemble: Leading Lady of the Nineteenth-Century Stage: A Biography.* New York: Dial Press, 1982.

Graulich, Melody, and Elizabeth Klimasmith, eds. *Exploring Lost Borders: Critical Essays on Mary Austin.* Reno: University of Nevada Press, 1999.

Hall, David D. *Cultures of Print: Essays in the History of the Book.* Amherst: University of Massachusetts Press, 1996.

Halverson, Cathryn. *Maverick Autobiographies: Women Writers and the American West, 1900–1936.* Madison: University of Wisconsin Press, 2004.

Haywood, Chanta M. *Prophesying Daughters: Black Women Preachers and the Word, 1823–1913.* Columbia: University of Missouri Press, 2003.

Holly, Carol. "Nineteenth-Century Autobiographies of Affiliation: The Case of Catharine Sedgwick and Lucy Larcom." In *American Autobiography: Retrospect and Prospect,* edited by Paul John Eakin, 216–34. Madison: University of Wisconsin Press, 1991.

Horowitz, Helen Lefkowitz. *The Power and Passion of M. Carey Thomas.* New York: Alfred A. Knopf, 1994.

Huff, Cynthia. "Textual Boundaries: Space in Nineteenth-Century Women's Manuscript Diaries." In *Inscribing the Daily: Critical Essays on Women's Diaries,* edited by Suzanne L. Bunkers and Cynthia Anne Huff, 123–38. Amherst: University of Massachusetts Press, 1996.

Humez, Jean M. *Harriet Tubman: The Life and the Life Stories.* Madison: University of Wisconsin Press, 2003.

Jemison, Mary. *A Narrative of the Life of Mrs. Mary Jemison.* Edited by James E. Seaver. 1824. Ann Arbor, Mich.: Allegany Press, 1967.

Jewel, Adele M. "A Brief Narrative of the Life of Mrs. Adele M. Jewel." Ann Arbor, Mich.: Dr. Chase's Steam Printing House, 1869.

Jewett, Sarah Orne. "Looking Back on Girlhood," *Youth's Companion* 65 (January 7, 1892): 5–6.

Kaplan, Amy. "Manifest Domesticity." *American Literature,* 70, no. 3 (Sept, 1998): 581–606.

Kelley, Mary. *Empire of Reason: Women, Education, and Public Life.* Chapel Hill, North Carolina: University of North Carolina Press, 2006.

———. "Introduction." In *The Portable Margaret Fuller,* edited by Mary Kelley, ix–xxxiv. New York: Penguin Books, 1994.

———. *Private Woman, Public Stage: Literary Domesticity in Nineteenth-Century America.* 1984. Chapel Hill: University of North Carolina Press, 2002.

Kemble, Fanny. *Journal of a Residence on a Georgian Plantation in 1838–1839.* New York: Harper & Brothers, 1863.

———. *The Terrific Kemble: A Victorian Self-Portrait from the Writings of Fanny Kemble,* edited by Eleanor Boyle. London: H. Hamilton, 1978.

Kerber, Linda K. "Separate Spheres, Female Worlds, Woman's Place: The Rhetoric of Women's History." In *No More Separate Spheres!: A Next Wave American Studies Reader,* edited by Cathy N. Davidson and Jessamyn Hatcher, 29–65. Durham, N.C.: Duke University Press, 2002.

Kilcup, Karen L., and Thomas S. Edwards, eds. *Jewett and Her Contemporaries: Reshaping the Canon.* Gainesville: University of Florida Press, 1999.

Kolodny, Annette. "Inventing a Feminist Discourse: Rhetoric and Resistance in Margaret Fuller's *Woman in the Nineteenth Century.*" In *Reclaiming Rhetorica: Women in the Rhetorical Tradition,* edited by Andrea A. Lunsford, 137–66. Pittsburgh: University of Pittsburgh Press, 1995.

———. *The Land before Her: Fantasy and Experience of the American Frontiers, 1630–1860.* Chapel Hill: University of North Carolina Press, 1984.

Kraditor, Aileen S. *Up from the Pedestal: Selected Writings in the History of American Feminism.* Chicago: Quadrangle Books, 1968.

Krentz, Christopher. "Introduction." In *A Mighty Change: An Anthology of Deaf American Writing, 1816–1864,* edited by Christopher Krentz, xi–xxxiii. Washington, DC: Gallaudet University Press, 2000

Krupat, Arnold. "Native American Autobiography and the Synecdochic Self." In *American Autobiography: Retrospect and Prospect,* edited by Paul John Eakin, 171–94. Madison: University of Wisconsin Press, 1991.

Larcom, Lucy: "Beginning to Work." In *A New England Girlhood: Outlined from Memory.* New York: Houghton Mifflin; Cambridge: Riverside Press, 1889.

Lee, Jarena. *The Life and Religious Experience of Jarena Lee, a Colored Lady, Giving an Account of Her Call to Preach the Gospel.* 1836. Cincinnati: Printed and Published for the Author, 1839.

Lee, Rachel C. *The Americas of Asian American Literature: Gendered Fictions of Nation and Transnation.* Princeton: Princeton University Press, 1999.

———. "Journalistic Representations of Asian Americans and Literary Responses, 1910–1920." In *An Interethnic Companion to Asian American Literature,* edited by King-Kok Cheung, 249–73. New York: Cambridge University Press, 1997.

Ling, Amy. *Between Worlds: Women Writers of Chinese Ancestry.* New York: Pergamon Press, 1990.

———. "Creating One's Self: The Eaton Sisters." In *Reading the Literatures of Asian America,* edited by Shirley Geok-lin Lim and Amy Ling, 305–18. Philadelphia: Temple University Press, 1992.

MacLane, Mary. "Mary MacLane Meets the Vampire on the Isle of Treacherous Delights." *Butte Evening News,* March 27, 1910.

———. *Tender Darkness: A Mary MacLane Anthology.* Edited by Elisabeth Pruitt. Belmont, CA: Abernathy and Brown, 1993.

———. *The Story of Mary MacLane.* 1902. Helena, MT: Riverbend, 2002.

"Madeleine." *Madeleine: An Autobiography.* 1919. New York: Persea Books, 1986. 206–239.

Mobley, Marilyn Sanders. *Folk Roots and Mythic Wings in Sarah Orne Jewett and Toni Morrison: The Cultural Function of Narrative.* Baton Rouge: Louisiana State University Press, 1991.

Myerson, Joel. *Critical Essays on Margaret Fuller.* Boston: G. K. Hall, 1980.

Namias, June. *White Captives: Gender and Ethnicity on the American Frontier.* Chapel Hill: University of North Carolina Press, 1993.

Nelson, Dana D. "Representative/Democracy: Presidents, Democratic Management, and the Unfinished Business of Male Sentimentalism." In *No More Separate Spheres!: A Next Wave American Studies Reader,* edited by Cathy N. Davidson and Jessamyn Hatcher, 325–54. Durham, N.C.: Duke University Press, 2002.

———. "Women in Public." In *The Cambridge Companion to Nineteenth-Century American Women's Writing,* edited by Dale M. Bauer and Philip Gould, 38–68. Cambridge: Cambridge University Press, 2001.

Padilla, Genaro M. *My History, Not Yours: The Formation of Mexican American Autobiography.* Madison: University of Wisconsin Press, 1993.

Painter, Nell Irvin. *Sojourner Truth: A Life, a Symbol.* New York: W. W. Norton and Company, 1996.

Peake McDonald, Cornelia. *A Woman's Civil War: A Diary with Reminiscences of the War from March 1862.* Edited by Minrose C. Gwin. Madison: University of Wisconsin Press, 1992.

Pease, Donald E. *Visionary Compacts: American Renaissance Writings in Cultural Context.* Madison: University of Wisconsin Press, 1987.

Pérez, Eulalia. "An Old Woman and Her Recollections." In *Three Memoirs of Mexican California.* As recorded in 1877 by Thomas Savage. Edited and translated by Vivian C. Fisher, 74–82. Berkeley: Friends of the Bancroft Library, University of California at Berkeley, 1988.

Pierce, Yolanda. "African-American Women's Spiritual Narratives." In *The Cambridge Companion to Nineteenth-Century American Women's Writing*, edited by Dale M. Bauer and Philip Gould, 244–61. Cambridge: Cambridge University Press, 2001.

Pruitt, Elisabeth, ed. *Tender Darkness: A Mary MacLane Anthology*. Belmont, Calif.: Abernathy & Brown, 1993.

Quimby, Harriet. "How I Made My First Big Flight Abroad: My Flight Across the English Channel." *Fly Magazine*. Leslie-Judge Co., June 1912.

Rowe, John Carlos. *Literary Culture and U.S. Imperialism: From the Revolution to World War II*. New York: Oxford University Press, 2000.

Ruoff, A. LaVonne Brown. *American Indian Literatures: An Introduction, Bibliographic Review, and Selected Bibliography*. New York: Modern Language Association of America, 1990.

Rupp, Leila. *A Desired Past: A Short History of Same-Sex Love in America*. Chicago: University of Chicago Press, 1999.

Sánchez, Rosaura. *Telling Identities: The Californio Testimonios*. Minneapolis: University of Minnesota Press, 1995.

Santamarina, Xiomara. *Belabored Professions: Narratives of African American Working Womanhood*. Chapel Hill: University of North Carolina Press, 2005.

Schlissel, Lillian. *Women's Diaries of the Westward Journey*. New York: Schocken Books, 1982.

Schlissel, Lillian, Vicki Ruíz, and Janice J. Monk. *Western Women: Their Land, Their Lives*. Albuquerque: University of New Mexico Press, 1988.

Scott, John Anthony. *Fanny Kemble's America*. New York: Crowell, 1973.

Seaver, James E., ed. *A Narrative of the Life of Mrs. Mary Jemison*. 1824. Ann Arbor, Mich.: Allegany Press, 1997.

Shea, Daniel B. "The Prehistory of American Autobiography." In *American Autobiography: Retrospect and Prospect*, edited by Paul John Eakin, 25–46. Madison: University of Wisconsin Press, 1991.

Sherman, Sarah Way. *Sarah Orne Jewett: An American Persephone*. Hanover: University of New Hampshire/University Press of New England, 1989.

Smith, Sidonie. *Moving Lives: Twentieth-Century Women's Travel Writing*. Minneapolis: University of Minnesota Press, 2001.

——. "Cheesecake, Nymphs, and 'We the People': Un/National Subjects About 1900." *Prose Studies: History, Theory, Criticism* 17.1 (1994): 120–40.

Smith, Sidonie, and Julia Watson. *Reading Autobiography: A Guide for Interpreting Life Narratives*. Minneapolis: University of Minnesota Press, 2001.

——. "Situating Subjectivity in Women's Autobiographical Practices." In *Women, Autobiography, Theory*, edited by Sidonie Smith and Julia Watson, 3–54. Madison: University of Wisconsin Press, 1998.

——, eds. *Women, Autobiography, Theory*. Madison: University of Wisconsin Press, 1998.

Smith-Rosenberg, Carroll. *Disorderly Conduct: Visions of Gender in Victorian America*. New York: Alfred A. Knopf, 1985.

——. "The Female World of Love and Ritual: Relations between Women in Nineteenth-Century America." In *Women's America: Refocusing the Past*, edited by Linda K. Kerber and Jane Sherron De Hart, 168–82. New York: Oxford University Press, 2000.

Stewart, Jeffrey C. "Introduction." In *Narrative of Sojourner Truth: A Bondswoman of Olden Time, With a History of Her Labors and Correspondence Drawn from Her "Book of Life,"* by Olive Gilbert, xxxiii–xlvii. New York: Oxford University Press, 1991.

Temple, Judy Nolte. "Fragments as Diary: Theoretical Implications of the *Dreams and Visions* of 'Baby Doe' Tabor." In *Inscribing the Daily: Critical Essays on Women's Diaries,* edited by Suzanne L. Bunkers and Cynthia Anne Huff, 72–85. Amherst: University of Massachusetts Press, 1996.

Thomas, M. Carey. *The Making of a Feminist: Early Journals and Letters of M. Carey Thomas.* Edited by Marjorie Housepian Dobkin, 90–93, 116–19, 124, 130–35. Kent, Ohio: Kent State University Press, 1979.

Truth, Sojourner. Speech at the Akron Women's Rights Convention. *Anti-Slavery Bugle,* June 21, 1851. In *Narrative of Sojourner Truth,* edited by Margaret Washington, 117–18. New York: Vintage Books, 1993.

Tubman, Harriet. "Testimony." 1855. In *A North-Side View of Slavery. The Refugee: or the Narratives of Fugitive Slaves in Canada. Related by Themselves, with an Account of the History and Condition of the Colored Population of Upper Canada,* edited by Benjamin Drew, 30. Boston: John P. Jewett and Company, 1856.

Washington, Booker T., Norman Barton Wood, and Fannie Barrier Williams. *A New Negro for a New Century: An Accurate and Up-to-Date Record of the Upward Struggles of the Negro Race. The Spanish-American War, Causes of It; Vivid Descriptions of Fierce Battles; Superb Heroism and Daring Deeds of the Negro Soldier . . . Education, Industrial Schools, Colleges, Universities and Their Relationship to the Race Problem.* Chicago: American Publishing House, 1900.

Watson, Julia. "Bringing Mary MacLane Back Home: Western Autobiographical Writing and the Anxiety of Place." In *Western Subjects: Autobiographical Writing in the North American West,* edited by Kathleen Boardman and Gioia Woods, 216–46. Salt Lake City: University of Utah Press, 2004.

Welter, Barbara. "The Cult of True Womanhood: 1820–1860." *American Quarterly* 18.2 (1966): 151–74.

White-Parks, Annette. *Sui Sin Far/Edith Maude Eaton: A Literary Biography.* Urbana: University of Illinois Press, 1995.

Wiegman, Robyn. *American Anatomies: Theorizing Race and Gender.* New Americanists. Durham, N.C.: Duke University Press, 1995.

Williams, Fannie Barrier. *The New Woman of Color: The Collected Writings of Fannie Barrier Williams, 1893–1918.* Edited by Mary Jo Deegan. DeKalb: Northern Illinois University Press, 2002.

Wink, Amy. *She Left Nothing in Particular: The Autobiographical Legacy of Nineteenth-Century Women's Diaries.* Knoxville: University of Tennessee Press, 2001.

Winnemucca (Hopkins), Sarah. *Life Among the Piutes: Their Wrongs and Claims.* Edited by Mrs. Horace Mann. 1883. Reno: University of Nevada Press, 1994.

Wong, Hertha Dawn. *Sending My Heart Back across the Years: Tradition and Innovation in Native American Autobiography.* New York: Oxford University Press, 1992.

Wong, Sau-ling Cynthia. "Immigrant Autobiography: Some Questions of Definition and Approach." In *American Autobiography: Retrospect and Prospect,* edited by Paul John Eakin, 142–70. Madison: University of Wisconsin Press, 1991.

Xiao-Huang-Yin. "Between the East and the West: Sui Sin Far—the First Chinese American Woman Writer." *Arizona Quarterly* 7 (1991): 49–84.

Zagarri, Rosemarie. "The Postcolonial Culture of Early American Women's Writing." In *The Cambridge Companion to Nineteenth-Century American Women's Writing,* edited by Dale M. Bauer and Philip Gould, 19–37. Cambridge: Cambridge University Press, 2001.

Zanjani, Sally Springmeyer. *Sarah Winnemucca.* Lincoln: University of Nebraska Press, 2001.

Zitkala-Ša (Gertrude Simmons Bonnin). *Dreams and Thunder: Stories, Poems, and the Sundance Opera.* Edited by P. Jane Hafen. Lincoln: University of Nebraska Press, 2001.

———. "Impressions of an Indian Childhood." *The Atlantic Monthly* 85.507 (January 1900): 37–47.

———. "An Indian Teacher among Indians." *The Atlantic Monthly* 85.509 (March 1900): 381–86.

———. "The School Days of an Indian Girl." *The Atlantic Monthly* 85.508 (February 1900): 185–94.

———. "Why I am a Pagan." *The Atlantic Monthly* 90.542 (December 1902): 801–803.

Wisconsin Studies in Autobiography

William L. Andrews
General Editor

Robert F. Sayre
The Examined Self: Benjamin Franklin, Henry Adams, Henry James

Daniel B. Shea
Spiritual Autobiography in Early America

Lois Mark Stalvey
The Education of a WASP

Margaret Sams
Forbidden Family: A Wartime Memoir of the Philippines, 1941–1945
Edited, with an introduction, by Lynn Z. Bloom

Charlotte Perkins Gilman
The Living of Charlotte Perkins Gilman: An Autobiography
Introduction by Ann J. Lane

Mark Twain
*Mark Twain's Own Autobiography: The Chapters from
    the* North American Review
Edited, with an introduction, by Michael Kiskik

Journeys in New Worlds: Early American Women's Narratives
Edited by William L. Andrews

American Autobiography: Retrospect and Prospect
Edited by Paul John Eakin

Caroline Seabury
The Diary of Caroline Seabury, 1854–1863
Edited, with an introduction, by Suzanne L. Bunkers

Marian Anderson
My Lord, What a Morning
Introduction by Nellie Y. McKay

American Women's Autobiography: Fea(s)ts of Memory
Edited, with an introduction, by Margo Culley

Frank Marshall Davis
Livin' the Blues: Memoirs of a Black Journalist and Poet
Edited, with an introduction, by John Edgar Tidwell

Joanne Jacobson
Authority and Alliance in the Letters of Henry Adams

Cornelia Peake McDonald
*A Woman's Civil War: A Diary with Reminiscences of the War,
    from March 1862*
Edited, with an introduction, by Minrose C. Gwin

Kamau Brathwaite
The Zea Mexican Diary: 7 Sept. 1926–7 Sept. 1986
Foreword by Sandra Pouchet Paquet

Genaro M. Padilla
*My History, Not Yours: The Formation of Mexican American
    Autobiography*

Frances Smith Foster
Witnessing Slavery: The Development of Ante-bellum Slave Narratives

Native American Autobiography: An Anthology
Edited, with an introduction, by Arnold Krupat

American Lives: An Anthology of Autobiographical Writing
Edited, with an introduction, by Robert F. Sayre

Carol Holly
Intensely Family: The Inheritance of Family Shame and the Autobiographies of Henry James

People of the Book: Thirty Scholars Reflect on Their Jewish Identity
Edited by Jeffrey Rubin-Dorsky and Shelley Fisher Fishkin

G. Thomas Couser
Recovering Bodies: Illness, Disability, and Life Writing

José Angel Gutiérrez
The Making of a Chicano Militant: Lessons from Cristal

John Downton Hazlett
My Generation: Collective Autobiography and Identity Politics

William Herrick
Jumping the Line: The Adventures and Misadventures of an American Radical

Women, Autobiography, Theory: A Reader
Edited by Sidonie Smith and Julia Watson

Carson McCullers
Illumination and Night Glare: The Unfinished Autobiography of Carson McCullers
Edited by Carlos L. Dews

Marie Hall Ets
Rosa: The Life of an Italian Immigrant

Yi-Fu Tuan
Who Am I?: An Autobiography of Emotion, Mind, and Spirit

Henry Bibb
The Life and Adventures of Henry Bibb: An American Slave
With a new introduction by Charles J. Heglar

Suzanne L. Bunkers
Diaries of Girls and Women: A Midwestern American Sampler

Jim Lane
The Autobiographical Documentary in America

Sandra Pouchet Paquet
Caribbean Autobiography: Cultural Identity and Self-Representation

Mark O'Brien, with Gillian Kendall
How I Became a Human Being: A Disabled Man's Quest for Independence

Elizabeth L. Banks
Campaigns of Curiosity: Journalistic Adventures of an American Girl in Late Victorian London
With a new introduction by Mary Suzanne Schriber and Abbey L. Zink

Miriam Fuchs
The Text Is Myself: Women's Life Writing and Catastrophe

Jean M. Humez
Harriet Tubman: The Life and the Life Stories

Voices Made Flesh: Performing Women's Autobiography
Edited by Lynn C. Miller, Jacqueline Taylor, and M. Heather Carver

Loreta Janeta Velazquez
The Woman in Battle: The Civil War Narrative of Loreta Janeta Velazquez, Cuban Woman and Confederate Soldier
With a new introduction by Jesse Alemán

Cathryn Halverson
Maverick Autobiographies: Women Writers and the American West, 1900–1936

Jeffrey Brace
The Blind African Slave: Or Memoirs of Boyrereau Brinch, Nicknamed Jeffrey Brace
as told to Benjamin F. Prentiss, Esq.
Edited and with an introduction by Kari J. Winter

Colette Inez
The Secret of M. Dulong: A Memoir

Before They Could Vote: American Women's Autobiographical Writing, 1819–1919
Edited by Sidonie Smith and Julia Watson